DATE DUE

OC 23 '92 DE 9 '03			
NO 2 '92 AP 2 9 '04			
DE 7 '07			
AP 1 '95 AG 4 '05			
AP 26 '96 MY 3 1 '07			
JY 11 '96			
AG 8 '97			
DE 3 '97			
JY 23 '98			
OC 1 '98			
MY 25 '99			
NO 7 '01			
NO 26 '01			
NO 21 '05			

HOW TO OBTAIN YOUR U.S. IMMIGRATION VISA WITHOUT A LAWYER

By

Benji O. Anosike, B.B.A., M.A., Ph.D.

Copyright, © 1990, by Benji O. Anosike

Library of Congress Cataloging-in-Publication Data

Anosike, Benji O.
    How to obtain your U.S. immigration visa without a lawyer / by
Benji O. Anosike.
        p.   cm.
    Includes bibliographical referencs and index.
    ISBN 0-932704-10-7 : $23.95
    1. Emigration and immigration law--United States--Popular works.
I. Title.
KF4819.6.A56   1990
34273'082--dc20
[347.30282]
                                                    90-49637
                                                    CIP

Published by:

Do-It-Yourself Legal Publishers,
298 5th Avenue
New York, N.Y. 10001

Printed in the United States of America

ISBN: 0-932704-10-7
Library of Congress Catalog Card No.: 90-49637

TABLE OF CONTENTS

APPENDICES

FOREWORD:

THE PUBLISHER'S MESSAGE

*Of all the mighty nations in the East or in the West
This glorious Yankee nation is the greatest and the
    best;
We have room for all creation and our banner is
    unfurled,
Here's a general invitation to the people of the world.
Come along, come along, make no delay,
Come from every nation, come from every way....*

So read a passage from a 19th Century American Ballad

To All Our Dear Readers:

The subject matter of immigration to the United States of America - simply, the governing laws, ways and means, and procedures by which persons may officially gain entry into, or stay in the United States - has always been a "hot," deeply felt subject for America, in deed the world, for as long as the United States has existed as a nation. In the interest of brevity, suffice it to say, simply, that the United States can legitimately lay claim to its reputation as a "nation of immigrants" - a nation whose citizens are overwhelmingly the sons and daughters and descendants of persons who came to the United States from other lands. With the subject of immigration, one at once finds the one subject about which there's so common an experience shared by all of us AMERICANS; hence the great emotions and ambivalence with which this matter has been treated historically in America!

It requires no great intellect, therefore, for one to see that a working knowledge of, or at least familiarity with the matter of who gets to be selected for or admitted into the country, or excluded or expelled from it, and how and why, is a subject matter that is of crucial interest and importance to a great many American citizens as well as foreign nationals the world over.

What this Manual Will Do For You

HOW TO OBTAIN YOUR U.S. IMMIGRATION VISA WITHOUT A LAWYER, is primarily concerned with one fundamental but limited aspect of the immigration issue:'the knots and bolts' of securing a U.S. entry visa; exposition of what the officially prescribed requirements and procedures are by which the foreign national may qualify for a visa under the laws and regulations of the immigration authorities; and the actual preparation and assembling of such requirements and its filing with the immigration authorities who grant the visa. In brief, with a working knowledge or mastery of the contents of this manual, YOU (any foreign national) will

---

*Quoted from "The Rights of Aliens" by David Carliner,p.25.

know what and what requirements and qualifications you need to have in order to be eligible for grant of entry permit into the United States, or to stay in the country if already admitted; and, even more important, you will, solely by YOURSELF and without any "expert" assistance, be able to undertake all the filing procedures necessary for you to apply for and obtain the type of entry visa, immigrant or non-immigrant, which you desire and qualify for, or be able to maintain yourself in lawful status as an alien in the United States. And, if you are a U.S. citizen or a permanent resident already, you will be able to determine whether or not you qualify to bring your family members to the U.S., and how to actually do so; and if you are an official of a corporation or business or institution, you will be able to master the process by which you can hire a foreign national for work for you in a vital capacity.

One fundamental premise underlies this manual: whatever else may be said to be involved in obtaining an entry visa by which an alien can become lawfully admitted into (or to remain in) the United States, the process itself is, at its most basic level, primarily a clerical and ministerial operation, requiring no complex "legal" procedures or expertise or some specialized technical theories of law or public policy calling for a lawyer or other such professional, but merely knowledge of the types of documentations or other evidence you need present to establish your eligibility for a given class of visa and the ability to write up or gather such documentations for the benefit of the immigration authorities.

The National Scope - And Purpose - Of This Manual

HOW TO OBTAIN YOUR U.S. IMMIGRATION VISA aims, first and foremost, at providing at "street level" to the people directly affected - to the aliens and foreign nationals themselves who seek or desire entry into or to stay in the United States - the practical tools and knowledge with which they can, themselves, seek their objectives, and in a relatively inexpensive, affordable and accessible way open to all the world over. Similarly, the handbook is aimed at providing vital knowledge of the basics involved for the benefit of the non-specialists engaged in various religious, civic and community organizations, voluntary agencies, and other recognized public interest groups across the United States who counsel and assist aliens with various immigration-related needs and problems inside and outside the United States.

This manual could not be more timely or its contents more relevant or needed for our present times. Even as we speak, as this book goes to press (and, even as you, the reader, probably goes through the contents herein!), the world increasingly promises to get still smaller and smaller. With astronomical technological changes continuing to occur all over the world and rapidly transforming the world into one "interrelated global environment," and with the historic revolutionary upheavals which have been occurring in the recent history of Asia, Eastern Europe and other parts of the world and which promise to sweep away (or at least chip away at) the major historical differences and barriers between social, economic and political systems among peoples and nations of the world, one thing is almost certain, namely, the attraction and the attractiveness of the United States as the "land of opportunity" and the "last beacon of hope" for those in search of political freedom or economic betterment throughout the world, is all too likely to increase, not decrease. The sounds and signs are around us, and every bit of evidence suggests that America of the immediate future is likely to see not less, but a lot more discussions and concerns centering around such immigration-related historic anxieties as the "influx" of "illegal aliens," the need for "defense of American borders" or the "amnesty program", and the issue of the "undocumented aliens", the "boat people", "refugees", and so on and so forth. This manual, it is hoped and intended, will help America - and the citizens of the world - to better understand and cope with such matters or developments, and in a more responsible and rational manner.

Long-standing Recognition By All of the Need for a Guidebook of this Kind

In deed, immigration administrators and workers, policy makers, volunteer agencies and operatives, and even legal practitioners who work in the area of immigration matters, are all seemingly united in a common recognition of the crying need for a practical manual such as this book. And many of them, frustrated and unable to find practical guide books or programs for use in their day-to-day work or encounters with their immigrant clients, have from time to time bemoaned the inavailability or inaccessibility of such practical materials.

Writing as far back as 1986, C. James Cooper, Jr., one among the crop of legal practitioners in the field of immigration who are truly respectable and credible, draws a powerful but vivid portrait of the kind of reality in America's immigration world which now underlies the rationale for the publication of the present manual. Cooper sums it all up this way:

"I have felt for a long time that there has been a need for an immigration program that would give people a better understanding about our immigration laws and policies. There are very few, if any public sources for this information.

Public libraries, generally, do not...Even if they do, it is difficult to find information on some of the "dos and don'ts" of immigration.

The (U.S.) Immigration Service is very helpful in giving you the necessary immigration forms; however, they cannot legally give you advice. I have had many clients who relied on advice from well intended friends and relatives which was either misleading or misunderstood......

Qualified immigration attorneys (lawyers) are a good source of information...However, in many cases you may not need to consult with an immigration attorney. Other times, you may only need one consultation to clarify some problem area or to get an assessment on whether you have a good chance of getting what you want or whether you should anticipate some problems.....

There are many things you can do by yourself without the need for any legal assistance....(and a handbook of the type will hopefully).....
guide you through some of these areas by giving you practical points on what has worked in the past and to prepare you for any potential problems.

For those areas which could cause problems (from what you may discover from the knowledge you gather from your reading of the handbook), it may be worth your time and expense to consult an attorney at least once...As a result, you will have a better understanding about your situation and can then decide if you want to proceed (by yourself) after the consultation.

.(Indeed, even) if you decide you'd(rather) use the services of an attorney to prepare your entire case, (still you can benefit by reading such a guidebook, for)...the more information you have about our immigration system the better are your chances for getting a visa. Experience shows us that the most successful people are those who have the best information. I assure you, as an attorney with many years (over 35 years) of experience, that clients who have understood the immigration system and knew what to expect, were usually successful. This is due in large part, because such clients knew what to anticipate, and, as a result, were easily able to contribute relevant information....they were more relaxed and confident in any contacts they had with either (the) Immigration or the Consulates*

Translated, **the central point is**: whichever route you, the alien, intend to go, whether, on the one hand, you will choose to file for the American entry or residency visa yourself and completely pursue it by yourself; or, on the other hand, you will choose to engage the services of an immigration lawyer to do it for you in part or in whole, having this practical handbook in hand would still be to your invaluable advantage and helpfulness as a visa seeker, and might even spell the critical difference between your sucessfully obtaining one and your not obtaining one!!

Here's the Fundamental Essence and Message

In point of fact, the point of **HOW TO OBTAIN YOUR U.S. IMMIGRATION VISA WITHOUT A LAWYER** should not be mistaken or misundestood. We emphasize that the cardinal aim of this manual is neither to debunk the actual or potential usefulness of employing the services of a competent immigration lawyer at all times and in all circumstances ever, nor to advocate solely a do-it-yourself approach by the alien or the non-professional in all circumstances. Rather, the objective position of the manual is that, equipped with a basic understanding of the workings and process, the non-lawyer and non-specialist could do just as good a job as, perhaps even a better job (and definitely a less expensive one!) than the average lawyer in applying for or securing the average U.S. visa. And it is specifically contended that this is so especially with respect to the more usual, routine types of cases which, as a rule, are generally clerical and straightforward, hardly involving any complex or technical issues of law or policy.

The Publisher's Continuing Gratitude to You, Our Readers

It remains for us to assure our readers that we have diligently researched, checked and counter-checked every bit of the information contained in this manual to ensure its accuracy and up-to-dateness. Nevertheless, we humans have never been noted for our infallibility, no matter how hard the effort! Furthermore, details of most laws and procedures do change from time to time, and those partaining to immigration are by no means exempted or immune from this rule. With respect to immigration specifically, the details of the rules and procedures (though not of the laws, regulations or basic principles) by which the processing of visa applications is carried out, and the standards of liniency or stringency by which the decisions are made, often differ from one immigration district or U.S. Consulate abroad to another. Nor, further, is this relatively short manual conceivably intended to be an encyclopedia on the subject, possibly containing or meant to contain the answers and solution to every issue on the subject.

---

*Quoted from "AMERICAN IMMIGRATION TAPES"(Text), Allterra Visas, Ltd., 1986 pp. 1-2. Passage is quoted in such extensive detail as it makes the present publisher's intended point so well.

THE READER IS THEREFORE FOREWARNED that this manual is sold with this disclaimer: the Publisher (or editors or author) does NOT make any guarantees whatsoever, or purport to engage in rendering legal or other professional service, or to substitute for a lawyer, an immigration counselor or consultant, or a personal adviser and the like. Where any such professional help or other expert assistance is legitimately necessary in particular situations, it should be sought accordingly.

Our profound thanks and gratitude go to the **following persons and organizations:** Denver, Colorado's **C. James Cooper, Jr,** the immigration legal practitioner and authority, the author of "The American Immigration Tapes," and its "Form Book," whose illustrated printed forms (and other information) are extensively reproduced in this manual for illustrative purposes; immigration lawyer and autho**r Dan P. Danilov** of Seattle, Washington, and his publisher, Self-Counsel Press, Inc., from whose book ("Immigrating TO The U.S.A.") a limited number of select forms are reproduced for our own illustrative purposes; lawyer and author ("The Greencard Book") **Richard Madison** of New York city, from whose publication we reproduced a few select forms or tables for their great value as illustrative tools; and many, many others too numerous to mention herein. All have, in one way or the other, and by your deed, pioneering works and/or research in the field - and by your ever unselfish readiness to share and to disseminate the fruits thereof - made the present undertaking both more purposeful and easier for the present publisher.

Finally, we'd like to remind you, our readers: Please note that we continue to love hearing from you on your immigration ideas, aspirations experiences or problems. As always, just drop us a few lines at our address below(we prefer written communications, please). With us, you, the readers, are the KING or QUEEN! We value and welcome your feedback - always!!

Thank you all again.

— **Do-It-Yourself Legal Publishers**
298 *Fifth Avenue,*
New York, N.Y. 10001

New York, NY
August, 1990.

Alien Students Learn More Education Is the Key

By MARVINE HOWE

It was Rap Day at John Dewey High School last week, and most of the workshops focused on sex and drugs. But in room 343, it was standing room only as students, teachers and professionals discussed the really hot topic of the times — the rights of illegal immigrant children.

Lawyers and other experts emphasized to the students that New York City's public schools are open to all young people, whether or not they are in the country legally. They also passed out Board of Education leaflets welcoming "undocumented and documented immigrants" in six languages.

"But if I can't get a job, why should I get an education?" an Asian teenager asked, expressing the frustration of many undocumented students. For illegal teen-agers, the 1986 Immigration Reform and Control Act has been both an opportunity and an obstacle. The act offered illegal aliens a brief amnesty in which to become legal, but also created stiff penalties for employers who hire illegals.

"Hope," responded Kathleen Jarvis, who heads the Advocates for Children's Immigrant Student Rights Project. "Eventually that law is going to change, so get your foot in the door and acquire a skill the United States needs."

Train Parents and Staff

Although figures vary widely for New York City's undocumented population, Columbia University's Center for Social Sciences conservatively estimated that after the expiration of the amnesty in May 1988, 250,000 undocumented aliens remained in the country, including 46,000 children.

The visit to John Dewey, in the Coney Island section of Brooklyn, was part of a program to help immigrant schoolchildren cope with the new system, and part of a day of discussions at the school. It was organized by the City Bar Association in New York and Advocates for Children, a non-profit organization. They train school staff and parents, run seminars for students, and operate a telephone help line.

About 40 students signed up for the workshop. At least 80 showed up.

"There's a great need to reach out to immigrant schoolchildren who are afraid to ask for help," said Laurie Milder, director of the Bar Association's Community Outreach Law Program. She said about 60 immigration lawyers have volunteered their time.

Can They Get Financial Aid?

More than 1,000 of John Dewey's 3,000 students are foreign-born, and Ms. Milder and the other speakers faced a barrage of questions.

Are illegals entitled to go to college? Can they get financial aid? How can an illegal student get a green

During Rap Day at John Dewey High School lawyers and other experts tried to assuage some students' fears that being undocumented immigrants would prevent them from getting jobs. Kathleen Jarvis, of the Advocates for Children's Immigrant Student Rights Project, was at right.

The New York Times/Vic DeLucia

Many youths are surprised to find that they can go to college.

card — permanent resident status? If an illegal student gives birth to a child here, can the mother stay in the country?

Ms. Jarvis told them that the 17 colleges of the City University of New York are open to undocumented students and do not require a student to show a Social Security number. Later she described the case of a 17-year-old star athlete in a Brooklyn high school who had been offered athletic scholarships by 13 universities. But, because she was an illegal immigrant, from the West Indies, and all the schools insisted on having a Social Security number, she had to go to CUNY.

Undocumented students used to pay nonresident tuition, double that of residents, in the city's colleges, but now they are eligible for the residents' rate.

Undocumented students are not yet eligible for Federal or state financial aid, Ms. Jarvis said. "But we advise you to take one or two courses because you'll hear about scholarships; it's like the lottery, you've got to be in it to win it."

Robert Washington, an immigration lawyer and former teacher, told the audience that while the amnesty period was over, there were other ways to become legal. Sponsorship by a close relative or acquisition of skills listed by the Labor Department as needed in the United States. Such categories include priest, minister or religious worker, physical therapist or someone of outstanding scientific or artistic ability.

An immigration judge would probably let the undocumented mother of an American-born baby stay "because the policy has been to keep families together as a general rule," Mr. Washington said.

Ms. Jarvis later described the case of a pregnant illegal teen-ager who was thrown out of her home and moved to a shelter. Lawyers said she was entitled to some welfare benefits

"because she was carrying a U.S. citizen child," Ms. Jarvis said.

After the session ended — with a burst of applause — Enid Margolies, assistant principal, gathered a dozen students to prolong the discussion.

"Now maybe there's a chance for me to continue my studies," a Haitian boy of 14 said excitedly, explaining that he had not known City University accepted undocumented students. His parents had left him with an aunt, who is a United States resident, and she was willing to adopt him but her husband was reluctant.

A Cuban boy of 17, who came here more than four years ago, asked how to get a green card "so I can study and go into the Navy."

For specific problems, the students were told to call the Immigrant Students Legal Rights Helpline at (718) 729-8866.

In the past, most calls came from school counselors, but now it is mainly students who want to go to college, Ms. Jarvis said. Since undocumented students are generally afraid to disclose their identity, they are promised confidentiality and asked only their first name, age, country of origin and school.

CHAPTER ONE

THE VARIOUS KINDS OF VISAS BY WHICH ALIENS MAY BE ADMITTED INTO THE UNITED STATES.

Under the immigration Laws and regulations of the United States, the term *"ALIEN"* is used to denote *"any person not a citizen or a national of the United States"*. In other words, every person applying for entry to the United States — unless he or she is a U.S. citizen or a national — is an *"alien"* under the parlance of the U.S. immigration authorities.

A. THE TWO MAJOR GROUPINGS OF U.S. VISAS: IMMIGRANT AND NON-IMMIGRANT GROUPS.

In the broadest term, entry visas to gain admission into (or to remain in) the United States, are classified into two major categories: **THE IMMIGRANT AND NON-IMMIGRANT CATEGORIES.** The "IMMIGRANT" visa category is for the alien who is intent on entering the United States for permanent stay or residence therein; and the NON-IMMIGRANT visa category, on the other hand, is for the alien who is intent on entering the United States for a temporary, specified period of time and for limited purposes (such as to visit or to do business or study, and the like).

For an alien applying for a visa, it is most important that he or she properly determines, first, whether he or she falls under the "immigrant" or the "non-immigrant" category, and, secondly, the particular subclassification within such immigrant or non-immigrant category to which he or she belongs. For, it is only when an applicant knows this information, that he can apply for the proper type of entry visa for which he is eligible, and which when obtained, may not later be subject to revocation or subject the alien recepient to possible exclusion from entry into the United States by the immigration authorities at the port of entry, or to deportation even after having been admitted into the U.S.

We detail below in the rest of this chapter, the different classes of aliens which comprise each of these two major categories of visa.

B. THE NON-IMMIGRANT VISA CAREGORY

As stated earlier above, a non-immigrant is, in a word, simply an alien entering or seeking to enter the United Stated for a temporary, specified or definite period of time. Under the U.S. immigration laws and rules of operation, here's the so-called **"basic rule"** by which the U.S. consular and immigration authorities determine who is a non-immigrant: every alien person applying for a visa to enter the United States is simply "presumed" to be an intending immigrant — unless and until he or she can satisfactorily show the consular or immigration officers that he or she is not. That is, unless he or she shows that he/she can qualify for one of the non-immigrant classifications.

Here is how Section 214 (b) of the Immigration and Nationality Act. (8 U.S.C. 1184 (b)), puts it: "Every alien shall be presumed to be an immigrant until he establishes to the satisfaction of the consular officer at the time of application for a visa, and (to) the immigration officer, at the time of application for admission, that he is entitled to a non-immigrant status under Sec. 101 (a) (15)".

To sum it all up in simple terms, what this **"basic rule"** has come to mean for the visa applicant in practical terms, is this: it matters little what claims you make in your visa application as to your being an intending non-immigrant; the real task for you is that you be ready and able to establish, to the satisfaction of the officials who have to consider your visa application, that you are not actually an intending immigrant, instead; and, unless you are able to satisfactorily present such proof, the officials will simply consider ("presume") you to be a probable or intending immigrant and thus reject such application for a non-immigrant visa!

CHART I.
The Alien's Visa and Entry Process into the United States

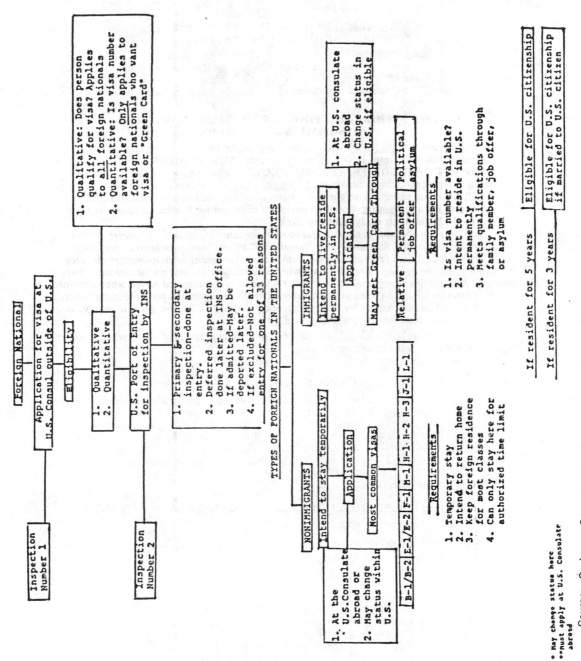

Foreign National

Application for visa at U.S. Consul outside of U.S.

Inspection Number 1

Eligibility
1. Qualitative
2. Quantitative

1. Qualitative: Does person qualify for visa? Applies to all foreign nationals
2. Quantitative: Is visa number available? Only applies to foreign nationals who want visa or "Green Card"

U.S. Port of Entry for inspection by INS

Inspection Number 2

1. Primary & secondary inspection—done at entry.
2. Deferred inspection done later at INS office.
3. If admitted—May be deported later.
4. If excluded—Not allowed entry for one of 33 reasons

TYPES OF FOREIGN NATIONALS IN THE UNITED STATES

NONIMMIGRANTS

Intend to stay temporarily

Application

1. At the U.S.Consulate abroad or
2. May change status within U.S.

Most common visas

B-1/B-2 | E-1/E-2 | F-1 | H-1 | H-2 | H-3 | J-1 | L-1

Requirements
1. Temporary stay
2. Intend to return home
3. Keep foreign residence for most classes
4. Can only stay here for authorized time limit

IMMIGRANTS

Intend to live/reside permanently in U.S.

Application

1. At U.S. consulate abroad
2. Change status in U.S. if eligible

May get Green Card Through

Relative | Permanent job offer | Political asylum

Requirements
1. Is visa number available?
2. Intent to reside in U.S. permanently
3. Meets qualifications through family member, job offer, or asylum

Eligible for U.S. citizenship | If resident for 5 years

Eligible for U.S. citizenship if married to U.S. citizen | If resident for 3 years

• May change status here
•• Must apply at U.S. Consulate abroad

Source: C. James Cooper's "American Immigration Tapes (Text)," p. 233. Reproduced by Permission.

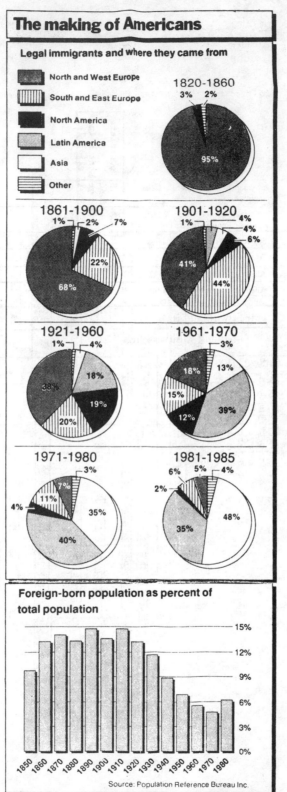

The making of Americans

Legal immigrants and where they came from

CHART 2.

Legend:
- North and West Europe
- South and East Europe
- North America
- Latin America
- Asia
- Other

1820-1860
3% 2% 95%

1861-1900
1% 2% 7% 22% 68%

1901-1920
4% 1% 4% 6% 41% 44%

1921-1960
1% 4% 18% 38% 19% 20%

1961-1970
3% 18% 13% 15% 39% 12%

1971-1980
3% 7% 11% 4% 35% 40%

1981-1985
6% 5% 4% 2% 35% 48%

Foreign-born population as percent of total population

15% 12% 9% 6% 3% 0%

1850 1860 1870 1880 1890 1900 1910 1920 1930 1940 1950 1960 1970 1980

Source: Population Reference Bureau Inc.

As cited in The New York Times,
Sunday, April 10, 1988 p.E5.

C. THE DIFFERENT CLASSES OF THE NON- IMMIGRANT VISAS

In all, there are at least 16 basic "classes" into which the non-immigrant visa category is divided, meaning that in order for an alien to qualify or be classifiable as a "non-immigrant" of any kind, he (or she) must be able to show that he falls within at least one of these classes.

(CHART 3)

Those Classes are as Follows:

VISA CLASSIFICATION SYMBOL	CLASS OF NON-IMMIGRANT	MAXIMUM ADMISSION PERIOD
A - 1	Foreign Government officials or employees and their immediate families.	Duration of status
A - 2	Attendants, Servants, or personal employees of A - 1 aliens	Duration of their status
A -3	Employees of A - 1 or 2 - 2 aliens and their immediate families	1 year
B - 1	Temporary Visitors for business	6 months
B - 2	Temporary Visitors for pleasure	6 months
C - 1, C - 3	Aliens in transit through the U.S.	Not more than 29 days.
C -2	Aliens in transit to or from the United Nation Headquarters	Duration of status in transit to U.N.
TROV	Transit without visa	Next available flight
D - 1	Crewmen remaining with vessel or aircraft	Time carrier is in port not to exceed 29 days
D - 2	Crewmen discharged from vessel or aircraft	Not to exceed 29 days from arrival
E - 1	Treaty trader, his spouse or child, if accompanying or following to join him	1 year
F - 1	A student coming to pursue a full course of study at a qualified institution.	Duration of status
F - 2	The Spouse or minor child(ren) of the F-1 alien	Same as in F - 1
G - 1, G - 2, G - 3, G - 4	A foreign government representative to, officer or employees of, an international organization and their immediate families.	Duration of status
G - 5	Attendants, servants, or personal employees of G - 1, G - 2, G - 3 and G - 4 aliens, and their immediate families.	1 year
H - 1	Temporary worker: of distinguished merit and ability, coming to perform exceptional services requiring such qualities.	2 years with possible 1 year extensions up to 5 years.
H - 2	Temporary worker in short supply: worker coming to perform skilled or unskilled work where labor shortages exist.	2 years
H - 2A	Agricultural workers who until June 1987, had previously been admitted to the U.S. for temporary periods in the H - 2 category.	
H - 3	Temporary worker coming as an "Industrial Trainee"	Length of program
H - 4	Spouse and minor children accompanying or following to join H - 1, H - 2 or H - 3 alien	Duration of H-1, H-2 or H-3
I	Bona fide representative of foreign press, radio, film, or other information media, coming solely to engage in such vocation, and his spouse or minor child(ren) if accompanying or following to join him.	1 year

J - 1	So-called "Exchange Visitor": a bona fide student, scholar, trainee, teacher, professor, research assistant, specialist, leader in a specialized field of knowledge or skill, or similar person, coming to participate in a program designated by the U.S. Secretary of State for the purpose of pursuing such activity.	Duration of status
J - 2	Spouse and minor children of J - 1 alien, if accompanying or following to join him	Same as J -1
K - 1	Alien financees and fiances of U.S. citizens.	90 days
K - 2	Children of K-1 aliens	same as K - 1
L - 1	Intra- company transferees	1 year intervals extendable to 3 years.
L - 2	Spouses and minor children accompanying or following to join L-1 alien.	same as for L - 1 above
M - 1	Vocational student	Duration of status
"NATO alien" - 1, 2, 3, and 4.	NATO official; member state representative or a member of his staff; immediate family member of any of these	Duration of status
NATO - 5, 6, 7.	NATO "expert", or member of a civilian component, accompanying or attached to a force under the North Atlantic Treaty Organization (NATO); or an attendant, servant, or personal employee of any of these, or member of his immediate family,	1 year

D. THE IMMIGRANT VISA CATEGORY

As you may recall, we defined the IMMIGRANT VISA (p. 1) as that category of visas which is meant for an alien intending to enter the United States to live permanently. (This contrasts, of course, with the NON-IMMIGRANT VISA, whose purpose, on the other hand, is for a temporary stay in the United States in order to undertake a specific limited task!).

By what underlying principle do the immigration authorities make the determination as to who is an intending "immigrant" and who is not ?

Essentially, the rule of thumb by which such determination is made basically flows directly from the key provision [section 214 (b)] of the Immigration and Nationality Act which we have earlier cited above (see pp above), namely, that "every alien shall be presumed to be an immigrant until he (can) establish...... that he or she falls within one of the non-immigrant classess". Put another way, if you do not readily appear to the immigration authorities to be a non-immigrant, you are automatically "presumed" to be (taken to be) an intending immigrant; and hence your application will be treated and evaluated accordingly by the same standards as are used for an immigrant visa applicant.

As defined by the immigration law, the goal of an intending immigrant is to be "lawfully admitted for permanent residence" in the United States. A central point made absolutely clear from the said law's definition herein, is this: *that the key element in being able to qualify as such a lawful permanent resident of the United States, which is to say, for being granted an "Immigrant" type of visa, is the INTENT of the alien himself to make the United States his permanent home.* Thus, in contrast to the non-immigrant, who is expected not to stay permanently in the U.S., the immigrant alien must, on the other hand, intend to reside in the United States permanently.

E. THE IMMIGRANT VISA CATEGORY: CERTAIN LIMITS WHICH APPLY TO THE NUMBER OF VISAS ISSUABLE FOR EACH CLASS

As explained above (pp. 1 & 5), one key difference between the non-immigrant visa and the immigrant visa, is the differential length of time for which the holder of one type of visa is expected to stay in the United States, in contract to the holder of the other type of visa. Apart from this, however, there is one other major area of difference (among others) between the two broad types of visas or aliens: in so far as the immigrant visas are concerned, a numerical limitation applies to the number of such visas which may be issued each year. (No such limitation applies with respect to non-immigrants, on the other hand.)

Employed primarily as a device for controlling the number of immigrant visas issued (or of immigrants allowed into the U.S.), **the immigration law imposes a numerical limitation on the number of immigrant (but not non-immigrant) visas which may be granted each year.** What this means, in practical terms is that an alien seeking an immigrant type of visa, even if fully meeting all the **"qualitative"** requirements prescribed for eligibility for such a visa (e.g.. having the correct family relationship to a U.S. citizen, or the professional, financial, health or moral status required), will still not be able to obtain the immigrant visa, unless he shall have also met the **"quantitative"** requirement — i.e.., unless an immigrant visa number is available for him under the numerical limitation rule.

F. THE BASIC STRUCTURE OF THE NUMERICAL LIMITATION PROVISION

Basically, the applicable law allows an over-all 270,000 immigrant visas (exclusive of vasas granted to those who qualify as "immediate relatives" and "special immigrants") to be made available to all applicants world-wide each and every year. Out of this over-all number of immigrant visas allowed world-wide per year (270,000), each independent foreign nation is allowed a share of not more than 20,000 visas for each year.

Where an independent foreign nation has a colony or dependency, (e.g. the Royal colony of Hong Kong), that colony or dependency is limited to an annual share of 5,000 out of the 20,000 visa ceiling alloted to the independent nation.

There are two groups of intending immigrants who are exempt from, and hence are not subject to, the numerical limitation requirement. These are aliens who qualify either as "IMMEDIATE RELATIVES" of U.S. citizens (defined as the spouse, and unmarried minor children and the parents of U.S. citizens), or as so-called "SPECIAL IMMIGRANTS."* Thus, all other applicants for immigrant visa (that is, with the exception of those qualifying as "immediate relatives" or "special immigrant"), are subject to the constraints of the numerical limitation of 20,000 immigrant visas per independent nation, per year,

---

*The number of "special immigrants" who get to be admitted into the U.S. each year has been said to be "so limited as to merit only brief treatment" by one 1987 account by one immigration law authority, which estimated that such persons number approximately 3,000 to 6,000 per year world-wide. This group include the following: U.S. permanent resident aliens returning from temporary visits abroad; former citizens who lost their citizenship through marriage or through service in allied armed forces during World War II; ministers of religious denominations having bona fide organizations in the U.S. needing their services, and their immediate families; present or former employees of the U.S. government abroad with 15 years of service, and their immediate families, and other persons. (See more detailed account of this group on pp. 42-3)

G. DIFFERENT CLASSES OF IMMIGRANT VISAS: THE EIGHT "PREFERENCES"'

In all, within the numerical limitation of 20,000 immigrant visas allowed each country per year under the immigrant procedure, the order and percentages in which such visas are made available to applicants are set in terms of eight categories — called **"PREFERENCES"**.

The Eight Immigrant visa "Preferences" are as follows:

1. **First Preference Category:**

   Up to 20% of the over-all annual limit of 270,000, first, to unmarried sons and daughters over 21 year of age, of U.S. citizens.

2. **Second Preference Category:**

   Up to 20% of the over-all annual limit of 270,000, plus visas not required for the First Preference category, next, to spouses, and <u>unmarried</u> sons and daughters of aliens lawfully admitted to the U.S. for permanent residence (i.e. "Green Card" holders living in the U.S.)

3. **Third Preference Category:**

   Up to 10% of the overall annual limit, goes next to members of the professions and persons of exceptional ability in the sciences or the arts.

4. **Fourth Preference Category:**

   Up to 10% of the over-all annual limit of 270,000, plus visas not required by the first three preference categories above, next, to <u>married</u> sons and daughters of U.S. citizens.

5. **Fifth Preference Category:**

   Up to 24% of the over-all annual limit of 270,000, plus visas not required for the first four preference categories above, next, to brothers and sisters of U.S. citizens.

6. **Sixth Preference Category:**

   Up to 10% of the over-all annual limit of 270,000, next, to skilled and unskilled workers determined by the U.S. Secretary of Labor to be in short supply in the U.S.

7. **Seventh Preference Category:**

   Up to 6% of the over-all annual limit of 270,000, next, to refugees and political asylees who qualify as "Conditional entrants" for admission into the United States.

8. **NON-PREFERENCE: Preference Category:**

   Any visas left unused from the above enumerated seven preference classes (if any), are made available to NON-PREFERENCE immigrants according to strict chronological order in which such applicants come. Non-preference status is presumed until an applicant establishes the right to either one of the above seven preferences, or to "immediate relatives" or "special immigrant" status.

CHART 4: THE IMMIGRANT PREFERENCE CHART

Who May Qualify	Prefer-ence	Necessary Forms		General Information
		For Those Applying Inside the U.S.	For Those Applying Outside the U.S.	
1. Husband or wife of a United States citizen.	**No Numerical Limitations** ("Immediate Relative" of U.S. Citizen)			There is no numerical limitation for an immediate relative of a United States citizen as shown to your left.
2. Child under 21 years of age of a United States citizen.		I-130 I-485 G-325A I-134 FD-258 I-486A		There is NO requirement for a Labor Certification.
3. Orphan adopted outside the United States by a United States citizen.			I-130 OF-230	Remember that a United States citizen must be over 21 years old to petition for his or her parents. But you do not need to be over 21 years old if you are a United States citizen and petitioning for your husband or wife.
4. Orphan coming to the United States to be adopted by a United States citizen.			I-600 (orphans only)	
5. Parent of a United States citizen over 21 years old.				
Unmarried sons and daughters over 21 years of a United States citizen.	First Preference	I-130 I-485 G-325A I-134 FD-258 I-486A	I-130 OF-230	This preference comes under the numerical limitation of 58,000. The United States citizen parent will petition for the **Unmarried** sons or daughters, not **Married** sons or daughters. A Labor Certification is NOT needed.
Husband or wife and all **Unmarried** children of a lawful permanent resident alien.	Second Preference	I-130 I-485 G-325A I-134 FD-258 I-486A	I-130 OF-230	The lawful permanent resident alien is the same as the I-151 or green card holder. He or she will petition for their immediate family as shown to your left. You cannot petition for your **Married** sons and daughters. There are numerical limitations of 58,000. A Labor Certification is NOT needed.

Who May Qualify	Preference	Necessary Forms		General Information
		For Those Applying Inside the U.S.	For Those Applying Outside the U.S.	
A professional or highly skilled person. (Scientists, doctors, etc.) Must have exceptional ability in his or her field.	Third Preference	I-140 ETA 750. A & B		Will need a "Job Offer" from a prospective employer and a Labor Certification. There are no age limits or marital requirements. There are numerical limitations of 29,000.
A **Married** son or daughter of a United States citizen. (Must be married at time of application for admission.)	Fourth Preference	I-130 I-485 G-325A I-134 FD-258 I-486A	I-130 OF-230	The mother or father must be a United States citizen and will petition for his or her **Married** son or daughter. A Labor Certification is NOT needed. There are numerical limitations of 29,000.
A brother or sister of a United States citizen over 21 years of age.	Fifth Preference	I-130 I-485 G-325A I-134 FD-258 I-486A	I-130 OF-230	The United States citizen who is petitioning for his or her brother or sister must be over 21 years of age. It does not matter how old the beneficiary is. A Labor Certification is NOT needed. There is a numerical limitation of 69,600. (All unused allocations from previous preferences will be used here according to the respective hemisphere.)
Needed skilled or unskilled workers. Mechanics, agriculture workers, union trades, etc. (The magic word here is **needed**. Jobs must be ones for which there' are NO qualified or willing, available U.S. workers at "prevailing wages".)	Sixth Preference	I-140 ETA 750A & B		The skill or labor to be performed must be in short supply. A job offer from a perspective employer and a Labor Certification will always be needed. There are numerical limitations of 29,000.

Preference	Who May Qualify	Necessary Forms	General Information
Seventh Preference	A conditional entry by a refugee because of persecution of race, religion, political beliefs, are fleeing a communist controlled country or have been "uprooted" because of a catastrophic disaster as declared by the President of the United States.	I-589	Entering the United States as a refugee generally carries a wide range of interpretation. If it is a catastrophic disaster, then you must keep in mind that it has to be declared as such by the President of the Untied States. There is a general numerical limitation of 17,400. A refugee will need to "petition" or have a "sponsor." A Labor Certification is NOT needed.
Nonpreference	Non-Preference Immigrants are those who are unable to qualify for any of the previously mentioned seven preferences. A Non-Preference immigrant may include a "business investor." If you are financially secure and not dependent upon working in the United States.	I-526 (For aliens immigrating as investors)	You will petition for yourself. A business investor must invest at least $40,000. The numerical limitation depends upon the number of immigrant visas left over from the seven preferences. (You can only use those numbers that are left over.)

H. AVAILABILITY OF IMMIGRANT VISA NUMBER: HOW TO DETERMINE IF YOUR VISA NUMBER IS AVAILABLE

The availability of immigrant visas is published each month by the Visa Section of the U.S. Department of State. Since each "PREFERENCE" category is alloted a set percentage of the world-wide number of visas allowed for the year, the State Department necessarily keeps track of the number of visas used up by each foreign nation in the course of the year, as well as the number used in each preference category. In each month, the Department publishes a statement — the **VISA OFFICE BULLETIN** — listing the visa availability world-wide for each preference category and individually by each country. (See an illustrative sample of this Bulletin on pp. 13-14)

Only a limited number of immigrant visas are, of course, available within the numerical system for each foreign country and within each preference category. Consequently, there is established a method by which to determine the order in which aliens are to receive consideration for an immigrant visa.

In general, an immigrant visa applicant is "charged" to the country of the applicant's birth (and not the country of his citizenship or nationality), and this determines the country against whose annual allotment of 20,000 visas a particular applicant is to be charged. As often happens, the waiting list for certain countries (e.g. Mexico, the Phillipines, India or Hong Kong) is longer than for other countries. When such a situation exists, the law would permit what is know as an **"alternate chargeability"** or **"cross-chargeability"** under certain circumstance. Thus, for example, if your spouse or parent was born in a different country having a shorter waiting list, you will be permitted to have your visa charged against your spouse's or parent's country of birth, thus allowing you to secure an entry visa sooner than you probably would otherwise have.

As a rule, when the demand from any single country exceeds the 20,000-Visa limit in a given year, then for the year following, the visa availability for the natives of that country will be allocated according to the preference percentages for world-wide allocation of available visas.*

In such instances, the State Department establishes a cutoff date before which a visa applicant must have established a priority date in order for a visa to be made available for the applicant in that category. To put it differently, when natives of a particular country have used, or are projected to use, more than their country's visa allotment for any particular year, a date is established for each preference category for that country before which a priority date must have been established in order for a visa to be made available for an applicant in that category from that country.

In this manner, the State Department is able to distribute visas so that the allotments for each preference category are maintained on a world-wide basis while the ceiling for each country is preserved.

I. YOUR VISA "PRIORITY DATE"

Immigrant visa petitions are considered chronologically on the basis of the **"priority date"** assigned to the application. Because the number of immigrant visas is limited, a visa is given to the applicant (the beneficiary of the visa petition) with the earliest date. Thus, for example, if two persons with approved Labor Certifications and approved SIXTH Preference Petitions both apply for an immigrant visa on the same day at the same U.S. consulate abroad, the

---

*Such countries falling under this category are listed individually and clearly indentified in the U.S. State Department's Visa Office Bulletin. For example, in 1982, natives of the People's Republic of China used up their full allotment of 20,000 immigrant visas for the year. Hence, in the following year, 1983, visas where required to be distributed to that country's natives on the basis of set percentages for each preference category as follows:

Since not more than 10% of the available visas may be used world-wide in the Third Preference category, then no more than 10% of the visas available to the Chinese natives may be used in the Third Preference category in the year 1983, and so on and so forth. This way, by using the system of allocation, it is ensured that visas will be available in each preference category for that foreign state. For, otherwise, all 20,000 available visas might be used only by persons qualifying in the first few (top) preference categories, and the result will be that visas will be totally unavailable in the lower preference categories.

person with the earliest PRIORITY DATE will get the first visa that becomes available for the Sixth Preference for their particular country — that is, in the order of the priority date (also called "preference date") assigned to their respective applications.

The central importance of an alien's priority date is that it is the date used to determine, in effect, the alien's place on the "waiting list" for a visa as contained in the Visa Bulletin put out monthly by the U.S. State Department.

An alien whose application for a visa is in the stage of being processed, may check the priority date of his application by checking this Bulletin. (see sample of the Bulletin on pp. 13-14   ). According to a new regulation effective June 20, 1986, with respect to those aliens whose petitions for the visa are based on having secured an approved LABOR CERTIFICATION, the Priority Date is the date on which a particular alien's application for Labor Certification (see   p. 141) was first received and stamped by the local Employment Service in the U.S. It will be his Priority Date in the NON-PREFERENCE Visa Category. Then, if the alien later files a petition for a visa and has a THIRD or SIXTH preference petition approved based upon a profession or occupation, the alien is now placed into a higher preference — that is, the alien's THIRD or SIXTH preference priority date will be that same date on which the approved Labor Certification was first received by the Employment Service (and not the date on which the preference petition was submitted or approved). This, in other words, helps the alien, since he gets the advantage of the earlier priority date.

Here is the way this works in practice. Let's restate the basic rule in question here: an immigrant visa can be issued to an alien in the NON-PREFERNCE or THIRD preference or SIXTH preference category, only if there is an unused "available" visa from within the limited number of visas alloted the alien's country for the particular category in which the alien seeks to apply for the priority date. Another way the principle is often stated, is to say that the visa can be given the alien only if his priority (preference)date is "current" or "available". The visa is immediately "available" for a particular alien if the "waiting list" that existed shall have reached the priority date of the alien so that he does not have to wait on a list; and an alien's priority date is "current" for the alien's country and his preference category if any alien in that country and preference category may immediately apply for a visa inasmuch as there would be no waiting list for his country and preference category at the particular time.

To sum it all up, the point that is important for you to know and to remember, is this: *that for you to get an immigrant visa in your hands, you ultimately must meet not only the usual "qualitative" eligibility requirements for qualifying, but also the "quantitative" eligibility requirements — meaning that the visa number must be available for your country of birth at the very time you apply for the visa.* Thus, you may meet all the procedural ("qualitative") requirements prescribed for a visa and thus become "qualitatively" qualified for visa issuance in the THIRD or SIXTH preference, but if a current visa number is not available for you (meaning that you are not "quatitatively" eligible), you still will not be able to get a visa, nevertheless. (The same thing goes, of course,if you happen to meet the quantitative eligibility requirements, but lack the qualitative requirements).

EXAMPLE: Assume that in July 1986, the PRIORITY DATEfor available visa numbers for the THIRD preference (as published in the State Department's visa Bulletin), is January, 1987, and further assume that your U.S. employer filed for your Labor Certification with the Employment Service on September 1, 1985 — that is, the date on which the application for your Labor Certification was filed with the Employment Service. In other words, here your own particular priority date will come before the current priority date for the THIRD preference group as a whole (Jan. 1, 1986), meaning that a visa number would be immediately available to you.

---

*   For an alien seeking immigration based on close family relationship, the "priority date" is the date the visa petition is filed with the INS in the U.S.; for those based on an offer of permanent employment in the Third or Sixth preference categories, the "priority date" may be either the date the employer filed an application, or if an alien coming under a "blanket" Labor Certification under the Department of Labor's Schedule "A", it is the date of filing of the visa petition with the INS.

HOW TO USE THE VISA TABLE*

The State Department publishes a *Visa Bulletin* each month which reports the status of the various priorities. *See Figures* 5a, 5b *and* 5c *beginning on this page.* The *Bulletin* changes each month. To use the visa table, the reader looks down the left hand column of the table *(See Figure* 5b on page 14 *)* until the correct Place of Birth is found. If it is not listed separately, the "All Foreign States..."category at the top of the list is used. The column headings are then read to the right until the proper preference category is found. For Labor Certificate cases, this would be either the 3RD, 6TH, and/or NONPREFERENCE. Finally, the reader looks at the date or entry which appears at the intersection of the Place of Birth line and the proper Preference column.

IF ENTRY IS "C"

If the entry is "C", it means that visas are available for any properly qualified applicant with any priority date. "C" means current.

IF ENTRY IS "U"

The entry "U" means Unavailable. No immigrant visas are available for any alien in that preference no matter how old his priority date. The waiting list is probably quite long, and the State Department will not be able to issue visas in that preference for that Place of Birth until the table entry changes.

IF ENTRY IS A DATE

If the visa table entry is a date, the alien must wait for the table date to be later than his priority date. The alien's priority date must be earlier than the table date for there to be a visa available for him. If the alien's priority date is not earlier, the alien must wait for the table entry to become "C" or until the date shown is later than his date.

U.S. DEPARTMENT OF STATE
Bureau of Consular Affairs

VISA OFFICE

WASHINGTON, D.C.

Number   Volume

IMMIGRANT NUMBERS FOR JULY

Figure 5a

A. STATUTORY NUMBERS

1. This bulletin summarizes the availability of immigrant numbers during July. Consular officers are required to report to the Department of State all qualified applicants for numerically limited visas; and the Immigration and Naturalization Service reports the demand of all qualified applicants for adjustment of status. Allocations were made, to the extent possible under the numerical limitations, for the demand received by June 5th in the chronological order of the reported priority dates. If the demand could not be satisfied within the statutory or regulatory limits, the class or foreign state or dependent area, in which demand was excessive, was deemed to be oversubscribed. The cut-off date for an oversubscribed category is the priority date of the first applicant who could not be reached within the statutory or regulatory limits. Only applicants who have a priority date earlier than the cut-off date may be allotted a number. Immediately that it becomes necessary, during the monthly allocation process, to recede a cut-off date, supplemental requests for visa numbers will be honored only if the priority dates falls within the new cut-off date.

2. Issuances of visas are governed by provisions of Section 203 (a) of the Immigration and Nationality Act, as amended, which prescribes preference classes as follows:

First preference (unmarried sons and daughters of U.S. citizens): 20% of the over-all limitation of 270,000 in any fiscal year;

Second preference (spouses and unmarried sons and daughters of aliens lawfully admitted for permanent residence): 26% of over-all limitation; plus any numbers not required for first preference;

Third preference (members of the professions or persons of exceptional ability in the sciences and arts): 10% of over-all limitation;

Fourth preference (married sons and daughters of U.S. citizens): 10% of over-all limitation plus any numbers not required by the first three preference categories;

Fifth preference (brothers and sisters of U.S. citizens 21 years of age or over): 24% of over-all limitation, plus any numbers not required by the first four preference categories;

Sixth preference (skilled and unskilled workers in short supply): 10% of over-all limitation;

Nonpreference (other immigrants); numbers not used by the six preference categories.

*This discussion on the Visa Bulletin, and Tables 5a, 5b and 5c set forth herein, are reproduced for illustrative purposes, courtesy of Richard Madison's "The GreenCard Book."

July

Figure 5b

(For Illustration only, Entries are not Actual)

THE VISA TABLE

3. A labor certification under Section 212 (a) (14) or satisfactory evidence that the provisions of that section do not apply to the alien's case is a prerequisite for nonpreference classification. Since all beneficiaries of approved third and sixth preference petitions are required to have a labor certification in support of the preference petition, such applicants are thereby entitled also to the non-preference classification.

4. Section 203(b) of the Immigration and Nationality Act provides that visas be given to applicants in order of preference classes. However, Section 202(e) of the Act provides that, whenever the maximum number of visas have been made available to natives of a foreign state or dependent area in any fiscal year, in the next following fiscal year visas will be made available by applying the preference limitations to the foreign state (20,000) or dependent area (600) limitations. Foreign states and dependent areas listed below benefit under the provisions of Section 202(e) of the Act.

5. On the chart below the listing of a date under any class indicates that the class is oversubscribed (See paragraph 1): "C" means current, i.e., that numbers were available for all qualified applicants; and "U" means unavailable, i.e., that no numbers were available.

			PREFERENCE				
FOREIGN STATE	1ST	2ND	3RD	4TH	5TH	6TH	NONPREF-ERENCE
ALL FOREIGN STATES AND DEPENDENT AREAS EXCEPT THOSE LISTED BELOW	C	C	C	C	01-08-80	05-01-80	U
CHINA	C	12-08-80	04-15-80	02-15-79	01-08-77	09-22-79	U
INDIA	C	C	09-01-75	C	09-08-79	01-08-80	U
KOREA	C	C	C	C	09-08-78	01-08-80	U
MEXICO	C	01-01-72	C	04-22-78	09-22-77	01-08-80	U
PHILIPPINES	C	12-22-78	06-01-69	10-15-74	02-01-70	05-08-78	U
ANTIGUA	C	05-01-80	C	C	04-13-76	10-28-65	U
BELIZE	C	05-21-79	C	11-05-79	03-12-76	10-27-77	U
HONG KONG	C	09-08-76	09-12-69	03-22-77	04-22-71	03-02-78	U
ST. CHRISTOPHER-NEVIS	C	03-06-80	C	C	03-31-78	10-21-63	U

CA/VO -

Figure 5c

B. RECAPTURED CUBAN (SILVA) NUMBERS

1. Recaptured Cuban (Silva) numbers may be issued to those principal alien immigrant visa applicants born in independent countries of the Western Hemisphere, who registered with U.S. Consulates between July 1, 1968 and December 31, 1976, inclusive, and their spouses and children who are accompanying or following to join pursuant to 8 U.S.C. Sec. 1153(a)(9).

2. The reporting of demand for Recaptured Cuban (Silva) numbers; the allocation of numbers; and the establishing of the cut-off dates listed below follow the procedures outlined on page 1 of this bulletin, paragraph A.1., except that Silva allocations were made for demand received by May 10th.

COUNTRY

ARGENTINA	01-01-77	GUATEMALA	01-01-77
BAHAMAS	01-01-77	GUYANA	01-01-77
BARBADOS	01-01-77	HAITI	01-01-77
BOLIVIA	01-01-77	HONDURAS	01-01-77
BRAZIL	01-01-77	JAMAICA	01-01-77
CANADA	01-01-77	MEXICO	08-01-75
CHILE	01-01-77	NICARAGUA	01-01-77
COLOMBIA	01-01-77	PANAMA	01-01-77
COSTA RICA	01-01-77	PARAGUAY	01-01-77
CUBA	01-01-77	PERU	01-01-77
DOM. REPUBLIC	01-01-77	SURINAM	01-01-77
ECUADOR	01-01-77	TRINIDAD	01-01-77
EL SALVADOR	01-01-77	URUGUAY	01-01-77
GRENADA	01-01-77	VENEZUELA	01-01-77

C. PANAMA CANAL NUMBERS

1. The Panama Canal Act of 1979 (PL96-70) provides for the admission of 15,000 former employees of the Panama Canal Company or Canal Zone Government at the rate of no more that 5,000 visas a year. At the present time visas are available to qualified applicants on a "current" basis.

CA/VO -

J. HERE'S A SIMPLE LAYMAN'S WAY TO DETERMINE YOUR VISA NUMBER AVAILABILITY OR PRIORITY DATE

The Visa Office Bulletin, published each month by the U.S. State Department (see a sample on p13-14), reports on the status of the various priority dates and lists the visa numbers issued each month. And, a general way by which an alien would ordinarily try to determine whether a visa number for his particular visa preference category is available, or when his priority date has become current, is by looking up such information from the monthly visa Bulletin ; and if the alien should find that the date shown in the Bulletin for his country and preference is current and available (at the time that his petition is either filed or the decision is made on the petition), then he can conclude that he is eligible to get a visa.

The process, though, of doing even that — of going through the monthly visa Bulletin and trying to read and interpret the figures in the visa table by oneself — could often be unnecessarily confusing and burdensome, especially for a lay person. Hence, our simple advice is this: don't even bother yourself trying to do it yourself; let the immigration experts and personnel in the field do the work for you. Just call up or visit any of the following parties in your area and ask for help in providing you with the information: a U.S. consular officer; a U.S. Immigration and Naturalization Service officer; the Visa Office Section of the U.S. State Department in Washington D.C. (Phone No.'s (202) 663-1514 or (202) 632-1972), or a local lawyer or organization experienced and active in U.S. immigration matters. Ask to be informed about your status with respect to immigrant visa priority dates, whether the visa number for your particular preference category is available, and whether your priority date is "current". When calling, remember that visa numbers for the next month usually begin to be available during the last part of the present month.

```
╔═══════════════════════════════════════════╗
║  A NOTE TO YOU ABOUT SOME POSSIBLE         ║
║                                            ║
║  CHANGES IN THE PRESENT LAW                ║
╚═══════════════════════════════════════════╝
```

As of the writing of this book, there is an active move in the U.S. Congress to revise and overhaul the overall limit on legal immigration to the United States for the first time since 1924. Under a bill principally sponsored on the Senate side by Senators Edward M. Kennedy and Allan K. Simpson, and on the House side by Reps. Charles S. Schumer and Bruce A. Morrison, the following major changes are proposed to be made.

On the Senate side which in July 1989 did pass a bill containing these proposed changes, the following are the most important new features: i) a new (higher) over-all limit of 630,000 immigrants per year will be allowed, making it an increase of some 136,000 per year over the 1988 level, not counting refugees; ii) the proporti-on of immigrants selected each year on the basis of jobs or occupational skills (i.e., essentially those falling under 3rd and 6th preference categories) would be doubled, raised from its present 10% to a new level of 20%; iii) family reunifica-tion would still remain an overriding goal of U.S. immigration policy, and to ens-ure that, an increased number of visas - some 480,000 of the 630,000 immigrant vis-as issuable overall per year - would go to aliens on the basis of having a U.S. family relationship, while the balance of 150,000 visas would be admitted as "ind-ependents"; however, of the 480,000 visas issuable on the basis of family relatio-nships, a greater proportion of this will be made available to the spouses and young children of permanent resident aliens, while, on the other hand, eligibility for married brothers and sisters, in-laws, nieces, and nephews of U.S. citizens would be curtailed; iv) of the 150,000 visas reserved for "independents" - i.e., reserved for immigrants whose entry would not be based on family ties - a new category is created of some 54,000 visas per year which will be alloted to foreig-ners who have special skills needed by the U.S. but do not necessarily have jobs waiting for them or employers ready to hire or sponsor them, plus there's created a new category of some 30,000 visas to be alloted to 3rd and 6th preference categ-ories but reserved for professionals and skilled and unskilled workers who have jobs waiting for them in the United States; v) in selecting out the 54,000 immigr-ants to be granted a visa each year under the newly created category on the basis of possession of specially needed occupational skills, the government will make such selections on the basis of a **"point system"**, awarded for education, occupati-onal training, work experience, and age, with credit going to those in 21 to 44 years old bracket; and vi) the current visa system of no limit on the number of "immediate relatives" (spouses, minor children, and parents of U.S. citizens) who can enter the United States, would remain the same, but the proposed legislation would stipulate that the number of visas to be made available for immigrants who are not "immediate relatives", cannot fall below the 1988 level of 216,000, there-by guaranteeing current American citizens a minimum number of visas for their ext-ended family members; and vii) the proposed overall ceiling of legal immigants per year (630,000) will be reviewed and adjusted every three years, following certain prescribed procedures.

On the House of Representatives' side, on the other hand, the latest version of the bill sponsored by Rep. Morrison which last came up for final action in August 1990, would allow up to an overall ceiling of 775,000 legal immigrants per year, of which 520,000 will be based on family relationship, and 75,000 on job skills and professional qualification; plus, it would also allow for admission of another 55,000 "diversity" immigrants a year from areas that have not obtained many visas in recent years, such as Ireland and Africa.

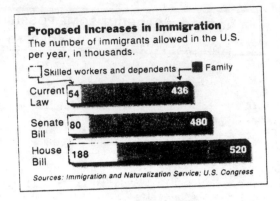

Proposed Increases in Immigration
The number of immigrants allowed in the U.S. per year, in thousands.

☐ Skilled workers and dependents ⬛ Family

Current Law	54	436
Senate Bill	80	480
House Bill	188	520

Sources: Immigration and Naturalization Service; U.S. Congress

As had apparently been envisioned originally by the sponsors and supporters of the new legislation, the principal objective behind it was to provide greater access to immigration for countries in Western Europe deemed to be, in Senator Kennedy's words, "the older sources of immigration"; the supporters had seemingly felt that the current 1965 immigration law, which had abolished the prior practice of setting quotas on immigrant visas, had come to place Europeans at a disadvantage lately, in that in recent years about 90% of legal immigrants qualified for visas on the basis of having a U.S. relative, and secondly, because lately more than 70% of all legal immigrants has come, not from Europe, but from Asia, Latin America, and the Caribbeans. As Senator Alfonse M. D'Amato of New York had summed it up: "Family reunification is a goal we all support. But what about those who have no immediate relatives in the United States? The present law shuts them out because they are from countries like Ireland or Italy, whose great days of immigration are long past". (N.Y. Times, Feb. 14,1988,"Key Senators Back Immigration Shift").

Nevertheless, as of the time of this manual going to press, a new national consensus and perspective seems to have evolved on the subject. The overriding consideration underlying this major overhaul of the immigration selection laws and policies now seems to be for the imperatives of the U.S. national economy, essentially for the purposes of recruiting and ensuring steady supply of foreign skilled workers and professionals for the growth needs of the U.S. economy and global competition in the years ahead. As Representative Morrison of Connecticut, a leader of the campaign for the new immigration legislation in the House, summed it us: "The debate has definitely shifted. In the past, few people focused on legal immigration as an economic issue. But a growing body of evidence shows that immigration creates jobs and stimulates demands...labor shortages can be a barrier to economic growth." ("Congress Acts to Admit More Skilled Immigrants," N.Y. Times,Aug. 15,1990).

By what date,specifically, will the proposed revisions actually become law? Or,what will be the actual or final provisions of the revised law? That remains to be seen for now. These much is certain already,though: that a new immigration legislation would probably be enacted in the foreseeable future,more likely within a matter of months; and that such new law will principally embody a new system, much along the lines sketched above, for permanent residency (i.e., immigrant) visa selection and allocation to aliens seeking legal admission to the United States!

CHAPTER TWO

THE NON-IMMIGRANT VISA CATEGORY: THE MAJOR SUB-CLASSES & THE SPECIAL CHARACTERICTICS AND ELIGIBILITY STANDARDS WHICH APPLY TO EACH.

In the preceding Chapter One, (pp. 1-5   ), we explained that the immigration visas are divided into two broad, catch-all categories — the immigrant and non-immigrant categories. And in Section C thereof   (pp. 4-5   ) we listed the various classes into which the non-immigrant category is subdivided. In this present Chaper, we shall discuss the <u>nonimmigrant</u> visa category, more specifically, the specific and specialized procedures, and the eligibility standards and qualifications that are applicable to each major class within the nonimmigrant visa category. For, though nonimmigrant visas as a class have many characteristics in common, strictly speaking virtually every nonimmigrant visa classification has some specific and specialized standards and requirements that are uniquely applicable to it.

The following are the types of nonimmigrants to be discussed below:

1. Temporary Visitors ("B" Visa) (at pp. 18-19)

2. Academic Students ("F" Visa) (pp. 19-20)

3. Vocational Students ("M" Visa) (pp. 20   )

4. Exchange Students ("J" Visa) (pp. 21-22   )

5. Temporary Workers of Distinguished Merit & Ability ("H" - 1" Visa) (pp 22-3   )

6. Temporary Services or Labour Workers ("H - 2" Visa) (pp 23-4   )

7. Industrial Trainees ("H - 3" Visa) (pp. 24   )

8. Intra-Company Tranferees ("L" Visa) (pp. 25-6   )

9. Treaty Traders & Treaty Investors ("E - 1" & "E - 2" Visas) (at pp. 26-8   )

10. Foreign Government Officials ("A - 1", "A - 2" & "A - 3" Visas) (pp. 28   )

11. "In Transit" Aliens ("C" Visa) (p. 28-9   )

12. Crewmen ("D" Visa) (p. 29)

13. Foreign Government Representatives to, and Employees of International Organizations ("G" Visa) (at pp. 29   )

1. TEMPORARY VISITORS (B - 1 & B - 2 Visa)

This is the largest category of nonimmigrants applying to go to the United States on a temporary basis, either for business purposes **(B - 1 Visa)**, or for pleasure **(B - 2 Visa).** According to the U.S. Foreign Affairs Manual; it is the explicit policy objective of the U.S. Government that the processing of the visitor's visa applications be expedited for "the facilitation of international travel both for its cultural and social advantage to the world and for its economic significance". Nevertheless, it has equally been true that, over the years, an increasing number of temporary visitors have used the devise of the nonimmigrant visa as an avenue by which to enter the U.S. only to remain permanently as overstays. For this reason, the immigration authorities have had to set forth a number of restrictions and criteria for admission, the aim being to attempt to limit the flow of temporary visitors only to those persons who are bona-fide nonimmigrants.

Basically, to qualify, you, the alien applicant, must be able to show the following:

(i) that you have a permanent residence in your foreign country which you have no intention of abandoning;

(ii) that you intend to enter the U.S. only for a temporary period of specifically limited duration; and

(iii) that you are doing so "to engage solely in legitimate activities relating to business or pleasure".

The following, for example, have been considered acceptable activities for visitors for pleasure (B - 2) applicants: tourism, social visits to relatives and friends, visits for health purposes or to participate in amateur sports or music contest and like activities, providing no payment is given for such participation. And such activities as the following have been considered acceptable activities for visitors for business (B - 1)applicants: taking of orders in the U.S. for a specialized product or service to be filled in a foreign country, negotiating in conferences or seminars of scientific, business or professional nature, visiting to instal or repair machinery or equipment which was purchased overseas or to train others for such activities, and the undertaking of independent research, participation in Board of Directors meetings or in professional athletic events involving payment limited to the prize money.

In making the determination as to whether to qualify an applicant as a visitor, here are the kind of factors the consular officials would generally consider:

(i) Are the arrangements you have made for meeting the expenses of your visit and return passage sufficiently adequate to make it unnecessary for you to have to obtain employment in the U.S.?

(ii) Might you have to work for pay in the U.S. or attend a school full-time?

(iii) Are your financial arrangements in any way dependent on assurances that relatives or friends in the U.S. will provide all or part of your financial support? If so, are there "forceful and compelling" ties between you and such sponsors which would lead the consular official to believe that the sponsors' assurances will in deed be undertaken?

(iv) Does it seem that you have "specific and realistic plans" for undertaking those things for which you are applying to make the visit, or, on the other hand, are your intentions merely "vague and uncertain"?

(v) Is the period of time for which you are planning to visit consistent with the stated purpose of your trip? And have you established with "reasonable certainty" that you will leave the U.S. upon completion of the stated purpose of your trip?

(vi) Is there any indication that you (the applicant) gave conscious consideration to your proposed period of stay, or are your intentions simple expressed in terms of remaining in the U.S. for the maximum time the U.S. authorities will allow or for the period for which friends and relatives have invited you?

(vii) Are you the principal wage earner for your family? If so, can you satisfactorily explain how your spouse and children will be provided for in your absence, and why you would wish to be separated from your family for a lengthy period of time, if it so applies:

(viii) Do you have reasonably permanent and well paying employment or business, or social or family relationships in your homeland significant enough to make you want to return home? *

As is the case in most visa application situations, it is on you (the visa applicant) that the whole burden falls to demonstrate to the satisfaction of the consular and immigration authorities that you have no intention of abandoning your foreign residence for good and that you will depart the U.S. voluntarily at the end of your authorized stay.

If a B - 1 or B - 2 visa issuance is approved, the visa will be stamped in your passport. Thereafter, so long as your visa has not expired and is still valid at the time, you may seek entry into the U.S. at a designated port of entry.

STUDENT & EXCHANGE VISITOR
CLASSES ("F", "M" & "J" Types of Visa)

Within the foreign "student" category of classes are the following three types of visas:

(i)   the "academic" student visa (called "F - 1" Visa)
(ii)   the "vocational " student visa (called "M - 1"), and
(iii)   the "foreign exchange" student visa (called "J - 1"),

2.   ACADEMIC STUDENTS ("F" Type Visa)

The "F" nonimmigrant visa class applies to the principal alien, and he (or she) is admitted in "F - 1" status, while his spouse and minor children, if applicable, are admitted in "F - 2" status.

Basically, to qualify as a nonimmigrant student, you should be able to demonstrate the following to the satisfaction of the U.S. consular officer (by providing adequate evidence and documentations to him):

(i) that you have a residence in a foreign country which you have no intention of abandoning;

(ii) that you are a "bona fide student qualified to pursue a full course of study" in the U.S.;

---

* If you are young, single and without permanent employment in your home country (e.g., a recently graduated student), expect to find it really difficult, probably impossible, to be issued a visa, no matter what financial guarantees are made on your behalf by a U.S. sponsor. Likewise, aliens with immediate family members permanently residing in the U.S. might have to demonstrate substantial ties to their home country to assure visa issuance.

(iii) that you seek to enter the U.S. "temporarily and solely for the purpose of pursuing such a course of study at an established institution of learning in the United States", one approved by the U.S. Attorney General for attendance by nonimmigrant students;

(iv) that you will, in fact, engage in a "full course of study" in the U.S.;

(v) that you have sufficient money or financial support* for at least the first year so that you won't need to engage in employment in the U.S,;

(vi) that you will be able to understand the English language well enough as to be able to carry out your studies; and, most important,

(vii) that you intend to leave the U.S. upon completion of your course of study.

First, before you even begin to apply for the F-1 visa, you shall have FIRST applied to and been accepted by an "accredited" school in the United States which is approved by the U.S. Attorney General for foreign student attendance. (Qualified schools are common, and include any Federal, state or local educational institutions, schools listed in the U.S. Department of Education publications, or a secondary school operated by a college or university listed in the said publications.) Upon your being accepted by the institution, the institution sends you (the alien student) a form, FORM 1-20A-B, with the first page of the form completed by the insitution. (See sample of Form 1-20A-B reproduced on pp. 73-7)

Thereafter, to apply for the F - 1 visa, you (the student) will apply at the American consulate in your home country by providing the consulate officer with Form 1 - 20 A – B. Under the immigration rules, the mere presentation by the student of a valid Form 1-20A-B is treated as "prima facia evidence" — that is, as a probable cause to believe — that the student will engage in a full course of study in the U.S., and that the institution in question is an accredited school duly approved by the Immigration and Naturalization Service (INS) for attendance by foreign students. It should be noted, however, that such evidence alone is not always accepted as final or conclusive by the consular or immigration personnel, and that they may atimes (as they are entitled to do under the law) make their own independent determination on the issue.

One principal *basis on which many student visa applications are* denied *is the lack of conviction on the part of the consular officer that the* prospective *student, if given admission into the U.S., will leave the United States upon completing his stated course of study, and that he would not, instead, seek employment and remain permanently in the U.S. thereafter.* Hence, you had better be well prepared to present substantial evidence to the consular officer demonstrating your intent to return to your home country — e.g., evidence of your ties to your home country, of availability of employment in your home country in the field of your intended specialization.

---

* In determining whether adequate financial support is available to you, you are permitted to count such funds, if any, as you are to derive from sources such as fellowships or work study programs from the U.S. school, scholarship or assistantship grants, such as research projects or lecturing or performance of other academic functions. Students will, however, need to attach Certification from the institution that they will also pursue a full course of study in addition to these other activities.

3. VOCATIONAL STUDENTS ("M" Type Visa)

The "M" nonimmigrant visa is the type of visa issued to the foreign student who is specifically limited to undertaking a full course of vocational training, as opposed to pure academic education. (The M - 1 is for the principal alien, while the M - 2 visa applies to his or her spouse and minor children). To qualify, the vocational training program must be undertaken in an established vocational or other recognized nonacademic institution. Training in such programs as the following, for example, have been considered acceptable for vocational students: training to qualify as an automobile mechanic, welder, secretary, computer programer, television repairing, book-keeping, health care technician, and so on.

What qualifications are required of you to be eligible for an M visa? Basically, the requirements for qualification for an M - 1 visa are essentially the same as those for the F - 1 visa (see pp. 19-20 above), but with just one exception: the M - 1 applicant must intend to study at a vocational or nonacademic institution. Thus, as a vocational, as opposed to academic student, you will have to apply for a FORM 1 - 20 M - N (instead of the FORM 1 - 20 A - B used for the F - 1 academic student visa). Thereafter, exactly as in the academic visa situation, you file the said Form 1 - 20 M - N with the U.S. consular officer in your home country to apply for the M - 1 visa (see illustrative sample copy of Form 1 - 20 M - N on pp. 73-7)

NOTE: As a rule, the consular officer, however, will not usually qualify you for an M vocational student status unless you can demonstrate that the vocational training you seek is not available in your own country, and that the particular training or skill you seek to acquire is needed in your country.

It's somewhat of significance for M-1 applicants to further note that the M category of students was carved out of the F student category by the Congress in June 1982 and made a separate category of its own, for this specific reason: to permit closer INS supervision over students whose programs were essentially vocational in nature. The INS had felt that vocational students required shorter periods of time to complete their programs, and that because of the difficulty involved for the INS in separating out vocational students from other students, it was difficult to determine whether such students had over-stayed beyond the period required to complete their vocational training. In addition, the INS felt it needed a way of separating out the vocational student applicant since many of them had often enrolled in programs which involved skills and training which could not readily be put to use in the students' home country, thereby increasing the likelihood that such students would remain in the U.S. and seek employment upon completion of their programs. Hence, the central concern of the INS in regard to the M visa applicant, is to police closely the conditions for entry and maintenance of status of such persons.

4. EXCHANGE STUDENTS ("J" Type Visa)

The exchange student visa, the so-called "J - 1" visa, has been characterized by one expert as "the most difficult type of student visa" for the alien to have. The central source of this "difficulty" has to do with the fact that a special restriction exists with regard to exchange students (and exchange visitors who come under the J nonimmigrant category for business and industrial trainees) which does not apply to other nonimmigrant categories. Thus, under a unique legal restriction which applies to no other nonimmigrant categories, the J - 1 visa holder must return to his or her home country for a period of at least 2 years immediately upon completing his or her original academic program

In brief, what this requirement means in practical terms, is this: the J-1 visa holder who has spent any time at all living in the United States, cannot apply to change or adjust his status to a Permanent Resident status as an immigrant; nor can he even apply to change his status from the "J-1" nonimmigrant status to another nonimmigrant status — until and unless he shall have first gone back to his country and lived there for the required two-year period immediately following his authorized period of study in the U.S..

The professed rationale and intent behind the exchange student or visitor program, is said to be primarily to help the so-called "Third World" countries to implement or speed up their economic development by providing them with professionals of high skills and training designed to go back and assist in developing such under-developed conditions. With such professed mission in mind, the immigration authorities have generally had a policy of strict enforcement of two-year foreign residency requirement in most instances.

NOTE however, that under a provision of the Immigration Act (Section 212 (e) thereof), the J - 1 visa holder is allowed to avoid the 2 — year foreign residence requirement, and may also immediately adjust his status to permanent residents in the U.S., under one condition: if he applies for and receives a **WAIVER** from the Department of Justice's INS. Such a waiver may be granted under the following conditions: (1) if the J-1 alien can show that he (or she) is married to a U.S. citizens or lawful permanent resident and that departure from the U.S. would bring "exceptional hardship" upon the alien's spouse (or upon a minor child of the alien, who is either a U.S. citizen or permanent resident); or (ii) if the alien can establish that he would be subject to persecution " on account of race, religion or political opinion" if he were to return to his country; or (iii) if the alien's home country gives a statement in writing to the Secretary of State stating that it has no objection to such a waiver being granted to the alien. In all circumstances **however,** the waiver is adjudicated by the U.S. Attorney General's office, and is generally granted "upon the favourable recommendation" of the USIA supporting a waiver, which is often. times based on the request of a U.S. Government agency or the INS. (To apply, the alien files Form I-612, "Application for waiver of the foreign Residence Requirement", with the INS).

Foreign nationals who use or seek the J visa essentially fall into four groups:

(i) students seeking to pursue graduate or post-graduate progams at a U.S. University;

(ii) scholars and other experts, often University professors, seeking to undertake research or to train others in their skills;

(iii) foreign medical doctors coming to U.S. medical institutions or hospitals to receive specialized or advanced training in certain medical specialties; and

(iv) persons from business or industrial organizations who seek to come to the U.S. to receive training in particular occupational skills, or in a particular company's methods and techniques, or an introduction to U.S. business or industrial techniques.

How do you qualify to receive a J - 1 visa? Essentially, the requirements you need to demonstrate to the local U.S. Consular Officer in your home country, are the same as those required for the F - 1 student situation (pp. 19-21 above).

To apply for a J - 1 visa as an exchange student or visitor, you (the alien applicant) will present a FORM IAP-66 (see same reproduced on p. 78) to the consular officer located in your home country. (You shall have, in other words, first applied to and been accepted by a U.S. educational institution approved by the Department of State for exchange visitor program, which would then have provided you with Form IAP-66, duly signed by the school authorities). The consular officer will determine at the time of the visa application whether or not you will be subject to the 2—year foreign residency requirement, and if so, he is required to notify you of that condition, and to make a notation of that requirement on the form IAP-66.

TEMPORARY WORKER CLASSES ("H" & "L" Type Visas)

This is one of the most commonly applied for nonimmigrant visa categories by aliens. Basically, this category falls into four main classifications, three of which fall under the "H" classification, with the last one falling under the "L" classification. They are:

(a) The "H - 1" or Distinguished merit and Ability Temporary Worker (pp. 23 below);

(b) The "H - 2" or Labor/Services Temporary Worker (pp. 23-4 below);

(c) The "H - 3" or industrial Trainee Temporary Worker (pp. 24 below); and

(d) The "L - 1" Intra-company Transferee (pp. 25-6 below).

(The dependents, that is, the spouses and minor children accompanying or following to join the principals under any of the "H" categories, are classified as having "H - 4" status, while their counterparts accompanying or following to join the L - 1 principal are classified as having "L - 2" status. Such dependents are not permitted to work, except that the children are allowed to go to school).

To apply for any H or L type visa, the application is initiated by "petition" (as opposed to an "application"), meaning that a sponsoring "petitioner", that is, another person other than the alien, say the alien's employer-to-be who is located in the U.S., would have first applied for a visa on behalf of the alien (the "beneficiary"). The said petitioner files this petition on your (the visa "beneficiary's") behalf by completing FORM 1-129B and filing it on the alien's behalf with an office of the Immigration and Naturalization Service in the United States. (see illustrative sample copy of Form 1-129B on pp 83~88. Now, if the INS approves the petition, it sends a notice of such approval to the U.S. consulate in the country in which the alien beneficiary is residing. The U.S. consulate, in turn, notifies the alien of the approval of the petition filed on his behalf, and, thereafter, the alien now makes his own direct application for the visa to the consulate ("STEPS" 5 of   Chapter 6, at pp. 68   ).

HOW TO QUALIFY UNDER EACH OF THE "H" OR "L" CLASSIFICATIONS

5. H-1 TEMPORARY WORKER: THE DISTINGUISHED MERIT AND ABILITY TEMPORARY WORKER.

Workers coming under this category are defined as aliens having "distinguished merit and ability". To qualify for a visa under the H - 1 category, an alien would   usually have to have a level of skill and recognition far beyond that ordinarily available in his field of expertise. Such persons are usually prominent in their field, often with a high level of competence and education, such as advanced university degrees.

As C. James Cooper Jr., a widely experienced immigration legal expert, sums it up, "in almost all cases where the H - 1 status is sought, the Immigration Service will require either proof of international renown, or at a minimum, a university degree related to the work which the foreign national intends to perform in the United States." ["American Immigration Tapes: Text", (1986)at P. 19]

Cooper Lists two principal ways by which one may establish oneself as a person of distinguished merit and ability: first, apart from the person meeting the INS's routine definition of a professional (which includes formal qualification as an architect, engineer, lawyer, physician, surgeon, and school and college teacher), he or she should also have at least a Bachelor's degree in his field, and, most preferably, a higher academic degree such as a Master's or a Ph.D. Then, a second way of demonstrating this, is for the applicant to be "a person of prominence, renown or pre-eminence in his or her specialized field" — through such proofs as newspaper articles by or about the alien, membership in international societies in which such membership is based on outstanding achievement, receipt of distinguished awards recognized as contributing immensely in the alien's field of specialization, listing in the "Who's who" almanac of internationally recognized persons in one's field, remuneration in high figures in one's profession.

Cooper advises applicants to "always remember that you have the burden of proving that you are a person of international renown and that even though you may not qualify (in the eyes of the immigration service)..... you may very well be eligible if you list all your accomplishments, awards and other internationally accepted standards of recognition. This is certainly not a time to be modest about your accomplishments".

6. THE LABOR OR SERVICES TEMPORARY WORKERS ("H - 2" Visa)

To qualify for a visa under this H - 2 category, an alien need not have an exceptional skill or ability. In deed, he need not have any skill or ability per se—he (or she) may be skilled, or semi-skilled, or totally unskilled. What is of relevance here, is that the position the H -2 applicant seeks to fill be temporary in nature, and that the work in question be one for which there is a demonstrated shortage of American workers willing and able to perform it, as officially certified by the U.S. Department of Labor.

Note that, unlike the H — 1 category, for which no LABOR CERTIFICATION is required, such certification from the U. S. Department of Labor is required with respect to the H - 2 category, stating that the Department so determines that no qualified U.S. worker is available to fill the position in question. (see pp. 141-154) for procedures by which a Labor Certification may be obtained).

Typical of the H - 2 workers, are the agricultural workers who could previously be admitted to the United States during harvest time, ski instructors who come only during the ski season, or sales clerks who only work during the Christmas sale seasons. Effective from June 1987, however, a new subdivision of the H - 2 category, namely the "H - 2 A" Agricultural Workers classification, was created by the Immigration Reform and Control Act of 1986. By this, the agricultural worker who previously had been admitted as part of the H-2 category, may henceforth be admitted as an H-2A worker. The H-2A classification is subject, however, to the same requirements as the H-2 category regarding labor certification, etc, with the same application forms used and identical procedures followed.

7. INDUSTRIAL TRAINEES ("H - 3" VISA)

To qualify for a visa under the H - 3 category, there are basically three key essentials:

(i) the alien must be coming to the U.S. to participate in a bona fide established training program under an American company or employer;

(ii) the alien must be able to show that the skill or training he or she will receive in the United States is not readily available in his or her home country or elsewhere; and

(iii) the alien must show that the training and his stay in the United States is for a temporary period, and that he intends to leave the U.S. after the program is completed.

Many large U.S. corporations (industrial establishments, organizations, firms, etc. in the fields of agriculture, commerce, finance, government, transportation, and the professions) often have training programs which involve both classroom instruction and on-the-job training. A typical H - 3 candidate, for example, would be, say, an alien from an agriculturally backward Third World country who wishes to learn some of the American agricultural techniques and technologies for increasing crop production which have made the United States so pre-eminent in the world in agricultural productivity.

In making a determination as to whether an alien qualifies for an H - 3 classification, a number of principles have been established over the years by which the Immigration Service officials assess the applicants. In sum, however, the most significant consideration for an H - 3 program seems to boil down to this: that an alien trainee not engage in what is termed "productive employment", if such employment will displace an American resident. The Immigration Service's overriding concern is that the alien trainee not be performing productive employment, as opposed to (and in the guise of) genuine job training. Hence, as a rule, if the INS authorities should believe that the amount of productive employment involved is excessive in comparison to the job training or instruction to be received, the petition will usually be denied.

Hence, to ensure approval of his H - 3 petition, the petitioning U.S. employer must typically back up his petition with adequate supporting documents. The employer must document the following: that an actual training program exists; that the program involves considerable hours of classroom instruction as well as of on-the-job training without supervision; that the training is not for the purpose of recruiting and training aliens merely to staff U.S. firms, but would actually provide the alien with training which is unavailable outside the U.S.; that the training is purposeful (is actually meant to impart skill or experience), and not just incidental to giving an alien productive employment.

8. INTRA-COMPANY TRANSFEREE ("L" Visa)

The L — 1 visa, formally called the "INTRA-COMPANY TRANSFEREE" visa, is commonly viewed among immigration experts as **probably the best of the family of four nonimmigrant temporary worker visas.** The specific objective of the U.S. Congress in passing the law which brought about this nonimmigrant category in 1970, was to ease the way for large international companies to transfer foreign employees and personnel to the United States for tours of duty therein so as to strengthen international trade with other countries of the world. Consequently, in the law creating the L --1 program, Congress used a broad, unambiguous language which made it apparent that many small business entities, even individual investors, could take advantage of the L category as well.

One great attraction of the L - 1 visa comes from the fact that it is easier for the intra-company transferee, if he is an executive or a manager, to change his (or her) status to a permanent resident status if his U.S. company can show that it needs his services permanently. The ease of changing to such permanent residency status stems from several factors: for one thing, such a Transferee(if an executive or a manager) is not required to get a certification from the U.S. Department of Labor as to whether or not there is a shortage of labor; secondly, unlike the situation with respect to other nonimmigrant temporary worker categories (e.g. the H - 1 category), the L - 1 visa holder need not maintain a domicile in a foreign country, as long as his intent and the intent of the employer is for his (the alien's) services to be utilized in the United States temporarily. Furthermore, the alien may have served in one capacity in foreign country and yet fill a different position in the United States. Nor is the alien required to be employed on a full-time basis by his would-be employer in the U.S. Finally, the initial approval period for the L - 1 transferee is three years, and may be extended in increments of one year.

Typical of those who use the L -- 1 visa, are executives of foreign-based parent organizations needing to travel to the United States frequently to oversee the operations of their U.S. subsidiaries. Frequently, multinational companies with subsidiaries or branch offices in both the U.S. and a foreign country have need to transfer their executive or those with specialized expertise in and out of the United States, enabling such executive to readily make multiple trips in and out of the United States to oversee business operations or problems as the need arises.

Simply, you qualify for intra-company transferee (L - 1) visa if you (the alien) meet the following requirements:

(i) you are seeking to enter the U.S. for a temporary period;

(ii) to perform services of a managerial or executive nature, or involving specialized knowledge;

(iii) with the same company or an affiliate or subsidiary of the company, with which you have been employed overseas for one year (or more) immediately preceding the time of your visa application.

A rather central question that follows, is: how do you define the key terms "managerial", "executive", or "specialized knowledge", as described in the above listed requirements? Let's make one thing clear outright, to begin with: there is no objective or simple definition or test available under the immigration law or regulations by which this determination can be made. As in most other areas of the immigration laws or procedures, we are dealing here with a matter which depends highly on the subjective discretion and disposition of the particular consular or immigration official who handles your visa application. And this reality still becomes more especially true and acute with respect to positions which may be said to fall under the so-called "grey area" — that is, those involving lower level type of managers (foreman, office managers, and the like), as differentiated from the top management types of positions (e.g., the principal partners or the directors or officers of the corporation) for whom the status may be more readily easy to categorize.

True enough, in the end, your fate may well wind up still being determined by what one obscure immigration or consular official thinks! Nevertheless, it still wouldn't hurt you to have a fair guideline by which to attempt a definition of what is needed. Here is one expert's rather vivid but useful definition of the above-named three key terms:

"Show me a person who can hire and fire employees (whom he supervises and controls), and I will show you a manager. On the other hand, show me a person who has authority to sign company checks and to make policy decisions and I will show you an executive. Show me a person who has proprietary knowledge (i.e., that type of knowledge which is unique to or used in a particular business, e.g. customer lists, trade secrets or a secret recipe) which is essential to the operation of a business, and I will show you a person with specialized knowledge". (C. James Cooper, Jr. P. 23.)

9. TREATY TRADERS ("E - 1") & TREATY INVESTORS ("E-2") CLASSES.

Types "E - 1" and "E - 2" visas, more formally called the TREATY TRADER and TREATY INVESTOR visas, respectively, are, in a word, meant for the business-oriented aliens who want to come to the United States in order to direct and develop the operations of a business in which they have invested substantial funds or in which sizable trade takes place.

The E type visas are a highly unique visa. For, though they are a non-immigrant type of visas, **they are nevertheless viewed as the closest thing within the nonimmigrant classification to the immigrant (i.e permanent resident)** visa. For one thing, an alien having a treaty trader (E - 1) or a treaty investor (E - 2) status, need not maintain a domicile in a foreign country, as one would be required to do under most other nonimmigrant categories. Furthermore, there is no requirement that the intended stay in the U.S. should be temporary, which means that a holder of an E visa may stay in the U.S. for an indefinite period of time so long as he or she continues to maintain the business enterprise for which he had secured the visa. Equally worthy of note, is that the E visa is typically issued for up to 4 or 5 years, depending on the treaty country involved. The initial period of stay is limited to one year, but an unlimited number of extensions is possible in two-year increments.

Do you qualify for an E type visa? Here are the basic requirements you are to meet:

(i) you (i.e. the alien applicant for the visa) must be a "national" (that is, a <u>citizen</u>, but not necessarily a native) of a country with which the U.S. has signed a treaty for trade and navigation (see list of such countries below);

(ii) you should be able to prove to the consular and immigration officials that you have the <u>intent</u> in good faith, and will be able, to depart the U.S. upon the termination of your visa status.

(iii) the trade you seek to carry on must be on a "substantial" scale and international in scope, principally between the U.S. and your foreign country, and carried on by you (the alien) on your own behalf or as agent of a foreign person or company so engaged.

(iv) the company which you represent shall have been incorporated under law or be otherwise formally registered for business purposes within the foreign treaty country of which you are a citizen.

(v) more than 50% of the trade involved must take place between your country and the U.S.

(vi) you (the alien visa applicant) must be actively managing either your own business or your employer's; if in another's employ, such employer or company must have the same nationality as yours (the treaty country), with at least 50% of the U.S. organization owned by nationals of your (the treaty) country; you must be employed in a supervisory or executive capacity, or, if employed in lesser capacity, you should have specialized skills or qualifications such that your services are essential to the operations of your company or employer.

(According to the U.S. Foreign Affairs Manual, most E - 2 visas go, not to large foreign corporations requiring multi-million dollar investments, but to businesses requiring relatively small investments, such as grocery stores or restaurants).

As for the treaty INVESTOR or E - 2 situation, as compared to the treaty trader or E - 1 situation, the qualifications are essentially identical to those enumerated above except that the treaty investor applicant needs to show that he is entering the United States for the sole purpose of <u>investing</u> a "substantial" amount of capital, or that he has so invested already; that the business enterprise in which he has made, or intends to make such investment, is actual, and is a genuine bona-fine business either already existing or in the process of formation, and not merely a fictitious paper operation.

According to the guideline given by the U.S. Foreign Affairs Mannual, in general whether an alien's investment qualifies as "**substantial investment**", would depend on the type of business, the nature of the business operation required, and whether the investment has already been made or is simply in the process of being made. The central question to be determined here by the examining consular or immigration official in making such determination, is essentially this: does the type of investment offered by the particular alien applicant in the particular line of business, seem to be "substantial" within the context of the particular business, in relation to the kind of funds which would ordinarily be necessary to effectively operate in that type of business?

The Foreign Affairs Manual provides, for the benefit of consular and immigration examiners, two tests by which such determination should be attempted: (1) the "**relative**" **test,** wherein the amount invested by the alien should be weighted against the total value of the particular enterprise in question (more appropriate when investment is in an ongoing established business); or (2) the so-called "**proportionality**" **test,** wherein the amount invested by the alien should be weighted against the amount normally considered necessary to establish a viable enterprise of the type contemplated (more applicable when the alien is in the process of investing in a new business).

THE TREATY COUNTRIES

As of this writing (if uncertain, you can always check with your local U.S. consulate), the countries with which the United States has entered into the appropriate treaty qualifying them for both E - 1 and E - 2 visa privileges, are the following:

Argentina	Iran	The Phillipines
Austria	Italy	Spain
Belgium	Japan	Suriname
China (Taiwan)	S. Korea	Switzerland
Colombia	Liberia	Thailand
Costo Rica	Luxembourg	
	Netherlands	Togo
Ethiopia	Nicaragua*	The United Kingdom
France	Oman	Vietnam
Germany	Pakistan	Yugoslavia
Honduras	Paraguay	

In addition to the above countries, the following countries qualify ONLY for E - 1 (treaty trader) status: Bolivia, Brunei, Denmark, Estonia, Finland, Greece, Ireland, Israel, Latvia and Turkey.

How do you apply for an E - 1 or E - 2 visa from outside the United States? To apply, you do so by completing Forms 1-506 & 1-126 and filing them with the U.S. consular officer covering your area of residence or operations in your foreign country. (Illustrative sample Form 1 - 506 is reproduced at pp. 103-4. and Form 1 - 126 is at pp. 105-6)

---

* Note that on May 1, 1985, the U.S. give notice of abrogation of this treaty to Nicaragua, calling into question the status of the E visa holder from Nicaragua as of the effective date of such notice, which is May 1, 1986.

Under certain unique situations, an alien may have to apply for the treaty trader or investor visa from the United States. For example, an alien may qualify who is in the U.S., say on a business (B type) visa, and suddenly discovers a business opportunity in which he wishes to make substantial investment but finds that upon making such investment his presence is needed to manage the enterprise. In such situation, the alien will be applying, in effect, like one applying for adjustment of status (pp.161-170), while filing FORM I—526 and I—485.

10. FOREIGN GOVERNMENT OFFICIALS ("A - 1", "A - 2" and "A - 3" visas)

This category covers such officials as ambassadors, public ministers, and career diplomatic and consular officers of foreign governments and members of their immediate families.

Generally, for the United States to classify a diplomat or an official of a foreign government as qualified for the foreign government "official" designation, the foreign government involved must have been legally recognized by the United States. Otherwise, assuming that the alien involved is otherwise qualified for admission, he or she may simply be classified in such other category — e.g. as a temporary visitor, transit alien, or the like.

You may be eligible for a visa as an "official" if: you are regularly and professionally employed as a courier by the government to which you owe allegiance; if you are a foreign government representative to an international organization or are your government's official on official business. (Adequate proof and documentation to the consular officer regarding your asserted status, as well as details of the manner and destination of your journey,would usually be sufficient for a grant of the visa).

Persons in the A - 1 category are admitted for indefinite periods. However, those coming under A - 2 or A - 3 (i.e, the attendants and personal employees of A - 1 officials), are admitted initially for definite periods (usually 1 year), with extensions allowed in increments of no more than one year at a time upon application made by the alien. An application for extension of stay by persons coming under A - 2 or A - 3 categories, is made on FORM I -539, and is filed with the nearest immigration office with the necessary documentations (e.g. a statement from the employing official as to the applicant's current and intended employment) fully furnished.

11. IN TRANSIT ALIENS ("C" VISA)

The C visa is for the nonimmigrant who needs to make an immediate and continuous transit through the United States enroute to a final destination — for example, a Nigerian citizen who arrives in New York's John F. Kennedy Airport from, say, England, but needs to connect with a flight from New York to Nigeria, would be travelling on a "C" visa. Holders are not employable and not eligible to apply for change of status to any other type of visa. The alien shall have generally had,or will then apply for FORM I - 184 (permanent landing permit and identification card).

To qualify for issuance of a C visa, the alien must establish that he or she:

● is admissible, and is not ineligible for a nonimmigrant visa for any reason stipulated under the law (see Appendix A).

● seeks to enter the U.S. temporarily solely for the purpose of proceeding through the U.S. enroute to a specific foreign destination, or that he qualifies as a person entitled to pass in transit to and from the U.N. Headquarters by treaty arrangement.

● possesses a ticket or other assurance of transportation to his destination.

● has sufficient funds to enable him carry out the purpose of his transit journey.

● holds a valid foreign visa or other entry permit, if required by the country of destination.

● intends in good faith to depart the U.S. promptly upon the expiration of the period for which he is permitted to enter (usually no more than a maximum of 29 days).

12. CREWMEN ("D" VISA)

The **D visa** is the type of visa issued to crewmen (and women) aboard a vessel or an aircraft, the primary object of which is to enable them to get off for a short time while the vessel or aircraft is being repaired, refueled or serviced. Holders are not employable, and are not eligible to apply to change status to any other type of visa. The alien crewman will generally apply for and be issued a FORM 1 - 184 (permanent landing permit and identification card) by the immigration port authorities, and this enables him to gain entry into the U.S. territory proper.

13. FOREIGN GOVERNMENT REPRESENTATIVES TO & EMPLOYEES OF INTERNATIONAL ORGANIZATIONS ("G" VISA)

The **G visa** is the type of nonimmigrant visa issued to designated principal resident representatives of foreign governments to international organizations; to his deputies and other accredited officials on his staff; to an officer or employee of an international organization; to the attendant, servant or personal employee of a representative, official, or employee of the international organization; or to an immediate family member of any of the above mentioned groups.

To qualify for nonimmigrant status in this class, the alien claiming such status must be travelling to, or in transit through, the U.S. solely on official business connected with such an international organization. (Adequate proof and documentation to the consular office regarding your asserted status, as well as details of the manner and destination of your journey to and through the U.S., would usually be sufficient to win a grant of the visa).

Persons falling under the G - 1, G - 2, G - 3 and G - 4 classes (i.e., representatives to, and officials and employees of the international organizations) are admitted for indefinite periods, while persons falling under the G - 5 class (attendants, servants and personal employees of the foreign classes, and their familes) are admitted initially for definite periods (usually 1 year), with extensions allowed in increments of no more than one year at a time, upon application made by the alien. (Such application for extension is made on Form 1-539, and filed with the nearest immigration office in the U.S., with the necessary documentations, such as a statement from the employing officials as to the applicant's current and intended employment, fully furnished).

CHAPTER THREE

THE "K" VISA: A SPECIAL ENTRY VISA FOR FIANCES & FIANCEES ENGAGED TO MARRY U.S. CITIZENS

The **K visa** is singularly unique. Officially, it is classified as a <u>nonimmigrant</u> visa. However, in reality, it is almost like an immigrant visa, if not exactly one. Hence, we are devoting here a separate chapter solely to discussing the eligibility standards and the procedures involved in obtaining the K visa.

The K visa is, in short, for the alien living abroad who is a fiance or fiancee engaged to marry a United States citizen. The object of the K visa is to enable its alien holder, a fiance or fiancee of a U.S. citizen, to gain entry into the U.S. SOLELY for the alien to marry the U.S. citizen. If the alien is granted a visa, he or she must enter into the marriage with the U.S. citizen within 90 days of his or her entry into the U.S.; otherwise, the visa shall expire and the alien fiance or fiancee must return to his or her home country. No extensions are given on a K visa, the sole exception being in cases of illness or other like unforeseen emergencies; and no change of status to other categories, immigrant or nonimmigrant, is permissible for the K visa holder or the minor children accompanying such K visa holder, if any.

The K nonimmigrant category is unique in one major respect, namely: it differs from any other nonimmigrant classification in that it is the only nonimmigrant visa about which it is clear from the time of its issuance and at the time of the alien's entry into the U.S. at the border, that the alien nevertheless intends to remain in the U.S. <u>permanently.</u> (Under a provision of the Immigration Marriage Fraud Amendments of 1986, however, all K nonimmigrants upon marrying the U.S. citizen spouse, are subject to a 2—year period of "conditional permanent" residence, first).

A SUMMARY OUTLINE OF THE VISA & ENTRY PROCEDURES:

1.   The U.S. citizen engaged to the alien, prepares and files a "petition" (FROM 1 - 129F) in the United States with the local Immigration and Naturalization Service (INS) office in his area of residence there, naming the alien fiance or fiancee as the "beneficiary" to be granted a K visa to enter the U.S. (see sample FORM 1 - 129F reproduced on p. 2-3). The children of the alien, if applicable, may be included in the same petition. A second form, only recently introduced, FORM G - 325A, (see sample on p. 110), is also completed by the petitioner (and by the spouse-to-be) and submitted.

2.   Certain supporting documentations may generally be required of the petitioning U.S. citizen, among them: satisfactory evidence establishing that both parties have previously met and know each other in person within the past 2 years, and sworn statements (or other evidence) by the parties that they are legally free and are able to marry, and are both intent on marrying each other within 90 days of the alien partner's arrival in the United States.

3.   The INS routinely forwards a copy of the petition to its central office for an investigative check against the information held in its Fraudulent Petition Index File

4.   The INS looks over the petition and may approve or disapprove it. Assuming it is approved, the INS forwards the approved petition to the American Consulate in the foreign country in which the alien spouse-to-be lives. The consulate notifies the spouse-to-be that such petition has been approved and invites her (him) to appear for a visa interview and to submit certain documentations.

5.   The alien spouse-to-be assembles and submits the following documents to the U.S. consul:

> An application form from the U.S. consul, which she is to complete.

ii) a valid PASSPORT from her country (for herself, and for any minor child(ren) accompany, if applicable)

iii) her birth Certificate

iv) COURT ORDER of divorce from any previous marriage, if applicable.

v) a POLICE security clearance CERTIFICATE (with regard only to countries where the alien lived for 6 months or more since attaining the age of 16).

vi) report of MEDICAL EXAMINATION (Use Form OF 157 or equivalent)

vii) a SWORN STATEMENT of ability and intent to enter into a bona fide marriage with the U.S. citizen within 90 days of the alien's entry into the U.S.

Viii) PHOTOGRAPHS of both parties

ix) an "AFFIDAVIT OF SUPPORT" (a sworn statement of financial condition) or other proof supplied by the U.S. citizen showing that the alien will not be a "public charge" upon being admitted to the U.S. (See sample on p. 79)

6. The consular officials will review the documents submitted and conduct the visa interview with the alien spouse-to-be.

7. Assuming that all goes well, the alien will be issued a K visa. This visa must be used for travel within 4 months from issuance, or else a revalidation of the petition will become necessary each time the 4 months period expires.

The alien to whom the K visa is issued is given a sealed envelope by the consular officer; she presents this during immigration inspection upon her arrival at a U.S. border port of entry. (The envelope contains copies of the approved petition ,the statement by the beneficiary of ability and intention to marry, medical examination report and birth Certificates of the beneficiary and any of her children to whom a K visa was also issued). The K visa holder is given an INS. FORM 1 - 94 with employment authorization stamped on it; the children accompanying or later joining, are given the K - 2 visa.

Upon the alien's entry into the U.S., after the marriage takes place, the alien spouse will file to acquire the status of an immigrant alien, basically by submitting FORM 1 - 485 ("Application for status as Permanent Resident"), among others, in a procedure that is very similar to the adjustment of status procedure (pp.161-170).

NOTE: The forms are obtainable from the Publisher's FORMS DIVISION (see pp. 191-2). In completing them, read and closely follow the instructions accompanying or contained in them, including information on filling out *forms* and what supporting documents to provide.

FORM I-129F

UNITED STATES DEPARTMENT OF JUSTICE
IMMIGRATION AND NATURALIZATION SERVICE (INS)

Petition for Alien Fiancé(e)

OMB No. 1115-0054

DO NOT WRITE IN THIS BLOCK

Case ID#

A#

G-28 or Volag#

The petition is approved for status under Section 101(a)(15)(k). It is valid for four months from date of action.

Action Stamp

NOTE — READ INSTRUCTIONS CAREFULLY

Fee Stamp

AMCON: _____
☐ Personal Interview   ☐ Previously Forwarded
☐ Document Check
☐ Field Investigations

Leave Blank

REMARKS:

A. Information about you

1. Name (Family name in CAPS)   (First)   (Middle)
(Name of the U.S. citizen)

2. Address (Number and Street)   (Apartment Number)

(Town or City)   (State/Country)   (ZIP/Postal Code)

3. Place of Birth (Town or City)   (State/Country)

4. Date of Birth (Mo/Day/Yr)

5. Sex
☐ Male
☐ Female

6. Marital Status
☐ Married   ☐ Single
☐ Widowed   ☐ Divorced

7. Other Names Used (including maiden name)

8. Social Security Number

9. Alien Registration Number (if any)

10. Names of Prior Husbands/Wives

11. Date(s) Marriages(s) Ended

_____

_____

12. If you are a U.S. citizen, complete the following:
My citizenship was acquired through (check one)
☐ Birth in the U.S.
☐ Naturalization
  Give number of certificate, date and place it was issued

☐ Parents
  Have you obtained a certificate of citizenship in your own name?
  ☐ Yes   ☐ No
  If "Yes", give number of certificate, date and place it was issued

13. Have you ever filed for this or any other alien fiancé(e) or husband/wife before?   ☐ Yes   ☐ No
If you checked "yes," give name of alien, place and date of filing, and result.

B. Information about your alien fiancé(e)

1. Name (Family name in CAPS)   (First)   (Middle)

2. Address (Number and Street)   (Apartment Number)

(Town or City)   (State/Country)   (ZIP/Postal Code)

3. Place of Birth (Town or City)   (State/Country)

4. Date of Birth (Mo/Day/Yr)

5. Sex
☐ Male
☐ Female

6. Marital Status
☐ Married   ☐ Single
☐ Widowed   ☐ Divorced

7. Other Names Used (including maiden name)

8. Social Security Number

9. Alien Registration Number (if any)

10. Names of Prior Husbands/Wives

11. Date(s) Marriage(s) Ended

_____

_____

12. Has your fiancé(e) ever been in the U.S.?
☐ Yes   ☐ No

13. If your fiancé(e) is currently in the U.S., complete the following:
He or she last arrived as a (visitor, student, exchange alien, crewman, stowaway, temporary worker, without inspection, etc.)

Arrival/Departure Record (I-94) Number   **Date arrived** (Month/Day/Year)

Date authorized stay expired, or will expire, as shown on Form I-94 or I-95

INITIAL RECEIPT	RESUBMITTED	RELOCATED		COMPLETED		
		Rec'd	Sent	Approved	Denied	Returned

Form I-129F (Rev 5-4-89)Y

I-129F

B. (Continued) Information about your alien fiancé(e)

14. List all children of your alien fiancé(e) (if any)

(Name)	(Date of Birth)	(Country of Birth)	(Present Address)

15. Address in the United States where your fiancé(e) intends to live

(Number and Street)   (Town or City)   (State)

16. Your fiancé(e)'s address abroad

(Number and Street)   (Town or City)   (Province)   (Country)   (Phone Number)

17. If your fiancé(e)'s native alphabet is other than Roman letters, write his or her name and address abroad in the native alphabet:

(Name)   (Number and Street)   (Town or City)   (Province)   (Country)

18. Your fiancé(e) is related to you. ☐ Yes ☐ No

If you are related, state the nature and degree of relationship, e.g., third cousin or maternal uncle, etc.

19. Your fiancé(e) has met and seen you. ☐ Yes ☐ No

Describe the circumstances under which you met. If you have not personally met each other, explain how the relationship was established, and explain in detail any reasons you may have for requesting that the requirement that you and your fiancé(e) must have met should not apply to you.

20. Your fiancé(e) will apply for a visa abroad at the American Consulate in_____

(City)   (Country)

(Designation of a consulate outside the country of your fiancé(e)'s last residence does not guarantee acceptance for processing by that consulate. Acceptance is at the discretion of the designated consulate.)

C. Other information

If you are serving overseas in the armed forces of the United States, please answer the following:

I presently reside or am stationed overseas and my current mailing address is_____

I plan to return to the United States on or about_____

PENALTIES: You may, by law be imprisoned for not more than five years, or fined $250,000, or both, for entering into a marriage contract for the purpose of evading any provision of the immigration laws and you may be fined up to $10,000 or imprisoned up to five years or both, for knowingly and willfully falsifying or concealing a material fact or using any false document in submitting this petition.

Your Certification

I am legally able to and intend to marry my alien fiancé(e) within 90 days of his or her arrival in the United States. I certify, under penalty of perjury under the laws of the United States of America, that the foregoing is true and correct. Furthermore, I authorize the release of any information from my records which the Immigration and Naturalization Service needs to determine eligibility for the benefit that I am seeking.

(U.S. Citizen signs here as "petitioner")

Signature X_____   Date_____   Phone Number_____

Signature of Person Preparing Form if Other than Above

I declare that I prepared this document at the request of the person above and that it is based on all information of which I have any knowledge.

(Print Name)   (Address)   (Signature)   (Date)

FORM I-129F

G-28 ID Number _____

Volag Number _____

✦ U.S. GPO:1989-241-708/08814

CHAPTER FOUR

THE IMMIGRANT VISA ("GREEN CARD") CATEGORY: THE ROUTES TO ELIGIBILITY WHICH ARE BASED ON HAVING A FAMILY RELATIONSHIP WITH A U.S. CITIZEN OR "GREEN CARD" HOLDER.

As previously discussed (see pp. 1 & 5), the **IMMIGRANT** visa (also called by such names as "permanent resident" visa or the "Green Card") is that type of visa sought by that category of aliens who mean to live or remain **permanently** in the United States — in contrast to the NON-IMMIGRANT visa, meant for staying in the U.S. for a definite or limited period of time.

A. THE IMMIGRANT VISA SELECTION SYSTEM

As more fully outlined elsewhere (see pp. 6), the process of obtaining the right to lawful U.S. permanent Residency (immigrant visa status) is primarily governed by the immigrant visa "selection system" outlined under the immigration laws of the United States. The selection system is divided into two basic parts, namely:

(i) that part covering those classes of intending immigrants who are exempt from (i.e. are not subject to) any numerical limitations; and

(ii) that part dealing with those classes of intending immigrants who are subject to numerical limitations.

In this chapter, the concern will be limited to just those routes of gaining immigrant visa or permanent residency eligibility on the basis of one common denominator: the alien having some sort of <u>family relationship</u> with either a U.S. citizen or Permanent Resident. In this connection, *it should be taken note of that family relationships of varying kinds, as between aliens(i.e. non-U.S. nationals) and U.S. citizens or Permanent Residents, constitute the most important basis on which the overwhelming majority of immigrant visas are sought or granted every year. Hence, the great significance of this chapter.*

The reason why family relationship is so central is no mere accident: it has always been a deliberate and central policy aim of the immigration laws of the United States historically, to unify, reunite and prevent the separation of family members as much as possible.*

B. CATEGORIES OF IMMIGRANTS COVERED IN THIS CHAPTER

Included in this chapter, to cover all major categories of intending immigrants for which family relationship constitutes the basis of such claims to eligibility, are the following categories of immigrants:

(i) Those applying under the "immediate relatives" of U.S. citizens classification (i.e., a spouse or child of a U.S. citizen, or the parent(s) of such a citizen over 21 years of age).

(ii) other sons and daughters of U.S. citizens falling under the FIRST and FOURTH PREFERENCES on p. 7-9 (i.e., unmarried children over the age of 21 of the U.S. citizen, and the married children of U.S. citizen, respectively)

---

*A brief review of the classifications forming the basis for granting permanent immigrant visas (see pp. 7-10), will quickly show you, for example, that out of the total of seven "preferences, by which categories of eligible immigrants are selected, four of them relate to family relationships alone, aside from the separate "immediate relatives" and other family-related categories.

(iii) spouses, and minor or adult but unmarried sons and daughters of U.S. Permanent Resident aliens under the SECOND Preference on p- 7-8 above; and

(iv) the brothers and sisters of U.S. citizens under the FIFTH Preference on p. 7-9 above (the U.S. citizen sponsor must be 21 years of age or over).

C. A SOLE ADVANTAGE OF "IMMEDIATE RELATIVES" OF U.S. CITIZENS OVER OTHER KINDS OF FAMILY RELATIVES: NO WAITING FOR A VISA NUMBER

The reader will recall that, as previously noted (see pp. -   ), in so far as persons qualifying under the category of "immediate relatives" of U.S. citizens are concerned, such persons are exempt from numerical restrictions and are permitted to gain immigrant visas in no specific limited numbers. *The important point to be noted here, is that this exemption from numerical restrictions which applies to "immediate relative" applicant, does NOT apply to other aliens qualifying for immigrant visa on the basis of other kinds of family relationship.* To put it simply, for the reader, here is basically the one difference it makes to you in practical terms: if, on the one hand, your visa petition is based on an "immediate relatives" relationship, you would not have to worry about being put on or having to wait on a "waiting list" before you may be assigned a visa number; you would be assured of a visa number immediately upon your proof of qualification and documentations. However, if, on the other hand, your visa petition is based on a family relation-ship of any other kind other than as "immediate relative", then there must first need to be a visa number available at the time of your application before you may get a visa, meaning that you may have to go on a "waiting list" until it's your turn to get a visa number.* (See pp.   ,though, for full account of how the numerical limitation system works.)

This aside, the good news, though, is this: that other than this one difference, the basic procedures and substantive visa issues involved in all family relationship-based immigrant visa petitions are virtually the same. Hence, we have chosen to discuss all categories of family-based immigrant visa situations under this one chapter.

D. THE FIRST KEY PROBLEM AREA IN FAMILY-BASED IMMIGRANT VISA PETITIONS: ESTABLISHING THAT A FAMILY RELATIONSHIP ACTUALLY EXISTS

The most important issue involved in qualifying for per-manent residence visa in any one of the family-based prefe-rences, or as an immediate relative of a U.S. citizen, is

---

*By at least one expert account, the least backlogged category having the shortest waiting period or probably none at all, is the Ist Preference category, and the same is also true of the 4th Preference category for most countries. It is said that the major demand for immigrant visas based on close family relation, is in the 2nd and 5th preferences, and that both of these categories have experienced chronic backlogs in visa availability for most   countries since June 1982, with considerably greater backlogs (as much as 2 years) for persons in virtually all countries who apply in the 5th preference. (See Immigration Law & Business, by Austin T. Fragonen, et al., Vol. I, pp. 3-31-3-32.)

verification, determination and acceptance by the immigration authorities that a qualifying family relationship <u>does</u> <u>in</u> <u>fact</u> <u>exist</u> between the **sponsoring** petitioner (i.e.,the U.S. citizen or Permanent Resident), and the alien for whom the visa petition is filed, called the "beneficiary" of the petition. In this regard, being able to qualify as a **"CHILD"** as defined under the Immigration Act, determines eligibility for most of the family-based preference categories, particularly the First, Fourth,and Fifth preferences, and further determines eligibility with respect to qualifing as a "child" or a "lawful Permanent Resident" within the Second Preference category, or as a "child" or "parent" of a U.S. citizen.

The core relationship which serves as the defining factor for all family-based rights and benefits accorded under the immigration law, is the PARENT-CHILD relationship. Section 101 (6)(1) of the Immigration and Nationality Act defines the term "child" to include an unmarried person under the age of 21 years, who is:

a) a **legitimate child** ;

b) a **stepchild,** whether legitimate or illegitimate, as long as the child was not yet 18 years old when the marriage creating the status of stepchild occurred;

c) a **child legally legitimized** prior to the age of 18,provided the child is in the legal custody of the legitimizing parent at the time of the legitimization;

d) an **illegitimate*** child in relation to its natural mother, or in relation to its natural father if the father has or had a bona-fide parent-child relationship with the child;

e) an **adopted** child or children; and

---

*For immigration purposes, the rule is that the issue of whether a person is "illegitimate" is generally determined according to the law of the person's place or state of birth. For such countries which do not, for example,even make any distinction between legitimate and illegitimate children (e.g.,African cultures and those of South America), or for those in which laws have been adopted abolishing the making of any distinction concerning legitimacy as between children, the issue is virtually irrelevant for immigration purposes. In such situations, either of the natural parents may petition for the child as all children under such situations must in effect be deemed "legitimate".

**A few helpful pointers need to be noted on children falling under the "adopted" and "orphan" backgrounds. For an adoption to be recognized as valid for U.S. immigration purposes, the following general conditions must be met: if the adoption occurs in a foreign country, that country's adoption laws apply; if it occurs in the U.S., the adoption laws of the intended State of residence in the U.S. apply. The apotion must occur <u>before</u> the child's 16th birthday,and the child must have been in legal custody of,and lived with the adopting parents for at least two(2) years from after the adoption; you must be prepared to provide, in support of the petition for the child, that type of documentation required for an IMMIGRANT applicant who comes from the child's place of residence, as well as acceptable court papers or other documentations in proof that the adoption took place,in accordance with the laws of the place of the supposed adoption.

f) **orphans***, provided certain conditions apply.

The following are the types of showing often required to be provided to establish a valid child-parent relationship for immigration purposes:

- Evidence that the child lived with and was cared for as the child of the parent (or stepparent), or that the parent otherwise showed an active parental interest in the support and welfare of the child. (For example, proof of financial support, frequent visits or contacts with child by letter or other means, open acknowledgement of the child, evidence that the parent has held out the child as his own and provided for the child's needs, and, in general, any documented actions by the parent which reflect the existence of a parental relationship with the child).

- Documentary proof that the designated parent(s) are in fact the parent(s) — e.g. affidavits from persons present at the time of the pregnancy and birth of the child who can affirm the identity of the natural father and/or mother.

- Marriage Certificate or other proof of the marriage between the parents, where applicable.

- The child's birth certificate

- Evidence of the legal termination of prior marriages, if either parent was previously married.

- In general, <u>credible</u> evidence that a bona-fide blood relationship exists between the child and the designated parents — the blood relationship must be established by "Clear and convincing" evidence; this evidence may include a blood test if other evidence such as the father's name on the birth certificate or a judicial determination of paternity, is not available.

E. THE SECOND KEY PROBLEM AREA IN ESTABLISHING A FAMILY RELATIONSHIP: DETERMINING THAT A QUALIFYING MARRIAGE ACTUALLY EXISTS.

Next to the definition of "child", the definition of who qualifies as a "spouse" is the second most important issue involved in qualifying aliens as "family members" for the purposes of eligibility for issuance of immigrant visa. **The primary issue in most such matters, is this:** whether the underlying marriage upon which the claimed marital relationship is based is valid, including the validity of any prior divorces had by either spouse, if any.

---

* In respect to orphan children: generally, the orphan must have been a bona fide orphan, that is, both parents must have truly died or abandoned him, and where there's one surviving parent, he or she must have signed proper irrevocable surrender papers permanently giving up the child for adoption, with some showing that the surviving parent is incapable of supporting and caring for the child on his own; the petition for the adoption of the orphan must be filed <u>before</u> the child's 16th birth day; if the child is to be adopted in a foreign country, the adopting parents must show that they personally saw and approved of the child before the adoption was finalized.

The basic rules governing this are as follows: that a marriage must be. legally valid at its inception (from its very beginning); and the marriage must not have been entered into for the purpose of evading the U.S. immigration laws, i.e., as a fraudulent or "sham" marriage.*

One vital essential is that the alien spouse and the U.S. citizen or permanent resident must be parties to a legally valid marriage. In making a determination as to such a validity of the marriage, it is the law of the place where the marriage occurs that governs, in that the common view is that if the marriage happens to be valid at the place where it is contracted, the simple principles of comity dictate that it be recognized in other jurisdictions just as well.**

The exceptions when the above stated rules with respect to recognition of foreign contracted marriages do not apply and are hence not respected, include these:

i) when the parties to a marriage would be subject to criminal penalties for cohabiting in the U.S. jurisdiction where they reside or will reside; ii) where the marriage is deemed to be "against public policy" under U.S. social practices (e.g. a polygamous marriage or one between close relatives); and iii) where the parties to the marriage were not physically present at the marriage ceremony in the presence of each other, and the marriage was not consumated.; iv) in instances where one or both of the parties to the marriage have been previously married and then divorced, what may determine whether the present marriage of the parties is recognized as valid may well depend upon the validity of the prior marriage or marriages; thus, any such divorce(s) must be valid in the jurisdiction where the alien resided at the time of the divorce, and must also be accepted and deemed valid in the jurisdiction where the present marriage of the parties occurs.

Here are the major questions often posed on the issue of the marriage's validity:

1. Does the marriage in fact meet all the formal requirements of the jurisdiction (the place) in which it was entered into?

.2 Is the marriage recognized as a valid lawful marriage in the state of residence in the U.S.?

3. Does the marriage continue as a legal marriage, i.e., has no divorce or formal separation been entered into in the marriage in question?

4. Is it evident that the marriage was not entered into for the sole or primary purpose of obtaining an immigration benefit, such as an immigrant visa?

5. Were the parties entitled to enter into the current marriages on the basis that all prior marriages were legally terminated?

---

*As established over the years by the courts, the test for making the determination as to whether a marriage was fraudulent at its inception, is roughly this: the marriage is fraudulent "if the bride and groom did not intend to establish a life together at the time they were married." (Bark vs. INS, 511 F.2d 1200 (9th Circuit, 1975)).

**Note that all divorces granted by U.S. State courts are considered valid, as are subsequent marriages.

F. "SHAM MARRIAGE" PROVISIONS OF A NEW 1986 MARRIAGE FRAUD ACT.

Much of the documentations required to be supplied in support of visa petitions in which a marriage relationship is claimed, essentially centers on one question: establishing the *bona-fide* (the genuineness) of a marriage at its inception. Hence, the Immigration and Naturalization Service (INS) investigatory procedures are directed at the discovery of such marriage relationships that are sham or fraudulent. In deed, in 1986 the U.S. Congress, concerned about doing something about the growing issue of sham marriages, passed a law, the immigration **Marriage Fraud Act,** with provisions particularly designed to ferret out cases of sham marriages.

In this, the INS examiners are aided in the detection of fraudulent marriage relationships by a special provision of the new law. By this provision [Section 241(c) of the Marriage Fraud Act thereof] any marriage formed or terminated within 2 years before or after the admission of the alien to permanent residence in the U.S., is "presumed" to be a fraudulent marriage, and it is the alien's "burden" to prove that such is not the case.

The law provides that an alien "shall be deported as having procured a visa or other documentation by fraud" and "to be in the United States in violation of this Act", if he or she obtains lawful permanent status on the basis of a marriage,

> "Entered into less than two years prior to such entry of the alien and which, within two years subsequent to any entry of the alien into the United States, shall be judicially annulled or terminated, unless such alien shall establish to the satisfaction of the Attorney General that such marriage was not contracted for the purpose of evading any provisions of the immigration laws".

Particularly viewed with great abhorrence by the immigration authorities, is one particular variant of the marriage fraud, the situation commonly refered to as **"gigolo" marriages.** It refers to the situation in which a foreign national marries a U.S. citizen solely to procure an immigration benefit such as an immigrant visa, usually without the knowledge of the U.S. citizen. Often it such cases, the matter comes to light when the U.S. citizen spouse discovers that the foreign national is not interested in maintaining the marital relationship, but has rather used the marriage for the purpose of obtaining the immigration benefit.

G. MAJOR FRAUD COMBATING PROVISIONS OF THE MARRIAGE FRAUD LAW

The following are major provisions of the newly enacted law (the Marriage Fraud Act) designed to combat fraud in marriage for immigration purpose:

The **"alien spouse"** is defined specifically as aliens admitted to permanent resident status within two years of the marriage upon which the application for residency is based.

1. All "alien spouses" of U.S. citizens and Permanent Residents are now granted permanent residency status only "conditionally" for a period of two years, whenever the marriage upon which the immigration visa is based was formed within two years prior to the grant of the residence.

2. The couple is required to file a second visa petition within 90 days prior to the 2 years anniversary of the grant of conditional residence, so that the Immigration Service can re-evaluate the bona-fides of the marriage.

3. At any time during the two years of the alien spouse's conditional residency status, the Attorney General can in his discretion terminate such status and subject the alien to deportation, if the marriage is terminated by divorce or annulment during the two years following the grant of residence, or if during that period credible information comes to the attention of the Attorney General that the marriage in question was entered into for the purpose of procuring the alien's entry into the U.S. as an immigrant or that an unlawful fee or other payment was given for procuring the alien's permanent residency

4.   Approval of a SECOND Preference petition is barred for a spouse of a permanent resident if the permanent resident obtained his own residence through marriage to a citizen or another resident within 5 years of the filing of the new second preference petition. (Aimed at preventing aliens from entering into marriages to obtain immigration benefits, then divorcing the sponsoring spouse and remarrying another alien to seek immigration for him or her).

5.   A criminal penalty, up to 5 years in prison, and a fine of up to $250,000 is added for knowingly entering into a fraudulent or sham marriage. The alien spouse and the U.S. citizen spouse alike are subject to criminal charges under the marriage fraud law.

6.   A severe restriction is placed on approval of marriage-based petitions and adjustment of status applications when the alien beneficiary married while involved in deportation or exclusion or related judicial proceedings. In such instances, an immediate relative or preference petition cannot be approved for the alien beneficiary until the alien has resided outside the U.S. for at least a 2 years period from the date of the marriage. (Applies only to marriages taking place after Nov. 10, 1986).

7.   An alien can only qualify as a fiance(e) in the K nonimmigrant category if he or she has personally met the U.S. citizen sponsor within 2 years of the date of filing the K visa petition.

THE NEW YORK TIMES,
SUNDAY, JANUARY 27, 1985

The New York Times/Edward Hausner

María Clemencia Turcios de Silverio with her husband, Alejandro, and their son, Lisandro, at home in the Bronx.

U.S. Moving to Deport Wife of a Citizen

By LARRY ROHTER

Federal immigration authorities have begun deportation proceedings against a Salvadoran woman whose husband and 2-year-old son are American citizens. The action reverses earlier decisions that have allowed her to remain in New York City for nearly five years.

The woman, Maria Clemencia Turcios de Silverio, has been told by the New York office of the Immigration and Naturalization Service that she must leave the country by tomorrow or be deported. According to Barry Oppenheim, an attorney for Mrs. Silverio, the warning came in a meeting with immigration officials on Dec. 31.

Mr. Oppenheim said he was pleading Mrs. Silverio's case this weekend before immigration, consular and Congressional officials in an effort to delay the deportation.

Previous rulings on Mrs. Silverio's case would have guaranteed her the right to remain in the United States while her request for immigrant status was being processed. Being the spouse or parent of an American citizen normally entitles a foreigner to preferences in immigration.

"I cannot understand why this is happening," said Mrs. Silverio's husband, Alejandro, who came to New York City from the Dominican Republic in 1972 and was naturalized in 1981. "If I am an American citizen and have a wife, I cannot see the motive for them not wanting to give her the right to live here with me and our son."

Mr. and Mrs. Silverio were married July 7, 1983. They live in the Bronx with their son, Lisandro.

Illegal Entries Cited

The district director of the Immigration Service, Charles Sava, and his deputy, James A. Jasey, did not respond to several telephone calls concerning Mrs. Silverio's case. But Scott Blackman, head of the deportation branch, said Mrs. Silverio "has to leave the country because she has been ordered to leave."

When asked for details, Mr. Blackman said the "underlying reason" for Mrs. Silverio's forced departure was that she had been "found to be deportable" because she twice entered the country illegally in the late 1970's.

Immigration and Naturalization Service records show, however, that despite those offenses, immigration authorities on several occasions since 1980 have approved Mrs. Silverio's requests to remain in the United States.

In addition, an immigration judge ruled in November that, although Mrs. Silverio's illegal entry was "not to be condoned," her status as the spouse and mother of American citizens outweighed the earlier offense and warranted a suspension of the government's order of deportation.

No Deferral Offered

Under Federal law, immigration officials have wide discretionary powers and can defer action on deportation orders for various reasons, including family considerations.

But Mr. Blackman indicated that the Government was unwilling to give special treatment to Mrs. Silverio, arguing that she had failed to comply with directives to report to the United States consulate in Mexico for processing of her immigration requests.

"When she leaves, she can go to any country she chooses," he said.

But Mr. Oppenheim, Mrs. Silverio's attorney, said Mexico and the Dominican Republic, her husband's homeland, had refused to grant her entry visas because there was no guarantee that she would ever be readmitted to the United States.

According to Mr. Oppenheim, the immigration service also sent Mrs. Silverio's file to United States officials in El Salvador last month and failed to inform her of that change. Mr. Blackman, asked about this, said he had "no immediate knowledge" of the file's whereabouts.

Mrs. Silverio said she feared for her life if she were forced to return to El Salvador and apply for readmission to the United States. She said she was afraid her ties to the United States would make her a target of political assassins.

Mrs. Silverio's situation is further complicated by the fact that her husband was wounded by robbers at work last fall when he went to the aid of his employer. After surgery on his right arm, he is now undergoing rehabilitation and receiving disability payments.

Mrs. Silverio said that, if she were deported, her family might have to go on welfare, which could give the immigration authorities grounds to deny her re-entry.

Sham Marriage and Other Residency Ruses Increase

Jubilant House and Senate conferees congratulate one another after agreeing on immigration bill last week. They are, from left, Representatives Romano L. Mazzoli and Charles E. Schumer, Senator Alan K. Simpson and Representatives Peter W. Rodino Jr., Dan Lungren and Hamilton Fish Jr.

In Bureaucracy, Aliens Find Another Unprotected Border

By ROBERT PEAR

WASHINGTON

THE conventional photograph of an illegal alien shows a person wading across the Rio Grande. To be sure, tens of thousands do so, but there are more sophisticated ways to short-circuit the immigration process.

Moving against one such method, the House of Representatives voted late last month to increase Federal penalties for foreigners who use sham marriages with Americans to gain entry to the United States. The bill, which has many supporters in the Senate as well, is separate from the landmark legislation Congress sent to the President late last week, overhauling the nation's immigration law and prohibiting the hiring of illegal aliens. But the measures have the same basic purpose: to bar foreigners who are not entitled to be in this country.

The Census Bureau estimates that 3 million to 5 million aliens live here illegally, though others put the figure much higher. Many of the aliens entered the country legally as visitors or students and simply stayed. Most would be deportable if the Government could find them.

But a marriage to an American citizen automatically makes an alien eligible for the legal status of a permanent resident, because the unification of families has long been an overriding goal of American immigration policy. The number of aliens who gain permanent residence this way has increased dramatically, from 87,221 in 1981 to 124,093 in 1985, and it is expected to reach 140,000 this year, The Immigration and Naturalization Service estimates that 30 percent of the petitions filed in such cases involve marriage fraud.

"In some cases, a U.S. citizen is party to the sham marriage," said Representative Romano L. Mazzoli, Democrat of Kentucky. "In others, a U.S. citizen enters the marriage in good faith, only to find out later that he or she has been cruelly duped by a person who wanted no marriage,

Some who got in

Immigrants who have gained permanent resident status in the United States through marriage, as a result of professional or creative ability or by providing skilled or unskilled labor that is in short supply. (fiscal years)

	Marriage	Professional and creative ability	Skilled and unskilled labor
1981	87,221	8,103	11,873
1982	99,268	11,981	12,041
1983	107,349	12,338	12,708
1984	111,663	10,691	11,393
1985	124,093	10,947	11,425
1986	140,000*	10,000*	11,300*

*estimate Source: Immigration and Naturalization Service

but permanent residence in the United States."

Sam Bernsen, a lawyer who worked at the immigration service for more than 35 years, said: "Marriage to an American citizen cures many immigration problems. You don't need to wait for a visa number, you don't need a labor certification, and sometimes you can even get waivers of inadmissibility for such things as a criminal conviction."

Immigration officials also suspect extensive fraud in papers filed by employers and aliens seeking immigrant work visas. Project Strongtree, an investigation in progress for more than a year, has found that employers purporting to need foreign workers sometimes did not exist or were shell companies established only to obtain the labor certification needed for a visa. In other cases, immigration officials said, the company existed but the job was phony.

Employers often show help-wanted advertise-

ments to demonstrate that American workers were not available, a condition the law requires. But sometimes the job descriptions were tailored to the qualifications of a specific alien, or the ad was written so as to discourage Americans applicants. "We see all kinds of convolutions, manipulations and creative writing," said John F. Shaw, assistant commissioner of the immigration service in charge of investigations.

But Federal investigators are swamped with work, so fraudulent petitions of all kinds — more than 40 types of applications and petitions can be filed by or on behalf of aliens — often go undetected. Since 1975, according to I.N.S. officials, the number of petitions the agency acted upon rose 40 percent, to almost 2.2 million this year. In the same period, they said, the number of investigators declined 29 percent, to 700. Congress approved a substantial increase in the agency's budget for 1987.

Even when immigration officials suspect fraud, they often have difficulty proving it. To win a marriage fraud case, for example, the Government must show that an alien intended to circumvent the law at the time of the marriage. Under the House bill, aliens could still become permanent residents by marrying Americans, but if a marriage ended within two years the Government could revoke the alien's status and begin deportation proceedings.

Whether they entered the country legally or illegally, aliens often prolong their stays by using fraudulent birth certificates, drivers' licenses or Social Security cards, according to immigration officials. In Texas and other Southwestern states, such documents are readily available for a small price. The comprehensive immigration bill Congress approved last week sets new penalties, including a $2,000 fine and two years' imprisonment, for aliens caught using false identification.

But the lure of America's prosperity and freedom is so great that officials expect to see many ingenious types of fraud designed to circumvent the new restrictions.

CHAPTER 5

OTHER ROUTES, OTHER THAN A FAMILY RELATIONSHIP, FOR GAINING ELIGIBILITY FOR THE IMMIGRANT VISA

In the proceding Chapter 4 (pp. 34-41), we dealt with the single most principal basis on which the overwhelming majority of immigrant visa ("Green Card") applicants lay their claims to eligibility — namely, having a close family relationship of one kind or the other to a U.S. citizen or Green Card holder. In the present chapter, we shall concern ourselves with the other remaining major bases and considerations, other than family relationship, by which aliens may just as well establish eligibility for the immigrant visa.

The following such other bases for gaining eligibility shall be discussed below:

a) Being a "SPECIAL IMMIGRANT"

b) Being a "MEMBER OF THE PROFESSIONS" or a person of "EXCEPTIONAL ABILITY IN THE SCENCES OR THE ARTS" (That is, persons qualifying under the THIRD Preference category (7 & 8)

c) Possessing work skills for which a shortage of employable and willing workers exists in the U.S. (That is, persons qualifying under the SIXTH PREFERENCE category (p.7 & 9)

d) Being a REFUGEE OR POLITICAL ASYLUM SEEKER

e) Being an "IMMIGRANT INVESTOR"

f) Being a FOREIGN MEDICAL GRADUATE

A.   ELIGIBILITY BASED ON BEING A "SPECIAL IMMIGRANT"

One route by which a person could qualify for eligibility for admission into the United States as an immigrant, is to qualify as a ""SPECIAL IMMIGRANT." As defined under the immigration laws, **persons who fit into the following description are classified as "special immigrants":**

i) A person who is already lawfully admitted to the U.S. for permanent residence, who is returning to the U.S. from a temporary visit to a foreign country — that is, a person already possessing a valid immigrant visa or "Green Card".

ii) A former citizen of the United States, who lost such citizenship, say, through marriage to an alien, or through service in allied armed forces during World War II or other eligible wars. Such persons may re-apply for re-acquisition of citizenship, but must first be admitted to the U.S. as lawful permanent residents.

iii) A minister of religious denomination during the past two years, who is affliated to a bona-fide organization in the U.S. (and his spouse and children, if accompanying or following to join him), and who seeks to come to the U.S. solely to carry on the vocation of minister, and whose services are needed by the religious denomination to which he is affiliated.

iv) A present, or an honorably discharged or retired former employee, of the U.S. government in a foreign country (and his immediate family), who faithfully served the government for at least 15 years. (This group's eligibility is subject to the approval of the U.S. Secretary of State's Office).

v) Graduates of foreign medical school who entered the U.S. on an H or J temporary visa (pp. 21-4), and were licensed to practice and were practising medicine in a state as of January 9, 1987, and have continously lived and practiced medicine in the U.S. since the date of their entry.

vi) *G- 4 Special Immigrants. Retired employees of designated international organizations (principally the UN, the International Monetary Fund and the World Bank, as well as other lesser known organizations), and certain family members of current or retired employees, who have been present in the U.S., in the G - 4 nonimmigrant classification (see pp. 28-9))

G - 4 aliens eligible for the special immigrant status, fall into four classes:

1) Includes the unmarried son or daughter, not older than 25 years, of a present or former employee of a designated organization; **2)** The surviving spouse of a deceased employee of a designated organization; **3)** Certain retired employees of a designated organization themselves who shall have resided in the U.S. for at least 15 years before the date of retirement; and **4)** the spouse of a retired G - 4 employee who has obtained special immigrant status under this provision.

B. ELIGIBILITY BASED ON BEING A MEMBER OF A PROFESSION OR POSSESSING EXCEPTIONAL ABILITY IN THE SCIENCES AND ARTS

Another route by which an alien (a foreign national) could become eligible for admission to the United States as an _immigrant_, is through qualification within the so-called "THIRD Preference" category under the numerical limitation system of the immigration laws. (see pp. 6-15 for discussion of the numerical limitation system and the preference classifications. Readers will note from reading those sections that the THIRD preference category is alloted 10% of the 20,000 visa numbers allowed each country per year).

The following summarizes the major attributes required of an alien in order to qualify under this (the third) preference category:

i) The alien must be a member of the professions, or a person possessing exceptional ability in the sciences or the arts.

ii) The U.S. Department of Labor must have determined ("certified") that the skills possessed by the alien is in short supply in the United States (i.e., that there is a shortage of U.S. workers who are able, willing, qualified and available to do the same job), and that acceptance of such employment by the alien will not displace a U.S. worker or adversely effect his wages or working conditions.

iii) The qualifying alien must have had a permanent job offer by his U.S. based prospective employer for the position in question.

iv) The U.S.-based prospective employer must file a petition for a visa with the INS on behalf of the alien fully supported by the approved "Labor Certification" from the U.S. Department of Labor, except, of course, for instances where the occupation sought

---

*This is a new class of special immigrants created only in 1986 by the Immigration Reform Control Act. (8 U.S.C.) S1101 (a) (27) (1).

clearly falls under certain designated occupations which are exempt from the certification requirement.

Who qualifies as a professional or a person of "exceptional ability in the sciences and the arts" for our purposes here?

Defining a "professional." As generally defined by the immigration authorities and the courts, the term "professional" has variously been assigned to any of the following: achitects, engineers, lawyers, physicians, surgeons and teachers in elementary or secondary schools, colleges, academics, or seminaries, physicists, journalists, librarians, industrial designers, translators, mechanical technologists, experience as a specialized business executive, bank official, economist, mathematician, chemist, pharmacologist, etc.

A matter worthy of particular note in this connection is this: in defining who qualifies as "professional," the immigration authorities have for their purposes adopted a policy of not being rigid or fixed in such definition. Rather, they have deemed it more proper and useful to be flexible in defining qualification as a "professional" in each given instance, doing so on a case-by-case basis.*

The Immigration and Naturalization Service states the following as a guide for evaluating whether a particular job title or experience may qualify a worker to be considered a member of the profession:

"In short, it refers to a given status which requires knowledge of an advanced type in a given field of science or learning gained by prolonged course of specialized instruction and study.... The common denominator is the fact that (professions) require specialized training that is normally obtained through high education of a type for which a bacholor's degree can be obtained or through equivalent specialized instruction and experience in lieu thereof" (Mattter of Shin, ibid, as cited in Immigration Law and Buniess, Vol I, at pp. 3.78-3. 79)

In other words, to be considered a "professional" for immigration purposes, the underlying common denominator is that you possess that level of specialized training, instruction and experience which is normally acquired as a result of advanced education, and demonstrate knowledge of an advanced type in the particular field in which you claim competence.

As a rule, attainment of a university degree (usually a baccalaureate degree or it's equivalent) is normally considered a minimum prerequisite for a person to be considered a member of the professions. Nevertheless, a abaccalaureate degree, while a necessary condition, is not usually sufficient in all cases. In some occupations, more than a bachelor's degree (e.g. a Master's or even Ph.d degree) may be required to achieve status as a member of a profession, depending upon an analysis of the job description and requirements set forth in the Department of Labour's Dictionary of Occupational Titles.

In so far as obtaining an immigrant visa under the Third preference category is concerned, the reader should note that **qualifying the alien as a professional-level employee is the most important step.** (see chapter 8, pp. 141-154 for the general procedures for obtaining a Labour Certification for a U.S. employment)

Defining "Exceptional Ability."

Who qualifies as a person of 'exceptional ability' in the sciences or the arts under the third preference here under discussion?

In the first instance, as has been defined by the courts and the immigration authorities over the years, persons falling under these skill categories are classifiable as possessors of 'exceptional ability': entertainers, athletes, or artists.

Of great general assistance in making such a determination have been the body of decisions handed down by the courts. Clarifying the terms in a 1966 ruling, an administrative case law defined the term "exceptional ability" as follows:

* In the leading case on professional status, Matter of Shin, II. I & N 686 (Dist. Dir. 1966), the rationale for flexibility in assessing the term "profession" was thus noted: "the vocations included in the 'professions' in our modern highly industrialized society are constantly expanding, consistent with the greater knowledge and specialized training that such a society demands".

"(Contemplating) something more than what is usual, ordinary or common, and requires some rare or unusual talent, or unique or extraordinary ability in a calling which, of itself, requires talent or skill". (In matter of Frank 11.I & N 657 (Dist. Dir. 1966).

It should be taken particular note of by readers, that in defining what is acceptable as "exceptional ability" for immigration purposes, the immigration authorities have generally taken pains to emphasize that 'exceptional ability' under the THIRD preference category is not equivalent to the term 'distinguished merit and ability' as used in regard to the H - 1 nonimmigrant worker classification (pp.22-3).

To qualify in the Third preference category, the central point of departure seems to be this: the person may not merely hold some renown in his field sufficient to grant him consideration as a person of distinguished merit and ability, but he must also have international renown and recognition such that he could be considered a person of intenational ability in his field of science or the arts. In addition, the foreign national's exceptional ability in his given field of knowledge must also be shown to have the potential of benefiting the national economy, culture or welfare of the United States.

Here is how the Regional Commissioner of the INS set forth the principle in a famous 1967 ruling: "Exceptional ability" under the Third Preference classification, he states, contemplates "a broader field of activity, knowledge, and ability than that encompassed by H - 1 'distinguished merit and ability'."(In Matter of Kim, 121 & N. 758, as cited in Fragomen's Immigration Law and Business, Vol I at p. 3-88). The commissioner added that the attributes required for qualification for an H - 1 classification "could be confined to a specific, limited act or ability which is a limited part of the whole field", while qualification for the The Third Preference category contemplates prominence or pre-eminence in the field as a whole.

C. ELIGIBILITY BASED ON POSSESSING A WORK SKILL FOR WHICH THERE'S A SHORTAGE IN THE UNITED STATES.

Another route by which an alien (a foreign national) could gain eligibility for admission to the United States as an immigrant, is through qualification within the so-called "SIXTH Preference" category under the numerical limitation system of the U.S. immigration procedures.

There are close similarities between the THIRD Preference category aliens and the SIXTH Preference aliens. Like the THIRD Preference applicant, the SIXTH preference applicant must: i) have an offer of permanent employment in the United States; and ii) the alien's U.S. employer must have obtained a "Labor Certificate" (pp. 141-154) from the U.S. Department of Labor indicating that acceptance of such employment by the alien will not displace a U.S. worker or negatively affect his wages or working conditions.

There is one apparent major point of difference between the two categories, however. And that is this: on the one hand, the alien qualifying under the THIRD Preference category is more selective, limited just to skilled persons who qualify either as national or internationally eminent members of the professions or as persons of exceptional ability in the sciences or the arts; the SIXth Preference category, on the other hands, is more inclusive, extending more broadly to all aliens, whether skilled or unskilled or with or without university degrees, so long as they possess some skills for which a shortage of employable and willing persons exists in the United States. To put it another way, virtually any worker, skilled or unskilled, may quality under the SIXTH Preference category — so long as the necessary labor certification papers can be obtained for or by that alien for the job sought! Consequently, *in so far as qualifying for eligibility under the SIXTH preference is concerned, the practical reality is this: being able to secure the supporting LABOR CERTIFICATION for the job in question is almost 99 percent of the task!* (Procedures for obtaining an alien labor certification is outlined in Chapter 8, at pp.141-154).

Typical SIXTH preference occupations are such positions as these: domestic workers, child monitors, janitors, draftsmen, and similar nonprofessional occupations involving physical and manual labor.

NOTE: Readers should note that, in light of the fact that the Third Preference category is a more limited grouping than the Sixth Preference, any aliens who can qualify under the Third preference category can also receive SIXTH preference classification. Such a situation can be advantageous to an alien in certain limited instances when the backlog of visa availability for the particular country is shorter in the Sixth Preference category than in the Third Preference. A good example, for instance, would be the Philippines, where the priority date for the Sixth Preference petitions is known to be more than eight years ahead of the priority date for the Third Preference petitions.

D. ELIGIBILITY BASED ON BEING A REFUGEE OR POLITICAL ASYLUM SEEKER

Another route we shall address here by which an alien could gain eligibility for admission to the United States as an immigrant, is through qualification as a REFUGEE seeking political asylum.

Under the SEVENTH PREFERENCE category within the numerical limitation system (see pp. 7 & 10 above), foreign nationals who qualify as refugees or political asylees may obtain U.S. permanent residency (i.e. an immigrant status), and without need to have obtained either a labor certification or a U.S. job offer.

Conditions for Qualification:

Under the **Refugee Act. of 1980,** to qualify for the refugee or political asylee status (also called the **"conditional entrant"** status in reference to the fact that such person has to meet certain special conditions to qualify), the alien has to meet one or more of the following conditions:

    i)   he (she) must have been fleeing from his home country either to escape actual persecution or because he merely has "a well founded fear of persecution:........on account of race, religion, nationality, membership in a particular social group or political opinion", or

    ii)   he must have been fleeing from either a communist or communist-dominated country, or from a country within the "general area of the Middle East" (defined as the area between and including Libya on the West; Turkey on the north, Pakistan on the east, and Saudi Arabia and Ethiopia on the South); or

    iii)   he must have been uprooted from his homeland by catastrophic natural calamity, civic disturbance or military operation as defined by the President of the United States, and cannot return to his usual home.

The standards for "refugee" and "asylum" status are virtually identical. The difference is only one of slight technically: the refugee is one from a third country outside his homeland who then seeks admission to the United States; in contrast, an asylee (one applying for asylum) must already be in the United States or at a port of entry thereof. (For example, an Iranian in France who seeks admission to the U.S. on the claim of persecution is a "refugee"; however, if he were already in the U.S., even if he could not have a passport or a visa, he would be thought of as an "asylum" seeker)

Do you get accorded automatic refugee or asylee status just merely for the fact that you managed to make your way to the United States (or a port of entry thereof) screaming 'persecution' 'persecution'? Not at all! In deed, by current estimates, in recent times there are anywhere from 30,000 to 40,000 applications each and every year flooding in worldwide in quest for asylum in the United States, of which only a fraction, about 25% thereof, is granted by the Immigration Service. (In 1984, for example, there were 32, 344 such applications, of which just 8,278 were granted. See the Table below on p. 47)

To be sure, the alien applicant has a right to expect one thing:not to be returned to the country where he or she would face persecution. This does not mean, though, that he has an automatic right to asylum in the United States. In deed, the reader should know that an alien, even if fully and legally eligible for asylum in the United States, still does not have an automatic right to it and may nevertheless be turned down by the U.S. authorities. *The point, simply, is that in the final analysis what gets to be decided depends almost entirely on one factor: the "discretion" and disposition of the Immigration and Naturalization Service (INS) officers.* As provided for by the Refugee Act of 1980, and supported by several court rulings since, aliens with well-founded fear of persecution "may be granted asylum in the discretion of the Attorney-General". In practice, there is an annual limitation, fixed by the U.S. Attorney general or the President, on how many asylum applications will be granted. And generally, such determination as to who to grant asylum is justified on the humanitarian concerns and the national interest of the United States. The officials of the INS, which is an agency of the

U.S. Attorney General's Department of justice, are said by one source to "almost always" base their determinations solely on the "advisory opinion" (written report of recommendation) supplied them by the U.S. State Department's Bureau of Asylum and Humanitarian Affairs on every such application submitted.

A crucial issue upon which most asylum cases almost always rests, is this: being able to establish to the satisfaction of the INS (and the State Department) officials, just **what constitutes a "well-founded fear of persecution" on the part of a given alien?** The standards set by Federal Courts for assessing this seem to amount to the following i) some "objective facts" (i.e. elements such as presentation of testimony, written documentations or other evidence) must support the alien's subjective fears of persecution, his fears that he would face danger in his homeland or that other people there had suffered persecution for similar reasons; ii) the alien must present "specific facts" tending to show that he will be so singled out for persecution; and iii) as handed down in the 1987 Supreme Court's 9 - 3 decision (INS. v Cardoza-Fonseca), an applicant need not have to show that there's a "clear probability" that he would be persecuted in his home country but simply that "persecution (in the home country) is a reasonable possibility". As the Court put it, in its rather liberal interpretation of the law, an applicant probably meets the objective eligibility standard for asylum if he demonstrates " a 10 percent chance of being shot, totured, or otherwise persecuted".*

TABLE 6

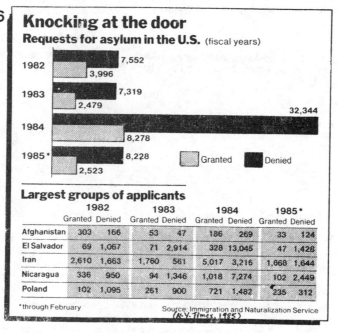

Knocking at the door
Requests for asylum in the U.S. (fiscal years)

Year	Granted	Denied
1982	3,996	7,552
1983	2,479	7,319
1984	8,278	32,344
1985*	2,523	8,228

Granted   Denied

Largest groups of applicants

	1982		1983		1984		1985*	
	Granted	Denied	Granted	Denied	Granted	Denied	Granted	Denied
Afghanistan	303	166	53	47	186	269	33	124
El Salvador	69	1,067	71	2,914	328	13,045	47	1,428
Iran	2,610	1,663	1,760	561	5,017	3,216	1,668	1,644
Nicaragua	336	950	94	1,346	1,018	7,274	102	2,449
Poland	102	1,095	261	900	721	1,482	235	312

*through February   Source: Immigration and Naturalization Service
(N.Y. Times, 1985)

* Note, however, that the sweeping "discretionary" powers granted the Attorney General under the Refugee Act, still remain.   overriding, nevertheless, and that his view on any given application still prevails. In practice, the fact, for example, that a person genuinely feared that he might be injured in a civil strife or violence in his country, has been dismissed by the Carter and Reagan Administration officials as insufficient grounds to grant asylum, as they contend that many who come from, say, Pakistan, Haiti, Guatamala, San Salvdor and other Central and latin American countries are fleeing poverty and economic conditions, and not political persecution. Accordingly, by recent State department account, applicants from a handful of strife-torn and/or poor countries, such as Cuba, Haiti, Iran, EL Salvador, and Nicaragua, comprise two-thirds of the requests for asylum in recent years, while the most often approved are those from Iran, Afghanistan, South Africa and Ethiopia.

To file for an immigrant visa within the "refugree" or "political asylum" classification, here's the basic procedure: the alien who is outside the United States, may apply for "conditional entrant" status by simply reporting to the nearest American consulate to him and following the instruction they give him. (The consulates will usually give you all the necessary forms you will need along with the directions on filling them out and undertaking the processing procedures). Upon approval of the application, the alien will be "paroled" into the U.S. but he will not actually become a permanent resident alien until he has been in the U.S. at least two years.

If you are **within** the United States, then you will need to obtain and file the following forms with the INS: FORM 1-589, "Request for Asylum in the United States", with accompanying Addendum to Form 1-589. (See samples of form on pp. 49-53; & FORM G – 325A (Biographic Information), sample is on pp. 110; and Form FD – 258 (Fingerprint Card), sample is on p. 72 . There are no specific supporting documents required for this application. However, any documentary (or other) evidence you can provide tending to establish that you would, indeed, be subjected to persecution in your native country, will be highly useful: evidence such as newspaper or magazine clippings or affidavits from persons from your home country testifying in support of your claim and describing any relationship you may have had with your government or with any U.S. enterprises or world organizations within your country that will support your claim.

NOTE: The prescribed printed forms necessary for filing for the visa covered in this chapter may be ordered from the Publisher's Form Division (see pp. 191-2).

FORM I-589

REQUEST FOR ASYLUM IN THE UNITED STATES

Page I

stration and Naturalization Service

| INS Office: | Denver, Colorado |
| Date: | |

| Family Name | First | Middle Name: NMN | 2. A number (if any or known) |

All other names used at any time (include maiden name if married)
None

| 3. Sex | ☐ Male / XX Female | 4. Marital status | ☐ Single ☐ Divorced / XX Married ☐ Widowed |

I was born: (Month) **July** (Day) **4** (Year) **1957** in (Town or City) **Addis Ababa** (State or Province) **Shoa** (Country) **Ethiopia**

| Nationality — at birth: **Ethiopian** | At present: **Same** | Other nationalities: **None** |

If stateless, how did you become stateless?
I am stateless because I left Ethiopia without an exit visa (permission from the present regime), and would not return to my country, since I know I would be imprisoned for life or killed.

| Ethnic group: **Amahra** | 7. Religion: **Christian/Coptic** | 8. Languages spoken: **Amahric, English, French** |

Address in United States (In care of, C/O, if appropriate)
(Number and street) **████ Colorado Boulevard,** (Apt. No.) (City or town) **████,** (State) **Denver, Colorado** (Zip Code) **████**
10. Telephone number (include area code) **303-████**

Address abroad prior to coming to the United States
(Number and street) **████** (City) **Nairobi** (Province) **Kenya** (Country)

My last arrival in the U.S. occurred on: (Mo/Day/Yr) **May 9, 1982**
As a ☐ Visitor XX Student ☐ Stowaway ☐ Crewman ☐ Other (Specify)

At the port of (City/State) **New York City, New York**
Means of arrival (Name of vessel or airline and flight number, etc.) **P.A. 189**

XX was ☐ was not inspected
Date authorized stay expires (Mo/Day/Yr) **May 31, 1984**

My nonimmigrant visa number is **A 2████** (If none, state "none"), it was issued by the U.S. Consul on **May 31, 1982** (Mo/Day/Yr)
at **Nairobi, Kenya** (City, County)

Name and location of schools attended	Type of school	From Mo/Yr	To Mo/Yr	Highest grade completed	Title of degree or certification
r L.O.P.H. School, Addis Ababa	Elementary/ Secondary	9·/66	8/74	8th	Promoted
nilk II Comprehensive Sec. School, Addis Ababa	Compre.	9/74	8/77	12th	Graduated

What specific skills do you have?
Typing, IBM key punch operator, children's counselor at YWCA

| 16. Social Security No. (if any) **None** |

Name of husband or wife (wife's maiden name)
Yilma ████

My husband or wife resides XX with me ☐ apart from me (if apart, explain why)
Address (Apt. No.) **████** (No. and street) **Colorado Boulevard, ████** (Town or city) **Denver,** (Province or state) **Colorado,** (Country) **████**

m I-589
v. 3-1-81)

NOTE: This form (and the addendum on p.53), reproduced here by courtesy of Denver, Colorado immigration attorney, C. James Cooper, Jr., is an actual application submitted on behalf of a political asylum seeker from Ethiopia. The supporting documents in this case were hundreds of pages long; however, what is included herein is only but a few excerpts from some of the documentations so as to give the reader just an idea of what is often needed to get a political asylum, especially when the applicant happens to come from certain countries.

(OVER)

S A M P L E S H E E T

in the U.S. is spouse making separate application for asylum? ☒Yes ☐No (If not, explain why)

11. U.S. are children included in your request for asylum? ☐Yes ☐No (If not, explain why)

N/A

I have ___1___ Sons or daughters as follows: (Complete all columns as to each son or daughter. If living with you, state "with me" in last column; otherwise give city and state of foreign country of son's or daughter's residence).

Name	Sex	Place of birth	Date of birth	Now living at
▓▓▓▓▓	M	Addis Ababa	3/31/78	▓▓▓▓ ▓▓▓▓ Addis Ababa

Relatives in U.S. other than immediate family

Name	Address	Relationship	Immigration status
▓▓▓▓▓	▓▓▓ Pennsylvania St. ▓▓▓, Colorado	Brother	Political Asylee
▓▓▓▓▓	▓▓▓ Dexter Street ▓▓▓ Colorado	Sister	Same as above
▓▓▓▓▓	▓▓▓ Pennsylvania St. ▓▓▓, Colorado	Sister	Same as above

Other relatives who are refugees but outside the U.S.

N	Relationship	Country where presently located
▓▓▓	Cousin	Kenya
▓▓▓	Cousin	Kenya

List all travel or identity documents such as national passport, refugee convention travel document or national identify card

Document type	Document number	Issuing country or authority	Date of issue	Date of expiration	Cost	Obtained by whom
ssport	P04▓▓▓	Ethiopia	11/15/80	11/16/82	$100	myself

Why did you obtain a U.S. visa?

I intended to travel to the United States, where I have friends and relatives.

7. If you did not apply for a U.S. visa, explain why not?

N/A

Date of departure from your country of nationality (Mo/Day/Yr)

September 23, 1981

29. Was exit permission required to leave your country? ☒Yes ☐No (If so, did you obtain exit permission ☐Yes ☒No (If not, explain why) I was denied exit permission by my government to travel to U.S. as a punishment for non participation in its political activities. My brother-in-law, who is a station manager for Ethiopian Airlines in Nairobi with the help of some influential friends was able to get me out of the country to Nairobi.

(2)

FORM I-589

42. Have you been recognized as a refugee by another country or by the United Nations High Commissioner for Refugees? ☐ Yes ☒ No (If yes, where and when)

43. Are you registered with a consulate or any other authority of your home country abroad? ☐ Yes—Give details ☒ No—Explain why not

I have not contacted them, not only because they would not recognizë me, but also I have absolutely no intention to ever get involved with them. I feel very worried about the safety of my parents and my son should the present regime learn of my whereabouts.

44. Is there any additional information not covered by the above questions? (If yes, explain)

Because of the conditions that have developed in my country, I would never return there, even if forced to do so. I fear for my child's and parents' safety but am more fearful of my own life if I returned to Ethiopia.

45. Under penalties of perjury, I declare that the above and all accompanying documents are true and correct to the best of my knowledge and belief.

November 4, 1983

(Signature of Applicant)   (Date)

(Interviewing Officer)

ACTION BY ADJUDICATING OFFICER

(Adjudicating Officer)

Advisory opinion requested ☐

(Date of Interview)

☐ GRANTED   ☐ DENIED

(Date)

(Date)

(4)

30. Are you entitled to return to country of issuance of your passport ☐ Yes ☒ No Travel document ☐ Yes ☐ No Or other document ☐ Yes ☐ No (If not, explain who) I will not be able to return to my country, since I left without permission and through contacts of my brother-in-law, who will be in great trouble if I were to return. In addition, my return will mean my imprisonment for leaving, because of the restriction the Kebele (political cell unit) has put me.

31. What do you think would happen to you if you returned? (Explain) My life would be in jeopardy. It was my refusal to participate in the Kebele and the youth league that turned my life into a nightmare. Accusation, of being a remnant of the old regime, a Christian, to that of being a sympathizer of the Ethiopian People's REvolutionary Party (EPRP) and the Ethiopian Democratic Union (EDU) were directed at me, which led to repeated interrogation in the Kebele, followed by detention and imprisonment in the Kebele.

32. When you left your home country, to what country did you intend to go? Even though I intended to travel to the United States, I was forced to stay in Nairobi with my brother-in-law for nine months, because of the travel restrictions to the U.S. and Western Europe my government put on me due to non-participation in its program.

33. Would you return to your home country? ☐ Yes ☒ No (Explain) I have seen enough horrors in my country to never want to go back under its existing conditions. The new regime makes no distinction between young or old, men or women. The new regime's brutality embraces all who still believe in God, family, and the traditions that have existed for thousands of years. I would be subject to physical abuse and tortu:

34. Have you or any member of your immediate family ever belonged to any organization in your home country? ☐ Yes ☒ No (If yes, provide the following information relating to each organization: Name of organization, dates of membership or affiliation, purpose of the organization, what, if any, were your official duties or responsibilities, and are you still an active member. (If not, explain) I have only been affiliated with the Ethiopian Orthodox Trinity Church as a member of the youth choir. However, my brother, Asmareye ~~~~~~~, was accused of being a member of the E.P.R.P., and was taken by the Kebele one morning, who advised my family that he died. We never received his body. My cousin, Nardos ~~~~~~, was held by the Kebele on similar charges, and was killed with three bullets, which necessitated our paying $300 in order to bury her. Both my brother and my cousin were 17 years of age.

35. Have you taken any action that you believe will result in persecution in your home country? ☒ Yes ☐ No (If yes, explain) I left Ethiopia without an exit visa, which is punishable by long-term imprisonment and possibly death. While in Ethiopia, I refused to participate in the Kebele's political activities, and because of that, have been imprisoned, interrogated, tortured and denied attendance at work, church or social activities.

36. Have you ever been ☒ detained ☒ interrogated ☐ convicted and sentenced ☒ imprisoned in any country? ☒ Yes ☐ No (If yes, specify for each instance: what occurred and the circumstances, dates, location, duration of the detention or imprisonment, reason for the detention or conviction, what formal charges were placed against you, reason for the release, names and addresses of persons who could verify these statements. Attach documents referring to these incidents, if any).

    SEE ATTACHED SHEET   **(p.53 herein)**

37. If you base your claim for asylum on current conditions in your country, do these conditions affect your freedom more than the rest of that country's population? ☒ Yes ☐ No (If yes, explain) While every Ethiopian has been affected by the change, I was affected a great deal more because of the label put on my father as a former landlord, my strong ties to my religion, and the suspicion put on my family and me as E.P.R.P. and E.D.U. supporters and the resulting murders of my brother and cousins. It is these family and religious reasons and my personal disinterest in the present regime which forced me to flee from one province to another to elude the constant harrassment by the Kebele people.

38. Have you, or any member of your immediate family, ever been mistreated by the authorities of your home country/country of nationality? ☒ Yes ☐ No. If yes, was it mistreatment because of ☐ Race ☐ Religion ☐ Nationality ☐ Political opinion or ☐ Membership of a particular social group? Specify for each instance: what occurred and the circumstances, date, exact location, who took such action against you and what was his/her position in the government, reason why the incident occurred, names and addresses of people who witnessed these actions and who could verify these statements. Attach documents referring to these incidents.

    SEE ATTACHED SHEET   **(p. 53 herein)**

39. After leaving your home country, have you traveled through (other than in transit) or resided in any other country before entering the U.S.? ☒ Yes ☐ No (If yes, identify each country, length of stay, purpose of stay, address, and reason for leaving, and whether you are entitled to return to that country for residence purposes. I stayed in Nairobi, Kenya, for nine months after leaving Ethiopia and before my arrival [in] the United States. I was helped by my brother-in-law, who is a station manager for the [Eth]iopian Airlines. Because of his help and his American friends, I was able to get to the [Unit]ed States. I would not be able to return to Kenya, since I have no residency status

[Why did] you continue traveling to the U.S.? Because my brother and sisters were here and offered to help me. [—] (I am now married to him) was also here, and friends of both of us.

[Did you apply] for asylum in any other country? ☐ Yes—Give details ☒ No—Explain why not [I] have always believed that no other country would match America's [dedication to] freedom, justice and equality for all. The United States' [esteem for] religious, racial and political diversity is a well-known fact

    (3)   (over)

42. Have you been recognized as a refugee by another country or by the United Nations High Commissioner for Refugees? ☐ Yes ☒ No   (If yes, where and when)

43. Are you registered with a consulate or any other authority of your home country abroad?   ☐ Yes—Give details ☒No—Explain why not

I have not contacted them, not only because they would not recognizë me, but also I have absolutely no intention to ever get involved with them. I feel very worried about the safety of my parents and my son should the present regime learn of my whereabouts.

44. Is there any additional information not covered by the above questions? (If yes, explain)

Because of the conditions that have developed in my country, I would never return there, even if forced to do so. I fear for my child's and parents' safety but am more fearful of my own life if I returned to Ethiopia.

45. Under penalties of perjury, I declare that the above and all accompanying documents are true and correct to the best of my knowledge and belief.

_____   November 4, 1983
        (Signature of Applicant)   (Date)

_____   _____
    (Interviewing Officer)   (Date of Interview)
ACTION BY ADJUDICATING OFFICER   ☐ GRANTED   ☐ DENIED

_____   _____
    (Adjudicating Officer)   (Date)

Advisory opinion requested ☐   _____
                                                              (Date)

30. Are you entitled to return to country of issuance of your passport ☐ Yes ☒ No   Travel document ☐ Yes ☐ No   Or other document ☐ Yes ☐ No   (If not, explain why.) I will not be able to return to my country, since I left without permission and through contacts of my brother-in-law, who will be in great trouble if I were to return. In addition, my return will mean my imprisonment for leaving, because of the restriction the Kebele (political cell unit) has put me.

31. What do you think would happen to you if you returned? (Explain) My life would be in jeopardy. It was my refusal to participate in the Kebele and the youth league that turned my life into a nightmare. Accusation of being a remnant of the old regime, a Christian, to that of being a sympathizer of the Ethiopian People's REvolutionary Party (EPRP) and the Ethiopian Democratic Union (EDU) were directed at me, which led to repeated interrogation in the Kebele, followed by detention and imprisonment in the Kebele.

32. When you left your home country, to what country did you intend to go? Even though I intended to travel to the United States, I was forced to stay in Nairobi with my brother-in- law for nine months, because of the travel restrictions to the U.S. and Western Europe my government put on me due to non-participation in its program.

33. Would you return to your home country? ☐ Yes ☒ No (Explain) I have seen enough horrors in my country to never want to go back under its existing conditions. The new regime makes no distinction between young or old, men or women. The new regime's brutality embraces all who still believe in God, family, and the traditions that have existed for thousands of years. I would be subject to physical abuse and tortu:

34. Have you or any member of your immediate family ever belonged to any organization in your home country? ☐ Yes ☒ No. (If yes, provide the following information relating to each organization: Name of organization, dates of membership or affiliation, purpose of the organization, what, if any, were your official duties or responsibilities, and are you still an active member. (If not, explain) I have only been affiliated with the Ethiopian Orthodox Trinity Church as a member of the youth choir. However, my brother, Asmareye ▮▮▮▮▮▮, was accused of being a member of the E.P.R.P., and was taken by the Kebele one morning, who advised my family that he died. We never received his body. My cousin, Nardos ▮▮▮▮▮▮, was held by the Kebele on similar charges, and was killed with three bullets, which necessitated our paying $300 in order to bury her. Both my brother and my cousin were 17 years of age.

35. Have you taken any action that you believe will result in persecution in your home country? ☒ Yes ☐ No (If yes, explain) I left Ethiopia without an exit visa, which is punishable by long-term imprisonment and possibly death. While in Ethiopia, I refused to participate in the Kebele's political activities, and because of that, have been imprisoned, interrogated, tortured and denied attendance at work, church or social activities.

36. Have you ever been ☒ detained ☒ interrogated ☐ convicted and sentenced ☒ imprisoned in any country? ☒ Yes ☐ No (If yes, specify for each instance: what occurred and the circumstances, dates, location, duration of the detention or imprisonment, reason for the detention or conviction, what formal charges were placed against you, reason for the release, names and addresses of persons who could verify these statements. Attach documents referring to these incidents, if any).

     SEE ATTACHED SHEET   (p.53 herein)

37. If base your claim for asylum on current conditions in your country, do these conditions affect your freedom more than the rest of that country's population? ☒ Yes (If yes, explain) While every Ethopiian has been affected by the change, I was affected a great deal more because of the label put on my father as a former landlord, my strong ties to my religion, and the suspicion put on my family and me as E.P.R.P. and E.D.U. supporters and the resulting murders of my brother and cousins. It is these family and religious reasons and my personal disinterest in the present regime which forced me to flee from one province to mother to elude the constant harrassment by the Kebele people.

38. Have you, or any member of your immediate family, ever been mistreated by the authorities of your home country/country of nationality? ☒ Yes ☐ No. If yes, was it mistreatment because of ☐ Race ☐ Religion ☐ Nationality ☐ Political opinion or ☐ Membership of a particular social group? Specify for each instance: what occurred and the circumstances, date, exact location, who took such action against you and what was his/her position in the government, reason why the incident occurred, names and addresses of people who witnessed these actions and who could verify these statements. Attach documents referring to these incidents.

     SEE ATTACHED SHEET   (p. 53 herein)

39. After leaving your home country, have you traveled through (other than in transit) or resided in any other country before entering the U.S.? ☒ Yes ☐ No (If yes, identify each country, length of stay, purpose of stay, address, and reason for leaving, and whether you are entitled to return to that country for residence purposes.) I stayed in Nairobi, Kenya, for nine months after leaving Ethiopia and before my arrival in the United States. I was helped by my brother-in-law, who is a station manager for the Ethiopian Airlines. Because of his help and his American friends, I was able to get to the United States. I would not be able to return to Kenya, since I have no residency status there.

40. Why did you continue traveling to the U.S.? Because my brother and sisters were here and offered to help me. My fiance (I am now married to him) was also here, and friends of both of us.

41. Did you apply for asylum in any other country? ☐ Yes—Give details ☒ No—Explain why not Because I have always believed that no other country would match America's idealism for freedom, justice and equality for all. The United States' tolerance for religious, racial and political diversity is a well-known fact world-wide.

SAMPLE SHEET

(3)   (over)

(FORM I-589-ATTACHMENT)
REQUEST FOR ASYLUM IN THE U.S. - ~~Getaneh~~ Hirut

Response to Question 36:

I have been detained, interrogated, tortured and imprisoned numerous time
in my country, Ethiopia. Several reasons were cited for these harrass-
ments: my family connections (former landowners); the alleged membership
of my brother and cousin to the now-defunct, Ethiopian Peoples Revolutionary Party, which resulted in their murder during the operation
referred to as "red against white" terror; my strong religious belief;
my refusal to participate and convert to the new tenets of the communist
philosophy to which the youth league adheres, all of which resulted in
my being looked upon as anti-government.

Most of my detention, interrogation, torture and imprisonment took place
at Higher 13, Kebele 11. The new regime has sliced the city into
Kebeles to restrict movement of the inhabitants and to gain virtual
control over the lives of the people. Each Kebele has unrestricted
power to detain, interrogate, torture, imprison, and even the right to
kill within each one's jurisdiction. The Kebeles are comprised of
people who belonged to the lowest strata during the former regime and
they used their newly-acquired power to settle scores on the people
who had scorned them prior to the present regime take-over.

The Kebele staff in the district in which I lived were former koolies
(street sweepers, day laborers and simple loafers), who showed no
mercy and used their uninhibited power ruthlessly. I owe my life to a
former koolie who used to do odd jobs for our family and never forgot
the humane way my family treated him. He was responsible for my
releases and the application of minimal methods of torture, compared
to other people, who were put to extreme pains.

There were no formal charges, no records kept, no representation by a
lawyer, no public disclosures--in short, there were no legal or formal
procedures followed in any of these arrests, detentions and even death.
Any Kebele member can conduct his/her own investigations. During the
period of 1975-1979, at the height of the Kebele power, I was summoned
and detained frequently. I would be beaten with a leather-covered wire
whip on any place of my body, and have some deep scars as a result of
that; I would be tied up, so that my body looked in the shape of a ball
and suspended with a stick in my mouth. Movement was impossible. The
longest detention (most detentions lasted two to three days at a time)
was in June of 1977, where I was questioned on the whereabouts of my
brother and cousin and the extent of my involvement and sympathy to
their cause. I was kept for two weeks in our Kebele cell with a number
of other students crammed in one room. I maintained my innocence and
lack of interest in politics and cited my previous interrogations which
had produced no results for the Kebele. I was finally released with
the help of the former koolie, who still showed kindness to.me.

From then on it became a routine to be summoned by one of the members
of the Kebele for more interrogation. It was a mere exercise of authority
with no foundations to the variety of accusations. Since they had
absolute authority, no one checked on their erratic behavior. I could
    keep my salaried job or go to church or attend social functions.
    were only allowed to work for the Kebele or attend their propaganda
lectures every night, and if I did neither, I was imprisoned. The torture and threats of rape filled my life with constant terror and night-
mares.

Response to Question 38:

As mentioned in the response to Question 36, I was tortured, scarred
and threatened with rape. My brother and a first cousin were murdered
because of their so-called affiliation with the E.P.R.P. We have
never received the body of my first cousin for burial. My father (a
landowner) was charged with corruption as a member of the former
regime, even though he was never involved in such activites, and he is
harrassed by being assigned to night guard duties, although he is old
and in poor health, and held a high position in the community prior to
the present regime take-over. My husband, Yilma ████ can verify
these statements. Mis-treatment happened so often from 1975 that I
am unable to state certain dates of these many occurrences.

Western Nations Are Raising Barriers to Refugees

By HENRY KAMM
Special to The New York Times

GENEVA, March 25 — While 12 million people are officially counted as refugees who have fled persecution or violence in their homelands, the Western nations that have been the principal upholders of the right of asylum are raising barriers to keep them out.

Those nations are afflicted, in a phrase that has gained currency among refugee workers, with "compassion fatigue." The main reason is a growing perception of an unending flow of people from lands of poverty in search not of safety but of economic betterment. The exiles' assertions that they are seeking political asylum are met with increasing disbelief.

Challenges to the requests for asylum affect not only recent refugee groups, such as Central Americans in the United States and Iranians and Sri Lankans in Europe, but also Vietnamese boat people, who for many years were granted refugee status, if not always asylum, without serious question.

1.6 Million Indochinese Accepted

Today, in the United States, Western Europe, Canada and Australia — which have so far taken in 1.6 million out of the 1.7 million Indochinese refugees — official and public attitudes have never been so negative.

And at the Office of the United Nations High Commissioner for Refugees, the exiles' chief international advocate, and among governmental specialists and private refugee organizations, a new pessimism is widespread.

"All the organizations that deal with refugees, national or international, are aware that procedures to determine who is and who is not a refugee are now being used to accept as few as possible and not to determine who needs protection and who does not," Jean-Pierre Hocke, the High Commissioner, said in an interview here.

Throughout Western Europe, where since 1986 the number of asylum seekers has for the first time risen above 200,000 annually — it was only in 1980 that the number reached 100,000 — acceptance rates have sunk alarmingly. Nations are reticent about statistics, but according to the disparate figures made available to the High Commissioner's office, acceptance rates now average from 7 percent to 14 percent.

Governments say little about the number of people turned back at their borders before they can present asylum requests. In an exception, the West Germany Interior Minister, Friedrich Zimmermann, was reported by the news magazine Der Spiegel to have said 124,000 aliens were denied entrance last year.

Switzerland, which before this decade averaged 70 percent acceptance, is down to about 7 percent. The West German approval rate has dropped from 16 percent in 1986 to short of 12 percent in the first six months of last year. In France, considered one of the more liberal nations in asylum policy, acceptances declined from 40 percent in 1986 to 32 percent since then.

'Reaction of Hostility'

"A general reaction of hostility, fear toward refugees has become apparent, sometimes virulent in nature," said Michel Moussali, representative of the High Commissioner's office to the European Community. "Several countries have decided to revise their procedures and adopt restrictive and dissuasive measures, with the declared aim of preventing the arrival of false refugees but in fact striking indiscriminately at economic migrants and true refugees."

Measures have been adopted by the United States, which automatically puts under detention, often for as long as two years, Central American asylum seekers who arrive with documents that are judged to be "not in order," said Roger Winter, director of the United States Committee for Refugees, a nongovernmental organization.

He also cited the interdiction at sea of more than 18,000 Haitian asylum seekers. "Such highly visible actions that our Government has taken contribute to the undermining of refugee protection," Mr. Winter said in a telephone interview.

The United States Immigration and Naturalization Service reported in March that requests for political asylum from Central Americans had gone up from 7,000 in 1985 to more than 50,000 in 1988.

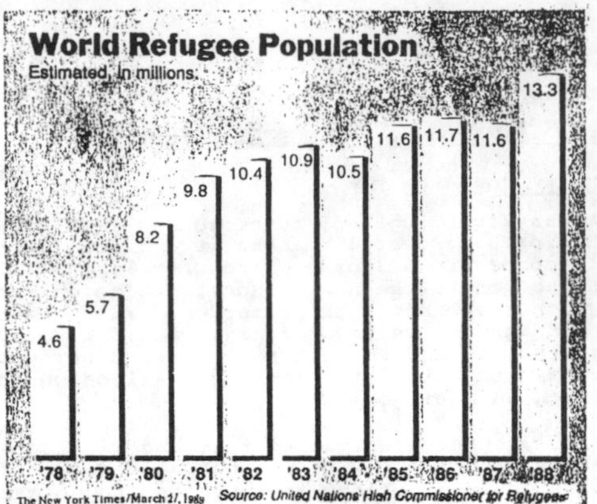
World Refugee Population
Estimated, in millions:
4.6
5.7
8.2
9.8
10.4
10.9
10.5
11.6
11.7
11.6
13.3
'78
'79
'80
'81
'82
'83
'84
'85
'86
'87
'88
Source: United Nations High Commissioner for Refugees
The New York Times/March 27, 1989

Denmark's Attitude: Sternness Gains

In Western Europe, policies described as "humane deterrence" have been generally adopted since the mid-1980's. They include increasingly restrictive visa requirements, penalties levied on airlines that deliver travelers without visas, denial of work permits while asylum applicants wait, often for years, for final decisions on their requests, reduction of welfare payments and other benefits during the waiting period and long-term lodging in barracks-like collective quarters, without minimal privacy.

Symptomatic, yet surprising because of a long history of humanitarianism, is the change in Denmark's attitude. "I think we've reached a point where it can't get worse," said Finn Slumstrup, information director of the Danish Refugee Council.

When in 1985 and 1986 the number of people granted asylum annually rose from around 1,000 to more than 6,500, a vocal minority began to warn that Danish homogeneity and national culture were threatened. The fact that many of the refugees were from Lebanon, Sri Lanka and Iran and joined about 23,000 migrant workers from Turkey, added a racist, and an anti-Muslim, note to the campaign, Mr. Slumstrup said in a telephone interview.

A revised immigration law and stern administrative procedures followed in 1986. Together, they made it difficult for asylum seekers to be admitted into Denmark.

As a result of the range of restrictive measures, the number of people granted asylum in Denmark has been cut in half since 1987.

"There is still sympathy for refugees, but they must be the 'right' refugees," Mr. Slumstrup said. "Boat people lived up to the image. They were undernourished, dressed in rags. They can't be reasonably well-dressed and well-fed, like the jet people of the 80's."

The United Nations agency operates under an international convention concluded in 1951 that defines a refugee as a person who, "owing to well-founded fear of being persecuted for reasons of race, religion, nationality, membership of a particular social group or political opinion, is outside the country of his nationality."

"The convention responded to the outflow of refugees from Eastern Europe," Mr. Hocké said. "Persecution was the key word, and it concerned individuals. Today, nine-tenths of the refugees are to be found in the third world. It means large groups fleeing from violence, not individuals needing protection from persecution."

Attitudes began to change in the early 1980's; the term "compassion fatigue" was first used in 1980, by Senator Alan K. Simpson of Wyoming. That period saw mass arrivals in Europe of asylum seekers fleeing from war in Lebanon and the revolutionary regime in Iran and culminating in the scattered arrivals of about 50,000 Tamils asking for shelter from civil strife in Sri Lanka.

"It is the high number of non-Europeans that caused the negative reactions," said Robert Van Leeuwen, deputy head of the Regional Bureau for Europe and North America of the High Commissioner's office. "The public, not helped by politicians who fail to play their educative role, is becoming more xenophobic. There is significant racism, and then the politicians play to that."

Refugee officials in general, while noting restrictive American measures toward Caribbean and Latin American asylum seekers, believe that the immigrant character of the United States and its multiracial makeup have kept negative attitudes there at a lower level.

Claims of Persecution: Harder Scrutiny

Mr. Hocké said that increasingly traditional asylum countries no longer accept a refugee's subjective judgment that the fear that impelled him to flee was well-founded. Young Tamil men have been told by most European Governments that they could have escaped from the conflicting pressures of their Government and the Tamil rebel groups to other regions of Sri Lanka instead of taking the long trip westward.

Most of the Tamils remain in the limbo of awaiting final rulings; fewer than 100 are believed to have been deported so far.

While the High Commissioner's office has maintained a stand on behalf of Tamil refugees in Europe, many in the organization and other refugee workers are concerned over a significant revision of its 14-year-old policy of support for asylum claims by Vietnamese boat people, the largest group of refugees leaving their country to apply for permanent asylum.

In an interview, the head of the agency's Asian activities went so far as to denounce the earlier policy.

"It is fairly obvious that for a number of historic and political reasons we didn't handle the Indochinese refugees very wisely," said Sergio Vieira de Mello, director of the High Commissioner's regional bureau for Asia. He was discussing the policy of recognizing their refugee status without individual screening.

Mr. Vieira de Mello noted that Hong Kong had now instituted severe screening measures and that Thailand and Indonesia had adopted a policy of pushing off refugee boats.

A Plan of Action: Caveats Introduced

The High Commissioner, together with the United States and other principal resettlement countries, submitted a Plan of Action to a 35-nation conference in Kuala Lumpur, Malaysia, this month. Vietnam and Laos took part.

The plan, which was not made public, was adopted without significant change. It stresses legal emigration possibilities and urges the granting of temporary asylum in countries where boat people land. But it considers it "imperative" that "organized clandestine departures be deterred." It urges the enforcement of "official measures" against organizers of departures.

The document makes no reference to the United Nations Universal Declaration of Human Rights, whose Articles 13 and 14 state, "Everyone has the right to leave any country, including his own," and "Everyone has the right to seek and enjoy in other countries asylum from persecution."

By implication, the Plan of Action also appears to recognize the possibility of forced repatriation to Vietnam for those rejected in screening. "In the first instance every effort will be made to encourage the voluntary return of such persons," it says, adding that "alternative methods of return" are to be examined if "after the passage of reasonable time" voluntary return makes insufficient progress.

Last month, Simon Ripley, a Briton who served as legal consultant to the High Commissioner's office in Hong Kong, resigned in protest against the screening. In a report submitted with his resignation, Mr. Ripley noted that of 313 cases screened, only 2 were found to qualify for refugee status.

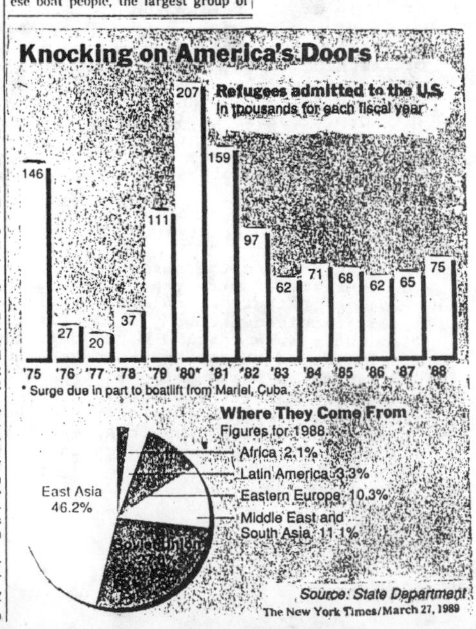
Knocking on America's Doors
Refugees admitted to the U.S.
In thousands for each fiscal year
146
27
20
37
111
207
159
97
62
71
68
62
65
75
'75
'76
'77
'78
'79
'80*
'81
'82
'83
'84
'85
'86
'87
'88
* Surge due in part to boatlift from Mariel, Cuba.
Where They Come From
Figures for 1988.
Africa 2.1%
Latin America 3.3%
Eastern Europe 10.3%
Middle East and South Asia 11.1%
East Asia 46.2%
Soviet Union
Source: State Department
The New York Times/March 27, 1989

E. ELIGIBILITY BASED ON BEING AN "IMMIGRANT INVESTOR"

Another route by which an alien (a foreign national) could gain eligibility for admission to the United States as an <u>immigrant</u>, is through qualification as a so-called "IMMIGRANT INVESTOR"

To qualify as an immigrant investor, an alien needs to meet the following requirements:

i)   Be able to establish that he or she has invested, or is actively in the process of investing, a minimum capital of $40,000 in U.S. funds in a commercial or agricultural enterprise producing some goods and services (not merely the buying of stock or bonds or placing money in the bank) in the United States.

ii)   The business that is established must expand the labor market, that is, it must employ at least one person (he/she must be a U.S. citizen or Permanent Resident) other than the alien or members of his immediate family, and the alien must be a principal manager in the business; and, perhaps most importantly,

iii)   A visa number from the "NON-PREFERENCE" category must be available to the alien <u>at the time of his/her application</u> for a visa.

The last of the above conditions (i.e., availability of a visa number in the non-preference classification), is probably the most difficult of all problems that the immigrant investor applicant quite often has to overcome. This is so because, though in theory there is an immigrant visa category called the "non-preference"category(See pp. 7 & 10),in practice, it turns out that there simply has not been even a single non-preference visa number available to any applicant as far back as since 1977. Not one! There has simply been a chronic backlog of non-preference applications for so long, necessitating a long, in deed impossible waiting periods for a visa number. And, what is more, virtually every expert in the field expects that this prevailing condition will continue for the foreseeable future!

Consequently, in light of the ever chronic backlog in this lowest of all immigrant preference categories, one major practical reality has been this: that aliens who might well have been able to qualify in the IMMIGRANT INVESTOR class have often chosen, in stead, to take other routes in seeking immigrant visa—usually the use of the labor certification. This way, with an approved labor certification (pp.141-154), such an immigrant investor alien would gain eligibility to be placed into either the THIRD (professional or skilled worker) preference category (pp. 7, 9 & 43), or into the SIXTH (skilled or unskilled worker) preference category (pp.7, 9 & 45 above).

To file for an immigrant visa within the "immigrant investor" classification, whether from outside or inside the United States, here's the basic procedure: The alien files Form I-526, "Request For Determination that Prospective Immigrant is an Investor" (sample p.60), and the form, OF222 (p. 58)Preliminary Questionaire to Determine Immigrant Status", with theUS Consulate abroad, or if already living in the U.S., he may file same with the INS office of where he is resident. Thereafter, when an immigrant visa number becomes available under the NONPREFERENCE category — a prospect which, you'll recall, rarely happens, if ever — you are sent a visa appointment date at that point. And that's when all the usual documentations (passports, photographs, medical exams, police certificates, etc., as listed in pp.112-116) will be required to be filed at the consulate. The rest of the routine procedure involved in visa operations — visa interview, investigation, port of entry inspection, and all the rest of them discussed in Chapter 7 of this manual, will follow accordingly.

F. ELIGIBILITY BASED ON BEING A FOREIGN MEDICAL GRADUATE

Finally, the last route we shall address here by which an alien could gain eligibility for admission to the United States as an <u>immigrant</u>, is through qualification as a FOREIGN MEDICAL SCHOOL GRADUATE as defined under the immigration laws.

Previously, until at least 1976, graduates of foreign medical schools had relatively easy access into the United sttes; aside from access to <u>nonimmigrant</u> entry for the purpose of receiving graduate medical training (.e.g. internship and residencies), the alien physicians were also able to gain admission to the United States as <u>immigrants</u> — by two basic routes, namely, under the THIRD preference (members of a profession) and the SIXTH preference (skilled-worker-in-short-supply) categories. Such alien physicians had, since 1965, enjoyed a rather privileged place, the "preferred position", on Schedule A of the U.S. Department of Labor's Pre-certification list, a schedule listing occupations in short supply in the U.S.

However, as from 1976, there was a new law passed — the **Health Professions Education Assistance Act.** — which brought about a radical change in the U.S. policy with respect to foreign medical graduates, radically reducing, in effect, the number of alien physicians practicising medicine in the United States. The U.S. Congress had become persuaded, in making this change of mind, that a shortage of U.S. doctors no longer existed, and that "there is no further need for affording preference to alien physicians and surgeons in admission to the United States......" Hence, the new 1976 law was passed placing severe restrictions on the ability of the foreign schooled physicians to enter the U.S., whether as an immigrant or a nonimmigrant.

Principally, the new law did this by creating a new ground for exclusion: foreign-schooled physicians seeking entry in the THIRD OR SIXTH preference (or Nonpreference) categories who were intent on working in the U.S. as medical professionals, were now to be excludable from entry unless the foreign medical school from which they graduated, were one deemed "accredited" by a body approved by the U.S. Secretary of Education.

Alternatively, however, a foreign-schooled physician would be exempt from this ground for exclusion with no requirement for "accredited" foreign medical school attendance, if he can meet either one of these requirements: if he has passed Parts I and II of the National Board of Medical Examination (NBMEE) or an equivalent examination (such as the Foreign Medical Graduate Examination in the medical Science or FMGE), and could demonstrate competence in spoken and written English; or, if he possesses demonstrable "national or international renown" — a term which, as is employed in practice, closely parallels the standard for physicians' required to qualify for "blanket" Labor Certification under Schedule A, Group II of the Department of Labor's regulations**. Then, in addition, such a "qualified" alien-schooled physician needs to meet one other requirement to fully qualify: he or she must obtain a labor certification from the U.S. Labour Department (pp. 141-154) — except for situations when the alien is applying to work in an area of the U.S. designated by the Department of Health and Human Resources as a **"health care manpower shortage area"** substantially short of physicians and surgeons, in which case the alien will not have to have a labor certification.

It should be noted, however, that the foreign medical graduate who enters the U.S. in the THIRD and SIXTH Preference categories are subject to the above-stated 1976 law's restrictions only on one other central condition: namely, when his basis of entry is to engage in a <u>medical field</u> of endeavor. On the other hand, such an alien, even though a physician and foreign trained, would be totally unaffected by and outside the scope of the exclusionary provision — in instances whenever such alien's line of work is outside the field of medicine and does not involve the performance of medical services***. In general, there is a common view, a kind of unwritten "litmus test" often adopted by the Immigration Service in making such a determination. If the MD degree is required by the employer, in part or in whole, for the performance of the position offered, then the alien is viewed as probably coming to the U.S. "principally to perform services as a member of the medical profession" as specified under the 1976 law. A key factor that is looked for by immigration officials in arriving at the determination, is: does the job offer requirement make an MD (i,e. medical) degree a mandatory requirement for the position, and is the position in question predominatly restricted to physicians?

---

* Apart from medical schools in the U.S. (including Puerto Rico), only medical schools in Canada have been determined by the Secretary of Education (now Health and Human Resources) to be so accredited. Thus, the Secretary has held that graduation from U.S. or Canadian medical school is equivalent to meeting the academic and language requirements prescribed.

**Falling outside the parameters of the 1976 law's restrictions, are, of course, the alien physicians who immigrates to the U.S. on the family relationship basis — as "immediate relatives", or as 1st, 2nd, 4th and 5th preference immigrants. Thus, those applying or qualifying for their visas on such other basis are not subject to the foreign trained physician exclusion prescribed under this law. Moreover, upon becoming a U.S. Permanent Resident by any other routes, such persons are absolutely free to practice medicine, providing the licensing requirements are met.

***For example, say you are an alien physician who has a Bachelor's degree in, say, dietetics or toxicology or physical therapy. You can apply to enter the U.S. as a dietician, or toxicologist or physical therapist, as the case may be, providing you are coming to the U.S. to actually practice the designated non-medical profession.

General Classes of Foreign Medical Graduates Who
Can Qualify for Admission to the United States

The following is a summary of some other classes of foreign medical doctors who could gain admission to the U.S. in immigrant or nonimmigrant status.

They are those qualifying as:

i)   H - 1 (Temporary Worker) nonimmigrants (pp. 22-3) (The alien must have been invited by a U.S. educational or research institution or agency to teach or do research).

ii) Participants in the nonimmigrant J - 1 "exchange visitor" program (see pp. 21-2   )

iii) Graduates of U.S. or Canadian medical schools

iv) Physicians of "national or international renown" (pp. 43-5   )

v)   Physicians of "exceptional ability" in the sciences or the arts.

vi) Physicains with religious commitments or affiliations to medical missionaries who are coming to the U.S. to engage in something other than medicine.

FORM FS-497A, also known as FORM OF-222

DEPARTMENT OF STATE
PRELIMINARY QUESTIONNAIRE TO DETERMINE IMMIGRANT STATUS

TO: THE UNITED STATES CONSUL AT	DO NOT WRITE IN THIS SPACE
	Instructions for _____
	Sent _____

INSTRUCTIONS

If a careful reading of Form DSL-852A indicates that you should file this form, please complete it and forward it to the designated consular office. This form must be completed in English and typed or printed in legible block letters. When this form is returned to you, please retain it as it must be attached to any future correspondence addressed to the consular office.

1. NAME   (Last name)   (First name)   (Middle names)

2. OTHER NAMES, ALIASES (If married woman, give maiden name and surnames of any previous spouses)

3. PRESENT ADDRESS (House number, street, city, state and ZIP code)

4. PLACE OF BIRTH (City, state or province, country)	5. DATE OF BIRTH (Month, Day, Year)

6. MARITAL STATUS   ☐ Single   ☐ Married   ☐ Widowed   ☐ Divorced

7. SEX ☐ Male ☐ Female	8. DISTINGUISHING MARKS OF IDENTIFICATION	9. Passport No._____ Issued by_____ Issue date_____

10. NAME AND BIRTHPLACE OF FATHER	11. MAIDEN NAME AND BIRTHPLACE OF MOTHER

12. NAME OF SPOUSE (Maiden or family name)   (First name)   (Middle name)

13. SPOUSE'S BIRTHPLACE (City, State or province, Country)	14. SPOUSE'S BIRTHDATE (Month, Day, Year)	15. WILL SPOUSE IMMIGRATE WITH YOU? ☐ Yes ☐ No

16. NAME AND BIRTHPLACE OF SPOUSE'S FATHER	17. NAME AND BIRTHPLACE OF SPOUSE'S MOTHER

18. IF YOU HAVE A SPOUSE, PARENT OR CHILD WHO IS A UNITED STATES CITIZEN OR ALIEN RESIDENT, PLEASE COMPLETE THE FOLLOWING:

NAME	RELATIONSHIP	STATUS IN U.S.	PRESENT ADDRESS

19. IF YOU HAVE ANY RELATIVES IN THE UNITED STATES OTHER THAN THOSE IDENTIFIED ABOVE, COMPLETE THE FOLLOWING:

NAME	RELATIONSHIP	STATUS IN U.S.	PRESENT ADDRESS

20. YOUR PRESENT STATUS IN THE UNITED STATES
☐ Parolee   ☐ Other (specify) _____
☐ Indefinite voluntary departure status   Alien registration number _____

21. NATIONALITY (Including former, if any)	22. PRESENT OCCUPATION OR VOCATION

FORM FS-497A
7-71

23. NAME AND ADDRESS OF PRESENT EMPLOYER

24. LIST UNMARRIED CHILDREN UNDER 21 YEARS, NOT U.S. CITIZENS, WHO WILL ACCOMPANY YOU

NAME OF CHILD	PLACE OF BIRTH (CITY, STATE OR PROVINCE, COUNTRY)	BIRTHDATE

25. IF YOU OR YOUR SPOUSE ARE NOW, OR HAVE BEEN, IN THE UNITED STATES, STATE:

☐ Applicant ☐ Spouse	WHERE WAS VISA OBTAINED	WHEN WAS VISA GRANTED (Month, Year)

CHECK TYPE OF VISA USED FOR SUCH ENTRY

☐ Immigrant   ☐ Government or international organization official or employee

☐ Exchange visitor   ☐ Other nonimmigrant (specify) _____

26. IF YOU OR YOUR SPOUSE PREVIOUSLY LIVED IN THE UNITED STATES, STATE:

DATE ADMITTED	DATE DEPARTED	REASON FOR DISCONTINUING RESIDENCE

27. LIST BELOW IN DATE ORDER ALL PLACES WHERE YOU, YOUR SPOUSE AND UNMARRIED CHILDREN NAMED ABOVE HAVE LIVED SINCE REACHING THE AGE OF 16. (It is not necessary to list the places where you have lived less than six months).

FIRST NAME OF FAMILY MEMBER	CITY OR TOWN, PROVINCE, COUNTRY	OCCUPATION	FROM (Month, Year)	TO (Month, Year)

28. MEMBERSHIP OR AFFILIATION IN ORGANIZATIONS IN EACH COUNTRY NAMED IN ITEM 27. CULTURAL, SOCIAL, LABOR OR POLITICAL.

ORGANIZATION	FROM	TO

I certify that all information given is complete and correct.

DATE	SIGNATURE

NOTE: If space above is insufficient to answer any questions properly, the additional information may be printed on a separate sheet of paper and attached to this form.

FORM 7-71 FS-497A OR OF 222

FORM I-526

REQUEST FOR DETERMINATION THAT PROSPECTIVE IMMIGRANT IS AN INVESTOR

UNITED STATES DEPARTMENT OF JUSTICE
Immigration and Naturalization Service

Form approved
OMB No. 43–R0514

REQUEST FOR DETERMINATION THAT PROSPECTIVE IMMIGRANT IS AN INVESTOR
in order to be relieved from labor certification requirement
of Section 212(a)(14) of the Immigration and Nationality Act

FILL IN WITH TYPEWRITER OR PRINT IN BLOCK LETTERS WITH BALLPOINT PEN. *DO NOT LEAVE ANY QUESTION UNANSWERED.* When appropriate insert "None" or "Not Applicable". If you need more space to answer fully any question on this form use a separate sheet of paper this size and identify each answer with the number of the corresponding question.

I hereby declare that I am seeking to become a lawful permanent resident of the United States for the purpose of engaging in an enterprise, and that I have invested, or am actively in the process of investing, in such enterprise capital totaling at least $40,000. On the basis of such investment, I request that the labor certification requirement of Section 212(a)(14) of the Immigration and Nationality Act be considered not applicable to me. I am submitting this request as part of my application to become a lawful permanent resident of the United States.

1. Applicant's Family Name (Capital Letters)　　(First name)　　(Middle name)　　(Maiden name, if married woman)

BRITTIAN,　　　　Sean　　　　R.

2. Birthdate (Month, day, year)　　Birthplace (City or town)　　(Country)
4/25/28　　　　Sydney　　　　　　Australia

3. Present Address (Number and street)　　(City or town)　　(Province or State, ZIP Code)　　(Country)
5560 East Holly Street　　Longview,　　Washington　98632　　U.S.A.

4. Name and Location of Enterprise
CORNETT DEVELOPMENT COMPANY
1113 South Main Street　　Longview,　　Washington　98632

5. Names and immigration status of partners (if applicable)　(co-shareholders)
Jonathan Peters
1113 South Main Street
Longview, Washington　98632
(Permanent Resident)

6. Percentage of partnership or stock owned by applicant
50%

7. Nature of enterprise (Describe briefly; include total number of persons employed or to be employed in the enterprise and relationship, if any, to the applicant. Give name, home address, immigration status, and relationship of at least one employee other than your spouse and children.) Investment Company; purchase bare land, sub-divide it with employee's help sell the lots or company will build with help of subcontractors single-family residences to sell to public on real estate contracts; will employ electricians, framers, plumbers and the like. I believe company will grow to have 5 - 15 employees within reasonable time.

8. Check one:　　☒ I have made the investment.　　　☐ I am actively in the process of making the investment.

9. The capital investment I made or am actively in the process of making consists of:
Cash　　$ 145,000.00
Other　　$_____　(describe) my personal business experience in development invest-
　　　　　　　　　　　　　　　　ments or real estate and managing
Other　　$_____　(describe) investment companies

TOTAL　$ 145,000.00 (invested May of 1976)

---

10. Describe briefly how you will engage in the enterprise, including the title of any job you will hold in it and the number of hours per week you will devote to the job. President - 40 hours (full time) of investment - construction company will supervise sub-contractors and obtain bid quotes and amounts and will sell houses to people and buy land for subdivision; will co-ordinate employees and work crews.

Form I-526 (Rev. 10-7-76)N

Over

OVER →

NOTE: This Form is reproduced herein for illustrative purposes only, courtesy of and from "Immigration to the U.S.A" by Dan P. Danilov (Self-Counsel Press, Inc.), pp.74-75.

FORM I-526

11. EXPERIENCE—Employment or training you have had which qualify you to engage in the enterprise:

Name and address of employer or trainer
Self-Employed investor of my own company called ENGLAND TRADING CO., LTD.

Name of Job	Date started month year	Date left month year	Kind of business
President-Owner of ENGLAND TRADING CO., LTD.	Over 25 yrs.	N/A	Mfr's representative for American, W. German, Swiss textile machinery & factories & real estate investment.

Describe in detail duties you performed, including use of tools, machines, or equipment, No. of hours per week.
President-General Manager: carry on day-to-day act of all business, negotiating contracts; communicating with factories; traveling to promote business in all countries; also invested in warehousing construction; land sub-division and land development; supervised building construction of aforesaid warehousing buildings.

Name and address of employer or trainer
Self-employed

Name of job	Date started month year	Date left month year	Kind of business
President & General Manager of ENGLAND TRADING CO., LTD.	Over 25 years	N/A	(See above)

Describe in detail duties you performed, including use of tools, machines, or equipment, No. of hours per week.

(See above -- ENGLAND TRADING CO. has been only business)

12. Describe any additional qualifications you possess for engaging in the enterprise.

N/A

13. List licenses (professional, journeyman, etc.) you have received.

N/A

14. I have attached the following documentary evidence (check each box applicable).

[X] Financial statements, such as balance sheet, or profit and loss statement.
[X] License or other official authorization to engage in business in U.S.
[X] Corporate charter or partnership agreement. [X] Lease or deed to premises. [ ] Cancelled checks.
[X] Bank statement showing bank balance. [X] Business contracts. [ ] Receipts.
[ ] Licenses received outside the U.S. [ ] School records, certificates or diplomas. [ ] Employment letters.
[X] Other (describe briefly).

15. If your native alphabet is in other than Roman Letters, write your name in your native alphabet below:

, N/A

16. (Signature of person preparing form, if other than applicant.) I declare that this document was prepared by me at the request of the applicant and is based on all information on which I have any knowledge.

Date: 10/22/ 78

Signature of Applicant
Sean A. Brittain

Date of signature October 22, 1978

Address of person preparing form, if other than applicant.

LAW OFFICES OF DAN P. DANILOV
3828 SEATTLE-FIRST NATIONAL BANK BLDG
SEATTLE, WASHINGTON 98154

Occupation: Lawyer

SAMPLE SHEET

CHAPTER SIX

SO YOU WANT A "NON-IMMIGRANT" TYPE OF VISA? HERE ARE THE STEP-BY-STEP PROCEDURES FROM START TO FINISH

The General Guidelines For Following This Chapter

In this chapter, we will deal with applying for the **"NON-IMMIGRANT"** types of visa or status (The equivalent treatment for the "IMMIGRANT" types of visa is outlined in Chapter 7, pp. 111-140)

The forms, instructions, and procedures outlined in this chapter are carefully arranged and organized in a system of orderly, simple "STEPS" — from "STEP 1" to "STEP 9". In each "step", you are told what to do (or to expect) and, where necessary, also provided with sample forms along with instructions on how to complete or make use of them.

BUT A WORD OF CAUTION IS NECESSARY: If you are to comprehend and follow this chapter, and hence be able to follow through in the processing of your visa application, one thing you must do is this: You Must Follow The "STEPS" ORDERLY AND ONE, (AND ONLY ONE) AT A TIME.

In preparing the forms and processing your visa application through the consular or immigration channels, take the steps strictly ONE at a time, following them EXACTLY in the same numerical order in which they are listed below in this chapter. In each step you come to, first read the instructions therein. This tells you how to proceed. Then, following what such instructions or information tell you to do, go one step (and only ONE step) at a time according to the order of the numbering. Do not skip around from step to step, or from page to page (unless, of course, if so instructed by the manual).

AND HERE THEY ARE, THE NINE (9) SIMPLE, SYSTEMATIC "STEPS" INVOLVED IN APPLYING FOR AND OBTAINING A NONIMMIGRANT VISA:

step 1: DETERMINE IN WHAT SPECIFIC "NONIMMIGRANT" VISA CATEGORY (OR CATEGORIES) YOU FALL UNDER.

(See Chapter 1, especially Sections B & C thereof (pp. 1-5), for the various classes into which applicants claiming nonimmigrant status fall).

NOTE THE VITAL NECESSITY OF THIS: As a matter of law, the immigration authorities may not approve a nonimmigrant visa application, unless the alien is first able to establish his qualification for the particular nonimmigrant category in which he claims membership to the satisfaction, first, of the consular officer (at the time of the application for the visa), and then secondly, to the satisfaction of the immigration inspection officer later (at the time of the alien's arrival for admission at the U.S. port of entry).

step 2: KNOW WHAT BASIC QUALIFICATIONS ARE REQUIRED OF ONE FOR ELIGIBILITY UNDER YOUR DESIGNATED VISA CATEGORY

(See Chapters 2 and 3, at pp. 17-33), and refer to the particular Sections therein having to do with the visa category you claim to fall under in STEP 1 above).

step 3: OBTAIN THE NECESSARY APPLICATION FORMS FOR THE TYPE OF VISA YOU SEEK.

For the added convenience of the readership, Do-it-yourself Legal Publishers makes available to its readers the standard, fully pre-sorted, all-in-one package of forms—containing the proper forms necessary for the particular type of visa you designate.

To order the Publisher's standard "all-in-one" immigration forms package, just complete the Order Form on p.191-2 and send it to the Publisher's legal Forms Division.

NOTE: Be sure to specify, exactly, what class of immigrant (or non-immigrant) visa you want to apply for (see Table on p. 4-5, 17-33). Aliens may order from the Publisher, whether they live (or are filing) in the United States or in a foreign land.

Note that aliens, who so prefer, may apply to their area's U.S. Consulate (if living abroad), or the immigration service offices for the forms. However, be forewarned: a common drawback experienced by most aliens in attempting to obtain forms through the Consulate or the INS, a long-standing source of frequent complaints and frustration experienced by aliens and legal and immigration practitioners alike, is the reality of long backlogs and delays in obtaining forms from these agencies; mail requests or phone calls to the agencies customarily go unanswered and the offices are overcrowded with applicants, manned by understaffed personnel, frequently necessitating that the applicant make a personal trip to the agency and quaranteeing that a better part of the work day is wasted!

 step 4: PROPERLY FILL OUT THE APPLICATION FORMS & BEGIN TO ASSEMBLE THE NECESSARY SUPPORTING DOCUMENTATIONS.

Note a few general rules in regard to completing the immigration forms. A truly important aid to anyone in preparing all such forms are the "blocks" provided on the forms; such blocks are generally self-explanatory and quite explicitly indicate the exact information required to be entered, and the order in which such information is to be put in in order for the information to contain in the space. Secondly, almost every immigration form has a set of "INSTRUCTIONS" on the body of the form, clearly telling the reader the purpose(s) for which the form is appropriate and giving some pointers on how to complete or file them, and guidelines on the information and supporting documents required to be furnished.

Hence, the first rule in completing the forms in this: in all instances, always be absolutely sure to read the forms and thoroughly understand the information required of you before filling them out. Be deliberately careful. Remember this: that the initial batch of forms you complete and submit are what is known as the "primary" documents, meaning that this is the documentary source which the consular and immigration authorities will probably go back to and refer to again and again, and against which they will cross-check any future documents and information from you for consistency. (In submitting supporting documents to the consular or INS officers, make it a point always, especially with regard to irreplaceable documents, to file only photostatic copies of the originals by first presenting the originals to them for their personal inspection and certification that the copies are the true copies. This precaution is necessary because the immigration services have a history of chronically losing important, often irreplaceable documents submitted by aliens. Furthermore, for any documents written in a foreign language, always submit a certified English translation as well).

For simplicity of comprehension to enable the reader to follow the process, here is the format we shall use here: we shall run down chapters 2 and 3 (pp.17-33) systematically, and for each NON-IMMIGRANT visa category designated therein, we shall list in this chapter: 1) the basic application and/or petition forms commonly used for the particular visa type; and (ii) the usual types of documentations commonly required for the particular visa type. And now, here they are:

FOR TEMPORARY VISITORS (B visa) (see pp. 18-19)

i) **Basic Forms commonly used:**
   FORM 156 (or **FORM FS -257₂** in the case of an alien whose personal appearance for interview has been waived by the consular officer for any reason). (See illustrated sample of Form on pp.70-71)

ii) **General Supporting Document For Most Nonimmigrant Situations* .**

● A valid **PASSPORT** for each applicable alien issued by the alien's country (used for proof of the alien's identity and nationality)

●**POLICE CERTIFICATE** (a certificate by the police or other appropriate law enforcement authorities in the foreign country reporting what their record shows, if any, regarding the alien), and/or **REPORT OF FINGERPRINTING** (use FORM ID - 258 or FD - 258, sampled on pp.) (Applies only to applicants 14 years of age or older. The fingerprinting may be made either at a U.S. consulate or a local police or other enforcement department, and the fingerprint card and report duly filled out and signed by the authorized official).

●Three (it may be more) passport-size **PHOTOGRAPHS** of each alien applying, showing a full front view of the facial features. The reverse side of each photo must be signed (full names) by the alien signing each application.

---

* NOTE: some of the supporting documents listed here may not apply or be required for your own particular visa classification or in your own particular case or consulate, and are only listed here as a general all-inclusive guide. Ultimately, the best source of what would specifically be required in a given case, is your consular official, and he will usually advice you of such details at the appropriate time.

● **REPORT OF MEDICAL EXAMINATION** (Exam. must usually be done by a doctor or medical facility specifically designated by the consular office).

● Documentary **EVIDENCE OF CLOSE FAMILY RELATIONSHIP** to an accompanying relative (usually a spouse or minor children), evidence such as marriage certificates, birth certificates, sworn declarations by witnesses of birth and family relationship, and the like.

● PROOF OF **THE ALIEN'S FINANCIAL STATUS:** some evidence showing that you (the principal aliens) are of sufficient financial means, enough that you will not seek to work in the U.S. (e.g. a letter from your prospective hosts in the U.S. stating the trip's purpose and possibly assuring your financial needs while you are in the U.S., an already purchased round trip ticket, your bank statements, and any other financial or property documentations.)

● Documentation appropriate to establish your maintenance of a residence in your home country and that you have no intention of abandoning such residency (e.g. evidence of a permanent job with a well-known employer in your home country, or of having close family ties therein).

2. FOR STUDENTS & EXCHANGE VISITORS ("F", "M" & "J" VISAS) (pp.19-22)

i) Basic Forms Commonly used:

FORM 1 - 20A—B (Applicable to those applying for F - 1 type visa only). As fully explained in pp. 20 , aliens have to apply to and secure this form directly from the intended school in the U.S. as it is not obtainable any other way. (See pp. 73-7 for illustrative sample of this form)

FORM IAP - 66 (Applicable to those applying for J - 1, "exchange student", type of visa (pp. 21-2). You should apply for and secure this form in the same manner indicated above for FORM 1 - 20 A - B users. See pp.78 for illustrative sample of this form).

FORM 1-20M—N. (Applicable to those applying for the "M" vocational type visa only. You should apply for and secure this form in the same manner indicated above for FORM 1 - 20 A — B users. Form 1 — 20 M - N is identical to Form 1 — 20 A - B reproduced as sample on pp. 73- 7)

ii) Supporting Documents:

● Same documents as those listed in p. 63-4 above under "General Supporting Documents for Most Nonimmigrant Situations" may apply here.

In addition, the following may be necessary:

● Documentation appropriate to establish that sufficient funds are or will be available to you to cover all expenses during the entire period of your study in the U.S.

(Example: AFFIDAVIT OF SUPPORT from the applicant's parent, sample Form on p. 79

NOTE, however, that the financial status of the person furnishing this affidavit is often closely evaluated by the consular officer to establish the person's ability to provide the support, and to probe the depth of his obligation and commitment.

● Documentation appropriate to establish that you (the alien) have "successfully completed a course of study equivalent to that normally required of an American student seeking enrollment at an institution at the same level".

● Substantial evidence, particularly with regard to your ties to your country, in proof that you intend to depart the U.S. upon completing your studies. (Examples: evidence of availability of employment in the alien's home country in the field in which the alien is undertaking studies, evidence of strong family ties in his home country to which he is likely to return).

3. FOR ALL H TEMPORARY WORKER CLASSES (H - 1, H - 2 & H - 3 Visas)

i) Basic form Commonly Used:

FORM 1 - 129B (Applicable for those applying for H-1 or Distinguished Merit and Ability temporary worker visa (pp.22-3),H - 2 or Labor/service temporary worker (pp.23-4) applicants. and the H-3 or Industrial Trainee temporary worker applicants (pp.24)

As more fully explained on P. 23 , this form is completed by the alien's U.S. employer-to-be, who then first files it with an INS office in the area of the job location in the U.S. (See pp. 83-5, 88-90, 89-7 and 99-101 for illustrative samples of this form)

ii) Supporting Documentations For All H Classes:

● Same documents as those listed in p. 63-4 above under "General Supporting Documents for Most Nonimmigrants Situations", may apply here.

In addition, the following may be necessary:

For H - 1 Visa Applicants:

● Statement containing a full and detailed description of the high education, technical training, specialized experience, or exceptional ability of the alien and the manner by which such qualifications were acquired. (see sample on pp. 86-7, 91, 128, 151-2)

● Certified copies of professional licenses held and distinguished awards received, school certificates and records showing periods of attendance major fields of study and degrees received.

● Letters and affidavits from former tutors or employers or recognized experts in the field testifying to the alien's technical training or specialized experience or exceptional ability.

● Published materials (newspaper or magazine articles, professional journal articles, etc.) by or about the alien.

FOR H-2 Visa Applicants:

● A copy of the LABOR CERTIFICATION from the Department of Labor confirming either that workers are not available in the U.S. for the job in question, or that no Labor Certification is required for it. (See pp. 141-154 for labor certification application procedures).

● Statement containing a full and detailed description of the conditions which make it critical that the alien be admitted to take the employment, and showing that the need for the position is temporary, reasonal, or recurrent in nature, and in what exact ways. (see pp. 91, 151-2)

For H - 3 Visa Applicants:

● Documentations appropriate to establish that an actual bona-fide training program exists with a U.S. employer, and that the program involves both considerable hours of classroom instruction and on-the-job training without supervision. (see "Explanatory Note" on p. 81, item #4)

● A statement describing the kind of training that is to be given the alien and setting forth the number of hours that will be devoted each to classroom instruction and to on-the-job training without supervision; the position or duties for which this training will prepare the alien trainee; a full explanation as to why it is claimed that such training cannot be obtained in the alien's country, the manner in which the alien came to the attention of the U.S. employer, and how he (she) was selected.* (see sample on p. 98)

● Proof of the alien's maintenance of a residence in his home country, and of his intention not to abandon it.

4.   FOR INTRA-COMPANY TRANSFEREES ("L" Visa) (see pp. 25-6)

i) Basic Forms Commonly Used:

FORM 1 –129B (Applicable for those applying for L - 1 visa, pp. 25-6   ). This form is completed by the alien's U.S. employer-to-be, who then first files it with an INS office in the area of the job location in the U.S. (See pp. 99-101 for illustrative sample of this form).

ii)   Typical Document Accompanying Form 1– 129B.

● Same documents as those listed on pp. 63-4 above under "General Supporting documents for Most Nonimmigrant Situations" may apply here.

---

* The INS Examinations Handbook) directs immigration examiners to scrutinize H - 3 petitions closely for the reason that there is a high incidence of fraud experienced in such petitions. It cites the following as what should serve as the "warning signs" for examiners in evaluating H - 3 petitions: (1) a proposed training program which deals in generalities with no fixed schedule, objectives or means of evaluation; (2) an elaborate proposed training program that is incompatible with the nature of the U.S. employer's business; (3) a training program on behalf of an alien who appears to already possess substantial expertise in the proposed field or in another field (4) a training program in a field for which there would be little or no need in the alien's native country; (5) a training program in which the U.S. employer claims no American will be displaced but no one can be found in the U.S. to fill the position; and (6) a training program in which the salary is far above the minimum wage level.

In addition, the following may be necessary:

Documentations appropriate to establish that the alien is a bona fide nonimmigrant intending to stay in the U.S. only for a temporary period (e.g. proof of alien's maintenance of a residence in his home country and that he has no intention of abandoning it).

Documentations or evidence showing that: qualifying corporate branches and qualifying employment positions are involved in the transfer; the U.S. subsidiary or affiliate has physical premises to operate its business (a lease or deed to an office space); the petitioning U.S. business entity and the overseas business are related as branches, subsidiaries or affiliates, and how, with the proper verfications duly attached (e.g. the last annual foreign federal or provincial tax return for the corporation, incorporation papers for both the foreign and U.S. corporations clearly showing shared ownership by the two, current profit/loss statement for the foreign corporation, etc). [For examples, see items cited in "Explanatory Note" on pp. 81-2]

● Evidence (attach a resume) showing the experience of the alien to assure that he or she has filled one of the qualifying positions outside the U.S. for the required one year period and a description of the capacity in which he / she was employed overseas.

● Evidence regarding the employer's intent to employ that alien in the U.S. temporarily, and a description of what capacity the alien would be employed in.

● Evidence showing the total number of shares of stock issued, the classes of stock ownership, the owners of the issued stock, and the percentage of ownership for each stock holder. (If possible, attach on Organization Chart showing the alien's standing in the overseas company's line of authority and another flow chart showing the connection with the U.S. company.) [See "Explanatory Note" on pp. 81-2, and sample letter on p. 102]

● A supporting covering letter by the U.S. subsidiary or affiliate attached, requesting the alien employee's transfer, and giving a full explanation (the "business necessity" letter) of why it is necessary that the particular worker be transferred, and his essentiality to the survival, well-being or progress of the U.S. company. [See sample letter on p. 102]

5. FOR TREATY TRADERS & INVESTORS (E-1 & E-2) (see pp. 26-8)

i) Basic Forms Commonly Used:

Form 1 - 506, "Application For Change of Nonimmigrant Status" (Used to change status of visitor to Treaty Investor status. See sample of form on p.103-4)

Form 1 - 539 (used to apply for an extension to remain in the U.S. See sample on p. 109
Form I-94, Arrival-Departure Record issued at entry into U.S.

Form 1 - 126 "A Report of Status by Treaty Trader or Investor" (Used to show maintenance of status, see sample on p.105-6).

NOTE: These forms are used by most nonimmigrant investors and traders who have already been admitted to the U.S. in a different nonimmigrant classification (e.g. as a visitor) and want to change to the status of a treaty investor or to extend their stay.

ii) Supporting Documentations For All "E" classes:

● Same documents as those listed in pp. 63-4 above, under "General Supporting Documents for Most Nonimmigrant Situation", may apply here.

In addition, the following may be necessary:

For the Treaty Trader (E - 1) case:

● Evidence indicating the nationality of the person or persons who own the stock, or the principal amount, of the business of the foreign company constituting the trading or investing entity. [In general, see items cited, for example, in "Explanatory Note," p. 82]

● Evidence of the nationality of the alien seeking the E visa (he does not have to be a citizen or national of the U.S. or a U.S. permanent resident).

● A statement of inequivocal intent to return to his home country when his E status ends.

● Invoices showing purchase prices for goods, equipment or machinery transferred to the U.S. for use in the business enterprise.

● Invoices showing that substantial volume of trade exists between the U.S. enterprise and the foreign business or company in the alien's country, the number of transactions, and whether there is a continuous course of trade.

SPECIAL FOR THE TREATY INVESTOR (E - 2) Case:

Documentation appropriate to establish that the alien possesses the required funds; that he actually invested or is in the process of investing the money in the business; that the business actually exists and has all the necessary licenses and other requirements to lawfully operate, and that he is a principal manager in the company.[See sample documentations listed in "Explanatory Note" p. 82]

(Examples of documents: corporate or business financial statements, bank books, copies of international bank money transfers, letters of credit and affidavits from bank, licenses to operate, partnership or incorporation papers as a U.S. company, invoices or leases or rent receipts for office or business space, photographs of the business enterprise showing the alien engaged in the conduct of his business, a list of prosective or actual employees, and any other documentation helping to establish that the alien does, in fact, intend to establish a bona-fide trade or investment company on a big scale).

6. **FOR FOREIGN GOVERNMENT OFFICIALS (A - 1, A - 2, & A - 3 VISAS p 28)**

(For the basic forms and/or supporting documentation required for application for A—1, A—2, or A-3 visas, see .p. 28 above for a brief outline)

7. **FOR TRANSIT ALIENS (C VISA) (pp. 28-9)**

(see pp. 28-9 for a brief outline of the basic forms and/or supporting documentations required).

8. **FOR CREWMEN (D Visa) (pp ·29)**

(See p. 29 for a brief outline of the basic forms and/or supporting documentations required.)

9. **FOR FOREIGN GOVERNMENT REPRESENTATIVES TO & EMPLOYEES OF INTERNATIONAL ORGANIZATIONS (G VISA)**

(See pp. 29 for a brief outline of the basic form and/or supporting documentations required).

10. **FOR FIANCES & FIANCEES ENGAGED TO MARRY U.S. CITIZENS (K VISA) (See pp. 30-3)**

i) **Basic Forms Commonly Used:**

FORM 1-129F, "Petition to classify status of Alien Fiance or Fiancee for Issuance of Nonimmigrant Visa". (see sample on p. 32-3)

FORM G -325A, "Biographic Data" (see sample of form on pp. 110) (Both forms are completed by the U.S. citizen to whom the alien is engaged to be married (called the "sponsor" or "petitioner") who then files them with an INS office in the U.S. naming the alien as the beneficiary).

ii) **Supporting Documents:**

Same documents as those listed in pp. 63-4 above under "General Supporting Documents for Most Immigrant Situations".

Same documents as those listed under Paragraph 5 (i) to (ix) on pp. 30-31

SUBMIT THE COMPLETED FORMS & SUPPORTING DOCUMENTATIONS TO ("FILE" THEM WITH) THE U.S. CONSULATE.

So, you have now finished filling out and assembling your application (or petition) papers — the forms as well as part or all of the supporting papers ("STEP 4" at pp.63-8 above). And now, what next?

The next order of business on your path to applying for and securing your visa to the U.S., is for you to *submit the papers to("file" them with) the appropriate U.S. officials for processing* — to the CONSULAR OFFICER in charge of nonimmigrant visa section at the U.S. Consulate or Embassy in your (the alien's) home country.

What happens next? The Consular officer will conduct a quick preliminary check of your application and the submitted supporting documents as to their format and contents to see that your submissions are at least complete and that the forms are completely filled out. The Consular officer will usually require you to "execute" (i.e. sign) the application form(s) in his presence. The Consular officer may tell you that certain necessary information or documentations are missing or improperly or incompletely filled in If that should happen, don't even worry about it. Simply request the official to tell you specifically what needs to be corrected or supplied, and make a note of what he says. Then make the corrections or obtain the missing documents and resubmit the papers accordingly.

In any case, assuming that the papers submitted seem at least complete and in order enough to be accepted, you will pay the consular officer the applicable filing fee, if any, and the officer will assign a "case number" to your application. (Make sure you collect a receipt of filing from the officer, for your records).

Now, the Consular officer will at this stage probably give you (or later send you) a list of instructions on the rest of the procedures still ahead to be undertaken: when and where to appear for the formal visa interview; how and where to take the medical examination, if applicable or not already taken; whether to, and how to complete FORM G - 325A (the standard Biographic Information form used mostly in immigrant visa cases to conduct security clearances); and a list of any further documentations not already submitted which the consular officer may deem necessary or appropriate in your particular case, and what have you.

Upon gathering and submitting all items required by the consular officer, the officer will set a date for you to be interviewed on your visa application — date for the so-called **VISA INTERVIEW** — and notify you to appear at the appointed time and place for the interview.

step 6: ATTEND THE VISA INTERVIEW

What happens at this all-important interview? First, recall a relevant point we emphasized very early on in this manual (pp.1 & 5), namely: that one fundamental rule central in all evaluations of nonimmigrant visa applicants, is the basic "presumption" that every alien seeking entry into the United States is an intending IMMIGRANT — until and unless he can satisfactorily establish to the consular official that he is qualified within a nonimmigant classification.

Simply summarized, it is safe for you to assume that much of the nonimmigrant visa interview you'll have, and what the consular officer will primarily focus on in such interview, will be largely colored by and related to this fundamental "presumption" under the law. *Primarily, the central interest of the interviewing consular officer's probe, and the thrust of his questions, will be aimed at uncovering the answer to this questions: what is your true, underlying "intent"?* He will ask questions to attempt to uncover, in short, whether you are truly what you claim you are, that is, a nonimmigrant who is truly intent on remaining in the U.S. only temporarily; or, on the other hand, if you are actually a fake, a pre-conceived immigrant at heart merely pretending to be a nonimmigrant just so that you can secure an easier or fast entry route into the U.S.

Hence, for you the alien, it is most important that you come to the interview prepared; you should be prepared to answer any and all questions the consul may possibly have for you on your application, and, more importantly, be prepared to show (by words and documentations) that you are in truth a genuine nonimmigrant .

A word or two of wisdom from one veteran expert who has been through scores of visa interviews in the course of his role as an immigration lawyer, seem directly fitting here as a general guide for the would-be visa interviewee:

"Whatever you do, never let the other side see you sweat. This point is very important. Everyone gets a little nervous when dealing with government officials. This is normal. But remember, immigration officials are law enforcement personnel and have carefully trained in the art of interviewing foreign nationals.. They have been taught that,generally, persons who appear to be nervous, ill at ease, who perspire, have sweaty palms and do not make direct eye contact, may be hiding something. Immigration officials are suspicious of anyone who appears to be uptight. Although it is understandable why a person would be nervous and full of anxiety under the scrutinizing eyes of an immigration or consular officer, you will be more successful if you understand the process and know what to expect. Therefore,your composure and mannerisms when dealing with an immigration or consular officer are very important. Although you should not act as though you know everything or be too confident, **you should try to be relaxed and appear to be as believable as possible. The impression you make may be the deciding factor on whether or not your visa will be granted"***

Finally, upon conclusion of the visa interview, if the consular officer approves your application, he (she) will stamp your passport with a notation of the type of nonimmigrant visa granted. Thereafter, when you are ready to travel you may apply for entry into the U.S. at any designated port of entry ("STEP 7" below).

step 7: SO YOU'VE OBTAINED YOUR VISA. JUST HOW DO YOU GET ACTUALLY ADMITTED INTO THE U.S.?

(Turn to Chapter 9, "Entering the United States..........", at pp.155-160)

step 8: EVEN WITH A VISA IN HAND, YOU CAN STILL BE "EXCLUDED" FROM ENTRY INTO THE U.S., OR BE "DEPORTED" AFTER ENTRY. HERE ARE SOME REMEDY POINTERS .

(Turn to Chapter 9, "Entering the United States.........", especially Section D thru. H thereof at pp.156-160)

step 9: YOU CAN CHANGE YOUR STATUS FROM "NON-IMMIGRANT" TO "IMMIGRANT" WHILE YOU'RE LIVING IN THE U.S. HERE'S HOW.

(Turn to Chapter 10, "Adjustment of status..." pp.161-178 for the full procedures).

* C. James Cooper, Jr. in "American Immigration Tapes: Text", pp 2-3.underscoring added.

SAMPLE OF FORM 156

p. 1 of 2 pgs.

SAMPLE
VISITOR (NONIMMIGRANT) VISA APPLICATION

Form Approved
O.M.B. No. 47–R0166

NONIMMIGRANT VISA APPLICATION

PART I

IMPORTANT: *ALL APPLICANTS MUST READ AND ANSWER THE FOLLOWING:*

(1) U.S. law prohibits the issuance of a visitor visa to persons who plan to remain in the United States indefinitely or who will accept employment there. A VISITOR MAY NOT WORK.

(2) A visa may not be issued to persons who are within specific categories defined by law as inadmissible to the United States (except when a waiver is obtained in advance). Complete information regarding these categories and whether any may be applicable to you can be obtained from this office. Generally, they include persons afflicted with contagious diseases (such as tuberculosis) or who have suffered serious mental illness; persons with criminal records involving offenses of certain kinds, including offenses against public morals; narcotic addicts or traffickers; persons who have been deported from the U.S.A.; persons who have sought to obtain a visa by means of misrepresentation or fraud; and persons who are, or have been members of certain organizations, including communist organizations and those affiliated therewith.

DO ANY OF THE FOREGOING RESTRICTIONS APPLY TO YOU?

☐ YES   ☒ NO

If YES, or if you have any question in this regard, personal appearance at this office is recommended. If it is not possible at this time, attach a statement of facts in your case to this application.

PART II

PLEASE PRINT THE FOLLOWING INFORMATION

1. LAST NAME Bermanti   **FIRST NAME** Samieu   **MIDDLE NAME**

2. OTHER NAMES (*Maiden, Professional, Religious, Aliases*) None   **3. NATIONALITY** Malaysia

4. DATE OF BIRTH (*Month, day, year*) 11/8/52   **5. PLACE OF BIRTH** (*City, State, Country*) Kuala Lumpur, Selangor,

6. PASSPORT NUMBER 011111   **7. DATE PASSPORT ISSUED** 3/14/75   **8. DATE PASSPORT EXPIRES** 3/14/80   **9. PASSPORT ISSUED AT** KualaLumpur

DO NOT WRITE IN THIS SPACE

B–1, B–2, OTHER _____

MULTIPLE OR _____ APPLICATIONS

INDEF., 48 MOS., OR _____ MOS.

LO _____ VISA NO. _____

ISSUED/REFUSED ON _____ BY _____

REFUSED: SECTION _____ INA

REVIEWED BY _____

Leave Blank

10. RESIDENTIAL ADDRESS (*Include apartment number and postal zone*)
14, Talan 21/32
Kuala Lumpur, Selangor
Malaysia
Home Telephone Number:

11. HAVE YOU EVER APPLIED FOR A UNITED STATES VISA OF ANY KIND? ☐ Yes ☒ No
(*If YES, state where, when and type of visa*)

12. NAME AND ADDRESS OF EMPLOYER OR SCHOOL
Food Universal Co.
Kuala Lumpur, Malaysia
Business Telephone Number:

13. INDICATE WHETHER:
☐ Visa was granted
☐ Visa was refused
☐ Application was abandoned
☐ Application was withdrawn

14. HAS YOUR U.S. VISA EVER BEEN CANCELED? ☐ Yes ☒ No

15. HAVE YOU EVER BEEN THE BENEFICIARY OF AN IMMIGRANT VISA PETITION OR INDICATED TO A U.S. CONSULAR OFFICER A DESIRE TO IMMIGRATE TO THE U.S.A.? ☐ Yes ☒ No

16. HAVE YOU EVER BEEN IN THE UNITED STATES? (*If YES, when and for how long?*) ☐ Yes ☒ No

OPTIONAL FORM 156 (Rev. 2–76)
(Formerly Form FS–257a)
Department of State
50156–102

COMPLETE ALL QUESTIONS ON REVERSE OF FORM ➤ OVER ➤

Form 156 is reproduced herein for illustrative purposes, courtesy of and from "Immigrating to the U.S.A" by Dan P. Danilov (Self-Counsel Press, Inc.), pp.98-99.

FORM OF 156   SAMPLE   p. 2 of 2 pgs.
(Back)

17. PRESENT PROFESSION OR OCCUPATION (*If retired, state past profession*) mechanic	18. SEX ☐ Female ☒ Male	19. MARITAL STATUS ☒ Married ☐ Single ☐ Widowed ☐ Divorced ☐ Separated

20. COLOR OF HAIR Black	21. COLOR OF EYES Brown	22. HEIGHT 5'4"	23. COMPLEXION Olive	

24. MARKS OF IDENTIFICATION
scar on left cheek

25. WHAT IS THE PURPOSE OF YOUR TRIP? to visit brother in Chicago, Ill.	26. HOW LONG DO YOU PLAN TO STAY IN U.S.A.? 6 months

27. AT WHAT ADDRESS WILL YOU RESIDE IN THE U.S.? 1827 Broadmore St. Chicago, Illinois 60607	28. NAME, RELATIONSHIP, AND ADDRESS OF SPONSOR, SCHOOL, OR FIRM IN U.S.A.

29. WHEN DO YOU INTEND TO ARRIVE IN THE U.S.A.? February 10, 79	30. DO YOU INTEND TO WORK OR STUDY IN THE U.S.A.? ☐ Yes ☒ No	31. WHO WILL PAY FOR YOUR TICKETS TO LEAVE THE U.S. AT THE END OF YOUR TEMPORARY VISIT?
32. WHO WILL FURNISH FINANCIAL SUPPORT? I will	33. HOW MUCH MONEY WILL YOU TAKE? $2000 U.S.	I will pay for my tickets

34. ARE ANY OF THE FOLLOWING IN THE U.S.A.? (*If YES, what is their status, i.e., student, working, etc?*)

☐ HUSBAND/WIFE no   ☐ FIANCE/FIANCEE no   ☒ BROTHER/SISTER working
☐ FATHER/MOTHER no   ☐ SON/DAUGHTER no

35. NAMES AND RELATIONSHIPS OF PERSONS TRAVELING WITH YOU none	36. HOW LONG HAVE YOU LIVED IN THIS COUNTRY? (*Country where you are applying for nonimmigration visa*) 6 years

37. PLEASE LIST THE COUNTRIES WHERE YOU HAVE LIVED FOR MORE THAN SIX MONTHS DURING THE PAST FIVE YEARS

Countries	Cities	Approximate Dates
Malaysia	Kuala Lumpur	April, 1972–present

38. TO WHICH ADDRESS DO YOU WISH YOUR VISA AND PASSPORT SENT?
14, Talan 21/32, Kuala Lumpur, Malaysia

39. I certify that I have read and understood all the questions set forth in this application, and the answers I have furnished on this form are true and correct to the best of my knowledge and belief. I understand that possession of a visa does not entitle the bearer to enter the United States of America upon arrival at a port of entry if he or she is found inadmissible.

DATE OF APPLICATION   May 5, 1978

APPLICANT'S SIGNATURE   Samien Bermanti

If this application has been prepared by a travel agency or another person in your behalf, the agent should indicate name and address of agency or person with appropriate signature of individual preparing form.

SIGNATURE OF PERSON PREPARING FORM _____

DO NOT WRITE IN THIS SPACE

37mm x 37mm
1½ inches x 1½ inches

—— PHOTO ——

Sign name on reverse side of photo

OPTIONAL FORM 156 BACK (Rev. 4–76)

FINGERPRINTS

FORM FD-258
APPLICANT
LEAVE BLANK

TYPE OR PRINT ALL INFORMATION IN BLACK

FBI   LEAVE BLANK

LAST NAME **NAM**   FIRST NAME   MIDDLE NAME

Sang   Kil

SIGNATURE OF PERSON FINGERPRINTED

RESIDENCE OF PERSON FINGERPRINTED

Clinton Street
Colorado, 80010

SIGNATURE OF OFFICIAL TAKING FINGERPRINTS

EMPLOYER AND ADDRESS   of fingerprinter
Aurora Police Department
Alameda Avenue
Aurora, Colorado

REASON FINGERPRINTED

Permanent Resident Applicant

ALIASES **AKA**

Sung

ORI

CITIZENSHIP **CTZ**
Korea

YOUR NO. **OCA**

FBI NO. **FBI**

ARMED FORCES NO. **MNU**

SOCIAL SECURITY NO. **SOC**

MISCELLANEOUS NO. **MNU**

COINSDNOO
USINS
DENVER, CO

DATE OF BIRTH **DOB**
Month 3 Day 3 Year 45

SEX M   RACE -   HGT. 5'7"   WGT. 160   EYES Brn   HAIR Blk   PLACE OF BIRTH **POB** Korea

LEAVE BLANK

CLASS

REF.

SAMPLE SHEET

| 1. R. THUMB | 2. R. INDEX | 3. R. MIDDLE | 4. R. RING | 5. R. LITTLE |
| 6. L. THUMB | 7. L. INDEX | 8. L. MIDDLE | 9. L. RING | 10. L. LITTLE |

LEFT FOUR FINGERS TAKEN SIMULTANEOUSLY   L. THUMB   R. THUMB   RIGHT FOUR FINGERS TAKEN SIMULTANEOUSLY

OVER→

NOTE: Upon filling in the applicable information in the upper part of this form, the actual "fingerprinting" is to be done by an appropriate official (e.g. a police officer or other law enforcement personnel). See Instructions on the back side of this Form.

FORM I-20A

(FOR NONIMMIGRANT "F-1" STUDENT STATUS)

Page 1 — Completed by the school where the student intends to study

FORM APPROVED
OMB. NO. 43-R0397

Name of Student—Family Name (Capital Letters)	First Name	Middle Name

Date of Birth (Mo., day, year)	Country of Birth	Country of Nationality

CERTIFICATE OF ELIGIBILITY

(FOR NONIMMIGRANT "F-1" STUDENT STATUS)

NOTE → **READ CAREFULLY THE INSTRUCTIONS ON PAGE 4**

Name of School

School Official To Be Notified of Student's Arrival in U.S.

Address of School (Include Zip Code)

Visa Issuing Post

It is hereby certified as follows:

1. This certificate is being issued to the student named herein for (Check one)

   a. ☐ Initial attendance at this school.   b. ☐ Continuation after a temporary absence outside the United States. His presently authorized stay, as it appears on Form I-94 in his possession, expires (month, day, year) _____   c. ☐ Other (specify) _____

2. The student named herein has been accepted for a full course of study in this school (If he must appear on or before a specified date, specify that date here _____.) He will be expected to carry a full program of study as defined by immigration regulation, 8 CFR 214.2(f)(la), and this institution. (Schools which devote themselves exclusively or primarily to vocational, business, or language instruction must complete the following: He will be expected to carry a minimum of _____ clock hours a week.) His major field of study is _____, normally requiring (specify length of proposed course) _____ and he is expected to complete his studies at this institution not later than _____.

3. The school has determined by a careful evaluation of the student's qualifications that the student has sufficient scholastic preparation to enable him to undertake a full course of study.

4. (Check one and fill in as appropriate.)

   a. ☐ Proficiency in the English language is required and the school has determined that the student has the required proficiency. Basis for determination: _____

   b. ☐ Proficiency in the English language is required. If the student lacks such proficiency, he will be:

   ☐ Enrolled in a full course of study of English in this school.

   ☐ Given special instruction in English, which will consist of _____

   c. ☐ Proficiency in the English language is not required. Explain: _____

5a. The present academic-year (or other academic-term of _____ months) cost for tuition and fees is $ _____; the average academic-year (or other academic-term) cost for living and incidental expenses is estimated to be $ _____. Total cost for academic-year (or other academic-term) is estimated to be $ _____. (Expenses for the summer period are not included in these figures.)

b. Estimated cost of living and incidental expenses for the summer period (or other non-academic period) of _____ months is $ _____.

6. Indicate how the student expects to meet the expenses estimated in items 5a and 5b above by completing the following (check and fill in as appropriate):

(Amount/Academic Year or other terms of _____ months)

☐ Scholarship/grant/assistantship from this school at $ _____ per _____ until _____ $ _____

☐ The student has been offered campus employment which will not displace a U.S. resident and will not affect the student's ability to carry a full course of study. The rate of pay is $ _____ per _____. $ _____ (enter estimated pay for academic year)

☐ Scholarship/grant/loan from another source (specify source _____) at $ _____ per _____ until _____. $ _____

☐ Personal or family funds (this school has received verification that these funds are available). $ _____

☐ Summer or other non academic year expenses will be met by (explain) _____ $ _____

_____

_____

Total: (Must at least equal items 5a and 5b above.) $ _____

7. This school (or if approval not in its own name, the _____ School District under which it operates or _____ School of which it is a part) was approved for attendance by nonimmigrant students by the Immigration and Naturalization Service on _____, file number _____. Such approval has not been revoked.

8. REMARKS _____

For immigration official	Signature of school official authorized by the school to issue Forms I-20A.
	Title	Date of issuance (This certificate expires 12 months after the date of issuance)

FORM I-20A

FORM I-20A

1. I seek to enter or remain in the United States temporarily and solely for the purpose of pursuing a full course of study at the school named on page 1 of this form.

2. Please print name in full	3. My maximum anticipated stay is (Months or Years)

4. My educational objective is

5. I am financially able to support myself for the entire period of my stay in the United States while pursuing a full course of study. (State source and amount of support:) (Documentary evidence of means of actual support must be attached to this form)

6. I last attended (Name of School)	(City)	(State)	(Country)

7. My major field of studies was	8. I completed such studies on (Date)

9. The person most closely related to me who lives outside the United States is:
(Name)   (Relationship)   (Address)

10. The person most closely related to me who lives in the United States is: (If you have no relative in the United States, give the name of a friend.)
(Name)   (Relationship)   (Address)

To Be Completed By the Student.

11. I understand the following:

a. A nonimmigrant student applying for admission to the United States for the first time after being issued an F-1 (student's) visa, will not be admitted unless he intends to attend the school specified in that visa. Therefore, if before he departs for the United States the student decides to attend some other school, he should communicate with the issuing American consular office for the purpose of having such other school specified in the visa. Any other nonimmigrant student will not be admitted to the United States unless he intends to attend the school specified in the Form I-20 or Form I-94 which he presents to the immigration officer at the port of entry.

b. A nonimmigrant student is not permitted to work off-campus for a wage or salary or engage in business while in the United States unless permission to do so has first been granted by the Immigration and Naturalization Service. A student who requires employment (1) because of economic necessity due to unforeseen circumstances arising after admission, or (2) to obtain practical training, may apply to the Immigration and Naturalization Service on Form I-538 for permission to accept such employment. Additional information concerning employment is set forth in Form I-538. The alien spouse or child accompanying or following to join a nonimmigrant student is not permitted to work in the United States.

c. A nonimmigrant student is permitted to remain in the United States only while maintaining nonimmigrant student status, and in any event not longer than the period fixed at the time of admission (or change to student classification) unless he applies to the Immigration and Naturalization Service on Form I-538 in accordance with the instructions on that form between 15 and 30 days prior to the expiration of the period of his authorized stay and obtains an extension of his stay.

d. Each year, every nonimmigrant student in the United States on the first day of January must submit by the 31st of January a written notice of his address to the Immigration and Naturalization Service. In addition, a notice must be sent within 10 days after every change of address. Regardless of whether he moves, each nonimmigrant student is required to file written notice of his address every 3 months. Printed forms obtainable at the United States immigration office or post office should be used in making the annual address report, the change of address report, and the 3-month address report.

e. At the time a nonimmigrant student departs from the United States, his temporary entry permit (Form I-94) is to be surrendered to a representative of the steamship or airline if he leaves via a seaport or airport, to a Canadian immigration officer if he leaves across the Canadian border, or to a United States immigration officer if he leaves across the Mexican border.

f. A nonimmigrant student may remain in the United States temporarily only for the purpose of pursuing a full course of study at a specified school. If, after being admitted, the student desires to transfer to another school, he must make written application on Form I-538 for permission to make such a transfer. The application must be submitted to the office of the Immigration and Naturalization Service having jurisdiction over the area in which the school from which he wishes to transfer is located. The application must be accompanied by Form I-20 completed by the school to which he wishes to transfer. He may not transfer until his application is approved. The application will be denied if the student failed to actually take a full course of study at the school he was last authorized by the Service to attend, unless he establishes that his failure to do so was due to circumstances beyond his control or was otherwise justified.

g. A student who seeks to re-enter the United States as a nonimmigrant student after a temporary absence must be in possession of the following documents: (i) A valid unexpired student visa (unless exempt from visa requirements); (ii) A passport valid for six months beyond the period of readmission (unless exempt from passport requirements); (iii) A current copy of Form I-20 (A and B). However, only the "A" copy of Form I-20 is required in the case of a nonimmigrant student returning from temporary absence outside the United States to continue attendance at the same school which the Immigration and Naturalization Service last authorized him to attend, in such case, Form I-20A may be retained by the student and used by him for any number of reentries within twelve months from the date of issuance, the certificate on page 2 of Form I-20A need not be completed, and Form I-20B should be destroyed.

h. A nonimmigrant student who does not register at the school specified in his temporary entry permit (Form I-94), or whose school attendance is terminated, or who takes less than a full course of study, or who accepts unauthorized employment, thereby fails to maintain his status and must depart from the United States immediately.

I CERTIFY THAT THE ABOVE IS CORRECT. I hereby agree to comply with the above and any other terms and conditions of my admission and any extension of stay. I hereby authorize the named school and any school to which I may subsequently transfer to release to the Immigration and Naturalization Service any information from my education records which the Service needs to know in order to determine if I am maintaining the lawful nonimmigrant status in which I was admitted to the United States under the immigration law. More specifically, I authorize the school to report, in writing, to the Immigration and Naturalization Service if I fail to register within 60 days of the time expected, if I fail to carry a full course of study, if I fail to attend classes to the extent normally required, if I am failing courses, if I become employed or if I terminate attendance at the named school and to provide the Service upon demand with my latest address.

Signature of Student	Address (City)	(State or Province)	(Country)	(Date)
X				
(Signature of Parent or Guardian if Student is Under 18 Years of Age)	(Address)		(Relationship)	(Date)

To Be Completed By the Student.

FORM I-20B

NOTICE AND REPORT CONCERNING
NONIMMIGRANT "F-1" STUDENT

UNITED STATES DEPARTMENT OF JUSTICE
Immigration and Naturalization Service

To Be Completed by the School

PART 1	Name of Student—Family Name (Capital Letters)	First Name	Middle Name

Date of Birth (Mo., day, year)	Country of Birth	Country of Nationality

NOTE ➡ READ CAREFULLY THE INSTRUCTIONS ON PAGE 4

Name of School

School Official To Be Notified of Student's Arrival in U.S.

Address of School (Include Zip Code)

Visa Issuing Post

PART II – NOTICE TO SCHOOL CONCERNING "F-1" STUDENT

As indicated herein, the above named student was admitted to or authorized to remain in the United States for a temporary period as a nonimmigrant student.

PLEASE REPORT PROMPTLY TO THE IMMIGRATION OFFICE HAVING JURISDICTION OVER YOUR SCHOOL THE OCCURRENCE OF ANY OF THE CIRCUMSTANCES DESCRIBED IN PART III, BELOW.

FAILURE TO SUBMIT REQUIRED REPORTS MAY RESULT IN WITHDRAWAL BY THE IMMIGRATION AND NATURALIZATION SERVICE OF ITS APPROVAL OF YOUR SCHOOL FOR ATTENDANCE BY NONIMMIGRANT STUDENTS.

For Immigration Official

PART III – REPORT BY SCHOOL CONCERNING "F-1" STUDENT

TO: Immigration and Naturalization Service

1. The student (Check one).

   (A) ☐ Did not register personally at this school within 60 days of the date expected.

   (B) ☐ Is carrying less than a full course of study or is attending classes to a lesser extent than normally required (explain in Remarks).

   • (C) ☐ Terminated attendance at this school **before** completion of the semester

   _____ (Give reason for termination in Remarks.)
   (Termination date)

   • (D) ☐ Terminated attendance at this school **upon** completion of the semester.

   _____ (Give reason for termination in Remarks.)
   (Termination date)

   • Do not report temporary discontinuance of attendance during a visit abroad, or because of acute illness or injury. However, if student fails to resume attendance this report must be submitted. A student who, on the basis of the recommendation of your school, has been authorized to accept employment for practical training in a field related to his course of studies is considered to be in attendance at your school during the authorized period of such employment. Please be guided accordingly in submitting reports concerning students who have been permitted to engage in practical training.

2. The student's last residence address in the U.S. was: (Apt. number and/or in care of)(Number and street)   (City or town)   (State)   (Zip Code)

3. The following information is furnished concerning the student's departure or planned departure from the United States:

Date of departure	Port of departure	Name of ship, airline, or transportation company
Address abroad		

4. Remarks:

Signature of school official	Title	Date

FORM I-20B (REV. 4-1-76) N

Page 3

SAMPLE SHEET

FOR FORMS I-20A & B

INSTRUCTIONS TO SCHOOL OFFICIALS

This certificate may be signed and issued only by an authorized school official in the United States after he has determined that the student is eligible. A false certification or improper issuance of this certificate to a student may result in revocation of the approval of your school for attendance by foreign students.

1. Before issuing this certificate you may wish to arrange to have the student tested for English language proficiency. If you wish to use a test of your own selection you may have it administered abroad by any person or agency you care to designate or by an American consular officer. Alternatively, if you wish to use a test which has been furnished to American consular officers by the Department of State, you should instruct the student to arrange with the consular officer to take the Department's English language examination. The results of any test administered by the consular officer will be forwarded direct to you.

   You should not issue this certification unless you are satisfied that the student meets the language and scholastic requirements to pursue the proposed course of study at your school, and that he is able to pay his expenses (including those of any accompanying spouse and children) during his stay in the United States. A copy of the evidence submitted by the student concerning scholastic preparation and ability to pay expenses must be retained by the school for the duration of the student's attendance there.

2. Complete page 1, and PART 1 of page 3, of this form for:

   a. Every **nonimmigrant** student whom you accept for admission to your school and who will apply for a visa and/or admission to the United States under Section 101 (a) (15) (F) (i) of the Immigration and Nationality Act;

   b. Every **nonimmigrant** student in the United States whom you accept for transfer to your school;

   c. Every alien in the United States who applies for a change to **nonimmigrant** student status and has been accepted to attend your school. (An alien who has been admitted or seeks admission to the United States for permanent residence is not classifiable as a nonimmigrant student. Forms I-20A and B should not be issued to any such alien.)

   Remove carbon interleaf and furnish I-20A and I-20B to the student. The Immigration and Naturalization Service, after authorizing admission (except in the case of a student returning from a temporary absence outside the United States to continue attendance at the same school), transfer, or change in status, will endorse and mail Form I-20B to the school. For procedure applicable in the case of a nonimmigrant student returning from a temporary absence outside the United States to continue attendance at the same school, see item 11g, page 2, of Form I-20A.

3. A student's spouse and minor children following to join him are not eligible for admission into the United States unless they present Form I-20A from the school in which the student is enrolled, stating that he is taking a full course of study, and the form is noted by the school to indicate the date of expiration of his authorized stay in the United States as shown on the student's Form I-94. When issuing Form I-20A for the use of his spouse and minor children, the school should fill in only the block giving the name and personal data relating to the student, the block giving name and address of the school, item 7 relating to school approval, and item 8, "Remarks", showing the date of expiration of the student's stay as, "Student's authorized stay in United States expires _____." In this instance, Form I-20B and the carbon interleaf should be destroyed.
   (date)

4. If the student fails to register, does not carry a full course of study, or does not attend classes as required, or if his attendance is terminated, fill in PART III of Form I-20B (page 3) and mail immediately to the office of the Immigration and Naturalization Service having jurisdiction over the area in which your school is located. (Please read PART II of Form I-20B for further instructions.)

INSTRUCTIONS FOR NONIMMIGRANT STUDENTS

1. Fill in page 2 of Form I-20A and complete and retain page 5 for your records. Do not fill in any other pages of the form.

2. If you are an applicant for admission to the United States, present both I-20A and I-20B to the American consular officer at the time of your visa application (unless you are exempt from visa requirements) and to the immigration officer upon your arrival in the United States. If you are exempt from visa requirements and are applying for admission to the U.S. for the first time as an F-1 student, present to the immigration officer documentary evidence of your ability to support yourself while pursuing a full course of study (see item 5, page 2 of I-20A). For procedure applicable in the case of a student returning from a temporary absence outside the United States to continue attendance at the same school, see item 11g, page 2, of I-20A.

3. If you are an applicant for permission to transfer to another school (or for transfer and extension of stay), mail or bring Form I-538 and both I-20A and I-20B to the office of the Immigration and Naturalization Service having jurisdiction over the area in which the school from which you wish to transfer is located, together with your temporary entry permit (Form I-94 ARRIVAL-DEPARTURE RECORD). (If your temporary entry permit is attached to your passport, the permit should be removed for this purpose.) **DO NOT SEND IN YOUR PASSPORT.**

4. If you are an applicant for change to nonimmigrant student status, apply on Form I-506 and attach both I-20A and I-20B. Apply at the office of the Immigration and Naturalization Service having jurisdiction over the area in which you are temporarily residing.

Severe penalties are provided by law for knowingly and wilfully falsifying or concealing a material fact in filling out this form.

FORM I-20A

FORM I-20A

Page 5

CERTIFICATE BY NONIMMIGRANT STUDENT UNDER SECTION 101 (a) (15) (F) (i)
OF THE IMMIGRATION AND NATIONALITY ACT

1. I seek to enter or remain in the United States temporarily and solely for the purpose of pursuing a full course of study at the school named on page 1 of this form.

2. Please print name in full

3. My maximum anticipated stay is (Months or Years)

4. My educational objective is

5. I am financially able to support myself for the entire period of my stay in the United States while pursuing a full course of study. (State source and amount of support:) (Documentary evidence of means of actual support must be attached to this form)

6. I last attended (Name of School)   (City)   (State)   (Country)

7. My major field of studies was

8. I completed such studies on (Date)

9. The person most closely related to me who lives outside the United States is:
(Name)   (Relationship)   (Address)

10. The person most closely related to me who lives in the United States is: (If you have no relative in the United States, give the name of a friend.)
(Name)   (Relationship)   (Address)

11. I understand the following:

a. A nonimmigrant student applying for admission to the United States for the first time after being issued an F-1 (student's) visa, will not be admitted unless he intends to attend the school specified in that visa. Therefore, if before he departs for the United States the student decides to attend some other school, he should communicate with the issuing American consular office for the purpose of having such other school specified in the visa. Any other nonimmigrant student will not be admitted to the United States unless he intends to attend the school specified in the Form I-20 or Form I-94 which he presents to the immigration officer at the port of entry.

b. A nonimmigrant student is not permitted to work off-campus for a wage or salary or engage in business while in the United States unless permission to do so has first been granted by the Immigration and Naturalization Service. A student who requires employment (1) because of economic necessity due to unforeseen circumstances arising after admission, or (2) to obtain practical training, may apply to the Immigration and Naturalization Service on Form I-538 for permission to accept such employment. Additional information concerning employment is set forth in Form I-538. The alien spouse or child accompanying or following to join a nonimmigrant student is not permitted to work in the United States.

c. A nonimmigrant student is permitted to remain in the United States only while maintaining nonimmigrant student status, and in any event not longer than the period fixed at the time of admission (or change to student classification) unless he applies to the Immigration and Naturalization Service on Form I-538 in accordance with the instructions on that form between 15 and 30 days prior to the expiration of the period of his authorized stay and obtains an extension of his stay.

d. Each year, every nonimmigrant student in the United States on the first day of January must submit by the 31st of January a written notice of his address to the Immigration and Naturalization Service. In addition, a notice must be sent within 10 days after every change of address. Regardless of whether he moves, each nonimmigrant student is required to file written notice of his address every 3 months. Printed forms obtainable at the United States immigration office or post office should be used in making the annual address report, the change of address report, and the 3-month address report.

e. At the time a nonimmigrant student departs from the United States, his temporary entry permit (Form I-94) is to be surrendered to a representative of the steamship or airline if he leaves via a seaport or airport, to a Canadian immigration officer if he leaves across the Canadian border, or to a United States immigration officer if he leaves across the Mexican border.

f. A nonimmigrant student may remain in the United States temporarily only for the purpose of pursuing a full course of study at a specified school. If, after being admitted, the student desires to transfer to another school, he must make written application on Form I-538 for permission to make such a transfer. The application must be submitted to the office of the Immigration and Naturalization Service having jurisdiction over the area in which the school from which he wishes to transfer is located. The application must be accompanied by Form I-20 completed by the school to which he wishes to transfer. He may not transfer until his application is approved. The application will be denied if the student failed to actually take a full course of study at the school he was last authorized by the Service to attend, unless he establishes that his failure to do so was due to circumstances beyond his control or was otherwise justified.

g. A student who seeks to re-enter the United States as a nonimmigrant student after a temporary absence must be in possession of the following documents: (i) A valid unexpired student visa (unless exempt from visa requirements); (ii) A passport valid for six months beyond the period of read-mission (unless exempt from passport requirements); (iii) A current copy of Form I-20 (A and B). However, only the "A" copy of Form I-20 is required in the case of a nonimmigrant student returning from temporary absence outside the United States to continue attendance at the same school which the Immigration and Naturalization Service last authorized him to attend, in such case, Form I-20A may be retained by the student and used by him for any number of reentries within twelve months from the date of issuance, the certificate on page 2 of Form I-20A need not be completed, and Form I-20B should be destroyed.

h. A nonimmigrant student who does not register at the school specified in his temporary entry permit (Form I-94), or whose school attendance is terminated, or who takes less than a full course of study, or who accepts unauthorized employment, thereby fails to maintain his status and must depart from the United States immediately.

I CERTIFY THAT THE ABOVE IS CORRECT. I hereby agree to comply with the above and any other terms and conditions of my admission and any extension of stay. I hereby authorize the named school and any school to which I may subsequently transfer to release to the Immigration and Naturalization Service any information from my education records which the Service needs to know in order to determine if I am maintaining the lawful non-immigrant status in which I was admitted to the United States under the immigration law. More specifically, I authorize the school to report, in writing, to the Immigration and Naturalization Service if I fail to register within 60 days of the time expected, if I fail to carry a full course of study, if I fail to attend classes to the extent normally required, if I am failing courses, if I become employed or if I terminate attendance at the named school and to provide the Service upon demand with my latest address.

Signature of Student   Address (City)   (State or Province)   (Country)   (Date)

X

(Signature of Parent or Guardian if Student is Under 18 Years of Age)   (Address)   (Relationship)   (Date)

NOTE ——► THIS PAGE IS TO BE COMPLETED AND RETAINED BY THE STUDENT FOR HIS RECORDS

FORM DSP-66
Presently, FORM IAP-66 **CERTIFICATE OF ELIGIBILITY FOR EXCHANGE VISITOR (J-1) STATUS**
Completed by the school

PLEASE DO NOT STAPLE THIS FORM (FILLED OUT BY SCHOOL)

DEPARTMENT OF STATE
BUREAU OF EDUCATIONAL AND CULTURAL AFFAIRS
CERTIFICATE OF ELIGIBILITY FOR EXCHANGE VISITOR (J - 1) STATUS

Form Approved
OMB No. 47-R0144

PART I — IT IS HEREBY CERTIFIED THAT:

1. _____ ( ) Male; ( ) Female
   (Family Name of Exchange Visitor) *(First Name)* *(Middle Name)*

born _____ in _____ , _____
   (Mo.) (Day) (Yr.) *(City)* *(Country)*

a legal permanent resident of _____ , whose position in
   (Country) *(Code)*

that country is _____ and whose U.S. address is or will be
   (Pos Code)

THE PURPOSE OF THIS FORM IS TO:
1 ( ) Begin a new program
2 ( ) Extend an on going program
3 ( ) Transfer to a different program
4 ( ) Replace a lost form
5 ( ) Permit the visitor's family to enter the U.S. separately.

2. will be sponsored by   University of
_____ to participate in Exchange Visitor Program No.   P- 1 - 168 , which is still valid and is officially described as follows:

A program to provide courses of study (undergraduate or graduate level), training, research, teaching, lecturing, or a combination thereof, in all the fields of study available at the University or institutions and installations under its control, for foreign students, trainees, guest instructors, visiting professors, and leaders in fields of specialized knowledge or skill.

3. This form covers the period from _____ to _____ (one year maximum.)
   (Mo.) (Day) (Yr.) *(Mo.) (Day) (Yr.)*

   If this form is for family travel or replaces a lost form, the expiration date on the exchange visitor's I-94 is _____ .

4. The category of this visitor is 1 ( ) Student, 2 ( ) Trainee, 3 ( ) Teacher, 4 ( ) Professor, 5 ( ) Research Scholar or Specialist, 6 ( ) International Visitor, 7 ( ) Professional Trainee, and the specific educational field or non-study activity to be engaged in is
   Code No. _____ , verbally described as follows:
   (Subj/Field Code)

5. During the period covered by this form, it is estimated that the following financial support (in U.S. $) will be provided to this exchange visitor by:

   a. ( ) The Program Sponsor in item 2 above $ _____ .
   Financial support from organizations other than the sponsor will be provided by one or more of the following:
   b1. ( ) U.S. Government Agency(ies): _____ (Agency Code), $ _____ ;b2. _____ (Agency Code), $ _____ .
   c1. ( ) International Organization(s): _____ (Int. Org. Code), $ _____ ;c2. _____ (Int. Org. Code),$ _____ .
   d. ( ) The Exchange Visitor's Government $ _____ .
   e. ( ) The binational Commission of the visitor's Country $ _____ .
   f. ( ) All other organizations providing support $ _____ .
   g. ( ) Personal funds $ _____ .

   (If necessary, use above spaces for funding by multiple U.S. Agencies or Intl. Organizations)

6. I.N.S. USE

7. _____
   (Name of Official Preparing Form) *(Title)*

   _____
   (Address)

   _____
   (Signature of Responsible Officer or Alternate R.O.) *(Date)*

PART II — ENDORSEMENT OF CONSULAR OR IMMIGRATION OFFICER REGARDING SECTION 212(e) OF THE I.N.A.

I, _____
   (Name)

_____
   (Title)

have determined that this alien in the above program
1. ( ) is not subject to the two year residence requirement;
2. ( ) is subject, based on: A. ( ) government financing and/or
B. ( ) the Exchange Visitor Skills List.

_____
(Signature of Officer) *(Date)*

PART III — STATEMENT OF RESPONSIBLE OFFICER FOR RELEASING SPONSOR (FOR TRANSFER OF PROGRAM)

Date _____ , Transfer of this exchange visitor from
program No. _____ sponsored by

to the program specified in item (2) is necessary or highly desirable and is in conformity with the objectives of the Mutual Educational and Cultural Exchange Act of 1961.

_____
(Signature of Officer) *(Date)*

FORM DSP-66
(6-75)   **Copy 1 - For Immigration and Naturalization Service**   Page 1

FORM I-134
U. S. Department of Justice
Immigration and Naturalization Service

OMB No. 1115-0062

Affidavit of Support

(ANSWER ALL ITEMS: FILL IN WITH TYPEWRITER OR PRINT IN BLOCK LETTERS IN INK.)

[The Sponsor's Name]

I, _____, residing at _____
(Name)   (Street and Number)

_____
(City)   (State)   (ZIP Code if in U.S.)   (Country)

BEING DULY SWORN DEPOSE AND SAY:

1. I was born on_____ at _____
(Date)   (City)   (Country)

   If you are **not** a native born United States citizen, answer the following as appropriate:

   a. If a United States citizen through naturalization, give certificate of naturalization number _____

   b. If a United States citizen through parent(s) or marriage, give citizenship certificate number _____

   c. If United States citizenship was derived by some other method, attach a statement of explanation.

   d. If a lawfully admitted permanent resident of the United States, give "A" number _____

2. That I am_____years of age and have resided in the United States since (date) _____

3. That this affidavit is executed in behalf of the following person:

Name		Sex	Age
Citizen of--(Country)	Marital Status	Relationship to Deponent	
Presently resides at--(Street and Number)	(City)	(State)	(Country)

Name of spouse and children accompanying or following to join person:

Spouse	Sex	Age	Child		Sex	Age
Child	Sex	Age	Child		Sex	Age
Child	Sex	Age	Child		Sex	Age

4. That this affidavit is made by me for the purpose of assuring the United States Government that the person(s) named in item 3 will not become a public charge in the United States.

5. That I am willing and able to receive, maintain and support the person(s) named in item 3. That I am ready and willing to deposit a bond, if necessary, to guarantee that such person(s) will not become a public charge during his or her stay in the United States, or to guarantee that the above named will maintain his or her nonimmigrant status if admitted temporarily and will depart prior to the expiration of his or her authorized stay in the United States.

6. That I understand this affidavit will be binding upon me for a period of three (3) years after entry of the person(s) named in item 3 and that the information and documentation provided by me may be made available to the Secretary of Health and Human Services and the Secretary of Agriculture, who may make it available to a public assistance agency.

7. That I am employed as, or engaged in the business of _____with _____
(Type of Business)   (Name of concern)

at _____
(Street and Number)   (City)   (State)   (Zip Code)

I derive an annual income of *(if self-employed, I have attached a copy of my last income tax return or report of commercial rating concern which I certify to be true and correct to the best of my knowledge and belief. See instruction for nature of evidence of net worth to be submitted.)* $_____

I have on deposit in savings banks in the United States $_____

I have other personal property, the reasonable value of which is $_____

Form I-134 (Rev. 12-1-84) Y   **OVER** ➞

Form I-134

I have stocks and bonds with the following market value, as indicated on the attached list
which I certify to be true and correct to the best of my knowledge and belief. $ _____
I have life insurance in the sum of $ _____
With a cash surrender value of $ _____
I own real estate valued at $ _____
With mortgages or other encumbrances thereon amounting to $ _____

Which is located at_____
(Street and Number   (City)   (State)   (Zip Code)

8. That the following persons are dependent upon me for support: *(Place an "X" in the appropriate column to indicate whether the person named is **wholly** or **partially** dependent upon you for support.)*

Name of Person	Wholly Dependent	Partially Dependent	Age	Relationship to Me

9. That I have previously submitted affidavit(s) of support for the following person(s). If none, state *"None"*

Name _____   Date submitted _____

_____

_____

10. That I have submitted visa petition(s) to the Immigration and Naturalization Service on behalf of the following person(s). If none, state none.

Name _____   Relationship _____   Date submitted _____

_____

_____

11. *(Complete this block only if the person named in item 3 will be in the United States temporarily.)*
That I ☐ do intend   ☐ do not   intend, to make specific contributions to the support of the person named in item 3. *(If you check "do intend", indicate the exact nature and duration of the contributions. For example, if you intend to furnish room and board, state for how long and, if money, state the amount in United States dollars and state whether it is to be given in a lump sum, weekly, or monthly, or for how long.)*

_____

_____

_____

OATH OR AFFIRMATION OF DEPONENT

I acknowledge at that I have read Part III of the Instructions, Sponsor and Alien Liability, and am aware of my responsibilities as an immigrant sponsor under the Social Security Act, as amended, and the Food Stamp Act, as amended.

I swear (affirm) that I know the contents of this affidavit signed by me and the statements are true and correct.

Alien's Sponsor signs here

Signature of deponent X_____

Subscribed and sworn to (affirmed) before me this _____ *day of* _____, 19_____

at _____. *My commission expires on* _____

Signature of Officer Administering Oath _____ *Title* _____

If affidavit prepared by other than deponent, please complete the following: I declare that this document was prepared by me at the request of the deponent and is based on all information of which I have knowledge.

_____

(Signature)   *(Address)*   *(Date)*

To Be filled in and signed by a Notary Public or ...

EXPLANATORY NOTE (To illustrate H, L and E Visa Cases employed in the Manual)

1. Various illustrative sample Forms reproduced in this manual (and the supporting letters, affidavits and other documentations thereto), are so reproduced herein by courtesy of C. James Cooper, Esq., a renowned Denver Colorado immigration law specialist; and these Cooper forms are particularly unique and well suited for our purposes for one reason: they are the true, actual forms and documentations used in actual petitions filed for various aliens by attorney Cooper, all of which visas were subsequently approved. The personal and business names, addresses, and other identifying details of sorts have been deleted in these forms, merely out of concern by Cooper to protect the privacy of his clients and the parties involved.

2. The particular **Form I-129B reproduced on pp.** 83-5, was filed specifically for an **H-1 VISA** for the position of an apparel Accounts Executive for a Hong Kong-based beneficiary (alien). Among the qualifications possessed by the beneficiary, are a Bachelor's Degree in Business Administration, an Associate Degree from the Fashion Institute, and work experience; the alien's qualifications were documented by submission of (among other things) copy of the Englewood Colorado employer's letter of offer of employment to the Hong Kong-based alien (see p. 81), an itemized job description of the position in question (see p. 87), as well as certified copies of the alien's degrees and transcripts, etc.

(See also p. 128 for another excellent sample **EMPLOYER LETTER** illustrative of the type of covering letter used in support of H-1 visa petitions. Here, the alien, originally from India, had entered the U.S. on an F-1 visa as a student. Then, after receiving his Master's Degree in Computer and Information Science and getting some work experience, the alien got a job offer for a **temporary** position; the prospective employer filed a petition (Form I-129B) for him for an H-1 visa. At the same time the employer filed the petition, the alien applied to change his status from F-1 (student), to an H-1 (temporary worker) by filing Form I-506.)

Note, however, that if this alien had gained entry already into the U.S., and is "in legal status" under another non-immigrant category (say, as a student, for example), the alien would, in addition, have to file an Application to Change his/her status on **Form I-506**, along with the Form I-129B petition. (If the alien was <u>NOT</u> in legal status, then he would have to designate a Consulate in a foreign country where he would apply for the H-1 visa from.)

3. The particular **Form I-129B reproduced on pp.** 88-90, was filed specifically for an **H-2 VISA** for a Mexican national whose job in the U.S. would be to train United States workers in the art of hand wiping tin on copper ware for a Denver Colorado company. Documentations submitted with the I-129B petition in support for the H-2 Visa request, included: i) letter of Labor Certification approval from the U.S. Department of Labor's office (see p. 92); ii) the application form used in applying for the labor certification, Form ETA 750A only (see p. 93); and iii) the Employer's Letter, a so-called "Business Necessity" letter (see p. 91), among other documentations. (Another sample BUSINESS NECESSITY LETTER is set forth on p. 152, for your information.)

4. The particular **Form I-129B reproduced on pp.** 95-7 was filed specifically for an **H-3 TRAINEE VISA** for a Swiss national who was then resident in Longmont Colorado, but on J-1 visa. The alien (he first applied for a Waiver of the 2-year requirement for the J-1 holders and was granted the waiver) was to be given business training in the management of the lumber business. Documents submitted with the I-129B petition for this H-3 visa request, included, among others, letter of employment/training from the sponsor (see p. 98), which clearly shows the general scope of the training, and more particularly, that the program has <u>both</u> classroom instruction as well as on-the-job training components.

5. The particular **Form I-129B reproduced on pp.** 99-101, was filed specifically for an **L-1 INTRA-COMPANY TRANSFEREE VISA** for an alien person who had been working in Bangkok, Thailand, as a Manager for the parent company there. The L-1 visa was to allow this employee to come to and remain <u>temporarily</u> in the U.S. (Denver, Colorado) for a period of 3 years for the purpose of setting up the subsidiary located in Denver and training U.S. workers for the subsidiary Documents submitted with the I-129B petition for this L-1 visa request, included, among others, the following: letter of employment from the U.S.

EXPLANATORY NOTE (Continued)

petitioner-employer (see p.102), a brochure of the company's products, numerous invoices and orders, certified copy of the Certificate of Incorporation of the business in the State of Colorado, certificate of stock ownership of the U.S. subsidiary, and other documentatioms to show the corporate relationship between the U.S. company in Colorado and the foreign parent company in Thailand.

6. The particular **Forms I-506** and **I-126** reproduced on pp. 103 and 105 ,respectively, were specifically filed in a successful actual case for an **E-2 TREATY INVESTOR'S VISA** for a French West Indian alien who happened to have come into the U.S. on a B-2 (i.e.,Tourist-Visitor's) visa, but then decided to invest in and work as a specialty cook in a restaurant in Duranja, Colorado. This,then, meant that he had to apply for change of his visa status from B-2 to an E-2 (i.e. INVESTOR'S) visa.

This particular case exemplifies a situation where the investor has some specialized knowledge and would be working in a minor technical capacity, rather than in a managerial or executive capacity. Among the documents submitted in support of this particular petition, were: i) supporting letter from the principal investors in the restaurant, a husband-and-wife team (see p.107); ii) the foreign investor's Form I-94 Arrival-Departure Record, which had been issued him by the Immigration Service at the time of his entry into the U.S.; iii) an AFFIDAVIT (sworn statement) by owners of the restaurant supporting the proposed investment by the alien (see p.108); and other documents, such as a certified copy of the deed to the restaurant building, the wine list and menu, media reviews of the restaurant, etc. (Form I-539, "Application for Extension of Temporary Stay," was apparently not submitted (or necessary) in this particular instance.)

SAMPLE FORM I-129B

**UNITED STATES
DEPARTMENT OF JUSTICE
Immigration and Naturalization
Service**

NOTE: See "Explanatory Note" on p.81, first, especially item 2 therein.

Form approved
OMB No. 43-R0348

Date Filed	Fee Stamp

**PETITION
TO CLASSIFY
NONIMMIGRANT
AS TEMPORARY
WORKER
OR TRAINEE**

File No.

(To be submitted in duplicate, with supplementary documents described in instructions, to the District Director having administrative jurisdiction over the place in the United States in which it is intended the alien(s) be employed or trained)

(THIS BLOCK NOT TO BE FILLED OUT BY PETITIONER)

The Secretary of State is hereby notified that the alien(s) for whom this petition was filed is (are) entitled to the nonimmigrant status checked below:

☐ H-1   ☐ H-3
☐ H-2   ☐ L-1

The validity of this petition will expire on _____
The admission of the alien(s) may be authorized to the above date.

REMARKS:

DATE
OF
ACTION
DD

DISTRICT

(PETITIONER NOT TO WRITE ABOVE THIS LINE)
(PLEASE FILL IN WITH TYPEWRITER OR PRINT IN BLOCK LETTERS IN INK)

I hereby petition, pursuant to the provisions of section 214(c) of the Immigration and Nationality Act, for the following: (Check one.)

H-1 ☒ Alien(s) of distinguished merit and ability to perform services of an exceptional nature requiring such merit and ability.

H-2 ☐ Alien(s) to perform temporary service or labor for which a bona fide need exists. (One who is to perform duties which are themselves temporary in nature.)

H-3 ☐ Alien trainee(s). (One who seeks to enter at the invitation of an individual, organization, firm, or other trainer for the purpose of receiving training in any field of endeavor. Incidental production necessary to the training is permitted provided a United States worker is not thereby displaced.)

L-1 ☐ Intra-company transferee. (One who has been employed continuously for one year and who seeks to enter in order to continue to render services to the same employer or a subsidiary or affiliate thereof in a managerial or executive capacity or in a capacity which involves specialized knowledge.)

1. NAME OF PETITIONER	2. DATE BUSINESS ESTABLISHED
▓▓▓▓ Inc.	February 19, 1976

3. ADDRESS (NUMBER, STREET, CITY, STATE, ZIP CODE)
▓▓▓ Parkway, ▓▓▓▓▓, Englewood, Colorado ▓▓▓

4. DESCRIPTION OF PETITIONER'S BUSINESS, INCLUDING ITS NATURE, NUMBER OF EMPLOYEES, AND GROSS ANNUAL INCOME
Importers and distributors in wearing apparel;
Employees, 19;
Gross annual income, $2,400,000.00

5. LOCATION OF AMERICAN CONSULATE AT WHICH ALIEN(S) WILL APPLY FOR VISA(S):

	(City in Foreign Country)	(Foreign Country)
	Hong Kong	

(If petition is to be made for more than one H alien and application for visas will be made at more than one American Consulate, a separate petition must be submitted for each consulate at which H visa applications will be made. Separate petition must be filed for each L-1 alien.)

6. THE ALIEN(S) WILL PERFORM SERVICES OR LABOR FOR OR RECEIVE TRAINING FROM THE FOLLOWING ESTABLISHMENT IN THE U.S.:
(Name of Establishment) ▓▓▓▓, Inc.

▓▓▓ DTC Parkway, Suite ▓▓	Englewood	Colorado	▓▓▓
(Street and Number)	(City or Town)	(State)	(Zip Code)

7. PERIOD REQUIRED TO COMPLETE SERVICES OR TRAINING		8. WAGES PER WEEK year	8A. HOURS PER WEEK	9. OVERTIME RATE
From (date) Date of approval To (date) 24 mos. thereafter	No. of days or months 24 mos.	$42,000.00	40	--

10. OTHER COMPENSATION (Explain)	10A. VALUED AT	11. BY WHOM PAID?
none	$ -- WEEKLY	Employer, ▓▓▓▓ Inc.

Form I-129B
(Rev. 6-20-66)N

RECEIVED	TRANS. IN	RET'D-TRANS OUT	COMPLETED

FORM I-129B

P.1 of 3 pgs.

(Page 2)

ALL PETITIONERS COMPLETE ITEMS 12A THROUGH 22. If petition is for more than one H alien, give required information for each additional alien in space provided on page 3 If the identity of the H aliens is not known at present, you must furnish information concerning them as soon as that information becomes known to you

12A. ALIEN'S NAME (Family name in capital letters)   (First name)   Dawning   (Middle name)   Zing Fong

12B. OTHER NAMES (Show all other past and present names, including maiden name if married woman.)   none

12C. NUMBER OF ALIENS INCLUDED IN THIS PETITION   1

13. ADDRESS TO WHICH ALIEN WILL RETURN   (Street and Number)   Flat B, 10th Flr., ▆▆▆▆▆   (City) Sheung Shing St., ▆▆▆▆   (Province)   (Country) Hong Kong

14. PRESENT ADDRESS   Same as #13 above

15. PROPOSED PORT OF ENTRY   San Francisco,CA

16. DATE OF BIRTH 5/21/58   **17. PLACE OF BIRTH** Hong Kong   **18. PRESENT NATIONALITY OR CITIZENSHIP** Hong Kong   **19. PRESENT OCCUPATION** Merchandiser

20. HAS AN IMMIGRANT VISA PETITION EVER BEEN FILED ON THE ALIEN'S BEHALF? ☐ YES ☒ NO
If "Yes", where was it filed?

21. HAS THE ALIEN EVER APPLIED FOR AN IMMIGRANT VISA OR PERMANENT RESIDENCE IN THE U.S.? ☐ YES ☒ NO
If "Yes", where did he apply?

22. TO YOUR KNOWLEDGE, HAS ANY VISA PETITION FILED BY YOU OR ANY OTHER PERSON OR ORGANIZATION FOR THE NAMED ALIEN(S) BEEN DENIED? ☐ YES ☒ NO
If you answered "yes", complete the following: Date of filing of each denied petition _____
Place of filing of each denied petition (city) _____
TO YOUR KNOWLEDGE, HAVE ANY OF THE NAMED ALIEN(S) EVER BEEN IN THE U.S.? ☐ YES ☐ NO (If "yes" identify each on Page 3)

23. NONTECHNICAL DESCRIPTION OF SERVICES TO BE PERFORMED BY OR TRAINING TO BE RECEIVED BY ALIEN(S) (THIS BLOCK NEED NOT BE COMPLETED IF PETITION IS FOR H-2 WORKERS) As an Apparel Account Executive, to supervise all overseas buying of fabric, samples and production, and to coordinate all fabrics and accessories with each factory for production

24. (If you are petitioning for an H-1 physician or nurse, complete this block.)
DOES THE LAW GOVERNING THE PLACE WHERE THE ALIEN'S SERVICES WILL BE PERFORMED RESTRICT HIM/HER FROM PERFORMING ANY OF THE DESIRED SERVICES? ☐ YES ☐ NO If the answer is "yes", attach statement listing the restricted services and setting forth the reason for the restriction. (See instructions for Physicians and Nurses.)

25. (If you are petitioning for a trainee complete this block.)
A. IS SIMILAR TRAINING AVAILABLE IN ALIEN'S COUNTRY? ☐ YES ☐ NO
B. WOULD ALIEN'S TRAINING RESULT IN DISPLACEMENT OF UNITED STATES WORKER? ☐ YES ☐ NO

26. (If you are petitioning for an L-1 alien complete this block.) (Check appropriate boxes.)
a. The alien has been employed in an ☐ executive; ☐ managerial capacity; ☐ in a capacity which involves specialized knowledge
by _____ since _____
    (name and address of employer)   (date)
b. The petitioner is ☐ the same employer ☐ subsidiary ☐ an affiliate of the employer abroad.

FILL IN ITEMS 27 THROUGH 31 INCLUSIVE ONLY IF PETITION IS FOR H-2 ALIEN(S)

27. DESCRIPTIVE JOB TITLE OF WORK TO BE PERFORMED BY ALIEN(S) (Use title which corresponds to that used in job order placed with state Employment Service or Agency by petitioner for same type of labor. Where work in more than one job classification is to be performed by aliens, state number to be employed in each job classification.)

28. IS (ARE) ALIEN(S) SKILLED IN WORK TO BE PERFORMED? ☐ YES ☐ NO ☐ UNKNOWN

29. IS ANY LABOR ORGANIZATION ACTIVE IN THE LABOR FIELD(S) SPECIFIED IN ITEM 27? ☐ YES ☐ NO
(If yes, specify organization(s) and labor field(s).)

30. IS THE PETITIONER INVOLVED IN, OR ARE THERE THREATENED, ANY LABOR RELATIONS DIFFICULTIES, INCLUDING STRIKES OR LOCKOUTS? (Specify)

31. I HAVE NOT BEEN ABLE TO FIND IN THE UNITED STATES ANY UNEMPLOYED PERSON(S) CAPABLE OF PERFORMING THE DUTIES OF THE POSITION(S) TO BE FILLED. THE FOLLOWING EFFORTS HAVE BEEN MADE TO FIND SUCH PERSON(S): (Complete only if labor certification not attached.)

ALL PETITIONERS FILL IN ITEMS 32 THROUGH 34B.

32. LIST DOCUMENTS SUBMITTED IN SUPPORT OF THIS PETITION. Petitioner's supporting letter; beneficiary's diplomas and school transcripts, resume

FORM I-129B

P.2 of 3 pgs.

SAMPLE SHEET

33. THE DOCUMENTS SUBMITTED HEREWITH ARE HEREBY MADE A PART OF THIS PETITION.

I am willing (according to) to post any bond required as a condition to the approval of this petition.
I agree that as soon as known I shall furnish the District Director to whom this petition is being submitted with the names of those alien(s) not named herein.
If the petition is for temporary worker(s), I certify that I have a bona fide need of such workers(s).
If the petition is for trainee(s), I certify he/she is coming to the United States to participate in a bona fide training program.
I certify that the statements and representations made in this petition are true and correct to the best of my knowledge and belief.

34A. SIGNATURE OF PETITIONER	DATE	34B. TITLE (Must be petitioner or authorized agent of petitioner)
William R.	3 -?-84	Pres

SIGNATURE OF PERSON PREPARING FORM, IF OTHER THAN PETITIONER

35. I declare that this document was prepared by me at the request of the petitioner and is based on all information of which I have any knowledge.

C. James Cooper, Jr.

999 18th St., #3220
Denver, Colorado 80202
(Address)

2/7/84
(Date)

If this petition is for more than one alien of distinguished merit and ability (H-1) or trainee (H-3), use spaces below to give required information. If additional space is needed, attach separate sheet executed in same general manner.

NAME	DATE OF BIRTH	PLACE OF BIRTH	NATIONALITY	OCCUPATION
PRESENT ADDRESS				
ADDRESS TO WHICH ALIEN WILL RETURN				
NONTECHNICAL DESCRIPTION OF SERVICES TO BE PERFORMED BY OR TRAINING TO BE RECEIVED BY ALIEN				

NAME	DATE OF BIRTH	PLACE OF BIRTH	NATIONALITY	OCCUPATION
PRESENT ADDRESS				
ADDRESS TO WHICH ALIEN WILL RETURN				
NONTECHNICAL DESCRIPTION OF SERVICES TO BE PERFORMED BY OR TRAINING TO BE RECEIVED BY ALIEN				

NAME	DATE OF BIRTH	PLACE OF BIRTH	NATIONALITY	OCCUPATION
PRESENT ADDRESS				
ADDRESS TO WHICH ALIEN WILL RETURN				
NONTECHNICAL DESCRIPTION OF SERVICES TO BE PERFORMED BY OR TRAINING TO BE RECEIVED BY ALIEN				

If this petition is for more than one (H-2) alien to perform temporary service or labor, use spaces below to give required information. If additional space is needed, attach separate sheet executed in same general manner. Identify each alien who has been in the U.S., by placing an "X" in the last column

NAME	NATIONALITY	DATE AND PLACE OF BIRTH	PRESENT ADDRESS	X

FORM I-129B

(End of Form)

P.3 of 3 pgs.

, INC.

EMPLOYER OFFER OF EMPLOYMENT
LETTER

TO:

Miss Dawning ████
Flat B, 10th Flr.
████████████
Sheung Shing St.
████████Hong Kong

April 3, 1984

Dear Dawning:

As we have discussed, I have offered you the position of Apparel Account
Executive with our company on a temporary basis, until we are able to locate,
hire and train an individual to fill this position on a permanent basis.

This letter is to confirm this offer and your acceptance of this position
at an annual salary of $42,000.00. This position's responsibilities
include the handling of all our clothing orders with each of the factories
in Hong Kong and Taiwan, coordinating all piece goods with each factory,
setting up production schedules that can be met, and setting up a file and
production system in our office that will correlate with those factories.

I became quite impressed with your experience and abilities in handling our
account with your employer in Hong Kong, and feel that you will add greatly
to the efficient organization of the development and production areas of our
business which will help increase our productivity.

As you are aware, the offer of the position of Apparel Account Executive is
subject to approval of our petition by the Immigration and Naturalization
Service.

Sincerely,

Bill ████████
Bill ████████

BG:jcb

NOTE: See "Explanatory Note" on P. 81,
especially the No. 2 paragraph thereof.

████████ Parkway ████████████████████ Englewood, Colorado 80111
Cable: ████████████ ● TWX ████████ ● FAX (303) ████████

NOTE: See "Explanatory Note" on p. 81,
especially the No. 2 paragraph thereof.

April 9, 1984

(EMPLOYER'S JOB DESCRIPTION)

TO WHOM IT MAY CONCERN:

As our Account Executive, Miss Dawning ▇▇▇ will be responsible for the management and coordination of all areas related to the development and production of our product lines. At the current time, we have five lines of skiwear fashions for a total of approximately 300 styles. We work a year in advance in this industry, and for each season our development and production encompass the following sequence of activities:

1. Research the current market and trends.
2. Identify design concept, price point, and style catagories for each line.
3. Anticipate trends for the coming season by working with fabric, trim, and color resources. (To include: Arthur Kahn, Seatex, Toray, Gore-Tex, Y.K.K. zippers, Sumitomo, Schoeller Textil, Pottendorfer, and AuMan.)
4. Select fabrics and colors for the new season, and order greige goods and lab dips from each vendor.
5. Coordination of trim and hardware colors with these resources to complement fabric colors.
6. Design, sketch, and detail styles for each line.
7. Adopt styles from sketches to be made into prototype samples.
8. Select factory to make prototype based upon equipment necessary to produce this style of garment.
9. Send designer sketch with detailed specification sheet to factory.
10. Upon receipt of prototype from factory, each style is reviewed and comments are made on the fit, detail, construction, and design elements. These comments are sent back to the factory.
11. Each prototype style that is considered for adoption into the line is then priced from the factory.
12. All fabrics, knit, trim, hardware, and accessories are coordinated to be delivered to the factory for sample production.
13. Styles are selected for each line, and details regarding fabric, insulation, knit, hardware, etc. are sent to the factory. Sample colors are selected, labeling defined, sizing established, and prices are set for our catalog.
14. Sample production is coordinated to meet the scheduled selling shows for our industry.
15. Sales for each style are projected and greige goods are booked for each fabric for production. Production space with each factory is also booked in anticipation of our needs for the coming season.
16. Based on sales and early projections, all elements for production are coordinated for delivery to the factory so that the product ship dates meet the delivery requirements of our customers.

Miss ▇▇▇'s education, experience, and ability to communicate in Chinese make her a most desireable candidate for this position. Her knowledge of textiles and garment construction, as well as, her experience in working in the same factories we use in Hong Kong and Taiwan will provide us with the strong communication link we do not currently have. Since she has been managing our account in Hong Kong, we feel she can help us to more efficiently organize our development and production areas (as listed) to meet the needs of our factories. We expect that her contribution will help us to increase productivity and effect more timely delivery of samples and production for better business. Miss ▇▇▇ salary will be $42,000.

Sincerely,

Bill ▇▇▇

SAMPLE
FORM I-129B
UNITED STATES
DEPARTMENT OF JUSTICE
Immigration and Naturalization
Service

**PETITION
TO CLASSIFY
NONIMMIGRANT
AS TEMPORARY
WORKER
OR TRAINEE**

Date Filed

Fee Stamp

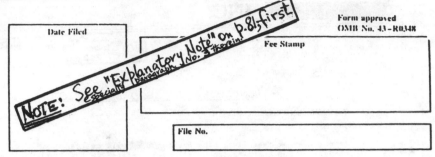

NOTE: See "Explanatory Note" on p.81, first especially paragraph No. 3 therein.

Form approved
OMB No. 43-R0348

File No.

(To be submitted in duplicate, with supplementary documents described in instructions, to the District Director having administrative jurisdiction over the place in the United States in which it is intended the alien(s) be employed or trained)

(THIS BLOCK NOT TO BE FILLED OUT BY PETITIONER)

The Secretary of State is hereby notified that the alien(s) for whom this petition was filed is (are) entitled to the nonimmigrant status checked below:

☐ H-1   ☐ H-3
☐ H-2   ☐ L-1

REMARKS:

The validity of this petition will expire on _____
The admission of the alien(s) may be authorized to the above date.

DATE
OF
ACTION
DD

DISTRICT

(PETITIONER NOT TO WRITE ABOVE THIS LINE)
(PLEASE FILL IN WITH TYPEWRITER OR PRINT IN BLOCK LETTERS IN INK)

I hereby petition, pursuant to the provisions of section 214(c) of the Immigration and Nationality Act, for the following: (Check one.)

H-1 ☐ Alien(s) of distinguished merit and ability to perform services of an exceptional nature requiring such merit and ability.

H-2 ☒ Alien(s) to perform temporary service or labor for which a bona fide need exists. (One who is to perform duties which are themselves temporary in nature.)

H-3 ☐ Alien trainee(s). (One who seeks to enter at the invitation of an individual, organization, firm, or other trainer for the purpose of receiving training in any field of endeavor. Incidental production necessary to the training is permitted provided a United States worker is not thereby displaced.)

L-1 ☐ Intra-company transferee. (One who has been employed continuously for one year and who seeks to enter in order to continue to render services to the same employer or a subsidiary or affiliate thereof in a managerial or executive capacity or in a capacity which involves specialized knowledge.)

1. NAME OF PETITIONER Rocky ▓▓▓▓▓▓▓▓▓▓▓ Co., Inc., a Colo. corp.	2. DATE BUSINESS ESTABLISHED 1950s

3. ADDRESS (NUMBER, STREET, CITY, STATE, ZIP CODE)
▓▓▓ Brighton Boulevard, Denver, Colorado, ▓▓▓▓

4. DESCRIPTION OF PETITIONER'S BUSINESS, INCLUDING ITS NATURE, NUMBER OF EMPLOYEES, AND GROSS ANNUAL INCOME
All processes involving tin;
Employees, 4;
Gross annual income, $150,000.00

5. LOCATION OF AMERICAN CONSULATE AT WHICH ALIEN(S) WILL APPLY FOR VISA(S):	(City in Foreign Country)	(Foreign Country)
	Juarez,	Mexico

(If petition is to be made for more than one H alien and application for visas will be made at more than one American Consulate, a separate petition must be submitted for each consulate at which H visa applications will be made. Separate petition must be filed for each L-1 alien.)

6. THE ALIEN(S) WILL PERFORM SERVICES OR LABOR FOR OR RECEIVE TRAINING FROM THE FOLLOWING ESTABLISHMENT IN THE U.S.:
(Name of Establishment) Rocky ▓▓▓▓▓▓▓▓▓▓▓▓ Co., Inc.
▓▓▓ Brighton Boulevard, Denver, Colorado ▓▓▓▓

(Street and Number)	(City or Town)	(State)		(Zip Code)

7. PERIOD REQUIRED TO COMPLETE SERVICES OR TRAINING			8. WAGES PER WEEK	8A. HOURS PER WEEK	9. OVERTIME RATE
From (date) 12/23/81	To (date) 12/31/82	No. of days or months 12 mos.	$200.00	40	--

10. OTHER COMPENSATION (Explain) None	10A. VALUED AT $ --	WEEKLY	11. BY WHOM PAID? Rocky ▓▓▓▓▓▓▓▓▓▓ Co.

RECEIVED	TRANS. IN	RET'D-TRANS OUT	COMPLETED

Form I-129B
(Rev. 6-20-80)M

FORM I-129B

(Page 2)

ALL PETITIONERS COMPLETE ITEMS 12A THROUGH 22. If petition is for more than one H alien, give required information for each additional alien in space provided on page 3. If the identity of the H aliens is not known at present, you must furnish information concerning them as soon as that information becomes known to you.

12A. ALIEN'S NAME (Family name in capital letters)   (First name)   Arturo   (Middle name)   NMN

12B. OTHER NAMES (Show all other past and present names, including maiden name if married woman.)   None   **12C. NUMBER OF ALIENS INCLUDED IN THIS PETITION**   1

13. ADDRESS TO WHICH ALIEN WILL RETURN   (Street and Number)   (City)   (Province)   (Country)
c/o Petro ~~_____~~, ~~____~~ Flacc Lourdes, Chihuahua, Chihuahua, Mexico

14. PRESENT ADDRESS   Same as #13 above   **15. PROPOSED PORT OF ENTRY**   El Paso, Texas

16. DATE OF BIRTH   1/7/46   **17. PLACE OF BIRTH**   Chihuahua, Chihuahua, Mexico   **18. PRESENT NATIONALITY OR CITIZENSHIP**   Mexican   **19. PRESENT OCCUPATION**   Tin hand-wiper

20. HAS AN IMMIGRANT VISA PETITION EVER BEEN FILED ON THE ALIEN'S BEHALF? ☐ YES ☒ NO
If "Yes", where was it filed?

21. HAS THE ALIEN EVER APPLIED FOR AN IMMIGRANT VISA OR PERMANENT RESIDENCE IN THE U.S.? ☐ YES ☒ NO
If "Yes", where did he apply?

22. TO YOUR KNOWLEDGE, HAS ANY VISA PETITION FILED BY YOU OR ANY OTHER PERSON OR ORGANIZATION FOR THE NAMED ALIEN(S) BEEN DENIED? ☐ YES ☒ NO
If you answered "yes", complete the following: Date of filing of each denied petition _____
Place of filing of each denied petition (city) _____
TO YOUR KNOWLEDGE, HAVE ANY OF THE NAMED ALIEN(S) EVER BEEN IN THE U.S.? ☐ YES ☐ NO (If "yes" identify each on Page 3)

23. NONTECHNICAL DESCRIPTION OF SERVICES TO BE PERFORMED BY OR TRAINING TO BE RECEIVED BY ALIEN(S) (THIS BLOCK NEED NOT BE COMPLETED IF PETITION IS FOR H-2 WORKERS)

24. (If you are petitioning for an H-1 physician or nurse, complete this block.)
DOES THE LAW GOVERNING THE PLACE WHERE THE ALIEN'S SERVICES WILL BE PERFORMED RESTRICT HIM/HER FROM PERFORMING ANY OF THE DESIRED SERVICES? ☐ YES ☐ NO If the answer is "yes", attach statement listing the restricted services and setting forth the reason for the restriction. (See instructions for Physicians and Nurses.)

25. (If you are petitioning for a trainee, complete this block.)
A. IS SIMILAR TRAINING AVAILABLE IN ALIEN'S COUNTRY? ☐ YES ☐ NO
B. WOULD ALIEN'S TRAINING RESULT IN DISPLACEMENT OF UNITED STATES WORKER? ☐ YES ☐ NO

26. (If you are petitioning for an L-1 alien, complete this block.) (Check appropriate boxes.)
a. The alien has been employed in an ☐ executive; ☐ managerial capacity; ☐ in a capacity which involves specialized knowledge
by _____ (name and address of employer) _____ since _____ (date)
b. The petitioner is ☐ the same employer ☐ subsidiary ☐ an affiliate of the employer abroad.

FILL IN ITEMS 27 THROUGH 31 INCLUSIVE ONLY IF PETITION IS FOR H-2 ALIEN(S)

27. DESCRIPTIVE JOB TITLE OF WORK TO BE PERFORMED BY ALIEN(S) (Use title which corresponds to that used in job order placed with state Employment Service or Agency by petitioner for same type of labor. Where work in more than one job classification is to be performed by aliens, state number to be employed in each job classification.)

Hand-wiping of tin

28. IS (ARE) ALIEN(S) SKILLED IN WORK TO BE PERFORMED? ☒ YES ☐ NO ☐ UNKNOWN

29. IS ANY LABOR ORGANIZATION ACTIVE IN THE LABOR FIELD(S) SPECIFIED IN ITEM 27? ☐ YES ☒ NO
(If "yes", specify organization(s) and labor field(s).)

30. IS THE PETITIONER INVOLVED IN, OR ARE THERE THREATENED, ANY LABOR RELATIONS DIFFICULTIES, INCLUDING STRIKES OR LOCKOUTS? (Specify)   No

31. I HAVE NOT BEEN ABLE TO FIND IN THE UNITED STATES ANY UNEMPLOYED PERSON(S) CAPABLE OF PERFORMING THE DUTIES OF THE POSITION(S) TO BE FILLED. THE FOLLOWING EFFORTS HAVE BEEN MADE TO FIND SUCH PERSON(S): (Complete only if labor certification not attached.)

ALL PETITIONERS FILL IN ITEMS 32 THROUGH 34B.

32. LIST DOCUMENTS SUBMITTED IN SUPPORT OF THIS PETITION.
Labor certification; employer's letter

FORM I-129B   P. 2 of 3 pgs.

33. THE DOCUMENTS SUBMITTED HEREWITH ARE HEREBY MADE A PART OF THIS PETITION.

I am willing (unwilling) to post any bond required as a condition to the approval of this petition.
I agree that as soon as known I shall furnish the District Director to whom this petition is being submitted with the names of those alien(s) not named herein.
If the petition is for temporary worker(s), I certify that I have a bona fide need of such worker(s).
If the petition is for trainee(s), I certify he/she is coming to the United States to participate in a bona fide training program.
I certify that the statements and representations made in this petition are true and correct to the best of my knowledge and belief.

34A. SIGNATURE OF PETITIONER.	DATE	34B. TITLE (Must be petitioner or authorized agent of petitioner)
Peter ▓▓▓	1/5/82	President

SIGNATURE OF PERSON PREPARING FORM, IF OTHER THAN PETITIONER

35. I ▓▓▓▓ this document was prepared by me at the request of the petitioner and is based on all information of which I have any knowledge.

C. James Cooper, Jr.   110 16th St., 14th Floor   Denver, Colorado 80202   1/5/82
(Signature)   (Address)   (Date)

If this petition is for more than one alien of distinguished merit and ability (H-1) or trainee (H-3), use spaces below to give required information. If additional space is needed, attach separate sheet executed in same general manner.

NAME	DATE OF BIRTH	PLACE OF BIRTH	NATIONALITY	OCCUPATION
PRESENT ADDRESS				
ADDRESS TO WHICH ALIEN WILL RETURN				
NONTECHNICAL DESCRIPTION OF SERVICES TO BE PERFORMED BY OR TRAINING TO BE RECEIVED BY ALIEN				

NAME	DATE OF BIRTH	PLACE OF BIRTH	NATIONALITY	OCCUPATION
PRESENT ADDRESS				
ADDRESS TO WHICH ALIEN WILL RETURN				
NONTECHNICAL DESCRIPTION OF SERVICES TO BE PERFORMED BY OR TRAINING TO BE RECEIVED BY ALIEN				

NAME	DATE OF BIRTH	PLACE OF BIRTH	NATIONALITY	OCCUPATION
PRESENT ADDRESS				
ADDRESS TO WHICH ALIEN WILL RETURN				
NONTECHNICAL DESCRIPTION OF SERVICES TO BE PERFORMED BY OR TRAINING TO BE RECEIVED BY ALIEN				

If this petition is for more than one (H-2) alien to perform temporary service or labor, use spaces below to give required information. If additional space is needed, attach separate sheet executed in same general manner. Identify each alien who has been in the U.S., by placing an "X" in the last column.

NAME	NATIONALITY	DATE AND PLACE OF BIRTH	PRESENT ADDRESS	X

FORM I-129B   (End of Form)   P. 3 of 3 pgs.

FROM:

Rocky ██████████ Co. Inc.

Brighton Boulevard, Denver, Colorado ██████
x x 3̶6̶x̶ S̶x̶x̶α̶x̶ x̶D̶x̶x̶x̶x̶x̶ K̶x̶b̶x̶x̶d̶x̶ x̶8̶0̶2̶0̶5̶x̶ 303-██████

Hot Dip Tinning -- Handwipe Tinning -- Electro Tin Plating

NOTE: Refer to "Explanatory Note" on p. 86, especially the No. 3 Paragraph therein.

EMPLOYER LETTER (Letter of Business Necessity)

January 5, 1982

TO: Immigration and Naturalization Service
1961 Stout Street
Denver, Colorado 80202

Name of the alien Beneficiary

Re: Mr. Arturo ████████████████

Gentlemen:

This letter is being written in support of the H-2 classification petition being filed herewith on behalf of Arturo ████████████████ to be employed by this company on a temporary basis as a hand-wiper of tin.

The Department of Labor has certified this individual to work temporarily in the United States for our company. As evidenced by such certified Alien Employment Application, ads were placed in newspapers in the United States, which resulted in no applicants for the job of the hand-wiping of tin.

Mr. ████████████████ abilities in the art of tin hand-wiping will be of benefit to our company, in that his sole purpose will be to train a U. S. citizen in this little-known art.

Yours very truly,

ROCKY ████████████ CO., INC.

Peter █████, President

SAMPLE SHEET

(DOL'S LETTER APPROVING CERTIFICATION)

Date: December 23, 1981

C. James Cooper, Jr.   Validity Date:
Attorney at Law   From -   12/23/81
14th Floor Penthouse   To   -   12/31/82
Petroleum Bldg.
Denver, Colorado 80202   Re: Form ETA 7-50A, Application for
                                    Alien Employment Certification

      Employer: Rocky ███████████ g   For: ███████████ , ARTURO
                 Co., Inc.   _____
                 Denver, Colorado   _____

                                        As: Hand Tinner   _____
                                             _____

The U. S. Department of Labor has certified the above application(s) for
admission of alien(s) for temporary employment in the United States.

The attached form ETA 750 should be submitted, together with your petition
(Form I-129B), to be filed at the Immigration and Naturalization Service
District Office.

Charles Vigil for
RAYMOND P. LAMB
Certifying Officer

cc: State ES Agency for   Colorado;

Attachment(s)

NOTE: → Only form ETA 750 A is needed for an H-2 temporary worker.
        In this case the Application was filed on August 5, 1981. Labor
        Certification as to the shortage of United States workers was not
        given until December 23, 1981. Generally, the Department of Labor
        tries to issue a certification more quickly for H-2 visas, than it
        does for applications for permanent employment.

NOTE: Refer to "Explanatory Note" on p. 81,
especially the third paragraph therein

SAMPLE

FORM
ETA 750A

U.S. DEPARTMENT OF LABOR
Employment and Training Administration

APPLICATION
FOR TEMPORARY
ALIEN EMPLOYMENT CERTIFICATION

P.I. OMB Approval No. 44-R1301

IMPORTANT: READ CAREFULLY BEFORE COMPLETING THIS FORM

PRINT legibly in ink, use a typewriter. If you need more space to answer questions on this form, use a separate sheet. Identify each answer with the number of the corresponding question. SIGN AND DATE each sheet in original signature.

To knowingly furnish any false information in the preparation of this form and any supplement thereto or to aid, abet, or counsel another to do so is a felony punishable by $10,000 fine or 5 years in the penitentiary, or b... (18 U.S.C. 1001).

PART A. OFFER OF EMPLOYMENT

NOTE: Refer to "Explanatory Note" on P. 8, especially the No. 3 paragraph therein.

1. Name of Alien *(Family name in capital letter, First, Middle, Maiden)*

▓▓▓▓▓▓▓▓▓▓, Arturo N.M.N.

2. Present Address of Alien *(Number, Street, City and Town, State ZIP Code or Province, Cou...)*

c/o Pedro ▓▓▓▓▓▓▓▓, ▓▓▓ Flacc Lourdes
Chihuahua, Chihuahua, Mexico

3. Type of Visa *(If in U.S.)*

None

4. Name of Employer *(Full name of organization)*

Rocky ▓▓▓▓▓▓▓., Inc.

5. Telephone *(Area Code and Number)*

303-▓▓▓▓▓▓

6. Address *(Number, Street, City or Town, Country, State,...)*

▓▓▓▓ Brighton Boulevard, Denver, Colorado ▓▓▓▓▓

7. Address Where Alien Will Work *(if different from item 6)*

N/A

8. Nature of Employer's Business Activity	9. Name of Job Title	10. Total Hours Per Week		11. Work Schedule *(Hourly)*	12. Rate of Pay	
		a. Basic	b. Overtime		a. Basic	b. Overtime
All processes involving tin	Hand-wiping of tin	40	N/A	7:30 a.m. 4:00 p.m.	$ 5.00 per hour	$ N/A per hour

13. Describe Fully the Job to be Performed *(Duties)*

The hand-wiping of tin on copper cooking ware and other types of copper utensils; the application of tin to heated and fluxed copper surfaces, either by a stick of pure tin, or in the molten state from a ladle, and then wiped and swirled over the surface by hand.

14. State in detail the MINIMUM education, training, and experience for a worker to perform satisfactorily the job duties described in Item 13 above.

15. Other Special Requirements

None

EDUCATION *(Enter number of years)*	Grade School	High School	College	College Degree Required *(specify)*
	6	6	0	None
				Major Field of Study
				None

TRAINING	No. Yrs.	No. Mos.	Type of Training
	1		Hand-wiping of tin

EXPERIENCE	Job Offered		Related Occupation		Related Occupation *(specify)*
	Yrs.	Mos.	Yrs.	Mos.	
	9	--	--		--

16. Occupational Title of Person Who Will Be Alien's Immediate Supervisor ➤ ➤ Owner/President

17. Number of Employees Alien will Supervise ➤ 0

◀ ENDORSEMENTS *(Make no entry in section - for government use only)*

1. QUALIFIED WORKERS CANNOT BE FOUND IN THE UNITED STATES.
2. EMPLOYMENT SERVICE POLICIES HAVE BEEN OBSERVED.
3. THIS CERTIFICATION IS VALID FROM 12/23/81 THROUGH 12/31/82

12/23/81
(DATE)

Charles R. Vigil for
(CERTIFYING OFFICER)
RAYMOND P. LAMB

Date Forms Received	
L.O. 8-5-81	S.O. 12/3/81
R.O. 12-17-81	N.O.
Ind. Code 5051	Occ. Code 5622.81014
Occ. Title HAND TINNER	

P. 1 of 2 pgs.

SAMPLE SHEET

18. COMPLETE ITEMS ONLY IF JOB IS TEMPORARY			19. IF JOB IS UNIONIZED *(Complete)*	
a. No. of Openings To Be Filled By Aliens Under Job Offer	b. Exact Dates You Exp. To Employ Alien		a. Number of Local	b. Name of Local
	From	To		
1	1/1/82	12/31/82	N/A	c. City and State

20. STATEMENT FOR LIVE-AT-WORK JOB OFFERS *(Complete for Private Household Job ONLY)*   N/A

Description of Residence		b. No. Persons Residing at Place of Employment			c. Will free board and private room not shared with anyone be provided?	("X" one)
("X" one)	Number of Rooms	Adults	Children	Ages		
☐ House		BOYS				☐ YES ☐ NO
☐ Apartment		GIRLS				

21. DESCRIBE EFFORTS TO RECRUIT U.S. WORKERS AND THE RESULTS. *(Specify Sources of Recruitment by Name)*

Prior to filing ETA 750, inquiries within the industry; newspaper advertisements.

Subsequent to filing of ETA 750, job offer filed with local Job Service Center; advertisements in The Denver Post, Denver, Colorado, and in the Phoenix Gazette of Phoenix, Arizona.

22. Applications require various types of documentation. Please read PART II of the instructions to assure that appropriate supporting documentation is included with your application.

23. EMPLOYER CERTIFICATIONS

By virtue of my signature below, I HEREBY CERTIFY the following conditions of employment.

a. I have enough funds available to pay the wage or salary offered the alien.

b. The wage offered equals or exceeds the prevailing wage and I guarantee that, if a labor certification is granted, the wage paid to the alien when the alien begins work will equal or exceed the prevailing wage which is applicable at the time the alien begins work.

c. The wage offered is not based on commissions, bonuses, or other incentives, unless I guarantee a wage paid on a weekly, bi-weekly or monthly basis.

d. I will be able to place the alien on the payroll on or before the date of the alien's proposed entrance into the United States.

e. The job opportunity does not involve unlawful discrimination by race, creed, color, national origin, age, sex, religion, handicap, or citizenship.

f. The job opportunity is not:

  (1) Vacant because the former occupant is on strike or is being locked out in the course of a labor dispute involving a work stoppage.

  (2) At issue in a labor dispute involving a work stoppage.

g. The job opportunity's terms, conditions and occupational environment are not contrary to Federal, State or local law.

h. The job opportunity has been and is clearly open to any qualified U.S. worker.

Colorado Division of Employment and Training 1655 Fox Denver, Colorado 80204

24. DECLARATIONS

DECLARATION OF EMPLOYER ▶ *Pursuant to 28 U.S.C. 1746, I declare under penalty of perjury the foregoing is true and correct.*

SIGNATURE X [signature]	DATE July 28, 1981

NAME *(Type or Print)* Peter ▓▓▓▓	TITLE President/Owner

AUTHORIZATION OF AGENT OF EMPLOYER ▶ *I HEREBY DESIGNATE the agent below to represent me for the purposes of labor certification and I TAKE FULL RESPONSIBILITY for accuracy of any representations made by my agent.*

ATURE OF EMPLOYER X [signature]	DATE July 28, 19..

NAME OF AGENT *(Type or Print) (if applicable)* C. James Cooper, Jr.	ADDRESS OF AGENT *(Number, Street, City, State, ZIP Code)* 110 16th Street, 14th Floor Denver, Colorado 80202

SAMPLE SHEET

FORM I-129B

UNITED STATES
DEPARTMENT OF JUSTICE
Immigration and Naturalization
Service

**PETITION
TO CLASSIFY
NONIMMIGRANT
AS TEMPORARY
WORKER
OR TRAINEE**

Date Filed	Fee Stamp
	File No.

Form approved
OMB No. 43-R0348

NOTE: See "Explanatory Note" on p.8; first paragraph #4

(To be submitted in duplicate, with supplementary documents described in instructions, to the District Director having administrative jurisdiction over the place in the United States in which it is intended the alien(s) be employed or trained)

(THIS BLOCK NOT TO BE FILLED OUT BY PETITIONER)

The Secretary of State is hereby notified that the alien(s) for whom this petition was filed is (are) entitled to the nonimmigrant status checked below:

☐ H-1 ☐ H-3
☐ H-2 ☐ L-1

REMARKS:

The validity of this petition will expire on _____. The admission of the alien(s) may be authorized to the above date.	DATE OF ACTION DD DISTRICT

(PETITIONER NOT TO WRITE ABOVE THIS LINE)
(PLEASE FILL IN WITH TYPEWRITER OR PRINT IN BLOCK LETTERS IN INK)

I hereby petition, pursuant to the provisions of section 214(c) of the Immigration and Nationality Act, for the following: (Check one.)

H-1 ☐ Alien(s) of distinguished merit and ability to perform services of an exceptional nature requiring such merit and ability.

H-2 ☐ Alien(s) to perform temporary service or labor for which a bona fide need exists. (One who is to perform duties which are themselves temporary in nature.)

H-3 ☒ Alien trainee(s). (One who seeks to enter at the invitation of an individual, organization, firm, or other trainer for the purpose of receiving training in any field of endeavor. Incidental production necessary to the training is permitted provided a United States worker is not thereby displaced.)

L-1 ☐ Intra-company transferee. (One who has been employed continuously for one year and who seeks to enter in order to continue to render his services to the same employer or a subsidiary or affiliate thereof in a managerial or executive capacity or in a capacity which involves specialized knowledge.)

1. NAME OF PETITIONER ████████ Co. (a division of the ████ Corporation)	2. DATE BUSINESS ESTABLISHED 1854

3. ADDRESS (NUMBER, STREET, CITY, STATE, ZIP CODE) ████ 28th Street, Boulder, Co. ████ (local ████)
   ████ Washington Avenue, Saginaw, Michigan ████ (home office)

4. DESCRIPTION OF PETITIONER'S BUSINESS, INCLUDING ITS NATURE, NUMBER OF EMPLOYEES, AND GROSS ANNUAL INCOME
   Petitioner is engaged in the business of the retailing of lumber and building materials. Petitioner is a division of an international corporate conglomerate with many divisions in the fields of agricultural machinery, credit and other enterprises throughout the world. employees: 7,151. Gross Annual Income: $25,809,692

5. LOCATION OF AMERICAN CONSULATE AT WHICH ALIEN(S) WILL APPLY FOR VISA(S):	(City in Foreign Country) Zurich	(Foreign Country) Switzerland

(If petition is to be made for more than one H alien and application for visas will be made at more than one American Consulate, a separate petition must be submitted for each consulate at which H visa applications will be made. Separate petition must be filed for each L-1 alien.)

6. THE ALIEN(S) WILL PERFORM SERVICES OR LABOR FOR OR RECEIVE TRAINING FROM THE FOLLOWING ESTABLISHMENT:
(Name of Establishment) ████ Co. (a division of the ████ Corporation)

████ 28th Street	Boulder	Colorado	████
(Street and Number)	(City or Town)	(State)	(Zip Code)

7. PERIOD REQUIRED TO COMPLETE SERVICES OR TRAINING			8. WAGES PER WEEK	8A. HOURS PER WEEK	9. OVERTIME RATE
From (date)	To (date)	No. of days or months	$175.00	48 hrs.	None
February 15.	August 15.	6 months			

10. OTHER COMPENSATION (Explain) None	10A. VALUED AT $ N/A WEEKLY	11. BY WHOM PAID? N/A

Form I-129B
(Rev. 2-25-76)N

	RECEIVED	TRANS. IN	RET'D-TRANS. OUT	COMPLETED

FORM I-129B

P. 1 of 3 pgs

ALL PETITIONERS COMPLETE ITEMS 12A THR   I 22. If petition is for more than one H alien, give requ   nformation for each additional alien in space provided on page 3. If the identity of the H al... .s is not known at present, you must furnish information concerning them as soon as that information becomes known to you.

12A. ALIEN'S NAME (Family name in capital letters)   (First name)   (Middle name)

~~████████~~   Andreas   Willi

OTHER NAMES (Show all other past and present names, including maiden name if married woman.) | **12C. NUMBER OF ALIENS INCLUDED IN THIS PETITION**   1

None

13. ADDRESS TO WHICH ALIEN WILL RETURN   (Street and Number)   (City)   (Province)   (Country)

~~████████~~   8157 Dielsdorf   Zurich   Switzerland

14. PRESENT ADDRESS   ███ Green Place Longmont, Colorado ███ | **15. PROCESS PORT OF ENTRY**   Chicago 8-15-77

16. DATE OF BIRTH   1-30-53 | **17. PLACE OF BIRTH**   Zurich, Switzerland | **18. PRESENT NATIONALITY OR CITIZENSHIP**   Swiss | **19. PRESENT OCCUPATION**   Trainee

20. HAS AN IMMIGRANT VISA PETITION EVER BEEN FILED ON THE ALIEN'S BEHALF? ☐ YES ☒ NO
If "Yes", where was it filed?

21. HAS THE ALIEN EVER APPLIED FOR AN IMMIGRANT VISA OR PERMANENT RESIDENCE IN THE U.S.? ☐ YES ☒ NO
If "Yes", where did he apply?

22. TO YOUR KNOWLEDGE, HAS ANY VISA PETITION FILED BY YOU OR ANY OTHER PERSON OR ORGANIZATION FOR THE NAMED ALIEN(S) BEEN DENIED? ☐ YES ☒ NO
If you answered "yes", complete the following: Date of filing of each denied petition _____
Place of filing of each denied petition (city) _____

TO YOUR KNOWLEDGE, HAVE ANY OF THE NAMED ALIEN(S) EVER BEEN IN THE U.S.? ☒ YES ☐ NO (If "yes" identify each on Page 3)
(as a tourist for 5 wks. from 7/16 to 8/27/76)

23. NONTECHNICAL DESCRIPTION OF SERVICES TO BE PERFORMED BY OR TRAINING TO BE RECEIVED BY ALIEN(S) (THIS BLOCK NEED NOT BE COMPLETED IF PETITION IS FOR H-2 WORKERS.)

Training for management of lumber retail business.

24. (If you are petitioning for an H-1 physician or nurse, complete this block.)
DOES THE LAW GOVERNING THE PLACE WHERE THE ALIEN'S SERVICES WILL BE PERFORMED RESTRICT HIM FROM PERFORMING ANY OF THE DESIRED SERVICES? ☐ YES ☒ NO If the answer is "yes", attach statement listing the restricted services and setting forth the reason for the restriction. (See instructions for Physicians and Nurses.)

(If you are petitioning for a trainee, complete this block.)
A. IS SIMILAR TRAINING AVAILABLE IN ALIEN'S COUNTRY? ☐ YES ☒ NO
B. WOULD ALIEN'S TRAINING RESULT IN DISPLACEMENT OF UNITED STATES WORKER? ☐ YES ☒ NO

26. (If you are petitioning for an L-1 alien, complete this block.) (Check appropriate boxes.)   not applicable
a. The ~~█████~~ been employed in an ☐ executive ~~██~~ managerial capacity; ☐ In a capacity which involves specialized knowledge
by _____ since _____
(name and address of employer) (date)
b. The petitioner is ☐ the same employer ~~████~~ ☐ an affiliate of the employer abroad.

FILL IN ITEMS 27 THROUGH 31 INCLUSIVE ONLY IF PETITION IS FOR H-2 ALIEN(S)

27. DESCRIPTIVE JOB TITLE OF WORK TO BE PERFORMED BY ALIEN(S) (Use title which corresponds to that used in job order placed with state Employment Service or Agency by petitioner for same type of labor. Where work in more than one job classification is to be performed by aliens, state ██████ to be employed in each job classification.)

28. IS (ARE) ALIEN(S) SKILLED IN WORK TO BE PERFORMED? ☐ YES ☐ NO ☐ UNKNOWN

29. IS ANY LABOR ORGANIZATION ACTIVE IN THE LABOR FIELD(S) SPECIFIED IN ITEM 27? ☐ YES ☐ NO
(If "yes", specify organization(s) and labor █████)

30. IS THE PETITIONER INVOLVED IN, OR ARE THERE THREATENED, ANY LABOR RELATIONS DIFFICULTIES, INCLUDING STRIKES OR LOCKOUTS? (Specify)

31. I HAVE NOT BEEN ABLE TO FIND IN THE UNITED STATES ANY UNEMPLOYED PERSON(S) CAPABLE OF PERFORMING THE DUTIES OF THE POSITION(S) TO BE FILLED. THE FOLLOWING EFFORTS HAVE BEEN MADE TO FIND SUCH PERSON(S). (Complete only if labor certification not attached.)

ALL PETITIONERS FILL IN ITEMS 32 THROUGH 34B.

32. LIST DOCUMENTS SUBMITTED IN SUPPORT OF THIS PETITION. 1. Letter from ~~████~~ regarding Training program. 2. Letter from Swiss Embassy 3. Letter from AIESEC-U.S.

FORM I-129B   P. 2 of 3 pgs.

SAMPLE (vertical, left margin)

33. THE DOCUMENTS SUBMITTED HEREWITH ARE HEREBY MADE A PART OF THIS PETITION.

I am willing (unwilling) to post any bond required as a condition to the approval of this petition.
I agree that as soon as known I shall furnish the District Director to whom this petition is being submitted with the names of those alien(s) not named herein.
If the petition is for temporary worker(s), I certify that I have a bona fide need of such worker(s).
If the petition is for trainee(s), I certify he is coming to the United States to participate in a bona fide training program.
I certify that the statements and representations made in this petition are true and correct to the best of my knowledge and belief.

A. SIGNATURE OF PETITIONER	DATE	34B. TITLE (Must be petitioner or authorized agent of petitioner)
By: *[signature]* ∞	Jan 31, 1979	*ZONE MANAGER*

SIGNATURE OF PERSON PREPARING FORM, IF OTHER THAN PETITIONER

35. I declare that this document was prepared by me at the request of the petitioner and is based on all information of which I have any knowledge.

(Signature)	(Address)	(Date)

If this petition is for more than one alien of distinguished merit and ability (H-1) or trainee (H-3), use spaces below to give required information. If additional space is needed, attach separate sheet executed in same general manner.

NAME	DATE OF BIRTH	PLACE OF BIRTH	NATIONALITY	OCCUPATION
PRESENT ADDRESS				
ADDRESS TO WHICH ALIEN WILL RETURN				
NONTECHNICAL DESCRIPTION OF SERVICES TO BE PERFORMED BY OR TRAINING TO BE RECEIVED BY ALIEN				

NAME	DATE OF BIRTH	PLACE OF BIRTH	NATIONALITY	OCCUPATION
PRESENT ADDRESS				
ADDRESS TO WHICH ALIEN WILL RETURN				
NONTECHNICAL DESCRIPTION OF SERVICES TO BE PERFORMED BY OR TRAINING TO BE RECEIVED BY ALIEN				

NAME	DATE OF BIRTH	PLACE OF BIRTH	NATIONALITY	OCCUPATION
PRESENT ADDRESS				
ADDRESS TO WHICH ALIEN WILL RETURN				
NONTECHNICAL DESCRIPTION OF SERVICES TO BE PERFORMED BY OR TRAINING TO BE RECEIVED BY ALIEN				

If this petition is for more than one (H-2) alien to perform temporary service or labor, use spaces below to give required information. If additional space is needed, attach separate sheet executed in same general manner. Identify each alien who has been in the U.S., by placing an "X" in the last column.

NAME	NATIONALITY	DATE AND PLACE OF BIRTH	PRESENT ADDRESS	X

Form I-129B   (End of Form)   P. 3 of 3 pgs.

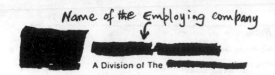

Name of the Employing company ↓

A Division of The ████████

TRAINING
PROGRAM LETTER

To Whom It May Concern:

Andreas ████████, an exchange student from Switzerland is requesting an "H-3" visa which would enable him to complete ████████████ Management Training Programm. We have encouraged him to do so, since it would be a tremendous value for him.

Andreas will be trained in marketing and sales of lumber and building-products. Approximately 25% of his time will be devoted to productive work while training. 75% will be training.

Classroomtraining or selfstudiing of slideshows, books and other company materials will take about 8 to 10 hrs. per week. (48-hour work week.) The trainee will be instructed in construction and architecture of american housing which is entirely different from the one in Switzerland. Much time will also be devoted to productknowledge and the operating procedures of the ████████ Company.

Approximately 24 to 26 hrs. are spent on the job training. The trainee will get acquainted with
- Warehousing: Stocking of materials, general operations of a warehouse and lumberyard
- Sales: Salestechniques and displays
- Advertising: specialtechniques involved in the lumberbusiness
- Inventory management: Management of stock and ordering materials.

This Training will enable Andreas to sell and market Lumber and other Buildingmaterials, also make him capable of managing smaller operations.

████████████ special trainingprogramm is considered to be the industries best. With 260 Lumberyards alone in the United States we are the true leaders in this field and today the world's largest lumber retailer. Hence our training provided in the United States cannot be duplicated anywhere else.

signed: ___████████████_____ , date: 2-5-1979

⎯ Kaj ████████ (Zonemanager of ████████████ in Colorado, a division of The ████████████

NOTE: Refer to "Explanatory Note" on p. 81, especially paragraph 4 therein.

SAMPLE

Department of Justice
igration and Naturalization Service

~~FORM I-129B~~ FORM I-129B

OMB No. 1115-0038
Approval Expires 9 86

P.1

PETITION TO CLASSIFY NONIMMIGRANT AS TEMPORARY WORKER OR TRAINEE

To be submitted in duplicate, with supplementary documents described in instructions, to the District Director having administrative jurisdiction over the place in the United States in which it is intended the alien(s) be employed or trained. L-1 blanket petition must be submitted to the District Director having jurisdiction over petitioner's main office.)

Date Filed

NOTE: Refer to "Explanatory Note" on p.81-2, especially paragraph 5 therein.

Fee Stamp

File No.

(THIS BLOCK NOT TO BE FILLED OUT BY PETITIONER)

The Secretary of State is hereby notified that the alien(s) for whom this petition was filed is (are) entitled to the nonimmigrant status checked below:

H-1   H-3
H-2   L-1
[ ] L-1 (blanket petition)

This petition is valid to _____
The admission of the alien(s) may be authorized to the above date.

DATE OF ACTION DD

REMARKS:

DISTRICT

☒ **NEW PETITION**   ☐ **PETITION EXTENSION**   ☐ **AMENDED BLANKET PETITION**

I hereby petition, pursuant to the provisions of section 214(c) on the Immigration and Nationality Act, for the following: (Check one.)

H-1 ☐ Alien(s) of distinguished merit and ability to perform services of an exceptional nature requiring such merit and ability.

; ☐ Alien(s) to perform temporary service or labor for which a bona fide need exists. (One who is to perform duties which are themselves temporary in nature.)

H-3 ☐ Alien trainee(s). (One who seeks to enter at the invitation of an individual, organization, firm, or other trainer for the purpose of receiving training in any field of endeavor. Incidental production necessary to the training is permitted provided a United States worker is not thereby displaced.)

L-1 ☒ Intra-company transferee. (One who has been employed abroad continuously for one year and who seeks to enter in order to continue to render services to the same employer or a subsidiary or affiliate thereof in a managerial or executive capacity or in a capacity which involves specialized knowledge.)

L-1 ☐ Intra-company transferee blanket petition. (A petitioner who had 5 executive or managerial L-1 petitions approved within the last year, and desires to bring into the United States employees who have been employed abroad continuously for one year who will continue to render services to the same employer or a subsidiary or affiliate thereof in a managerial or executive capacity.)

1. NAME OF PETITIONER	2. DATE BUSINESS ESTABLISHED
████████ (USA), Inc., a Colorado corp.	November 1984

3. ADDRESS (NUMBER, STREET, CITY, STATE, ZIP CODE)	TELEPHONE NUMBER
████. Federal Blvd., Denver, Colorado ████	303-████

4. DESCRIPTION OF PETITIONER'S BUSINESS, INCLUDING ITS NATURE, NUMBER OF EMPLOYEES, AND GROSS ANNUAL INCOME
Import/export/manufacture of Thai, Asian and contemporary furniture; Employees: projected, 5; gross annual income, projected, $1,000,000.

5. LOCATION OF AMERICAN CONSULATE AT WHICH ALIEN(S) WILL APPLY FOR VISA(S): (Not required for L-1 blanket petition)
(City in Foreign Country) Bangkok   (Foreign Country) Thailand

(If petition is for more than one H alien and application for visas will be made at more than one American Consulate, a separate petition must be submitted for each consulate at which H visa applications will be made. Separate petition must be filed for each L-1 alien.)

6. THE ALIEN(S) WILL PERFORM SERVICES OR LABOR FOR OR RECEIVE TRAINING FROM THE FOLLOWING ESTABLISHMENT IN THE U.S.: (Name of Establishment) (If L-1 blanket petition items 6-11 not applicable, show N/A) ████████ (USA), Inc.
████. Federal Blvd., Denver, Colorado, ████
(Street and Number)   (City or Town)   (State)   (Zip Code)
Attach list or itinerary if services will be performed at more than one location.

7. PERIOD REQUIRED TO COMPLETE SERVICES OR TRAINING	8. WAGES PER ~~XXX~~ Year	8A. HOURS PER WEEK	9. OVERTIME RATE
From (date) Date To (date) 36 mos. No. of days or months of approval thereafter 36 mos.	$25,000.00	40	--

10. OTHER COMPENSATION (Explain)	10A. VALUED AT	11. BY WHOM PAID?
--	$ -- WEEKLY	Petitioner/employer

Form I-129B (Rev 7-1-83)N

	RECEIVED	TRANS. IN	RET'D TRANS. OUT	COMPLETED

FORM H-129B P.2 (Page 2)

QUESTIONS 12A THRU 32 NEED NOT BE COMPLETED TO FILE EXTENSION OF VISA PETITION VALIDITY WITH CONCURRENTLY FILED I 539 APPLICA
TION FOR EXTENSION OF STAY.

ALL NEW PETITIONERS COMPLETE ITEMS 12A THROUGH 22, except L-1 blanket petitioners. If petition is for more than one H alien, give required information for each additional alien in space provided on page 3. If the identity of the H aliens is not known at present, you must furnish information concerning them as soon as that information becomes known to you.

12A. ALIEN'S NAME (Family name in capital letters)	(First name) Pawadee	(Middle name) NMN

12B. OTHER NAMES (Show all other past and present names, including maiden name if married woman.) None	12C. NUMBER OF ALIENS INCLUDED IN THIS PETITION 1

13. ADDRESS TO WHICH ALIEN WILL RETURN (Street and Number) (City) (Province) (Country)
Sukhumvit ███, Bangkok, Thailand

14. PRESENT ADDRESS Same as #13 above	15. PROPOSED PORT OF ENTRY N/A

16. DATE OF BIRTH 3/10/59	17. PLACE OF BIRTH. Thailand	18. PRESENT NATIONALITY OR CITIZENSHIP Thailand	19. PRESENT OCCUPATION Personal Executive Assistant to President

20. HAS AN IMMIGRANT VISA PETITION OR APPLICATION FOR PERMANENT LABOR CERTIFICATION EVER BEEN FILED ON THE ALIEN'S BEHALF? I YES XX NO
If "Yes", where was it filed?

21. HAS THE ALIEN EVER APPLIED FOR AN IMMIGRANT VISA OR PERMANENT RESIDENCE IN THE U.S.?   YES   XX NO
If Yes", where did he apply?

22. TO YOUR KNOWLEDGE. HAS ANY VISA PETITION FILED BY YOU OR ANY OTHER PERSON OR ORGANIZATION FOR THE NAMED ALIEN(S) BEEN DENIED?   YES XX NO
If you answered "yes", complete the following: Date of filing of each denied petition _____
Place of filing of each denied petition (city) _____
(TO YOUR KNOWLEDGE. HAVE ANY OF THE NAMED ALIEN(S) EVER BEEN IN THE U.S.?   I YES XX NO (If "yes" identify each on Page 3)

NONTECHNICAL DESCRIPTION OF SERVICES TO BE PERFORMED BY OR TRAINING TO BE RECEIVED BY ALIEN(S) (THIS BLOCK NEED NOT BE COMPLETED IF PETITION IS FOR H-2 WORKERS) As Personal Executive Assistant to the President, office management, recruitment of U.S. workers, communication with parent company, in the Thai language.

24. IS THE BENEFICIARY FULLY QUALIFIED UNDER THE GOVERNING LAWS IN YOUR JURISDICTION TO PERFORM THE DESIRED SERVICES (OR TO RECEIVE THE DESIRED TRAINING) AND ARE YOU AUTHORIZED TO EMPLOY THE BENEFICIARY TO SUBSTANTIALLY PERFORM SUCH SERVICES? XX YES   I NO (If "NO" or if beneficiary will be restricted in performance of services, please explain in detail on separate statement.

25. (If you are petitioning for a trainee, complete this block) N/A
A. IS SIMILAR TRAINING AVAILABLE IN ALIEN'S COUNTRY? I YES   NO
B. WOULD ALIEN'S TRAINING RESULT IN DISPLACEMENT OF UNITED STATES WORKER? : YES   NO
C. WILL YOU USE THE ALIENS TO OVERCOME A LABOR SHORTAGE? : YES : NO

26. (If you are petitioning for an L-1 alien, complete this block.) (Check appropriate boxes.) (Does not apply to L-1 blanket petition)
a. The alien has been employed in an   : executive: XX managerial capacity;   : in a capacity which involves specialized knowledge
████████ Co., Ltd.
by Sukhumvit Rd., ██████, Bangkok _____ since _____ October 1983 _____
(name and address of employer) (date)
b. The petitioner is : the same employer XX subsidiary : an affiliate of the employer abroad.

FILL IN ITEMS 27 THROUGH 31 INCLUSIVE ONLY IF PETITION IS FOR H-2 ALIEN(S)

27. DESCRIPTIVE JOB TITLE OF WORK TO BE PERFORMED BY ALIEN(S) (Enter title which was used by the Department of Labor in processing labor certification application.)

28. IS (ARE) ALIEN(S) SKILLED IN WORK TO BE PERFORMED? YES NO UNKNOWN

29. IS ANY LABOR ORGANIZATION ACTIVE IN THE LABOR FIELD(S) SPECIFIED IN ITEM 27? YES NO
(If "yes", specify organization(s) and labor field(s).)

30. IS THE PETITIONER INVOLVED IN. OR ARE THERE THREATENED. ANY LABOR RELATIONS DIFFICULTIES, INCLUDING STRIKES OR LOCKOUTS? (Specify)

31. I HAVE NOT BEEN ABLE TO FIND IN THE UNITED STATES ANY UNEMPLOYED PERSON(S) CAPABLE OF PERFORMING THE DUTIES OF THE POSITION(S) TO BE FILLED. THE FOLLOWING EFFORTS HAVE BEEN MADE TO FIND SUCH PERSON(S). (Complete only if labor certification not attached.)

32. If petition is for extension the petitioner must certify that all data from the previously approved petition remains the same. : YES : NO

ALL PETITIONERS MUST FILL IN ITEMS 33 & 34B.

FORM I-129B

P.3 (Page 3)

33. THE DOCUMENTS SUBMITTED HEREWITH ARE HEREBY MADE A PART OF THIS PETITION.

I am willing (unwilling) to post any bond required as a condition to the approval of this petition.
I agree that as soon as known I shall furnish the District Director to whom this petition is being submitted with the names of those alien(s) not currently identified. (does not apply to L-1 blanket petition)
If the petition is for temporary worker(s), I certify that I have a bona fide need of such worker(s).
If the petition is for trainee(s), I certify he/she is coming to the United States to participate in a bona fide training program.
I certify that the statements and representations made in the petition are true and correct to the best of my knowledge and belief.

34A. SIGNATURE OF PETITIONER	DATE	34B. TITLE (Must be petitioner or authorized employee of petitioner)
Vichol _____n		President

SIGNATURE OF PERSON PREPARING FORM, IF OTHER THAN PETITIONER

35. I declare that this document was prepared by me at the request of the petitioner and is based on all information of which I have any knowledge.

999 18th St., #3220
Denver, Colorado 80202

(Address)   (Date)

If this petition is for more than one alien of distinguished merit and ability (H-1), or trainee (H-3) use spaces below to give required information. If additional space is needed, attach separate sheet executed in same general manner.

NAME	DATE OF BIRTH	PLACE OF BIRTH	NATIONALITY	OCCUPATION
PRESENT ADDRESS				
ADDRESS TO WHICH ALIEN WILL RETURN				
NONTECHNICAL DESCRIPTION OF SERVICES TO BE PERFORMED BY OR TRAINING TO BE RECEIVED BY ALIEN				

NAME	DATE OF BIRTH	PLACE OF BIRTH	NATIONALITY	OCCUPATION
PRESENT ADDRESS				
ADDRESS TO WHICH ALIEN WILL RETURN				
NONTECHNICAL DESCRIPTION OF SERVICES TO BE PERFORMED BY OR TRAINING TO BE RECEIVED BY ALIEN				

NAME	DATE OF BIRTH	PLACE OF BIRTH	NATIONALITY	OCCUPATION
PRESENT ADDRESS				
ADDRESS TO WHICH ALIEN WILL RETURN				
NONTECHNICAL DESCRIPTION OF SERVICES TO BE PERFORMED BY OR TRAINING TO BE RECEIVED BY ALIEN				

If this petition is for more than one (H-2) alien to perform temporary service or labor, use spaces below to give required information. If additional space is needed, attach separate sheet executed in same general manner. Identify each alien who has been in the U.S., by placing an "X" in the last column.

NAME	NATIONALITY	DATE AND PLACE OF BIRTH	PRESENT ADDRESS	X

(End of the Form)

SAMPLE SHEET

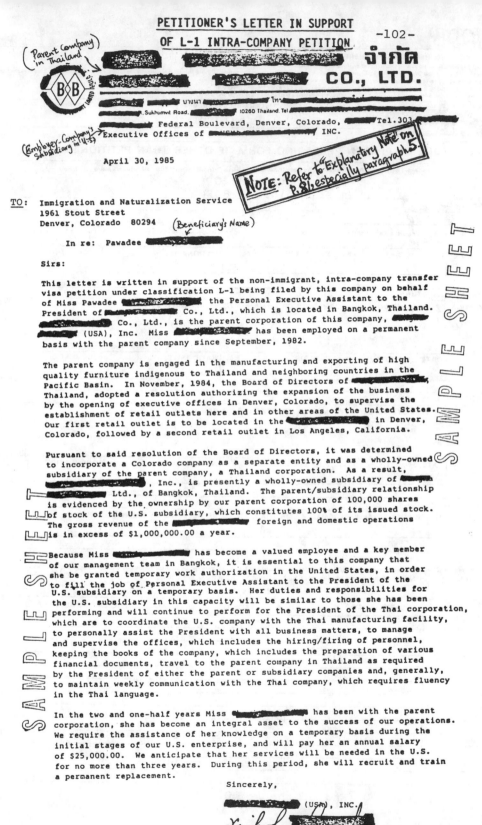

(Parent company in Thailand)

จำกัด

BB

CO., LTD.

บางนา ... 10260 Thailand. Tel ...

R. Sukhumvit Road, ...

Federal Boulevard, Denver, Colorado, ... Tel. 303 ...

Executive Offices of ... INC.

(Employer-Company's subsidiary in U.S.)

April 30, 1985

NOTE: Refer to Explanatory Note on P.81, especially paragraph 5.

TO: Immigration and Naturalization Service
      1961 Stout Street
      Denver, Colorado 80294   (Beneficiary's Name)

      In re: Pawadee ...

Sirs:

This letter is written in support of the non-immigrant, intra-company transfer visa petition under classification L-1 being filed by this company on behalf of Miss Pawadee ..., the Personal Executive Assistant to the President of ... Co., Ltd., which is located in Bangkok, Thailand. ... Co., Ltd., is the parent corporation of this company, ... (USA), Inc. Miss ... has been employed on a permanent basis with the parent company since September, 1982.

The parent company is engaged in the manufacturing and exporting of high quality furniture indigenous to Thailand and neighboring countries in the Pacific Basin. In November, 1984, the Board of Directors of ..., Thailand, adopted a resolution authorizing the expansion of the business by the opening of executive offices in Denver, Colorado, to supervise the establishment of retail outlets here and in other areas of the United States. Our first retail outlet is to be located in the ... in Denver, Colorado, followed by a second retail outlet in Los Angeles, California.

Pursuant to said resolution of the Board of Directors, it was determined to incorporate a Colorado company as a separate entity and as a wholly-owned subsidiary of the parent company, a Thailand corporation. As a result, ..., Inc., is presently a wholly-owned subsidiary of ... Ltd., of Bangkok, Thailand. The parent/subsidiary relationship is evidenced by the ownership by our parent corporation of 100,000 shares of stock of the U.S. subsidiary, which constitutes 100% of its issued stock. The gross revenue of the ... foreign and domestic operations is in excess of $1,000,000.00 a year.

Because Miss ... has become a valued employee and a key member of our management team in Bangkok, it is essential to this company that she be granted temporary work authorization in the United States, in order to fill the job of Personal Executive Assistant to the President of the U.S. subsidiary on a temporary basis. Her duties and responsibilities for the U.S. subsidiary in this capacity will be similar to those she has been performing and will continue to perform for the President of the Thai corporation, which are to coordinate the U.S. company with the Thai manufacturing facility, to personally assist the President with all business matters, to manage and supervise the offices, which includes the hiring/firing of personnel, keeping the books of the company, which includes the preparation of various financial documents, travel to the parent company in Thailand as required by the President of either the parent or subsidiary companies and, generally, to maintain weekly communication with the Thai company, which requires fluency in the Thai language.

In the two and one-half years Miss ... has been with the parent corporation, she has become an integral asset to the success of our operations. We require the assistance of her knowledge on a temporary basis during the initial stages of our U.S. enterprise, and will pay her an annual salary of $25,000.00. We anticipate that her services will be needed in the U.S. for no more than three years. During this period, she will recruit and train a permanent replacement.

                                        Sincerely,

                                        ... (USA), INC.

                                        Vichol ..., President

SAMPLE SHEET

SAMPLE FORM I-506

UNITED STATES DEPARTMENT OF JUSTICE
IMMIGRATION AND NATURALIZATION SERVICE

NOTE: Refer to "Explanatory Note" on p. 82, especially Paragraph 6 thereof.

P.I.

Form Approved
OMB No. 43-R0342

Fee Stamp

APPLICATION FOR CHANGE
OF NONIMMIGRANT STATUS

(Under Section 248 of the Immigration and N...

➡ Please read the Instructions o...

I hereby apply to have my status in the U... ...hanged to that of a nonimmigrant _____E-2_____
(Student, visitor, etc.)

I wish to remain in the United States in that ...w status until__as_long_as_I_am_eligible_____
(Month, Day, Year)

This application is submitted together with the required documents which are made a part hereof, and if applicable the fee of $10.

PRESS FIRMLY—LEGIBLE COPY REQUIRED. PRINT OR TYPE YOUR NAME EXACTLY AS IT APPEARS ON YOUR ARRIVAL-DEPARTURE RECORD FORM I-94. IF YOUR MAILING ADDRESS IN THE U.S. IS WITH SOMEONE WHOSE FAMILY NAME IS DIFFERENT FROM YOURS, INSERT THAT PERSON'S NAME IN THE C/O BLOCK.

1. YOUR NAME	FAMILY NAME (Capital Letters) ▓▓▓	FIRST Jules	MIDDLE Renaud	7. I AM IN POSSESSION OF PASSPORT
IN CARE OF	C/O Dominique A. ▓▓▓		FILE, NUMBER (If Known)	NUMBER:° 4▓▓▓
2. MAILING ADDRESS IN U.S.	NUMBER AND STREET (Apt. No.) ▓▓▓ Main Avenue			ISSUED BY (Country) French West Indies
	CITY ▓▓▓	STATE Colorado	ZIP CODE 81301	WHICH EXPIRES ON: (Month, Day, Year) July 26, 1988

3. DATE OF BIRTH (Month, Day, Year) Dec. 2, 1951	COUNTRY OF BIRTH F.W.I.	COUNTRY OF CITIZENSHIP France	8. I AM ATTACHING MY TEMPORARY ENTRY PERMIT FORM I-94
4. PRESENT NONIMMIGRANT CLASSIFICATION B-2	DATE ON WHICH AUTHORIZED STAY EXPIRES Jan. 6, 1984		9. I ENTERED WITH PASSPORT VISA NO. 007▓
5. DATE AND PORT OF LAST ARRIVAL IN UNITED STATES 8/7/83 – Miami, Fla.	NAME OF VESSEL, AIRLINE, OR OTHER MEANS OF LAST ARRIVAL IN U.S. Eastern Airlines		10. MY NONIMMIGRANT STATUS IN THE UNITED STATES ☐ HAS ☒ HAS NOT BEEN CHANGED SINCE MY ENTRY (If changed, give details)
6. THE PERMIT NUMBER ON MY FORM I-94 IS ▓▓▓			

FOR GOVERNMENT USE ONLY

Reclassification to

☐ STAY GRANTED TO (Date)

☐ Application DENIED V.D. TO (Date)

DATE OF ACTION

DO OR OIC OFFICE

11. MY PERMANENT ADDRESS OUTSIDE THE UNITED STATES IS: (Street) (City or Town) (County, District, Province or State) (Country)

Petit ▓▓▓, St. Barthelemy ▓▓▓ (Guadeloupe) F.W.I.

| 12. I RESIDED AT THE ADDRESS IN ITEM 11 FROM: (Month, Day, Year) December 2, 1951 | TO: (Month, Day, Year) present |

13. SINCE MY ENTRY INTO THE UNITED STATES I HAVE RESIDED AT THE FOLLOWING PLACES:

(Street and No.) (City or Town) (State)	FROM: (Month, Day, Year)	TO: (Month, Day, Year)
▓▓▓ Main Avenue, ▓▓▓ Colorado	August 8, 1983	Present Time

14. I DESIRE TO HAVE MY NONIMMIGRANT STATUS CHANGED FOR THE FOLLOWING REASONS:

See attached

15. I DID NOT APPLY TO THE AMERICAN CONSUL FOR A VISA IN THE NONIMMIGRANT STATUS WHICH I AM NOW SEEKING FOR THE FOLLOWING REASONS:

See attached

16. I SUBMIT THE FOLLOWING DOCUMENTARY EVIDENCE TO ESTABLISH THAT I WILL MAINTAIN THE NONIMMIGRANT CLASSIFICATION TO WHICH I WISH TO BE CHANGED:

Form I-126 with supporting documentation.

ATTACH YOUR FORM I-94 — °DO NOT SEND YOUR PASSPORT

RECEIVED	TRANS. IN	RET'D-TRANS OUT	COMPLETED

FORM I-506 (REV. 9-12-77)Y

17. (COMPLETE THIS BLOCK ONLY IF YOU ARE APPLYING FOR CHANGE TO STUDENT STATUS.)
THE COUNTRY IN WHICH I INTEND TO LIVE AND WORK AFTER I COMPLETE MY SCHOOLING IN THE UNITED STATES IS _____

(IF YOU ARE SEEKING TO ATTEND A VOCATIONAL OR BUSINESS SCHOOL, COMPLETE THE FOLLOWING ADDITIONAL STATEMENTS BY CHECKING THE APPROPRIATE BOXES.)

THE SCHOOLING I AM SEEKING ☐ IS ☐ IS NOT AVAILABLE IN MY COUNTRY.

I ☐ INTEND ☐ DO NOT INTEND TO ENGAGE IN THE OCCUPATION FOR WHICH THAT SCHOOLING WILL PREPARE ME.

18. MY OCCUPATION IS:
Chef

19. SOCIAL SECURITY NO. (If none, state "none")
None

20. I ☐ HAVE ☒ HAVE NOT BEEN EMPLOYED OR ENGAGED IN BUSINESS SINCE ENTERING THE UNITED STATES. IF ANSWER IS IN AFFIRMATIVE, COMPLETE THE FOLLOWING:
NATURE OF OCCUPATION OR BUSINESS IN WHICH I ☐ AM ☐ WAS EMPLOYED:

NAME OF EMPLOYER OR BUSINESS FIRM | ADDRESS

MY EMPLOYMENT OR ENGAGEMENT IN BUSINESS BEGAN ON: (Month, Day, Year) | AND ENDED ON: (Month, Day, Year)

MY MONTHLY INCOME FROM EMPLOYMENT OR BUSINESS ☐ IS ☐ WAS:

21. IF NOT EMPLOYED OR ENGAGED IN BUSINESS IN THE UNITED STATES, DESCRIBE FULLY THE SOURCE AND AMOUNT OF YOUR INCOME ABROAD AND HOW SUPPORTED WHILE IN THE UNITED STATES: (If applying for change to student status, see instruction #4.)
Am employed by ▓▓▓▓▓▓▓▓ in St. Barthelemy, F.W.I. -
on leave of absence - salary is $250/weekly plus bonus; savings of $9,000

22. I ☒ AM ☐ AM NOT MARRIED
Name of Spouse | Present address | Citizenship (Country)
Anne Gertrude ▓▓▓▓ | St. Barthelemy, F.W.I. | France

23. I HAVE TWO (Number) CHILDREN: (List children below)

Name	Age	Place of Birth	Present Address
Fabienne Anne ▓▓▓	5	F.W.I.	) St. Barthelemy, FWI
Donatienne ▓▓▓	3	F.W.I.	)

I HAVE FOUR (Number) OTHER RELATIVES IN THE UNITED STATES: (List relatives below)

Name	Relationship	Immigration Status	Present Address Miami, FL
Roger ▓▓▓	Half-brother	Perm.Res.	▓▓ SW 256 St., Homestead,
Leon ▓▓▓	Half-brother	Perm.Res.	Address unknown
Ribert ▓▓▓	Half-brother	Perm.Res.	Address Unknown
Ginette ▓▓▓	Sister-in-Law	E-2	▓▓ Main Ave., ▓▓▓▓, CO

24. N/A ☐ I HAVE ☐ HAVE NOT FILED THE ADDRESS REPORT REQUIRED BY THE ALIEN REGISTRATION ACT OF 1940 AS AMENDED AND BY SECTION 265 OF THE IMMIGRATION AND NATIONALITY ACT.

25. I ☐ HAVE ☒ HAVE NOT BEEN ARRESTED OR CONVICTED OF ANY CRIMINAL OFFENSE IN THE UNITED STATES OR IN ANY FOREIGN COUNTRY. IF ANSWER IS IN THE AFFIRMATIVE, GIVE DETAILS:

26. I certify that the above is true and correct to the best of my knowledge and belief. (If form prepared by other than applicant, that person must execute item 25.)

(Signature of Applicant)   9/30/83 (Date)

SIGNATURE OF PERSON PREPARING FORM, IF OTHER THAN APPLICANT
27. I declare that this document was prepared by me at the request of the applicant and is based on all information of which I have any knowledge.

(Signature) | 110 Sixteenth St., 14th Flr.
Denver, Colorado 80202 | 10/3/83
(Address) | (Date)

Response to Items 14 and 15 on Form I-506: [Attached To Form I-506]

14. I became associated with Dominique A. ▓▓▓▓ and his wife, Josseline M.L. ▓▓▓▓, as an employee in their restaurant, ▓▓▓▓▓▓, in St. Barthelemy in the French West Indies in 1975 as their master chef. I prepared the specialized Caribbean dishes, the pates, the pastries, the recipes for which are proprietary to the ▓▓▓▓▓▓ Restaurant, and the French bread, and was with them until early 1982.

15. Recently, I was invited by Mr. and Mrs. ▓▓▓s to visit their new restaurant in ▓▓▓▓, Colorado, with the possibility of investing in it and possibly going back to work for them. I felt I could not make a decision about investing in the restaurant, or accepting their offer of employment until I took a look at their restaurant, the city of ▓▓▓▓ and Colorado in general.

After seeing the ▓▓▓▓▓▓ Restaurant and much discussion with Mr. and Mrs. ▓▓▓▓, I concluded that my investing in their restaurant would be a wise, financial move for me and, because I always enjoyed working with them in the past, I would like to work with them again.

SAMPLE
FORM I-126

REPORT OF STATUS
BY TREATY TRADER OR INVESTOR

NOTE: Refer to "Explanatory Note" on P. 82, especially paragraph 6.

p. 1.

Read instructions on other side before filling out this report.

Registration Number

1. Name (Last, in capital letters)	(First)	(Middle)	2. Date of Birth
▓▓▓▓	Jules	Renaud	Dec. 2, 1951

3. Place of Birth (City or Town)	(State or Province)	(Country)	4. Present Nationality
▓▓▓▓		French West Indies	French

5. United States Mailing Address (Apt. No.) (No. and Street) (City or Town) (State) (Zip Code)
▓▓▓ Main Avenue, ▓▓▓▓, Colorado 81301

6. Foreign Residence (Street) (City or Town) (State or Province) (Country)
▓▓▓▓, St. Barthelemy (Guadeloupe) 97133 F.W.I.

7. Resided at above foreign address	From 12/2/51	To present	8. Date of Entry (Month, day, year) August 7, 1983

9. Port of Entry (City) Miami	(State) Florida	10. Name of vessel or other conveyance Eastern Airlines

11. Visa 007▓▓	Issued on (Mo., day, year) 8/5/83	Visa Issued at (City) Martinique	(Country) F.W.I.

12. Passport Number 4▓▓▓	Issued on (Mo., day, year) 7/27/83	Issued at (City) St. Barthelemy, F.W.I.	(Country)	Expiration Date 7/26/88

13. Information Concerning Business Engaged in Pursuant to Treaty of Commerce and Navigation with the United States:

A. Name of Country Signatory to Treaty with United States
France

B. Name and address of business or enterprise in which engaged or employed
▓▓▓▓ Restaurant, ▓▓▓ Main Avenue, ▓▓▓▓, Colorado, 81301

C. Nature of business or enterprise
French and Caribbean restaurant

D. List all countries engaged in trade with the company named in item B and the amount derived from each country
U.S. gross sales - projected, $500,000.00

E. Percentage of Business or Enterprise Owned by Nationals of Country of Which You Are a National: 100 % Are such Nationals residing abroad? YES_____ NO XX . If such Nationals are residing in the United States, list their immigration status.

F. Title of My Position or Occupation
Master Chef

G. Brief Description of My Duties
Preparation of all Caribbean dishes, which involve knowledge of the recipes which are proprietary secrets of ▓▓▓▓; baking daily French bread; preparing all patés and pastries (see approval of fellow employee dated 11/1/82 - ALPHA-L)

H. (Check box and fill in blank as appropriate)

[XX] I am an employee of the business or enterprise named in item 13B.

[XX] I am an independent developer or director of operations of the business or enterprise named in item 13B, in which I have personally invested or am in the process of investing cash or other capital in the amount of $ 35,000.00

14. Documents attached in support of this report (See Instructions)

[XX] Arrival-Departure Record (Form I-94)   [XX] Letter from Employer

[ ] Application for Extension of Stay (Form I-539)   [XX] Application for Change of Nonimmigrant Status (Form I-506)

Form I-126 (Rev.6-26-78)N   OVER   OVER→

15. Marital status

☒ Married	☐ Divorced	☐ Widowed	☐ Never Married

Name of Spouse

Anne Gertrude ▨▨▨▨

Nationality of Spouse	Passport Issued By (Country)	Expires on (Date)
French	Franch	July 26, 1988

Present Address of Spouse

▨▨▨▨▨▨▨▨ , St. Barthelemy, F.W.I.

16. Name of Children	Date of Birth	Country of Birth	Passport issued by (Country) and Expires On (Date)
Fabienne Anne ▨▨▨▨	1/8/78	F.W.I.	None
Donatienne ▨▨▨▨▨	1/12/80	F.W.I.	None

Note: If the children for whom you are seeking extension or change of nonimmigrant status do not residue with you, give their complete address on a separate attachment to this application.

17. I certify that all information furnished in this report is true and correct.

Date 9/30/83 _____ _Joblnce▨▨▨▨▨▨_

Signature of Treaty Trader or Investor or applicant seeking such status

18. Signature of person preparing form, if other than Treaty Trader or Investor or applicant seeking such status

I declare that this document was prepared by me at the request of the Treaty Trader or Investor or applicant seeking such status and is based upon all information of which I have any knowledge. _▨▨▨▨▨▨▨_

Signature

Date 10/3/83 _____ Address 110 16th St., 14th Floor, Denver, Colorado 80202

INSTRUCTIONS

If you were admitted to this country as a Treaty Trader prior to December 24, 1952, this report must be submitted annually, 30 days prior to each anniversary of your entry, to the immigration office having jurisdiction over your place of residence; and, in that case, no application for extension of temporary stay need be submitted.

If you are seeking to acquire status as a Treaty Trader or Investor, this report must be attached to your Application for Change of Nonimmigrant Classification, Form I-506.

If you acquired status as a Treaty Trader or Investor on or after December 24, 1952, this report must be attached to your Application for Extension of Temporary Stay (Form I-539).

Submit with this report your temporary entry permit (Form I-94, Arrival-Departure Record). If your temporary entry permit is attached to your passport, the permit should be removed for this purpose. DO NOT SEND IN YOUR PASS-PORT. However, you must be in possession of a passport valid for at least six (6) months beyond the date to which your stay may be extended.

If you are employed, submit with this report a letter from your employer stating your present and intended position and duties. Name and title or position of person signing the letter should be clearly indicated. If your employer is a person and not an organization, the letter from your employer should indicate whether or not he is an E-1 or E-2 nonimmigrant.

A Treaty Trader or Investor may include in this report any alien dependent spouse and unmarried, minor children who are in the United States. If this application includes your wife and children, their Forms I-94 must be submitted with the application. They too must be in possession of passports valid for at least six months beyond the expiration date of the extensions requested. In all other cases separate reports must be made.

DO NOT WRITE IN THIS SPACE

(For use of Immigration and Naturalization Service Officer)

☐ Status maintained   ☐ Status not maintained   ☐ See Form I-506 for action taken.

Date _____   _____

District Director

GPO 830-77

(End of Form)

SUPPORTING LETTER BY PRINCIPAL INVESTORS

NOTE: See "Explanatory Note" on pp. 81-2, especially Paragraph 6 thereof.

Restaurant Bar
■■ Main Avenue
303-■■■■

September 26, 1983

<u>TO</u>: U.S. Department of Justice
Immigration and Naturalization Service
Denver, Colorado

RE: Application for change of Status
of Jules Renaud ■■■■

Gentlemen,

I and my wife, Josseline ■■■ are partners in the operation of the ■■■■■ Restaurant in St. Barthelemy, French West Indies. Renaud ■■■ was employed by us at that location from 1975 through March of 1982 as our Master Chef. In 1982, my wife and I decided to establish a second ■■■■ Restaurant in Durango, Colorado, and acquired property at ■■ Main Avenue in Durango, where our restaurant is now located.

At that time, we investigated the labor market in Durango and were not able, unfortunately, to find experienced help with whom we could share our proprietary secrets relating to recipes for the sauces and salad dressings which make our French and Caribbean cuisine unique. We were fortunate that our assistant Manager in St. Barthelemy, Ginette ■■■, wanted to invest in our restaurant and work in Durango.

Our restaurant is slowly growing, and we feel that if we could re-employ our Master Chef, Renaud ■■■, at our restaurant in Durango, since he is interested in investing in our venture, our operation would move more quickly to the profit side of our ledger. We have been financially troubled, and Mr ■■■ investment will certainly alleviate that burden.

Attached hereto is a copy of the menu offered in St. Barthelemy, and a copy of the menu offered at our Durango restaurant, utilizing our proprietary secrets in the preparation of the various sauces, etc...

We are very anxious to have Mr ■■■ with us again, and request that you favorably consider his request for change of his status in the U.S. Thank you.

Very truly yours,

Dominique ■■■

STATE OF COLORADO)
) ss.
COUNTY OF LA PLATA)

AFFIDAVIT

DOMINIQUE A. ███████, being first duly sworn, deposes and states as follows:

1. That he is the holder of a non-immigrant "E-2" visa issued at Martinique, French West Indies, on February 16, 1982, which expires on February 16, 1986.

2. That the affiant and his spouse, JOSSELINE ███████ ███████ who is also the holder of a non-immigrant "E-2" visa which expires on February 16, 1986, are the owners of real property located in Durango, Colorado, with a street address of ███████ Avenue. A copy of the deed to this property is attached hereto.

3. That the affiant and his spouse have established a restaurant located at the above address known as the ███████ Restaurant, specializing in French and Caribbean cuisine.

4. That Jules Renaud ███████ had been employed by the affiant and his wife at their ███████████████ in St. Barthelemy, French West Indies, as their primary chef from November, 1975, to March 15, 1982, which position required specialized knowledge and training in the method of the operation of the restaurant.

5. That ███████████ is currently in the United States as a visitor, which non-immigrant status expires on January 6, 1984. A copy of his I-94 is attached hereto.

6. That the affiant and his wife wish to re-employ Mr. ███████ as the master chef of ███████████████ in Durango, and that Mr. Laplace wishes to invest in said restaurant.

7. That Jules Renaud ███████ is the brother-in-law of Ginette Josephe ███████ who is an employee of the ███████ Restaurant and an investor therein, and who was granted E-2 status on November 1, 1982.

_____
Dominique A. ███████

Subscribed and sworn to before me this 29th day of September, 1983.

My commission expires 11-1-86.

_____
Notary Public
949 Second Ave.
Durango, Co. 81301

FORM I-539

NOTE → **IMPORTANT** Please read attached instructions before filling out application. Use typewriter or print in block letters with ball-point pen. Be sure this application and the attached Form I-539A and address mailing label are legible. Do not leave any question unanswered. When appropriate, insert "none" or "not applicable". If you need more space to answer fully any question on this form use a separate sheet of paper this size, and identify each answer with the number of the corresponding question.

UNITED STATES DEPARTMENT OF JUSTICE
IMMIGRATION AND NATURALIZATION SERVICE

READ INSTRUCTIONS CAREFULLY
FEE WILL NOT BE REFUNDED

OMB No. 1115—0093
Expires 1-84

APPLICATION TO EXTEND TIME OF TEMPORARY STAY

FEE STAMP

I HEREBY APPLY TO EXTEND MY TEMPORARY STAY IN THE UNITED STATES

PRESS FIRMLY — LEGIBLE COPY REQUIRED. PRINT OR TYPE YOUR NAME EXACTLY AS IT APPEARS ON YOUR ARRIVAL—DEPARTURE RECORD FORM I-94. IF YOUR MAILING ADDRESS IN THE U.S. IS WITH SOMEONE WHOSE FAMILY NAME IS DIFFERENT FROM YOURS, INSERT THAT PERSON'S NAME IN THE C/O BLOCK.

6. DATE TO WHICH EXTENSION IS REQUESTED

1. YOUR NAME — FAMILY NAME (CAPITAL LETTERS)   FIRST   MIDDLE

IN CARE OF — C/O

7. REASON FOR REQUESTING EXTENSION

2. MAILING ADDRESS IN U.S. — NUMBER AND STREET (APT. NO.)   FILE NUMBER

CITY   STATE   ZIP CODE

3. DATE OF BIRTH (MO./DAY/YR.)   COUNTRY OF BIRTH   COUNTRY OF CITIZENSHIP

4. PRESENT NONIMMIGRANT CLASSIFICATION   DATE ON WHICH AUTHORIZED STAY EXPIRES

TELEPHONE NUMBER

5. DATE AND PORT OF LAST ARRIVAL IN U.S.   NAME OF VESSEL, AIRLINE, OR OTHER MEANS OF LAST ARRIVAL IN U.S.

8. REASON FOR COMING TO THE U.S.

THE ADMISSION NUMBER FROM MY I-94 IS: ▶

FOR GOVERNMENT USE ONLY

☐ EXTENSION GRANTED TO (DATE)

DATE OF ACTION

☐ EXTENSION DENIED V.D. TO (DATE)

DD OR OIC OFFICE

9. HAS AN IMMIGRANT VISA PETITION EVER BEEN FILED IN YOUR BEHALF?
☐ YES   ☐ NO   IF "YES", WHERE WAS IT FILED?

10. HAVE YOU EVER APPLIED FOR AN IMMIGRANT VISA OR PERMANENT RESIDENCE IN THE U.S.? ☐ YES   ☐ NO   IF "YES", WHERE DID YOU APPLY?

11. I INTEND TO DEPART FROM THE U.S. ON (DATE)

I AM IN POSSESSION OF A TRANSPORTATION TICKET FOR MY DEPARTURE ☐ YES   ☐ NO

12. PASSPORT NO. *   EXPIRES ON (DATE)   ISSUED BY (COUNTRY)

13. NUMBER, STREET, CITY, PROVINCE (STATE) AND COUNTRY OF PERMANENT RESIDENCE

14. MY USUAL OCCUPATION IS:

15. SOCIAL SECURITY NO. (IF NONE, STATE "NONE")

16. I ☐ AM   ☐ AM NOT MARRIED. IF YOU WISH TO APPLY FOR EXTENSION FOR YOUR SPOUSE AND CHILDREN, GIVE THE FOLLOWING: (SEE INSTRUCTIONS # 1)

NAME OF SPOUSE AND CHILDREN	DATE OF BIRTH	COUNTRY OF BIRTH	PASSPORT ISSUED BY (COUNTRY) AND EXPIRES ON (DATE)

NOTE IF SPOUSE AND CHILDREN FOR WHOM YOU ARE SEEKING EXTENSION DO NOT RESIDE WITH YOU, GIVE THEIR COMPLETE ADDRESS ON A SEPARATE ATTACHMENT TO THIS APPLICATION.

17. I (INSERT "HAVE" OR "HAVE NOT") _____ BEEN EMPLOYED OR ENGAGED IN BUSINESS IN THE UNITED STATES. (IF YOU HAVE BEEN EMPLOYED OR ENGAGED IN BUSINESS IN THE UNITED STATES, COMPLETE THE REST OF THE BLOCK.)

NAME AND ADDRESS OF EMPLOYER OR BUSINESS	INCOME PER WEEK	DATES EMPLOYMENT OR BUSINESS BEGAN AND ENDED

I certify that the above is true and correct

SIGNATURE OF APPLICANT   (Alien signs here)

X

DATE

SIGNATURE OF PERSON PREPARING FORM, IF OTHER THAN APPLICANT

I declare that this document was prepared by me at the request of the applicant and is based on all information on which I have any knowledge.

SIGNATURE   ADDRESS   DATE

ATTACH YOUR FORM I-94 OR I-144 — *DO NOT SEND YOUR PASSPORT

RECEIVED	TRANS. IN	RET'D. TRANS OUT	COMPLETED

Form I-539 (Rev. 5-4-89)N

FORM G-325A

-110-

U.S. Department of Justice

Immigration and Naturalization Service

FORM G-325A

BIOGRAPHIC INFORMATION

OMB No. 1115-0066

Approval expires 4-30-85

(Family name)	(First name)	(Middle name)	☐ MALE ☐ FEMALE	BIRTHDATE (Mo.-Day-Yr.)	NATIONALITY	FILE NUMBER A-
ALL OTHER NAMES USED (Including names by previous marriages)			CITY AND COUNTRY OF BIRTH			SOCIAL SECURITY NO. (If any)

	FAMILY NAME	FIRST NAME	DATE, CITY AND COUNTRY OF BIRTH (If known)	CITY AND COUNTRY OF RESIDENCE .
FATHER				
MOTHER (Maiden name)				

HUSBAND (If none, so state) OR WIFE	FAMILY NAME (For wife, give maiden name)	FIRST NAME	BIRTHDATE	CITY & COUNTRY OF BIRTH	DATE OF MARRIAGE	PLACE OF MARRIAGE

FORMER HUSBANDS OR WIVES (if none, so state) FAMILY NAME (For wife, give maiden name)	FIRST NAME	BIRTHDATE	DATE & PLACE OF MARRIAGE	DATE AND PLACE OF TERMINATION OF MARRIAGE

APPLICANT'S RESIDENCE LAST FIVE YEARS. LIST PRESENT ADDRESS FIRST.

STREET AND NUMBER	CITY	PROVINCE OR STATE	COUNTRY	FROM		TO	
				MONTH	YEAR	MONTH	YEAR
						PRESENT TIME	

APPLICANT'S LAST ADDRESS OUTSIDE THE UNITED STATES OF MORE THAN ONE YEAR

STREET AND NUMBER	CITY	PROVINCE OR STATE	COUNTRY	FROM		TO	
				MONTH	YEAR	MONTH	YEAR

APPLICANT'S EMPLOYMENT LAST FIVE YEARS. (IF NONE, SO STATE.) LIST PRESENT EMPLOYMENT FIRST

FULL NAME AND ADDRESS OF EMPLOYER	OCCUPATION (SPECIFY)	FROM		TO	
		MONTH	YEAR	MONTH	YEAR
				PRESENT TIME	

Show below last occupation abroad if not shown above. (Include all information requested above.)

THIS FORM IS SUBMITTED IN CONNECTION WITH APPLICATION FOR:	SIGNATURE OF APPLICANT	DATE
☐ NATURALIZATION ☐ STATUS AS PERMANENT RESIDENT	X	
☐ OTHER (SPECIFY):		
Are all copies legible? ☐ Yes	IF YOUR NATIVE ALPHABET IS IN OTHER THAN ROMAN LETTERS, WRITE YOUR NAME IN YOUR NATIVE ALPHABET IN THIS SPACE:	

PENALTIES: SEVERE PENALTIES ARE PROVIDED BY LAW FOR KNOWINGLY AND WILLFULLY FALSIFYING OR CONCEALING A MATERIAL FACT.

APPLICANT: BE SURE TO PUT YOUR NAME AND ALIEN REGISTRATION NUMBER IN THE BOX OUTLINED BY HEAVY BORDER BELOW.

COMPLETE THIS BOX (Family name)	(Given name)	(Middle name)	(Alien registration number)

CHAPTER 7

SO YOU WANT AN "IMMIGRANT" TYPE OF VISA? HERE ARE THE STEP-BY-STEP PROCEDURES FROM START TO FINISH.

The General Guidelines For Following This Chapter

In this chapter, we deal with the formalities as they relate to applying for the IMMIGRANT" types of visa or status. (The equivalent treatment for the "NON-IMMIGRANT" types of visa, is outlined in Chapter 6 (pp. 62-110).

The forms, instructions, and procedures outlined in this chapter are carefully arranged and organized in a system of orderly, simple "STEPS" — from "STEP 1" to STEP 9 ". In each "step," you are told what to do (or to expect)and provided with sample forms along with instructions on how to complete or make use of them.

BUT A WORD OF CAUTION IS NECESSARY: If you are to comprehend and follow this chapter, and hence be able to follow through in the processing of your visa application and ultimately secure a visa, one thing you must do is this: YOU MUST FOLLOW THE "STEPS" ORDERLY, AND ONE (AND ONLY ONE) AT A TIME.

In preparing the forms and processing your visa application through the consular or immigration channels, take the steps strictly ONE at a time, following them EXACTLY in the same numerical order in which they are isted below in this chapter. In each step you come to, first read the instructions therein. This tells you how to proceed. Then, following what such instructions or information tell you to do, go one step (and only ONE step) at a time according to the order of the numbering. Do NOT skip around from one step to another, or from page to page (unless of course, if so instructed by the manual).

AND HERE THEY ARE, THE TEN (10) SIMPLE SYSTEMATIC "STEPS" INVOLVED IN APPLYING FOR AND OBTAINING AN IMMIGRANT VISA:

step 1: DETERMINE IN WHAT SPECIFIC "IMMIGRANT" VISA CATEGORY (OR CATEGORIES) YOU FALL UNDER

(See Chapter 1, Sections D to G, (pp. 5- 10) for the various classes into which applicants claiming eligibility for immigrant status fall).

step 2: KNOW WHAT BASIC QUALIFICATIONS ARE REQUIRED OF ONE FOR ELIGIBILITY UNDER YOUR DESIGNATED VISA CATEGORY

(See Chapter 4 (pp. 34-41), and Chapter 5 (pp 42-61), and refer to the particular Section(s) therein which have to do with the visa category you claim to fall under in STEP 1 above. (See, also, Chapter 1, Sections H thru. J, for issues relating to determination of your visa "availability", "currency" and "priority dates").

step 3: OBTAIN THE NECESSARY APPLICATION FORMS FOR THE TYPE OF VISA YOU SEEK.

For the added convenience of the readership, Do-it- yourself Legal Publishers makes available to its readers the standard, fully pre-sorted, all-in-one package of forms—containing the proper forms necessary for the particular type of visa you designate.

To order the Publisher's standard "all-in-one" immigration forms package, just complete the Order Form on p.191-2 and send it to the Publisher's legal Forms Division. Aliens may order from the Publisher, whether they live (or are filing) in the United States or in a foreign land.

Note a few general rules in regard to completing the immigration forms. A truly important aid to anyone in preparing all such forms are the "blocks" provided on the forms: such blocks are generally self-explanatory and quite explicitly indicate the exact information required to be entered, and the order in which such information is to be put in the space. Secondly, almost every immigration form has a set of "INSTRUCTIONS" on the body of the form, clearly telling the reader the purpose(s) for which the form is appropriate and giving some pointers on how to complete or file them, and guidelines on the information and supporting documents required to be furnished.

Hence, the first rule in completing the forms in this: in all instances, always be absolutely sure to read the forms and thoroughly understand the information required of you before filling them out. Be deliberately careful. Remember this: that the initial batch of forms you complete and submit are what is known as the "primary" documents, meaning that this is the documentary source which the consular and immigration authorities will probably go back to and refer to again and again, and against which they will cross-check any future documents and information from you for consistency. (In submitting supporting documents to the consular or INS officers, make it a point always, especially with regard to irreplaceable documents, to file only photostatic copies of the originals by first presenting the originals to them for their personal inspection and certification that the copies are the true copies. This precaution is necessary because the immigration services have a history of chronically losing important, often irreplaceable documents submitted by aliens. Furthermore, for any documents written in a foreign language, always submit a certified English translation as well).

step 4: IS YOUR CLAIM TO VISA ELIGIBILITY BASED ON AN OCCUPATION OR A JOB OR LABOR SKILL? THEN, FIRST SEEK TO OBTAIN AN ALIEN "LABOR CERTIFICATION".

Essentially, this will apply to you ONLY IF you fall under the employment-based THIRD or SIXTH preference visa categories or under the IMMIGRANT INVESTOR or FOREIGN MEDICAL GRADUATE classifications (See Section B and Section C of chapter 5 (pp. 43-5) and Chapter 8, Section C (pp.55-7), for the complete procedures by which a Labor Certification is obtained).

step 5 : **HAVE YOUR U.S. "SPONSOR", A RELATIVE OR AN EMPLOYER, FILE A "PETITION" ON YOUR BEHALF.**

Recall what has been amply explained in several Sections of this manual (see, for example, pp. 6 & 8), namely, that the very initial act involved in applying for an immigrant visa, is for either a U.S. relative of the alien, or, where employment or job skill is the basis of the eligibility qualification*, then for the alien's prospective U.S. employer, to file a "petition" on behalf of the alien to sponsor the said alien for the immigrant visa. Hence, here we shall first list the PETITION Forms and the accompanying supporting documentations thereof necessary for the filing of such a petition by a U.S sponsor who must either be a relative or an employer.

NOTE THESE, HOWEVER: Be remined that the law was changed as recently as June 20, 1986 and that effective thereafter, the new rule is that anyone who files for and receives labor certification from the Department of Labor, must file a visa petition (form 1-140) within 60 days of receiving certification — even if a visa number is not available. And if this is not done, the person will lose his "priority date" for a visa number which was established when the certification application was filed with the DoL.

Furthermore, in the-employment-based situations, however, the employer usually shall have applied for and probably obtained a Labor Certification first, before making such a visa "petition". Or, more often than not, the employer will simply file the application for Labor certification (or, if a Schedule A Job, for "pre-certification") simultaneously with the visa petition. The employer will simply complete both the application forms for both the Labor Certification (pp. 41-54 of this manual) and the visa petition for classification of the alien under a THIRD or SIXTH preference visa category (STEP 5 on pp-   ), and submit the labor certification application to the immigration service along with the visa petition, with all applicable supporting documents for each attached. This approach is considered advantageous by many immigration lawyers and counsellors, the thesis being that, this way, the immigration official would have been in a position to determine, himself, that the alien is either exempt from labor certification (as a Sechedule A job applicant) or is deserving of an affirmative labor certification, thereby enabling the official to proceed speedily to the considering of the visa petition itself.

Basic Forms Needed by Sponsor in Petitioning for the Alien:

FORM 1-130. (This Form, called the "Petition" for short, is to be completed in all family relationship-based visa applications (i.e., the 1st, 2nd, 4th & 5th visa preference categories); it is completed by the U.S. citizen or Permanent Resident alien to whom the intending alien claims to have a close family relationship. See illustrative sample of Form 1-130 on pp. 120-22.) See, also, "Explanatory Note" on p. 171.

FORM 1-140. (This Form, in stead of the above-listed Form 1-130, is used for the petition when the basis for the claim to eligibility is job skills or occupation-related - i.e., the 3rd and 6th visa preference categories. Illustrative Form 1-140 is at pp. 123-5, 126-7, with "Explanatory Note" at p. 119)

. **FORM G-325A.** (The Biographic Information form - see illustrative sample on pp. 110). This form is to be completed in part by the sponsoring petitioner, and in part by the alien. The form is mostly used and applicable in petitions involving "Adjustment of Status" sitauations where the alien is already in the United States in a non-immigrant status and seeks to change to immigrant status (see pp. for adjustment of status procedures). However, the form may be required in initial immigrant visa petition situations.

To file the petition for the alien, the sponsoring petitioner (variously called the "sponsor" or the "petitioner"), upon completing the above forms, files them with the U.S. Immigration and Naturalization's District Office in the United States for the area in which the spons-

*NOTE: For the sake of simplicity to make this chapter less crowded and easier for the reader to follow, we list elsewhere the basic filing forms and the supporting documents (and procedures) needed for filing for a visa under the other two important "immigrant" sub-categories discussed in this manual — namely, the "IMMIGRANT INVESTOR" and "POLITICAL ASYLEE" groups. Hence, for aliens applying for an immigrant visa on the basis of being a Refugee or Political Asylum seeker, see such details in Chapter 5, Section D thereof (pp. 46-53), especially pp. 46; and for those applying on the basis of being an Immigrant Investor, see Chapter 5, Section E thereof (pp. 55   ).

or resides or the alien's prospective employment is located.(If the sponsor happens to be living outside the U.S., the petition may be filed by him at the nearest U.S. Consulate.) For petitions for which the basis is employment or occupation-related, the sponsoring U.S. employer will generally file a petition only when the alien is <u>outside</u> the United States, or, if the alien is already in the U.S., then only if his non-immigrant visa has expired or he has violated the terms of his non-immigrant visa (such as by dropping out of school or working without permission.) If the conditions are otherwise, it would ordinarily be the alien himself who has to file the petition, that is, as an "adjustment of status" case set forth in pp. 161 & 171.

Documentations Required in Support for the Sponsor's Petition, for Petitions Based on Family Relationships:

To be attached to the basic PETITION forms in support of the sponsors petition, are typically the following documents:

● BIRTH CERTIFICATE (or other equivalents, such as baptismal certificates, military service records,and the like) for <u>both</u> the petitioner and the alien "beneficiary" of the petition, to establish the relationship between the U.S. petitioner and the alien,if any.

● PROOF OF U.S. CITIZENSHIP OF PETITIONER, or of his/her U.S. Permanent Residency status (Form 1-551 or the "Green Card")

● MARRIAGE CERTIFICATE of the petitioner to the alien, if applicable.

● PROOF OF AGE of each alien (e.g. birth certificate or Declaration of age).

● ADOPTION DECREE (or other proof of legal adoption), if the alien is said to be an adopted child.

● DIVORCE DECREE (or death certificate thereof) from prior marriages by the petitioner and/or the alien, if any.

● MARRIAGE CERTIFICATE OF THE COMMON PARENTS of the petitioner and the alien(s), in cases, for example, involving a brother or sister sponsoring a brother or sister.

● "SECONDARY EVIDENCE" type of data — such as affidavits (sworn statements) from people attesting to the necessary facts as to the close family relationship claimed,or letters, correspondence and other proof of communications which had existed between the petitioner and the alien.

Documentations Required in Support for the Sponsor's Petition, for Petitions Based on 3rd or 6th Preference (Job-Related) Visa Categories:

● Approved LABOR CERTIFICATION.(See illustrative sample on pp.133 & 153 STATEMENT OF QUALIFICATION OF ALIEN,Form ETA750B.(See illustrative sample on pp. 131)

● JOB OFFER FOR ALIEN, Form ETA-750A.(See illustrative sample on pp. 129-130)

● Certified copies of CERTIFICATES, DIPLOMAS, SCHOOL TRANSCRIPTS, and other documents and proofs of educational qualification, job skills or professional status. [See "Explanatory Note" on p. 119, especially item 3]

● AFFIDAVITS FROM CREDIBLE AUTHORITIES OR EXPERTS testifying to alien's technical training or specialized experience.

● PUBLISHED MATERIALS BY OR ABOUT THE ALIEN in newspapers,magazines, professional journals, etc.

● Proof of PROFESSIONAL LICENSES, membership in professional societies, achievement awards, and the like.

● Affidavits from present or former Employers, professors or professional colleagues. [See examples on pp. 134 & 152]

● SUPPORTING LETTERS from the alien's U.S. petitioner-employer. [See pp. 134 & 152]

● CERTIFICATE AWARDS from trade union or technical schools, apprenticeship schools, etc.

● LICENSES or trade union certificates.

step 6: UPON APPROVAL OF THE SPONSOR'S "PETITION", THEN THE ALIEN HIMSELF NOW FILES AN "APPLICATION" FOR THE VISA

After the sponsoring relative or employer shall have filed his "petition" paper on behalf of the alien "beneficiary" of the petition (the subject of STEP 5 above), the Immigration and Naturalization Service (INS) will consider the petition. If the petition is approved, the INS will send the sponsor either a copy of the approved FORM 1 - 130 (or 1 - 140), or a **NOTICE OF APPROVAL OF VISA PETITION** (Form 1 - 191), and also send another copy to the American consulate in the alien's home country. Thereafter, the alien himself (or herself) is, in turn, notified of the approval by the U.S. consulate in his home country, with information and directives provided the alien regarding how he may make application at the local U.S. consulate for his immigrant visa, and what documentations to provide. From then on, it is all up to YOU, the alien, to make an "application" on your own to the U.S. consulate in your country for an IMMIGRANT visa.

TO FILE THE "APPLICATION" for your immigrant visa (it's now called an "application", as opposed to a "petition", which refers to what the alien's U.S. sponsor files), here's broadly what you do:

You (i.e., the alien) complete FORM 230, "Application for Immigrant Visa and Alien Registration" (see sample on pp.137-140), and Form G-325A, the Biographic Information (see sample of Form on pp.110).

Upon completion of these preliminary application forms, you (the alien) submit them to the U.S. Consulate's office in your country of residence; the required application fee (the U.S. Consul will give you the appropriate amount) should also be enclosed at this time.

Supporting Documents to be Attached to the Alien's Application:

● Alien's BIRTH CERTIFICATE (or, if not available, then an equivalent, such as a baptismal certificate).

● Three (it could be more) passport-size color PHOTOGRAPHS of each alien, showing a full front view of the facial features, with the reverse side of each photograph signed (in full names) by the alien signing each application.

● A PASSPORT for each alien issued by the alien's country and valid for at least the next 6 months or so.

● A POLICE CERTIFICATE for each accompanying family member of the alien who is over 16 years of age — obtainable from the police or other appropriate authorities in each of all the countries where each alien had resided for more than 6 months. (If the alien is applying from within the U.S., the REPORT OF FINGERPRINTING (Form ID 258, sampled on p 72) may be used instead. The print is taken at a local police station or a local INS Office and recorded on the pre-coded card, then sent to the consulate or INS for referral to the FBI for a clearance report).

● COURT AND PRISON RECORDS, if any, for each applicable alien.

● MILITARY RECORD for each alien, if applicable.

● REPORT OF MEDICAL EXAMINATION for each alien. (The examination must usually be performed by a doctor or medical facility specically designated by the Consulate, who then furnishes the report.)

● Documentary evidence which ESTABLISH THE CLOSE FAMILY RELATIONSHIP YOU CLAIM to have with your sponsoring U.S. petitioner, if applicable - e.g. marriage certificates, affidavits or sworn declaration of birth and family relationship by witnesses, correspondence and other proof of communication and family relationship which had existed between the petitioner and the alien.

● EMPLOYER'S OFFER OF EMPLOYMENT (see sample on pp. 87, 134, 151), OR if not obtainable or applicable, then AN AFFIDAVIT OF SUPPORT made out and sworn to by the sponsoring U.S. citizen or Permanent Resident and his/her spouse, if married, showing that such sponsor will financially support you (the alien) and that you will not become a "public charge" to the U.S. government if admitted. (See sample Form 1-134 on pp.79-80. A cover sheet to this form carries detailed instructions on the supporting documents, such as income records, statement of earning, bank records, evidence of property ownership, etc., to be attached).

● An approved Alien LABOR CERTIFICATION from the Dept. of Labor (if alien is filing under the THIRD or SIXTH preference or any other employment or skill-based classification), with the underlying documentary evidence upon which the certification has been obtained, attached. (When a labor certification is submitted, it's customary in such cases to also enclose an EMPLOYER'S LETTER OR OFFER OF EMPLOYMENT- like the ones reproduced on pp. 87, 134 & 151. For procedure used in an actual case, see "Explanatory Note" on p. 119.

Visa Processing By The Consular Officer

Now, you have filed your application with your area's U.S. Consular Office. What happens next? The consular official will conduct a quick, preliminary check of your application and the supporting documents as to their formats and contents to see that your submissions are at least complete and that the forms are completely filled out. The consular official will usually require you to "execute" (i.e. to sign) the applications form(s) in his presence. The consular official may tell you that certain necessary information or documentations are missing or improperly or incompletely filled out. If that should happen, don't even worry about it. Simply request the official to tell you specifically what and what need to be corrected or supplied and make a note of what he says. Then make the corrections or obtain the missing documents and resubmit the papers accordingly. You will pay the consular officer the application filing fees required.

In any case, assuming that the papers submitted seem at least complete and in order, the officer will assign a "case number" to your application. (Make sure you collect a receipt of filing from the officer, for your records).

Now, the consular officer will probably give you (or send you by mail), a list of instructions for the rest of the procedures still ahead to be performed: when and where, for example, to appear for the formal visa interview; how and where to take the medical examination, if applicable or not already taken; whether and how to complete the FORM G - 325A (the standard Biographic Information form used mostly in immigrant visa cases to conduct security clearances; a list of any further information or documentations the consular officer may deem necessary or appropriate in the given case, such as evidence of adequate financial support, or of the alien's family relationship with the American sponsor, and what have you.

Upon assembling and submitting all items required by the consular officer, the officer will set a date for you to be interviewed on your visa application — date for the VISA INTERVIEW — and notify you of the time and place to appear for the interview.

step ⑦ : ATTEND THE VISA INTERVIEW

What happens at this all-important interview? *To sum it all up, in brief the primary objective of the interview is to enable the interviewing consular office to better determine this: whether the facts set forth by the alien in the underlying visa petition and application papers (and, where applicable, in the Labor Certification Papers) are correct, or, on the other had, whether fraud or misrepresentation of the facts is involved in those application papers.* Does the alien, for example, truly possess the close family relationship to a U.S. citizen or Permanent Resident, or the occupational qualifications or other eligibility qualifications as claimed in the alien's petition or application papers? Hence, for the consular officer doing the interviewing, this face-to-face encounter is primarily an occasion to probe the alien more closely with a view to counter-checking and clarifying any still unclear questions or apparent contradictions occuring from the application papers, and to test for their consistency and to fill in any material gaps or omissions thereof.

In general, by almost every account, the one central issue about which most problems occur in immigrant visa interviews, has to do with verification of the aliens' claims as to the existence of a family relationship to a U.S. citizen or Permanent Resident alien, especially claims as to the existence of a marriage between the alien and his/her sponsoring U.S. petitioner.

As a rule, immigration officials scrutinize applications that are based on claimed family relationships, especially marriage relationships, of an alien to a U.S. citizen or Permanent Resident with a special degree of attention and carefulness. The belief prevalent among immigration officials, is that this category of immigrant visas is the most abused of all immigrant visa classifications, and that many aliens enter into "sh am" m arr i ages w ith U.S. c it izens or perm anent res idents w ith the sole intent of g a in ing el ig ib il ity for imm igr ant v is a through su ch a rel at ion but w ithout a genu ine intent ion to m a int a in the m ar it al rel at ionsh ip.

Hen ce, if the interv iew ing consul ar off icer should, even remotely, feel that the ex istence of a close f am ily rel at ionsh ip you cl a im (s ay, as between one spouse to another, or a p arent and a ch ild, or one brother or s ister to another. et c) is in any w ay not cred ible, you c an rest assured th at th is w ill be one are a of intense interest and quest ioing the consul ar off icer w ill con centr ate on. If, for ex ample, you are in a m arr i age rel at ionsh ip s itu at ion and h ad m arr ied wh ile tempor ar ily in the Un ited St ates, you should gener ally expe ct to be quest ioned closely by the interv iew ing off icer reg ard ing wh at your <u>pre con ce ived intent ion</u> m ight h ave been at the t ime of your last entry into the U.S. as a non-imm igr ant. And you should, in th at event, be prep ared to answer quest ions and to present cred ible ev iden ce suff ic ient to conv in ce the consul ar (or INS) personnel th at the m arr i age w as leg it im ate and w as not entered into fr audulently just so th at you c an g a in el ig ib il ity for an imm igr ant v is a. You'll be asked quest ions wh ich are intended to ver ify th at you and your U.S. spouse truly intended to est abl ish a l ife together in a bon a-f ide m ar it al relationship at the t ime th at you entered into the m arr i age.

For a helpful insight, you'll find reproduced on p. 172-3 a Questionnaire used by consular and immigration officials in interviews and investigations in which a major concern is to determine the bona - fides (the honesty or legitimacy) of a marriage. (See, also, Ch apter 4, section D and E (pp.35-40), and Ch apter 3, p.30 for more on the problem areas involved in est abl ish ing bon a f ide m ar it al and other f am ily rel at ionsh ips for imm igr at ion purposes.)

Perh aps, at th is po int there c an be no more f itt ing word of adv ice or w isdom for the would-be v is a interv iewee th an th at very aptly offered by C. J ames Cooper, a veter an expert who h as been through s cores of v is a interv iews in the course of h is profess ion al dut ies as an imm igr at ion l awyer: "Wh atever you do, never let the other s ide see you get a l ittle nervous when de al ing w ith government off ic i als. Th is is norm al. But remember, imm igr at ion off ic i als are l aw enfor cement personnel and h ave been c arefully tr a ined in the art of inverv iew ing fore ign n at ion als. They h ave been t aught th at, gener ally, persons who appe ar to be nervous , ill at e ase, who persp ire, h ave swe aty p alms and do not m ake d ire ct eye cont act, m ay be h iding someth ing. Imm igr at ion off ic i als are susp ic ious of anyone who appe ars to be upt ight. Although it is underst and able why a person would be nervous and full of anx iety under the s crut in iz ing eyes of an imm igr at ion or consul ar off icer, you w ill be more su ccessful if you underst and the pro cess and know wh at to expe ct. Therefore, your composure and m anner isms when de al ing w ith an imm igr at ion or consul ar off icer are very import ant. Although you should not a ct as though you know everyth ing or be too conf ident, **you should try to be relaxed and appear to be as believable as possible. The impression you make may be the deciding factor on whether or not your visa will be granted*.**

F in ally, upon the con clus ion of the v is a interv iew, if the consul ar off icer approves your v is a appl ic at ion on the spot (and, assum ing th at a v is a number under your preference category is immed i ately av a il able at the t ime), the consul ar off icer m ay inform you there and then of its approv al; the off icer w ill usu ally st amp your p assport w ith a not at ion of the type of (imm igr ant) visa gr anted you, to serve as your tempor ary "GREEN CARD" for the me ant ime. Often t imes, however, you w ill be informed of the v is a de cision through the m a il. There after, when you are ready to tr avel, you m ay apply for entry into the U.S. at a des ign ated port of entry ("STEP 8" below).

step 8: SO, YOU HAVE OBTAINED YOUR VISA. JUST HOW DO YOU GET ACTUALLY ADMITTED INTO THE U.S.?.

(Turn to Chapter 9, at pp. 155-160, "Entering the United States...,)" for the full procedures).

step 9: EVEN WITH A VISA IN HAND, YOU CAN STILL BE "EXCLUDED" FROM ENTRY INTO THE U.S., OR BE "DEPORTED" AFTER ENTRY. HERE ARE SOME REMEDY POINTERS.

Turn to Chapter 9, at pp.155-160 "Entering the United States........." , especially sections D thru. H. thereof, at pp.156-160).

step 10: YOU CAN CHANGE YOUR STATUS FROM "NONIMMIGRANT" TO "IMMIGRANT" WHILE YOU'RE LIVING IN THE U.S. HERE'S HOW.

(This issue is essentially applicable and relevant only to an alien in a non-immigrant classification. However, for the reader's information, see Chapter 10 (pp.161-171) for the full procedures).

THE NEW YORK TIMES, SUNDAY, FEBRUARY 24, 1980

SPOTLIGHT

He Gets Visas for the Famous

By SUSAN HELLER ANDERSON

LONDON — Well-heeled, well-educated and wanting a piece of America, hundreds of thousands of foreign business executives, professionals, skilled workers and heavy investors emigrate annually to the United States. In contrast to the impoverished or persecuted refugees who have historically flocked to American shores, they sport Savile Row suits and Vuitton luggage.

On hand to help them through the complicated entry process is a fast-growing group of legal professionals — the immigration lawyers. More than 1,200 attorneys are engaged solely in this specialty, which until five years ago was all but ignored in law schools.

One immigration lawyer is Richard D. Fraade of Beverly Hills and — since early this year — London. Attorney for some of the world's most prominent would-be Americans, Mr. Fraade is believed to be the first of the lawyers to open an office in London, the scene of much immigration activity. The United States Embassy's visa office on Grosvenor Square is the world's busiest and expects to issue a million visas in fiscal 1980, a 30 percent increase over 1979.

Under American law, every visiting alien must have a visa. About 80 percent of the visas issued here are for tourists and present little problem. The rest go to persons who want to work, either temporarily or permanently, and these people must enter a lengthy and complicated process that can take months and often years. The immigration lawyer finds ways to facilitate this process.

Parts of the immigration system are fraught with scandal and red tape. Some lawyers have mastered it by skirting the law, but no such charges have been made against Mr. Fraade and Embassy officials here say that immigration lawyers can perform a useful service.

"When Elton John comes to the U.S., he needs a temporary work permit," Mr. Fraade explained. "He's not going to queue up on Grosvenor Square." Of the more than 500 active clients on Mr. Fraade's books in Beverly Hills 90 percent are European.

Mr. Fraade's services have been employed by Roger Vadim, the film director, Joe Bugner, the boxer, Diana Dors, the actress, musicians Oscar Peterson and the Little River Band, Columbia Pictures, the University of Southern California, model agencies run by Eileen Ford, Wilhelmina and Johnny Casablancas, and virtually all of the toney French restaurants in Los Angeles. He has engineered temporary work permits for dozens of servants to the stars. Other clients are large employers of skilled workers, such as the California-based aircraft and silicon chip industries.

Describing himself as a "Europhile and Anglophile in particular," Mr. Fraade attires himself in English pin stripes and shirts bought from the international peacocks' shop, Turnbull and Asser. "I'm a suitoholic," he confessed. Having descended from Russian immigrants "of the pushcart variety," and having lived abroad, he said, helps him to identify with his clients. Shortly after he was born in Oklahoma City in 1942 his parents moved to New York, then, after the war, to Düsseldorf. "That gave me the introduction to Europe that marked me," said Mr. Fraade. The family later went West and Mr. Fraade was graduated from the University of California at Los Angeles. He attended Brooklyn Law School. "When I graduated in 1968 immigration law was not taught," he recalled.

"To stay out of the Army I taught school in Bedford Stuyvesant," he said, "then went into the special prosecutor's office under New York State Attorney General Louis Lefkowitz in 1970. Meanwhile, I continued traveling to Europe."

"Through friends I met girls coming to New York who wanted to work as models," he said. He moonlighted by shepherding their visa applications through the Labor and Justice Departments. In 1975 he returned to California, passed the bar and set up the immigration department for a large law firm. He started his own practice last August in Beverly Hills.

Last month he placed a discreet ad in the London Financial Times announcing the opening of his London office. He got enough responses to indicate there was a potential market here for his services. "Coming to England is a logical extension of what's been happening in my practice," he said.

"I charge a flat fee," Mr. Fraade said, "from $3,000 to $7,500 depending on the case. The lower figure is more usual. I also try to do some pro bono work taking immigrant cases for no fee." In London the fee is slightly higher.

For immigrant visas, priority is given to relatives of United States citizens. Only two categories apply to immigrants wishing to work who have no American relatives. The sixth-preference category — skilled and semiskilled workers — has a backlog of six to eight months. The third preference — professionals, scientists and artists — has no backlog. "Vadim is clearly third preference," Mr. Fraade said. "But a top chef? The law's not so clear." Some 90 percent of his clients seeking permanent residency are in the third- or sixth-preference categories and his job is often to convince visa officers of the validity of their claims. "Here the advocacy role can be helpful," said Alan Gise, United States consul general here.

Investors, however, are not given preference and, because the flow of immigrants is now so heavy that quotas are often filled by the preference categories alone, prospects are dim. Mr. Fraade has a solution.

On his latest trip he saw a client in Frankfurt whom he described as a top German industrialist. "He's convinced Europe is in a state of moral, economic and political decay and that Russia will take over. He won't make any more capital investments in Europe," Mr. Fraade said. "He wants to emigrate to America, the last bastion of capital enterprise. The structuring of a business affiliate lets him come on an E-2 Treaty-Investor visa — the next best thing to a green card." A "green card," which is in fact blue and white, is a permanent resident's permit.

Consular officials admit to mixed feelings about immigration lawyers but concede that, for corporations and investors in particular, they are useful. "The system is set up so no one should require a lawyer," Mr. Gise noted. "But in practice if you are an investor the immigration lawyer prepares the papers, oversees the transfer of funds, sees that requirements are met." Mr. Fraade has a client who wants to set up a subsidiary in California, which requires incorporation in that state. While his Beverly Hills office begins the incorporation procedure his brother Robert, in London, gathers the personal documents necessary for the client's visa, perhaps saving months.

Robin Laurance

Richard D. Fraade, immigration lawyer

EXPLANATORY NOTE (to illustrate 3rd and 6th Preference Cases used in the Manual)

1. Please take note that the sample petition Form I-140 reproduced and used here for illustrative purposes (pp. 126-7) , has long been superseded by a revised edition which is now currently in use as of June 1986 (see pp.123-5). However, we still employ the old, outdated form here for illustration, because of the fact that the petition of Mr. Arun (Doe) to be discussed here, concerns the same case and the same alien whose <u>actual</u> case has been used to illustrate the filing procedures for various other types of visa in this manual, courtesy of C. James Cooper, Jr., the Denver, Colorado immigration lawyer and specialist. As noted earlier in the preceding section, the names, personal and business addresses, and other identifying information of sorts have been deleted on these sample forms and documentations,merely out of concern to protect the privacy of the parties involved.

2. In this specific case, which, you should be reminded, is a true actual case previously processed, the alien, originally an Indian national from New Delhi therein, had first entered the U.S. on an F-1 student visa in August 1983. After having received a Master's Degree in Computer and Information Science and had some practical training, the alien got a job offer from a company in Fort Collins, Colorado, for a position as a Software and Development Engineer, a <u>temporary</u> position, which then meant that he needed an H-1 (temporary worker) visa. The alien's prospective employers filed a petition for an H-1 Visa for the alien, Form I-129B. (See samples of illustrative Form I-129B on pp. 83-5, 88-90, 99-101) Then, at the same time, since in this particular instance the alien was perfectly "in status" as a student at the time, the alien was qualified to file, and filed Form I-506 from .within the U.S. to change his status from his non-immigrant F-1 student status, to the non-immigrant H-1 (temporary worker) status. (See a sample Form I-506 on pp. 103 .) The application was granted and the alien's status changed to H-1 status. Then, subsequently, the alien's Colorado-based employer decided they needed his services <u>permanently</u>; the employer then started the process for securing permanent residence for the alien.

3. Since the alien's educational and work experience apparently qualified him for the **3rd Preference immigrant visa, first, the employer needed to apply for a certification** from the Department of Labor **(Labor Certification)** stating that there was a shortage of qualified, able, willing and available U.S. workers for the specific position in question; the employer employed and was granted this certification. (See Chap. 8, especially Section E at p.141; for labor certification procedures, generally; sample labor certification application form for Mr. Arun (Doe), Form ETA 750A & B, are reproduced on pp.129-132,and sample letter from the U.S. Department of Labor approving certification, is reproduced on p. 133 .) **Second,** at the same time, immediately after receiving the Labor Certification (i.e., <u>no later than</u> 60 days of receiving that), the employer **filed also the Form I-140 visa petition** with the Immigration Service to classify the alien under the 3rd (it could also have been the 6th) preference visa category.(Sample Form I-140 for Mr. Arun (Doe's) case is reproduced on pp. 126-7.)

4. And third, at the same time the I-140 petition was filed, the alien himself (he's formally called the "beneficiary" of the petition) also filed an Application to Adjust his Status to that of a permanent resident, **Form I-485,** attaching thereto various supporting documents - the employer's letters of offer of employment (seepp. 128 & 134), the Biographic Data Form G-325A' (see a blank copy of this form on p.110), certified copies of his college degrees and diplomas, fingerprints, photographs, medical examination reports, alien's Arrival-Departure Record, Form I-94, his approved Labor Certification notification letter (see copy on p. 133) and the underlying documentations on which it was granted, etc. (See sample of Mr. Arun (Doe's) Form I-485 on pp.135-6).

5. Finally, note that, in short, the procedure followed in the above situation (as in all such situations) is similar to the **ADJUSTMENT OF STATUS** process set forth in Chap. 10 of the manual, pp.161-17). Note, also, that with respect to the 6th Preference category job positions, you may not <u>simultaneously</u> file an Application to Adjust Status to Permanent Resident (Form I-485) at the same time that you file the Form I-140 petition. The reason this is so is that the 6th preference is generally noted for having chronic backlogs of visa numbers; and inasmuch as the rule is that an alien is <u>not</u> eligible to adjust his/her status in the U.S. if there is a backlog of visa numbers in the particular preference involved, you would have to designate in the petition (paragraph 18 of the current form at P.124) an American Consulate abroad closest to your residence to which your visa case should be sent for processing upon approval of the petition.

Form I-130
U.S. Department of Justice (INS)
Petition for Alien Relative

OMB No. 1115-0054

P. 1 of 3 pgs.

DO NOT WRITE IN THIS BLOCK — FOR EXAMINING OFFICE ONLY

Case ID#	Action Stamp	Fee Stamp
A#		
G-28 or Volag #		

(handwritten note, stamped diagonally) FORM IS SELF-EXPLANATORY. FIRST, CAREFULLY READ THE INSTRUCTIONS ACCOMPANYING THE FORM, BEFORE COMPLETING FORM.

Section of Law:
- ☐ 201 (b) spouse
- ☐ 201 (b) child
- ☐ 201 (b) parent
- ☐ 203 (a)(1)
- ☐ 203 (a)(2)
- ☐ 203 (a)(4)
- ☐ 203 (a)(5)

AM CON: _____

REMARKS:

Petition was filed on _____ (priority date)
- ☐ Personal Interview
- ☐ Pet .☐ Ben. "A" File Reviewed
- ☐ Field Investigations
- ☐ 204 (a)(2)(A) Resolved
- ☐ Previously Forwarded
- ☐ Stateside Criteria
- ☐ I-485 Simultaneously
- ☐ 204 (h) Resolved

Leave Blank

A. Relationship ☑

1. The alien relative is my:
☐ Husband/Wife ☐ Parent ☐ Brother/Sister ☐ Child

2. Are you related by adoption?
☐ Yes ☐ No

3. Did you gain permanent residence through adoption?
☐ Yes ☐ No

B. Information about you

1. Name (Family name in CAPS) (First) (Middle)

2. Address (Number and Street) (Apartment Number)

(Town or City) (State/Country) (ZIP/Postal Code)

3. Place of Birth (Town or City) (State/Country)

4. Date of Birth (Mo/Day/Year)

5. Sex ☐ Male ☐ Female

6. Marital Status ☐ Married ☐ Widowed ☐ Single ☐ Divorced

7. Other Names Used (including maiden name)

8. Date and Place of Present Marriage (if married)

9. Social Security number

10. Alien Registration Number (if any)

11. Names of Prior Husbands/Wives

12. Date(s) Marriage(s) Ended

13. If you are a U.S. citizen, complete the following:
My citizenship was acquired through (check one)
- ☐ Birth in the U.S.
- ☐ Naturalization
  Give number of certificate, date and place it was issued

  _____

- ☐ Parents
  Have you obtained a certificate of citizenship in your own name?
  ☐ Yes ☐ No
  If "Yes," give number of certificate, date and place it was issued

14a. If you are a lawful permanent resident alien, complete the following:
Date and place of admission for, or adjustment to, lawful permanent residence, and class of admission:

14b. Did you gain permanent resident status through marriage to a United States citizen or lawful permanent resident? ☐ Yes ☐ No

C. Information about your alien relative

1. Name (Family name in CAPS) (First) (Middle)

2. Address (Number and Street) (Apartment Number)

(Town or City) (State/Country) (ZIP/Postal Code)

3. Place of Birth (Town or City) (State/Country)

4. Date of Birth (Mo/Day/Year)

5. Sex ☐ Male ☐ Female

6. Marital Status ☐ Married ☐ Widowed ☐ Single ☐ Divorced

7. Other Names Used (including maiden name)

8. Date and Place of Present Marriage (if married)

9. Social Security number

10. Alien Registration Number (if any)

11. Names of Prior Husbands/Wives

12. Date(s) Marriage(s) Ended

13. Has your relative ever been in the U.S.?
☐ Yes ☐ No

14. If your relative is currently in the U.S., complete the following:
He or she last arrived as a (visitor, student, stowaway, without inspection, etc.)

Arrival/Departure Record (I-94) Number   Date arrived (Month/Day/Year)

Date authorized stay expired, or will expire as shown on Form I-94 or I-95

15. Name and address of present employer (if any)

Date this employment began (Month/Day/Year)

16. Has your relative ever been under immigration proceedings?
☐ Yes ☐ No Where _____ When _____
☐ Exclusion ☐ Deportation ☐ Rescission ☐ Judicial Proceedings

(stamped diagonally: SAMPLE)

INITIAL RECEIPT	RESUBMITTED	RELOCATED		COMPLETED		
		Rec'd	Sent	Approved	Denied	Returned

Leave Blank

Form I-130 (Rev. 02-28-87) N

16. List husband/wife and all children of your relative (if your relative is your husband/wife, list only his or her children).

Name	Relationship	Date of Birth	Country of Birth

17. Address in the United States where your relative intends to reside

(Number and Street)   (Town or City)   (State)

18. Your relative's address abroad

(Number and Street)   (Town or City)   (Province)   (Country)

19. If your relative's native alphabet is other than Roman letters, write his/her name and address abroad in the native alphabet:

(Name)   (Number and Street)   (Town or City)   (Province)   (Country)

20. If filing for your husband/wife, give last address at which you both lived together: From   To

(Name)   (Apt. No.)   (Town or City)   (State or Province)   (Country)   (Month)   (Year)   (Month)   (Year)

21. Check the appropriate box below and give the information required for the box you checked:

☐ Your relative will apply for a visa abroad at the American Consulate in _____
          (City)   (Country)

☐ Your relative is in the United States and will apply for adjustment of status to that of a lawful permanent resident in the office of the Immigration and Naturalization Service at _____ . If your relative is not eligible for adjustment of status, he or she will
          (City)   (State)
apply for a visa abroad at the American Consulate in _____
          (City)   (Country)

(Designation of a consulate outside the country of your relative's last residence does not guarantee acceptance for processing by that consulate. Acceptance is at the discretion of the designated consulate.)

D. Other Information

1. If separate petitions are also being submitted for other relatives, give names of each and relationship.

2. Have you ever filed a petition for this or any other alien before?   ☐ Yes   ☐ No
If "Yes," give name, place and date of filing, and result.

Warning: The INS investigates claimed relationships and verifies the validity of documents. The INS seeks criminal prosecutions when family relationships are falsified to obtain visas.

Penalties: You may, by law be imprisoned for not more than five years, or fined $250,000, or both, for entering into a marriage contract for the purpose of evading any provision of the immigration laws and you may be fined up to $10,000 or imprisoned up to five years or both, for knowingly and willfully falsifying or concealing a material fact or using any false document in submitting this petition.

Your Certification

I certify, under penalty of perjury under the laws of the United States of America, that the foregoing is true and correct. Furthermore, I authorize the release of any information from my records which the Immigration and Naturalization Service needs to determine eligibility for the benefit that I am seeking.

(The Petitioner signs here)   *Enter today's date*   *Your phone #*

Signature X_____   Date _____   Phone Number _____

Signature of Person Preparing Form if Other than Above

I declare that I prepared this document at the request of the person above and that it is based on all information of which I have any knowledge.

(Print Name)   (Address)   (Signature)   (Date)

Volag Number _____   G-28 ID Number _____

FORM
I-130

SAMPLE SHEET

NOTICE TO PERSONS FILING FOR SPOUSES IF MARRIED LESS THAN TWO YEARS

Pursuant to section 216 of the Immigration and Nationality Act, your alien spouse may be granted conditional permanent resident status in the United States as of the date he or she is admitted or adjusted to conditional status by an officer of the Immigration and Naturalization Service. Both you and your conditional permanent resident spouse are required to file a petition, Form I-751, Joint Petition to Remove Conditional Basis of Alien's Permanent Resident Status, during the ninety day period immediately before the second anniversary of the date your alien spouse was granted conditional permanent residence.

Otherwise, the rights, privileges, responsibilities and duties which apply to all other permanent residents apply equally to a conditional permanent resident. A conditional permanent resident is not limited to the right to apply for naturalization, to file petitions in behalf of qualifying relatives, or to reside permanently in the United States as an immigrant in accordance with the immigration laws.

> **Failure to file Form I-751, Joint Petition to Remove the Conditional Basis of Alien's Permanent Resident Status, will result in termination of permanent residence status and initiation of deportation proceedings.**

NOTE: You must complete Items 1 through 6 to assure that petition approval is recorded. Do not write in the section below item 6.

1. **Name of relative** (Family name in CAPS)   (First)   (Middle)

2. **Other names used by relative** (Including maiden name)

3. **Country of relative's birth**   4. **Date of relative's birth** (Month/Day/Year)

5. **Your name** (Last name in CAPS)   (First)   (Middle)   6. **Your phone number**

Action Stamp

SECTION
- [ ] 201 (b)(spouse)
- [ ] 201 (b)(child)
- [ ] 201 (b)(parent)
- [ ] 203 (a)(1)
- [ ] 203 (a)(2)
- [ ] 203 (a)(4)
- [ ] 203 (a)(5)

DATE PETITION FILED

- [ ] STATESIDE CRITERIA GRANTED

SENT TO CONSUL AT:

Leave Blank

CHECKLIST [✓]

Have you answered each question?
Have you signed the petition?
Have you enclosed:

- [ ] The filing fee for each petition?
- [ ] Proof of your citizenship or lawful permanent residence?
- [ ] All required supporting documents for each petition?

If you are filing for your husband or wife have you included:

- [ ] Your picture?
- [ ] His or her picture?
- [ ] Your G-325A?
- [ ] His or her G-325A?

Relative Petition Card
Form I-130A (Rev. 02-28-87) N

Current
FORM I-140

U.S. Department of Justice
Immigration and Naturalization Service (INS)

-123- (FRONT PG)

Petition for Prospective Immigrant Employee

p. 1 of 3 pgs.
OMB # 1115-0061

Leave blank

DO NOT WRITE IN THIS BLOCK

Case ID#

A#

G-28 or Volag#

Petition was filed on:

_____
(Priority Date)

Action Stamp

FORM IS SELF-EXPLANATORY. FIRST, CAREFULLY READ THE INSTRUCTIONS ACCOMPANYING THE FORM, BEFORE COMPLETING IT.

Fee Stamp

Petition is approved for status under section:
☐ 203(a)(3)   ☐ 203(a)(6)
Section 212(a)(14) certification
☐ Attached   ☐ Sched. A, Group _____

A. Information about this petition

This petition is being filed for a:
☑ 3rd Preference Immigrant
☐ 6th Preference Immigrant

(See instructions for definitions and check one block only)

B. Information about employer

1. **Name** (Family name in CAPS) (First) (Middle)   or   (Company Name)

2. **Address** (Number and Street)

(Town or City)   (State/Country)   (ZIP/Postal Code)

3. **Address where employee will work** (If different)
(Number and Street)

(Town or City)   (State/Country)   (ZIP/Postal Code)

4. **Employer is:**   ☐ an organization   ☐ a permanent resident
(check one)   ☐ a U.S. citizen   ☐ a nonimmigrant

5. **Social Security Number**   or   **IRS employer ID number**

6. **Alien Registration Number** (if any)

7. **Description of Business** (Nature, number of employees, gross and net annual income, date established) (If employer is an individual, state occupation and annual income).

8. **Have you ever filed a visa petition for an alien employee in this same capacity?**
☐ Yes   ☐ No   (If Yes, how many?)

9. **Are you and the prospective employee related by birth or marriage?**
☐ Yes   ☐ No

10. **Are separate petitions being filed at this time for other aliens?**
☐ Yes   ☐ No   (If Yes, list names)

11. **Title and salary of position offered**

12. **Is the position permanent?**   ☐ Yes   ☐ No
13. **Is the position full-time?**   ☐ Yes   ☐ No
14. **Is this a newly-created position?**   ☐ Yes   ☐ No
(If No, how long has it existed?)

C. Information about prospective employee

1. **Name** (Family name in CAPS) (First)   (Middle)

2. **Address** (Number and Street)   (Apartment Number)

(Town or City)   (State/Country)   (ZIP/Postal Code)

3. **Place of Birth** (Town or City)   (State/Country)

4. **Date of Birth**   5. **Sex**   6. **Marital Status**
(Mo/Day/Yr)   ☐ Male   ☐ Married   ☐ Single
☐ Female   ☐ Widowed   ☐ Divorced

7. **Other names used** (including maiden name)

8. **Profession or occupation and years held**

9. **Social Security Number**   10. **Alien Registration Number** (if any)

11. **Name and address of present employer** (Name)

(Number and Street)

(Town or City)   (State/Country)   (ZIP/Postal Code)

12. **Date employee began present employment**

13. **If employee is currently in the U.S., complete the following:**
He or she last arrived as a (visitor, student, exchange alien, crewman, stowaway, temporary worker, without inspection, etc.)

Arrival/Departure Record (I-94) Number   Date arrived (Month/Day/Year)

Date authorized stay expired, or will expire as shown on Form I-94 or I-95

14. **Has a visa petition ever been filed by or on behalf of this person?**
☐ Yes   ☐ No   (If Yes, explain)

INITIAL RECEIPT	RESUBMITTED	RELOCATED		COMPLETED		
		Rec'd	Sent	Approved	Denied	Returned

Leave blank

Form I-140 (Rev. 06-23-86) Y

SAMPLE SHEET

I-140

C. (continued) Information about prospective employee

15. List husband/wife and all children of prospective employee

Name	Relationship	Date of Birth	Country of Birth	Present Address

16. Employee's address abroad

(Number and Street)   (Town or City)   (Province)   (Country)

17. If your employee's native alphabet is other than Roman letters, write his/her name and address abroad in the native alphabet:

(Name)   (Number and Street)   (Town or City)   (Province)   (Country)

18. Check the appropriate box below and give the information required for the box you checked:

☐ The employee will apply for a visa abroad at the American Consulate in _____
(City)   (Country)

☐ The employee is in the United States and will apply for adjustment of status to that of a lawful resident in the office of the Immigration and Naturalization Service at _____ . If the employee is not eligible for adjustment of status, he or she will apply
(City)   (State)

for a visa abroad at the American Consulate in _____
(City)   (Country)

Warning: The INS investigates employment experience. If the INS finds that employment experience is false, the application is denied and the person responsible for providing false information may be criminally prosecuted.

Penalties: You may, by law, be fined up to $10,000, imprisoned up to five years, or both, for knowingly and willfully falsifying or concealing a material fact or using any false document in submitting this petition.

Your Certification

This petition may only be filed by one of the following:

I am   ☐ the employer

☐ the prospective employee (only allowed for 3rd preference)

☐ a person filing on behalf of and authorized by the prospective employee (only allowed for 3rd preference)

I certify, under penalty of perjury under the laws of the United States of America, that the foregoing is true and correct. Furthermore, I authorize the release of any information from my records which the Immigration and Naturalization Service needs to determine eligibility for the benefit that I am seeking.

Print Name _(Enter)_____   Title _____

Signature X_____   Date _____   Phone Number _____

Signature of Person Preparing Form if Other than Above

I declare that I prepared this document at the request of the person above and that it is based on all information of which I have any knowledge.

X

_____   _____   _____   _____
(Print Name)   (Address)   (Signature)   (Date)

G-28 ID Number _____

Volag Number _____

I-140

FORM I-140

SAMPLE SHEET

NOTE: Fill in items 1-5 below so that your petition approval can be recorded by the Immigration Service.

1. Name of Prospective Employee	A#
2. Other Names Used	
3. Country of Birth	4. Date of Birth
5. Name of Prospective Employer	

Action Stamp	Section	Priority Date
	☐ 203(a)(3)	
	☐ 203(a)(6)	Filing Date
		Sent to Consul at:

Leave Blank

Petition for Prospective Immigrant Employee
Form I-140 (Rev. 06-23-86) Y

CHECKLIST [✓]

☐ Have you filled in all the information required on the form?

☐ Have you signed the form?

☐ Have you enclosed the Labor Department forms ETA 7-50 A & B?

☐ Have you enclosed all other required documents?

☐ Have you enclosed the fee?

FORM I-140

(Good till June 1986; after that date, you must use new Form sampled pp.123-5)

UNITED STATES DEPARTMENT OF JUSTICE

IMMIGRATION AND NATURALIZATION SERVICE

OMB No. 1115-0061
Approval expires 4-86

PETITION TO CLASSIFY PREFERENCE STATUS OF ALIEN ON BASIS OF PROFESSION OR OCCUPATION

DATE RECEIVED	FEE STAMP

NOTE: Refer to "Explanatory Note" on p.119, especially paragraphs No. 4 & 3

TO THE SECRETARY OF STATE

Petition was filed on ___

Beneficiary's file number: A ___

Petition is approved for status under section ☐ 203(a)(3). ☐ 203(a)(6)

☐ Sec. 212(a)(14) certification attached.

☐ Blanket Sec. 212(a)(14) certification issued.

DATE OF ACTION DD	
DISTRICT	

REMARKS

PETITIONER IS NOT TO WRITE ABOVE THIS LINE

Read this form and the attached instructions carefully before filling in petition

Petition is hereby made to classify the status of the alien beneficiary named herein for issuance of an immigrant visa as ("X" one)

☒ **A THIRD PREFERENCE IMMIGRANT** — An alien who is a member of the professions, or who because of his exceptional ability in the sciences or arts will substantially benefit prospectively the national economy, cultural interests or welfare of the United States, and whose services are sought by an employer. (Sec. 203(a)(3), Immigration and Nationality Act, as amended.)

☐ **A SIXTH PREFERENCE IMMIGRANT** — An alien who is capable of performing skilled or unskilled labor, not of a temporary or seasonal nature, for which a shortage of employable and willing persons exists in the United States. (Sec. 203 (a) (6), Immigration and Nationality Act, as amended.)

(If you need more space to answer fully any questions on this form, use a separate sheet, identify each answer with the number of the corresponding question and sign and date each sheet.)

PART I — INFORMATION CONCERNING ALIEN BENEFICIARY

1. NAME (Last, in CAPS) (First) (Middle)	2. ALIEN REGISTRATION NO. (If any)	3. PROFESSION OR OCCUPATION
▓▓▓ Arun NMN		Development Engineer

4. OTHER NAMES USED (Married woman give maiden name)	5. DO NOT WRITE IN THIS SPACE	6. DOES BENEFICIARY INTEND TO ENGAGE IN HIS/HER PROFESSION OR OCCUPATION IN THE
None		UNITED STATES ☒ YES ☐ NO. IF "NO," EXPLAIN.

7. PLACE OF BIRTH (Country)	8. DATE OF BIRTH (Month, day, year)	
United Kingdom	9/17/61	

9. NAME OF PETITIONER (Full name of organization; if petitioner is an individual give full name with last in capital letters) ▓▓▓ Co., Colorado ▓▓ Operation	10. NUMBER OF YEARS OF BENEFICIARY'S EXPERIENCE (If none explain why.)
11. CITY AND STATE IN THE UNITED STATES WHERE ALIEN INTENDS TO RESIDE Ft. Collins, Colorado (City) (State)	Approx. 1 year

12. BENEFICIARY'S PRESENT ADDRESS (Number and street) (City or town) (State or province) (Country) (ZIP Code, if in U.S.)

▓▓▓ .Shields Street, ▓▓▓ , Ft.Collins,Colorado ▓▓▓

13. TO YOUR KNOWLEDGE, HAS A VISA PETITION EVER BEEN FILED BY OR ON BEHALF OF THIS BENEFICIARY BASED ON HIS/HER PROFESSION OR OCCUPATION? ☐ Yes ☒ No. If "Yes," give name of each petitioner and date and place of filing.

14. IF BENEFICIARY IS NOW IN THE U.S. (a) HE/SHE LAST ARRIVED ON **8/20/83**
(Month) (Day) (Year)

AS A **F-1**
(Visitor, student, exchange alien, temporary worker, crewman, stowaway, etc.) (b) SHOW DATE BENEFICIARY'S STAY EXPIRED OR WILL EXPIRE AS

SHOWN ON FORM I—94 OR I—95 (Show latest date) **12-2-87 H-1**

15. BENEFICIARY'S SPOUSE (If Unmarried, State Unmarried)	NAME (Last name) (First name) (Middle name) (Maiden name, if married woman) Not married			
	COUNTRY OF BIRTH	DATE OF BIRTH	PRESENT ADDRESS (No. and Street) (City or town) (State or Province) (Country)	

16. BENEFICIARY'S CHILDREN (If None State None)	NAME (Show M or S for married or single)	M.S.	BIRTHDATE	COUNTRY OF BIRTH	ADDRESS
	None				

Form I-140 (Rev. 5-5-83)N

RECEIVED	TRANS. IN	RET'D·TRANS. OUT	COMPLETED

—OVER— ➜

17. "X" THE APPROPRIATE BOX BELOW AND FURNISH THE INFORMATION REQUIRED FOR THE BOX MARKED.

☐ Alien will apply for a visa abroad at the American Consulate in _____
                                                                    (City in foreign country)   (Foreign country)

☒ Alien is in the United States and will apply for adjustment of status to that of a lawful permanent resident in the office of the Immigration and

Naturalization Service at ____Denver____   ____Colorado____   If the application for adjustment of status is denied
                              (City)   (State)

                                    Calgary, Alberta, Canada

the alien will apply for a visa abroad at the American Consulate in _____
                                                                    (City in foreign country)   (Foreign country)

PART II—INFORMATION CONCERNING EMPLOYER AND POSITION

18. NAME OF PETITIONER (Full name of organization, if petitioner is an individual give full name with last in capital letters)   TELEPHONE NUMBER

██████████ Co., Colorado ██████████ Operation   303-██████████

19. ADDRESS   (Number and street)   (Town or city)   (State)   (ZIP code)

██████████ Harmony Road, Ft. Collins, Colorado ██████

20. PETITIONER IS (X one)

☐ U.S. CITIZEN   ☐ PERMANENT RESIDENT ALIEN ("A" NUMBER _____)   ☐ NONIMMIGRANT   ☒ ORGANIZATION

21. NET ANNUAL INCOME   22. WILL BENEFICIARY BE EMPLOYED AT THE ABOVE ADDRESS? ☒ YES ☐ NO. IF "NO," GIVE ADDRESS
Excess of $6 Billion   WHERE THE ALIEN WILL WORK.

23. DO YOU DESIRE AND INTEND TO EMPLOY THE BENEFICIARY   ☒ YES ☐ NO.

24. HAVE YOU EVER FILED A VISA PETITION FOR AN ALIEN BASED ON PROFESSION OR OCCUPATION? ☐ YES ☐ NO. IF "YES," HOW
     MANY SUCH PETITIONS HAVE YOU FILED?

25. ARE SEPARATE PETITIONS BEING SUBMITTED AT THIS TIME FOR OTHER ALIENS? ☐ YES ☒ NO. IF "YES," GIVE NAME OF EACH ALIEN.

26. THE FOLLOWING DOCUMENTS ARE SUBMITTED WITH THIS PETITION AND ARE MADE A PART THEREOF.

Labor Certification and attached documents showing alien's qualifications for
third preference status;
Employer's offer of employment letter;
Employer's latest annual report

PART III—CERTIFICATION OF PETITIONER OR AUTHORIZED REPRESENTATIVE

27. This petition was prepared by: ("X" one) ☐ the petitioner ☐ another person

If petition was prepared by another person, Item 29 below must also be completed.

The petition may be completed and signed only by the following persons:

In third preference cases — by the beneficiary or by the person filing the petition on the beneficiary's behalf. If the petition is being filed by a person on
behalf of the alien beneficiary, Item 28 below must be completed by that person.

In sixth preference cases — by the employer who desires and intends to employ the beneficiary. If the employer is an organization, the petition must be completed and signed
by a high level officer or employee of the organization.

- -

I certify, under penalty of perjury under the laws of the United States of America that the foregoing is true and corre██ ██████████████

Executed on (date) ___12/31/85___   Signature _Marlene_ ██████████

If petitioner is an organization, print full name and title of authorized official who is signing petition in behalf of organization:

Name and Title ___Marlene ██████___   Personnel Representative   Date ___12/31/85___

28. DECLARATION OF PERSON FILING PETITION FOR THIRD PREFERENCE ON BEHALF OF ALIEN BENEFICIARY

I declare that I have been reque██████████ by the alien beneficiary to file this petition on his (her) behalf.

Marlene ██████   ██████ Harmony Road Ft.Collins   12/31/85
(Signature)   (Address—Number, Street, City, State and ZIP Code)   (Date)

29. SIGNATURE OF PERSON PREPARING FORM, IF OTHER THAN PETITIONER

I declare that this document was prepared by me at the request of the petitioner and is based on all information of which I have any knowledge

[signature]   999 Eighteenth St. Denver, CO   12/31/85
(Signature)   (Address—Number, Street, City, State and ZIP Code)   (Date)

TO PETITIONER: DO NOT FILL IN THIS BLOCK — FOR USE OF IMMIGRATION OFFICER

a. Corrections numbered ( ) to ( ) were made by me or at my request.

                                                          (Date)   (City)

     (Signature of petitioner or authorized member of petitioner's organization)   (Title)

b. The person whose signature appears immediately above was interviewed under oath and affirmed all allegations contained herein.

     (Date)   (City)   (Signature and Title)

(End of Form)

S A M P L E S H E E T

EMPLOYER LETTER IN SUPPORT OF H-1 PETITION

COLORADO ███████ OPERATION
███████ Harmony Road, Fort Collins, Colorado ██████ Telephone 303 ████

NOTE: See "Explanatory Note" on p.119

November 20, 1985

TO: U.S. Immigration and Naturalization Service

RE: Mr. Arun ██████

Dear Sirs:

We write this letter in support of our H-1 application on behalf of Mr. Arun ██████.

██████ Company is one of the largest U.S. electronics companies, employing 84,000 employees worldwide in research, development, manufacture, and sales of a broad line of electronic test equipment used in commercial and industrial application. ██████ ranks in the top 20 of all U.S. corporations in terms of export dollars.

The United States and HP are in great need of computer scientists highly trained in the areas of computer networking and operating systems. The lack of sufficient networking has been claimed by many in our industry as being the primary reason for the current slump in the computer industry. From our market research, we have found the lack of sufficient networking to be the biggest limiter to the success of our computer products.

For the past two years we have conducted aggressive recruiting and training programs aimed at filling our needs for computer scientists highly trained in networking and operating systems. We have not been successful; in 1984 we fell ten people short of our target and in 1985 we have fallen 5 short of our target.

In December of 1984 we found Mr. Arun ██████. Mr. ██████ met our qualifications extremely well. He obtained his masters degree in Computer Science from Ohio State University where he studied and researched networking and operating systems. Since that time he has become a key contributor on a very important networking product which will allow multi-vendor computer communication. His continued involvement in this project if required in order to avoid significant delays.

During this year it has become obvious to us that Arun has specific skills that are needed to accomplish the projects planned for development by Colorado ██████. Therefore, we are petitioning for an H-1 visa for him. We are requesting this for temporary employment 2 years beyond the approval of this application. During the temporary assignment, it is our hope that Arun will be able to train or recruit individuals to carry on these responsibilities.

Thank you for your time and consideration for this petition.

Sincerely,

███████

Sandy L. ██████
R&D Section Manager

SAMPLE

FORM ETA 750A

U.S. DEPARTMENT OF LABOR — -129-
Employment and Training Administration

APPLICATION FOR ALIEN EMPLOYMENT CERTIFICATION

IMPORTANT: READ CAREFULLY BEFORE COMPLETING THIS FORM
PRINT legibly in ink or use a typewriter. If you need more space to answer questions on this form, use a separate sheet. Identify each answer with the number of the corresponding question. SIGN AND DATE each sheet in original signature.

To knowingly furnish any false information in the preparation of this form and any supplement thereto or to aid, abet, or counsel another to do so is a felony punishable by $10,000 fine or 5 years in the penitentiary, or (18 U.S.C. 1001).

PART A. OFFER OF EMPLOYMENT

1. Name of Alien (Family name in capital letter, First, Middle, Maiden)

▓▓▓ Arun

2. Present Address of Alien (Number, Street, City and Town, State ZIP Code or Province, Country)

▓▓▓ Shields ▓▓▓, Fort Collins, Colorado, ▓▓▓, USA

3. Type of Visa (If in U.S.)

F-1 (practical training)

The following information is submitted as evidence of an offer of employment.

4. Name of Employer (Full name of organization)

▓▓▓., Colorado ▓▓▓ Operation

5. Telephone (Area Code and Number)

303-▓▓▓

6. Address (Number, Street, City or Town, Country, State, ZIP Code)

▓▓▓ Harmony Road, Fort Collins, Colorado, ▓▓▓

NOTE: Refer to "Explanatory Note" on p. 119, esp. paragraph 3

7. Address Where Alien Will Work (if different from Item 6)

N/A

8. Nature of Employer's Business Activity	9. Name of Job Title	10. Total Hours Per Week		11. Work Schedule (Hourly)	12. Rate of Pay	
		a. Basic	b. Overtime		a. Basic	b. Overtime
Manufacturer of computers, peripherals & software, electronic equip. etc.	Development Engineer (Software)	40	--	8:00 a.m. 5:00 p.m.	$ 30,240 per year	$ -- per hour

13. Describe Fully the Job to be Performed (Duties)

Architect, design and develop advanced networking and operating system software on UNIX-based technical workstations, using C language; apply strong academic background in operating systems, networking, UNIX and C language to 2K NCSS (2,000 Non-Commented Source Statement) operating system and networking-related software products.

D.O.T. 003.167-062

14. State in detail the MINIMUM education, training, and experience for a worker to perform satisfactorily the job duties described in Item 13 above.

EDUCATION (Enter number of years)	Grade School	High School	College	College Degree Required (specify)
	6	6	6	Bachelor and Master
				Major Field of Study Computer Science

TRAINING	No. Yrs.	No. Mos.	Type of Training

EXPERIENCE	Job Offered		Related Occupation		Related Occupation (specify)
	Number				
	Yrs.	Mos.	Yrs.	Mos.	
	0				

15. Other Special Requirements

16. Occupational Title of Person Who Will Be Alien's Immediate Supervisor

Project Manager

17. Number of Employees Alien will Supervise

0

ENDORSEMENTS (Make no entry in section - for government use only)

Date Forms Received

L.O.: MAY 0 2 1985	S.O.
R.O.: 6/19/85	N.O.
Ind. Code 35	Occ. Code 003167062
	Occ. Title Development Engineer

CERTIFICATION

PURSUANT TO THE PROVISIONS OF SECTION 212(A) (14) OF THE IMMIGRATION AND NATIONALITY ACT AS AMENDED I HEREBY CERTIFY THAT THERE ARE NOT SUFFICIENT U.S. WORKERS AVAILABLE AND THE EMPLOYMENT OF THE ABOVE WILL NOT ADVERSELY AFFECT THE WAGES AND WORKING CONDITIONS OF WORKERS IN THE U.S. SIMILARLY EMPLOYED.

10/8/85 Charles G. Vigil

Replaces MA 7-50A, B and C (Apr. 1970 edition) which is obsolete.

ETA 750 (Oct. 1979)

-OVER- ➡

18. COMPLETE ITEMS ONLY IF JOB IS TEMPORARY			19. IF JOB IS UNIONIZED *(Complete)*	
a. No. of Openings To Be Filled By Aliens Under Job Offer	b. Exact Dates You Expect To Employ Alien		a. Number of Local	b. Name of Local
	From	To		
N/A				c. City and State

20. STATEMENT FOR LIVE-AT-WORK JOB OFFERS   *(Complete for Private Household Job ONLY)*

a. Description of Residence		b. No. Persons Residing at Place of Employment				c. Will free board and private room not shared with anyone be provided?	*("X" one)*
("X" one)	Number of Rooms	Adults	Children		Ages		☐ YES ☐ NO
☐ House			BOYS				
☐ Apartment	N/A		GIRLS				

21. DESCRIBE EFFORTS TO RECRUIT U.S. WORKERS AND THE RESULTS. *(Specify Sources of Recruitment by Name)*

Employer has and will conduct such recruitment efforts as are appropriate and normal to the industry and customary for this company.

22. Applications require various types of documentation. Please read PART II of the instructions to assure that appropriate supporting documentation is included with your application.

23. EMPLOYER CERTIFICATIONS

By virtue of my signature below, I HEREBY CERTIFY the following conditions of employment.

a. I have enough funds available to pay the wage or salary offered the alien.

b. The wage offered equals or exceeds the prevailing wage and I guarantee that, if a labor certification is granted, the wage paid to the alien when the alien begins work will equal or exceed the prevailing wage which is applicable at the time the alien begins work.

c. The wage offered is not based on commissions, bonuses, or other incentives, unless I guarantee a wage paid on a weekly, bi-weekly or monthly basis.

d. I will be able to place the alien on the payroll on or before the date of the alien's proposed entrance into the United States.

e. The job opportunity does not involve unlawful discrimination by race, creed, color, national origin, age, sex, religion, handicap, or citizenship.

f. The job opportunity is not:

(1) Vacant because the former occupant is on strike or is being locked out in the course of a labor dispute involving a work stoppage.

(2) At issue in a labor dispute involving a work stoppage.

g. The job opportunity's terms, conditions and occupational environment are not contrary to Federal, State or local law.

h. The job opportunity has been and is clearly open to any qualified U.S. worker.

24. DECLARATIONS

DECLARATION OF EMPLOYER ➤ Pursuant to 28 U.S.C. 1746, I declare under penalty of perjury the foregoing is true and correct.

SIGNATURE	DATE
	4-22-85

NAME *(Type or Print)*	TITLE
▮▮▮ Company By Marlene ▮▮▮	Personnel Representative

AUTHORIZATION OF AGENT OF EMPLOYER ➤ *I HEREBY DESIGNATE the agent below to represent me for the purposes of labor certification and I TAKE FULL RESPONSIBILITY for accuracy of any representations made by my agent.*

SIGNATURE OF EMPLOYER	DATE
	4-22-85

NAME OF AGENT *(Type or Print)*	ADDRESS OF AGENT *(Number, Street, City, State, ZIP Code)*
C. James Cooper, Jr.	999 Eighteenth Street, Suite 3220 Denver, Colorado 80202

-OVER- ➡

PART B. STATEMENT OF QUALIFICATIONS OF ALIEN

FOR ADVICE CONCERNING REQUIREMENTS FOR ALIEN EMPLOYMENT CERTIFICATION: *If alien is in the U.S., contact nearest office of Immigration and Naturalization Service. If alien is outside U.S., contact nearest U.S. Consulate.*

IMPORTANT: READ ATTACHED INSTRUCTIONS BEFORE COMPLETING THIS FORM.

...nt legibly in ink or use a typewriter. If you need more space to fully answer any questions on this form, use a separate sheet. Identify each answer with the number of the corresponding question. Sign and date each sheet.

1. Name of Alien (Family name in capital letters)	First name	Middle name	Maiden name
████████	Arun	NMN	N/A

2. Present Address (No., Street, City or Town, State or Province and ZIP Code   Country)

████. Shields, ███, Fort Collins, Colorado, ████████ USA

3. Type of Visa (If in U.S.)
F-1 (prac. training)

4. Alien's Birthdate (Month, Day, Year)	5. Birthplace (City or Town, State or Province)	Country	6. Present Nationality or Citizenship (Country)
9/17/61	Southampton	United Kingdom	Indian

7. Address in United States Where Alien Will Reside

████████. Shields, Rd, Fort collins, Colorado, ████, USA

8. Name and Address of Prospective Employer If Alien has Job offer in U.S.

████████████., Colorado ████████ Operation

9. Occupation in which Alien Is Seeking Work
Development Engineer (Software)

10. "X" the appropriate box below and furnish the information required for the box marked

a. ☐ Alien will apply for a visa abroad at the American Consulate in ──────▶	City in Foreign Country	Foreign Country

b. ☒ Alien is in the United States and will apply for adjustment of status to that of a lawful permanent resident in the office of the Immigration and Naturalization Service at ──────▶	City	State
	Denver	Colorado

11. Names and Addresses of Schools, Colleges and Universities Attended (Include trade or vocational training facilities)	Field of Study	FROM Month	FROM Year	TO Month	TO Year	Degrees or Certificate Received
Ohio State University Columbus, Ohio	Computer Science	Sept.	1983	Dec.	1984	M.S.
Indian Inst. of Tech. Kanpur, India	Computer Science	Aug.	1978	May	1983	B.Tech.
Colvin Talugdars Coll. Lucknow, India	Maths, Science	July	1975	July	1977	Graduated

SPECIAL QUALIFICATIONS AND SKILLS

12. Additional Qualifications and Skills Alien Possesses and Proficiency in the use of Tools, Machines or Equipment Which Would Help Establish if Alien Meets Requirements for Occupation in item 9.

N/A

13. List Licenses (Professional, Journeyman, etc.)

N/A

14. List Documents Attached Which are Submitted as Evidence that Alien Possesses the Education, Training, Experience, and Abilities Represented

Diploma - school transcript

Endorsements	DATE REC. DOL
	O.T. & C.

(Make no entry in this section — FOR Government Agency USE ONLY)

(Items continued on next page)

-OVER- ──────▶

15. WORK EXPERIENCE. *List all jobs held during past three (3) years. Also, list any other jobs related to the occupation, seeking certification as indicated in item 9.*

a. NAME AND ADDRESS OF EMPLOYER

████████████████co., Colorado ████████ Operation
████. Harmony Road, Fort Collins, Colorado, █████

ε OF JOB	DATE STARTED Month Year	DATE LEFT Month Year	KIND OF BUSINESS
Development Engineer (Software)	Jan. 1985	to present	Design & Mfg. of computers, etc.

DESCRIBE IN DETAILS THE DUTIES PERFORMED, INCLUDING THE USE OF TOOLS, MACHINES, OR EQUIPMENT	NO. OF HOURS PER WEEK
Creates software; responsible for assignments involving research, development, or design of new products or maintaining existing products, which includes development of standards, algorithms, architectures, specifications, languages, networking, as well as problem analysis, planning, scheduling, establishing operating data, and conducting tests.	40

b. NAME AND ADDRESS OF EMPLOYER

NAME OF JOB	DATE STARTED Month Year	DATE LEFT Month Year	KIND OF BUSINESS

DESCRIBE IN DETAIL THE DUTIES PERFORMED, INCLUDING THE USE OF TOOLS, MACHINES, OR EQUIPMENT	NO. OF HOURS PER WEEK

...ME AND ADDRESS OF EMPLOYER

NAME OF JOB	DATE STARTED Month Year	DATE LEFT Month Year	KIND OF BUSINESS

DESCRIBE IN DETAIL THE DUTIES PERFORMED, INCLUDING THE USE OF TOOLS, MACHINES, OR EQUIPMENT	NO. OF HOURS PER WEEK

16. DECLARATIONS

DECLARATION OF ALIEN ►   *Pursuant to 28 U.S.C. 1746, I declare under penalty of perjury the foregoing is true and correct.*

SIGNATURE OF ALIEN ██████████████████	DATE 3/19/85

AUTHORIZATION OF AGENT OF ALIEN ►   *I hereby designate the agent below to represent me for the purposes of labor certification and I take full responsibility for accuracy of any representations made by my agent.*

SIGNATURE OF ALIEN ██████████████	DATE 3/19/85

ε OF AGENT *(Type or print)* C. James Cooper, Jr.	ADDRESS OF AGENT *(No., Street, City, State, ZIP Code)* 999 Eighteenth Street, Suite 3220 Denver, Colorado 80202

(End of Form)

U.S. Department of Labor

Employment and Training Administration
1961 Stout Street
Denver, Colorado 80294

(DOL'S LETTER APPROVING CERTIFICATION)

NOTE: Refer to "Explanatory Note" on p. 119, especially Item 3

Date: October 18, 1985

TO:Mr. C. James Cooper, Jr.
Attorney at Law for the Alien
999 - 18th Street, Suite #3220
Denver, Colorado 80202

Employer: ████████ Co.
          Fort Collins, Colorado

NAME OF THE ALIEN
██████, ARUN

OCCUPATION OF THE ALIEN
Development Engineer (Software)

DATE APPLICATION SUBMITTED
FOR PROCESSING
5/2/85

The U. S. Department of Labor has made a determination on your Application for Alien Employment Certification pursuant to Title 20, Code of Federal Regulations, Section 656.21, and as required by the Immigration and Nationality Act, as amended.

Form ETA 7-50A has been certified, and it is enclosed with the supporting documents.

All enclosures should be submitted to the Immigration and Naturalization Service District Office for consideration of the alien's application for adjustment of status (I-485), or with your petition (Form I-140).

Sincerely,

Becky Stuart

for CHARLES C. VIGIL
Certifying Officer

Attachments

cc: State Agency for State of Colorado;
     Alien - Mr. Arun ██████, ████████ Shields, ███, Ft. Collins, CO ███

SAMPLE SHEET

EXPLANATORY NOTE

This is Certification from the Department of Labor which is used by the Department of Labor office in Denver. Although the form is dated October 18, 1985, the alien's priority date for a visa number was May 2, 1985, which was the date the Application for Labor Certification was received by the State agency.

EMPLOYER'S OFFER OF EMPLOYMENT LETTER

(Name of Employing company)

COLORADO ████████ OPERATION
3404 East Harmony Road, Fort Collins, Colorado 80525, Telephone 303 226-3800

December 31, 1985

NOTE: See "Explanatory Note" on P. 119.

To: U.S. Immigration and Naturalization Service

RE: Mr. Arun ████████

Dear Sirs:

We write this letter in support of our application for permanent residency on behalf of Mr. Arun ████████.

████████ Company is one of the largest U.S. electronics companies, employing 84,000 employees worldwide in research, development, manufacture, and sales of a broad line of electronic test equipment used in commercial and industrial application. ████████ ranks in the top 20 of all U.S. corporations in terms of export dollars.

The United States and ██ are in great need of computer scientists highly trained in the areas of computer networking and operating systems. The lack of sufficient networking has been claimed by many in our industry as being the primary reason for the current slump in the computer industry. From our market research, we have found the lack of sufficient networking to be the biggest limiter to the success of our computer products.

For the past two years we have conducted aggressive recruiting and training programs aimed at filling our needs for computer scientists highly trained in networking and operating systems. We have not been successful; in 1984 we fell ten people short of our target and in 1985 we have fallen 5 short of our target. Considering this, we obtained labor certification from the Department of Labor for this position.

In December of 1984 we found Mr. Arun ████████. Mr. ████████ met our qualifications extremely well. He obtained his masters degree in Computer Science from Ohio State University where he studied and researched networking and operating systems. Since that time he has become a key contributor on a very important networking product which will allow multi-vendor computer communication. His continued involvement in this project if required in order to avoid significant delays.

Upon approval by the Immigration Service, the company intends to hire Mr. Chandra permanently at a yearly salary of $32,640.00.

Thank you for your time and consideration for this petition.

Sincerely,

████████ COMPANY

Thomas J. ████████
Personnel Section Manager

TJL/lb

Sample FORM I-485   APPLICATION FOR STATUS AS PERMANENT RESIDENT

(FEE STAMP)

	File No.

APPLICATION FOR THE BENEFITS OF SECTION:

☐ Sec. 208(b), I&N Act   ☐ Sec. 245, I&N Act

☐ Sec. 214(d), I&N Act   ☐ Sec. 249, I&N Act

☐ Sec. 13, Act of 9/11/57

(DO NOT WRITE ABOVE THIS LINE) (SEE INSTRUCTIONS BEFORE FILLING IN APPLICATION. IF YOU NEED MORE SPACE TO ANSWER FULLY ANY QUESTION ON THIS FORM, USE A SEPARATE SHEET AND IDENTIFY EACH ANSWER WITH THE NUMBER OF THE CORRESPONDING QUESTION. FILL IN WITH TYPEWRITER OR PRINT IN BLOCK LETTERS IN INK.)

1. I hereby apply for the status of a lawful permanent resident alien on the following basis: (Check one of the boxes below.)

A. ☐ As a person granted asylum under Section 207(a) to whom an immigrant visa is immediately available (Section 208(b), I&N Act). (No fee required.)

B. ☐ As a person who entered the U.S. with a visa issued to me as the fiancee or fiance of a U.S. citizen whom I married within 90 days after my entry, or as a child of such fiancee or fiance (Sec. 214(d), I&N Act).

C. ☐ As a former government official, or as a member of the immediate family of such official (Section 13, Act of September 11, 1957).

D. ☒ As a person to whom an immigrant visa is immediately available, other than one described above (Section 245, I&N Act).

E. ☐ As a person who has resided in the United States continuously since prior to July 1, 1924 (Section 249, I&N Act).

F. ☐ As a person who has resided in the United States continuously since a date on or after July 1, 1924, but before June 30, 1948 (Section 249, I&N Act).

G. ☐ As a motion to reopen or to reconsider my case in deportation proceedings before an immigration judge. (The fee for this request is $50.00.)

2. My name is (family in capital letters) (First Given) (Middle)
Arun   NMN

3. Sex: ☒ Male   ☐ Female   Phone number: 303-████

4. I reside in the United States at: (c/o) (Apt. No.) (No. and Street)
████. Shields Street, ████

(City) (State) (ZIP Code)
Fort Collins, Colorado, ████

5. Have you ever applied before for permanent resident status in the U.S.? ☒ No   ☐ Yes
(If "Yes", give the date and place of filing and final disposition.)

6. My file number is A-

7. I am a citizen of (Country): India

8. Date of Birth (Month) (Day) (Year): 9/17/61

9. Place of Birth (City or Town): Southampton   (County, Province, or State) (Country): United Kingdom

10. Name as appears on nonimmigrant document (Form I-94)
Arun ████

I last arrived in the United States at the port of (City and State)
New York, New York

on (Month) (Day) (Year): 8/20/83

by (Name of vessel or other means of travel): Pan Am

as a (visitor, student, crewman, parolee, etc.): F-1

I ☒ was   ☐ was not inspected.

11. My nonimmigrant visa, number ████ was issued by the United States Consul at (City) (Country)
New Delhi, India

on (Month) (Day) (Year): 7/8/83

12. I am ☒ single   ☐ married   ☐ divorced   ☐ widowed

13. I have been married ___0___ times, including my present marriage, if now married. (If you are now married give the following.)

a. Number of times my husband or wife has been married
N/A

b. Name of husband or wife (Wife give maiden name)

c. My husband or wife resides ☐ with me ☐ apart from me at Address (Apt. No.) No. & Street (Town or City) (Province or State) (Country)

14. a. I have _0_ sons or daughters as follows: (Complete all columns as to each son or daughter; if living with you state "with me" in last column; otherwise give city and state or country of son's or daughter's residence).

Name	Sex	Place of Birth	Date of Birth	Now living at
N/A				

b. The following members of my family are also applying for permanent resident status:

None

OVER

Form I-485 (Rev. 5-5-83) N

NOTE: Refer to the "Explanatory Notes" on P. 119, especially paragraphs 4 & 5 thereof. See also, P. 174.

	RECEIVED	TRANS IN	RETD TRANS OUT	COMPLETED

(Continues) ⟶

15. I list below all organizations, societies, clubs, and associations, past or present, in which I have held membership in the United States or a foreign country, and the periods and places of such membership. (*If you have never been a member of any organization, state "None".*)

None

16. I ☒ have not ☐ have been treated for a mental disorder, drug addiction or alcoholism. (If you have been, explain.)

17. I ☒ have not ☐ have been arrested, convicted or confined in a prison. (If you have been, explain.)

18. I ☒ have not ☐ have been the beneficiary of a pardon, amnesty, rehabilitation decree, other act of clemency or similar action. (If you have been, explain.)

19. APPLICANTS FOR STATUS AS PERMANENT RESIDENTS MUST ESTABLISH THAT THEY ARE ADMISSIBLE TO THE UNITED STATES. EXCEPT AS OTHERWISE PROVIDED BY LAW, ALIENS WITHIN ANY OF THE FOLLOWING CLASSES ARE NOT ADMISSIBLE TO THE UNITED STATES AND ARE THEREFORE INELIGIBLE FOR STATUS AS PERMANENT RESIDENTS:

Aliens who have committed or who have been convicted of a crime involving moral turpitude (does not include minor traffic violations); aliens who have been engaged in or who intend to engage in any commercialized sexual activity; aliens who are or at any time have been, anarchists, or members of or affiliated with any Communist or other totalitarian party, including any subdivision or affiliate thereof; aliens who have advocated or taught, either by personal utterance, or by means of any written or printed matter, or through affiliation with an organization, (i) opposition to organized government, (ii) the overthrow of government by force or violence, (iii) the assaulting or killing of government officials because of their official character, (iv) the unlawful destruction of property, (v) sabotage, or (vi) the doctrines of world communism, or the establishment of a totalitarian dictatorship in the United States; aliens who intend to engage in prejudicial activities or unlawful activities of a subversive nature; aliens who have been convicted of violation of any law or regulation relating to narcotic drugs or marihuana, or who have been illicit traffickers in narcotic drugs or marihuana; aliens who have been involved in assisting any other aliens to enter the United States in violation of law; aliens who have applied for exemption or discharge from training or service in the Armed Forces of the United States on the ground of alienage and who have been relieved or discharged from such training or service; medical graduates (other than those for whom Relative petitions have been approved) coming principally to perform services as members of the medical profession, unless they have passed Parts I and II of the National Board of Medical Examiners Examination (or an equivalent examination as determined by the Secretary of the Department of Health and Human Services) and who are competent in oral and written English.

Do any of the foregoing classes apply to you? ☒ No   ☐ Yes (*If answer is Yes, explain*)

20. *(COMPLETE THIS BLOCK ONLY IF YOU CHECKED BOX "A", "B", "C", or "D" OF BLOCK 1)*

APPLICANTS WHO CHECKED BOX "A" "B" "C" OR "D" OF BLOCK 1 IN ADDITION TO ESTABLISHING THAT THEY ARE NOT MEMBERS OF ANY OF THE INADMISSIBLE CLASSES DESCRIBED IN BLOCK 10 ABOVE MUST, EXCEPT AS OTHERWISE PROVIDED BY LAW, ALSO ESTABLISH THAT THEY ARE NOT WITHIN ANY OF THE FOLLOWING INADMISSIBLE CLASSES:

Aliens who are mentally retarded, insane, or have suffered one or more attacks of insanity; aliens afflicted with psychopathic personality, sexual deviation, mental defect, narcotic drug addiction, chronic alcoholism or any dangerous contagious disease; aliens who have a physical defect, disease or disability affecting their ability to earn a living; aliens who are paupers, professional beggars or vagrants; aliens who are polygamists or advocate polygamy; aliens who intend to perform skilled or unskilled labor and who have not been certified by the Secretary of Labor (see Instruction 10); aliens likely to become a public charge; aliens who have been excluded from the United States within the past year, or who at any time have been deported from the United States, or who at any time have been removed from the United States at Government expenses; aliens who have procured or have attempted to procure a visa by fraud or misrepresentation; aliens who have departed from or remained outside the United States to avoid military service in time of war or national emergency; aliens who are former exchange visitors who are subject to but have not complied with the two year foreign residence requirement.

Do any of the foregoing classes apply to you? ☒ No   ☐ Yes (*If answer is Yes, explain*)

21. I ☐ do not ☒ do intend to seek gainful employment in the United States. If you intend to seek gainful employment in the United States, state the occupation you intend to follow.

Development Engineer

(End of Form)

FORM
OF 230

FORM APPROVED
O.M.B. No. 47-RO150

OPTIONAL FORM 230 (English) (Rev. 7-79)
DEPT. OF STATE
50230-104

APPLICATION FOR IMMIGRANT VISA AND ALIEN REGISTRATION

INSTRUCTIONS: This form must be filled out in DUPLICATE by typewriter, or if by hand in legible block letters. All questions must be answered, if applicable. Questions which are not applicable should be so marked. If there is insufficient room on the form, answer on separate sheets, in duplicate using the same numbers as appear on the form. Attach the sheets to the forms. DO NOT SIGN this form until instructed to do so by the consular officer. The fee for filing this application for an immigrant visa is $5.00. The fee should be paid in United States dollars or local currency equivalent or by bank draft, when you appear before the consular officer.

WARNING: Any false statement or concealment of a material fact may result in your permanent exclusion from the United States. Even though you should be admitted to the United States, a fraudulent entry could be grounds for your prosecution and/or deportation.

1. Family name **DOE,**   First name **JOHN**   Middle name **JAMES**

2. Other names used or by which known (*If married woman, give maiden name*) **NONE**

3. Full name in native alphabet (*If Roman letters not used*) **NOT APPLICABLE**

4. Date of birth (Day) (Month) (Year) **16 Nov. 1961**	5. Age **30**	6. Place of birth (City or town) **NNEWI** (Province) (Country) **NIGERIA**

7. Nationality **NIGERIA**   8. Sex ☑ Male ☐ Female   9. Marital status ☐ Single (*never married*) ☑ Married ☐ Widowed ☐ Divorced ☐ Separated
Including my present marriage, I have been married .... times.

10. Occupation **Civil Engineer**   11. Present address **3 Nnewi Rd., Nnewi, NIGERIA**

12. Name, address, date and place of birth of wife/husband (*Give maiden name of wife*) **MARY DOLUE**

Date and place of marriage **Onitsha, Nigeria, June 17, 1986**

13. Names, addresses, dates and places of birth of all children. **none**

14. Person(s) named in 12 and 13 who will accompany or follow me to the United States **NONE**

15. Final address in the United States **127 HANCOCK ST. Brooklyn, New York 11217**

16. Person you intend to join (*Give name, address and relationship, if any*) **MARY (DOLUE) DOE - Wife 127 HANCOCK ST. Brooklyn N.Y. 11217**

17. Name and address of sponsoring person or organization (*If different from 16*)

18. Personal description
(a) Color of hair **Black**
(b) Color of eyes **Brown**
(c) Height **5** feet **11** inches
(d) Complexion **Dark**

19. Marks of identification **Scar on left cheek**

20. Purpose in going to the United States **To make home with wife**

21. Length of intended stay (*If permanently, so state*) **Permanently**

22. Intended port of entry **New York**

23. Do you have a ticket to final destination? **Yes**

THIS FORM MAY BE OBTAINED GRATIS AT CONSULAR OFFICES OF THE UNITED STATES OF AMERICA

NSN 7540-00-149-0919

Previous edition not usable

(Continues)—→

OF 230

OPTIONAL FORM 230 (English) (Rev. 7-79)   Page 2

24. Personal financial resources
    (a) Cash ...... $950 (U.S. dollar equivalent)   (c) Real estate (value) ...... None
    (b) Bank deposits ...... $1,520   (d) Other (describe) ...... None

25. Father's name, address, date and place of birth (*If deceased, so state giving year of death*)
    Eddy Doe, died Jan. 1, 1981

26. Mother's maiden name, address, date and place of birth (*If deceased, so state giving year of death*)
    Edna Doe, 2 Egun Rd, Lagos, Nigeria

27. Name, address and relationship of next of kin in home country (*If neither parent is living*)
    Not Applicable

28. List all places of residence for 6 months or more since your sixteenth birthday

City or town	Province	Country	Dates (From-To)	Calling or occupation
Nnewi		Nigeria	1/14/77 - 5/20/81	Student
Onitsha		Nigeria	5/20/81 - 4/10/85	Student
New York		U.S.A	4/11/85 - 5/2/86	Engr. Trainee
Nnewi		Nigeria	5/3/86 Present	Engineer

29. List all organizations you are now or have been a member of or affiliated with since your sixteenth birthday (*Include professional, vocational, social and political organizations*)

Name and address	Dates (From-To)	Type of membership and office held, if any
None		

30. List all languages, including your own, that you can speak, read and write

Language	Speak	Read	Write
Ibo	Yes	Yes	Yes
English	Yes	Yes	Yes

31. Inclusive dates of previous residence in or visits to the United States (*Give type of visa or status*) (*If never, so state*)
    April 11, 1985 to May 2, 1986 - resided in New York (student visa).

32. Have you ever been treated in a hospital, institution or elsewhere for a mental disorder. drug addiction or alcoholism? (*If answer is Yes, explain*)   Yes ☐ No ☑

33. Have you ever been arrested, convicted or confined in a prison, or have you ever been placed in a poorhouse or other charitable institution? (*If answer is Yes, explain*)   Yes ☐ No ☑

34. Have you ever been the beneficiary of a pardon, amnesty, rehabilitation decree, other act of clemency or similar action? (*If answer is Yes, explain*)   Yes ☐ No ☑

35. Have you ever applied for a visa to enter the United States? (*If answer is Yes, state where and when, whether you applied for a nonimmigrant or an immigrant visa and whether the visa was issued or refused*)   Yes ☐ No ☑

36. Have you been refused admission to the United States during the last 12 months? (*If answer is Yes, explain*)   Yes ☐ No ☑

37. Have you ever registered with a draft board under United States Selective Service Laws? (*If answer is Yes, explain*)   Yes ☐ No ☑

38. Have you ever applied for relief from training and service in the United States armed forces or departed from or remained outside the United States to avoid or evade military service? (*If answer is Yes, explain*)   Yes ☐ No ☑

39. Do you intend to enter the United States from Canada, Mexico or an island adjacent to the United States within two years after arrival in Canada, Mexico or such adjacent island? (*If answer is Yes, give the name of the transportation company by which you entered or intend to enter Canada, Mexico or such island*)   Yes ☐ No ☑

(Continues) ➝

OF 230

OPTIONAL FORM 230 (English) (Rev. 7-79)

40. United States laws governing the issuance of visas require each applicant to state whether or not he is a member of any class of individuals excluded from admission into the United States. The excludable classes are described below. You should read carefully the following paragraphs; your understanding of their content and the answers you give the questions that follow will assist the consular officer to reach a decision on your eligibility to receive a visa.

EXCEPT AS OTHERWISE PROVIDED BY LAW, ALIENS WITHIN ANY OF THE
FOLLOWING CLASSES ARE INELIGIBLE TO RECEIVE AN IMMIGRANT VISA:

(a) Aliens who are mentally retarded, insane, or who have suffered one or more attacks of insanity; aliens afflicted with psychopathic personality, sexual deviation, a mental defect, narcotic drug addiction, chronic alcoholism, or any dangerous contagious disease; aliens who have a physical defect, disease or disability affecting their ability to earn a living; aliens who are paupers, professional beggars, or vagrants; aliens convicted of a crime involving moral turpitude or who admit committing the essential elements of such a crime, or who have been sentenced to confinement for at least five years in the aggregate for conviction of two or more crimes; aliens who are polygamists, or who practice or advocate polygamy; aliens who are prostitutes, or who have engaged in, benefited financially from, procured or imported persons for the purpose of prostitution, or who seek entry to the United States to engage in prostitution or other commercialized vice, or any immoral sexual act; aliens who seek entry to perform skilled or unskilled labor and who have not been certified by the Secretary of Labor; and aliens likely to become a public charge in the United States.

Do any of the foregoing classes apply to you? Yes ☐ No ☑ *(If answer is Yes, explain)*

(b) Aliens who seek re-entry within one year of their exclusion from the United States, or who have been arrested and deported from the United States, or removed at Government expense in lieu of deportation, or removed as an alien in distress or as an alien enemy; aliens who procure or attempt to procure a visa or other documentation by fraud or willful misrepresentation; aliens who are not eligible to acquire United States citizenship, or who have departed from or remained outside the United States to avoid United States military service in time of war or national emergency; aliens who have been convicted of violating or for conspiring to violate certain laws or regulations relating to narcotic drugs or marihuana, or who are known or believed to be, or to have been, an illicit trafficker in narcotic drugs or marihuana; aliens seeking entry from foreign contiguous territory or adjacent islands within two years of their arrival therein on a non-signatory carrier; aliens who are unable to read and understand some language or dialect; aliens who, knowingly and for gain, have encouraged or assisted any other alien to enter, or attempt to enter, the United States in violation of law; aliens who are former exchange visitors who have not fulfilled the two-year foreign residence requirement; and aliens who are graduates of foreign medical schools destined to the United States to perform medical services are ineligible for a visa unless they have passed parts I and II of the NBME Exam or an equivalent exam as determined by the Department of Health, Education, and Welfare.

Do any of the foregoing classes apply to you? Yes ☑ No ☐ *(If answer is Yes, explain)*

Applicant overstayed time granted on student visa. Was ordered by the INS to depart; voluntarily departed from New York to Lagos, Nigeria, on 5/2/86, without deportation.

(c) Aliens who are, or at any time have been, anarchists, or members of or affiliated with any Communist or other totalitarian party, including any subdivision or affiliate thereof; aliens who advocate or teach, or who have advocated or taught, either by personal utterance, or by means of any written or printed matter, or through affiliation with an organization, (1) opposition to organized government, (2) the overthrow of government by force and violence, (3) the assaulting or killing of government officials because of their official character, (4) the unlawful destruction of property, (5) sabotage, or (6) the doctrines of world communism, or the establishment of a totalitarian dictatorship in the United States; aliens who seek to enter the United States to engage in prejudicial activities or unlawful activities of a subversive nature; and aliens who during the period beginning on March 23, 1933, and ending on May 8, 1945, under the direction of the Nazi Government of Germany, ordered, incited, assisted or otherwise participated in the persecution of any person because of race, religion, national origin, or political opinion.

Do any of the foregoing classes apply to you? Yes ☐ No ☑ *(If answer is Yes, explain)*

41. Were you assisted in completing this application? *(If answer is Yes, give name and address of person assisting you indicating whether relative, friend, travel agent, attorney or other)*   Yes ☐ No ☑

Name	*Address*	*Relationship*
NOT APPLICABLE		

(Continues) ⟶

OF 230

OPTIONAL FORM 230 (English) (Rev. 7–79)

42. The following documents are submitted in support of this application:

- ☑ Passport
- ☑ Birth certificate
- ☑ Police certificate(s)
- ☑ Marriage certificate
- ☐ Death certificate
- ☐ Divorce decree
- ☐ Military record

- ☑ Evidence of own assets
- ☑ Affidavit of support
- ☐ Offer of employment
- ☑ Medical record(s)
- ☑ Photographs
- ☐ Other (describe)
- ☑ Birth Certificate of Spouse

☐ Birth Certificates of unmarried children under age 21 who will not be immigrating at this time (*list those for whom birth certificates are not available or whose birth certificates are being submitted at this time in connection with a visa application.*)

DO NOT WRITE BELOW THE FOLLOWING LINE
The consular officer will assist you in answering parts 43 and 44

43. I claim to be exempt from ineligibility to receive a visa and exclusion under item .... in part 40 for the following reasons:

212(a)(14)

- ☐ Not Applicable
- ☐ Attached

Beneficiary of Waiver under
- ☐ 212(a)(28)(1)(i)
- ☐ 212(a)(28)(1)(ii)
- ☐ 212(b)(1)
- ☐ 212(b)(2)

- ☐ 212(e)
- ☐ 212(g)
- ☐ 212(h)
- ☐ 212(i)

Leave Blank

44. I claim to be a

☐ .... preference immigrant subject to the numerical limitation for ....

(*foreign state or dependent area*)

- ☐ Special immigrant not subject to limitation
- ☐ Immediate relative of a United States citizen

My claim is based on the following facts:

- ☐ I am (my .... is) the beneficiary of a .... petition.
- ☐ I am a returning resident alien.
- ☐ I derive foreign state chargeability under Section 202(b) through my ....
- ☐ Other (specify)

I understand that I am required to surrender my visa to the United States Immigration Officer at the place where I apply to enter the United States, and that the possession of a visa does not entitle me to enter the United States if at that time I am found to be inadmissible under the immigration laws.

I understand that any willfully false or misleading statement or willful concealment of a material fact made by me herein may subject me to permanent exclusion from the United States and, if I am admitted to the United States, may subject me to criminal prosecution and/or deportation.

I, the undersigned applicant for a United States immigrant visa, do solemnly swear (or affirm) that all statements which appear in this application have been made by me, including the answers to parts 32 through 41 inclusive, and are true and complete to the best of my knowledge and belief. I do further swear (or affirm) that, if admitted into the United States, I will not engage in activities which would be prejudicial to the public interest, or endanger the welfare, safety, or security of the United States; in activities which would be prohibited by the laws of the United States relating to espionage, sabotage, public disorder, or in other activities subversive to the national security; in any activity a purpose of which is the opposition to, or the control, or overthrow of, the Government of the United States, by force, violence, or other unconstitutional means.

I understand all the foregoing statements, having asked for and obtained an explanation on every point which was not clear to me.

You (applicant) sign here in presence of the U.S. Consul or official

X ....

(*Signature of Applicant*)

The relationships claimed in items 12 and 13 verified by documentation submitted to consular officer except as noted:

Subscribed and sworn to before me this .... day of ...., 19...... at ....

....

(*Consular Officer*)

TARIFF ITEM NO. 20

☆ U. S. Government Printing Office: 1979—281-187/5070

(End of Form)

CHAPTER 8

ALIEN LABOUR CERTIFICATION: THE PROCEDURES FOR OBTAINING A CERTIFICATE

As has been repeatedly discussed in various sections of this book (see, for example, pp. 43-5), a key prerequisite often needed by many aliens who seek admission to the United States, especially those who do so on the basis of employment offers or on labour or skills-related grounds, is what is known as an *approved LABOUR CERTIFICATION.* To put it simply, this is a document obtainable from a U.S. Department of Labour administrator, whereby the administrator states that upon his Department's study of the labour market in the given U.S. area, the Department determines ("certifies") that there are no U.S. citizens or Permanent Resident aliens who are able, willing, available and qualified to do the work the alien seeks, and that the alien's acceptance of the job will not displace a U.S. worker or adversely affect his wages or working conditions.

A. "SCHEDULE A" JOBS: THOSE CATEGORIES FOR WHICH LABOUR CERTIFICATION NEED NOT BE APPLIED FOR

As structured by the U.S. Government, there are certain specified occupations about which the U.S. Department of Labour (DOL) has determined that qualified U.S. workers are chronically in short supply—that is, that there are NO sufficient U.S. workers (citizens or permanent resident aliens) who are able, willing, qualified and available to do them. Such occupations are listed under what is called *"SCHEDULE A"* of the Department of Labour's *"Pre-certification" list* of occupations.

HERE IS THE CENTRAL POINT OF RELEVANCE HERE: for those occupations which fall under schedule A, the alien visa applicant or his U.S. employer does NOT have to file separate application for labour certification for them. For such occupations (i.e., Schedule A occupations), aliens qualified for them are said to have a *"blanket" labour certification,* that is, an automatic labour certification, and hence the aliens need *not* themselves personally apply for a labour certification for such occupations nor do they have to show the existence of a U.S. offer of employment. (Another term for such jobs needing no separate certification application, is "pre-certified" jobs).

The reader should be very clear, however, of what is being said here: occupations listed on SCHEDULE A are considered "pre-certified" in one special sense — in the sense that an alien visa applicant who can establish to the satisfaction of the immigration authorities that he (she) is qualified for such an occupation, is viewed as having been granted auomatic ("blanket") labour certification, and so needs not separately or personally apply for a labour certification (nor to show the existence of an offer of employment) before he may proceed to petition for a visa. The point here is that, while the alien claiming qualification for a Schedule A occupation needs not make a separate, specific independent application for a labour certification issuance, he nevertheless will still have to make an application for the particular Schedule A job in question, and, more importantly, demonstrate to the satisfaction of the immigration officials that he fully meets the qualifications for the particular schedule A job. Hence, it should be noted, a particular alien's "pre-certification", or his entitlement to a "blanket" certification under the "Schedule A occupation, is not necessarily "automatic" in the ordinary sense as the alien must first prove his qualification for a Schedule A job to the immigration service (or consular officer) on a case-by-case basis.

Occupations currently designated under Schedule "A" as of this writing (they frequently change),are listed in Table 7 below. As can be seen from that Table, Schedule A occupations are divided into four basic "GROUPS" - Groups 1, 11, 111, and 1v.

TABLE 7
SCHEDULE "A" JOB CLASSIFICATIONS
(No Labour Certification needed)

Group 1:

(a) Alien physicians who are willing to work in areas having a shortage of doctors, as determined by the Secretary of Health and Human Services.

(b) Physical therapists— people who have the equivalent of an American Bachelor's degree and have been licensed by the State where they will be working.

(c) Professional nurses who have passed the appropriate licensing examination and are considered to be registered nurses.

Group II:

Foreign national of exceptional ability and international fame in the sciences or arts (except for aliens in the performing arts), including college and university teachers and internationally famous foreign medical graduates.

Note: To qualify, a person must have a well documented international reputation, and also be a recipient of international prizes and awards in his (her) particular field of specialty and may also include listing in recognized international biographical works bearing eminent practitioners in his particular profession, or in articles appearing in international professional journals, and other documentations, which should be as extensive as possible.

Group III:

Religious workers coming to the United States to take a religious occupation such as preaching or teaching, religious workers with a religious commitment who are coming to the United States to work for nonprofit religious organizations. (Nuns, priests, ministers of recognized religions, ordained clergymen or women, brothers, monks, christian science practitioners, cantors, translators of religious books, etc, fit into this group.)

Group IV:

Managerial or executive personnel (intra-company transferees). This includes:

(a) People who have been admitted to the U.S. in order to work as intra-company transferees and who are currently working in managerial or executive positions with the same international corporation or a subsidiary or affiliate thereof where they were continuously employed abroad for one year before being admitted to the U.S. (See discussion on "L-1" nonimmigrant visa category on pp. 25 & 65)

(b) People who will be engaged in the U.S. in managerial or executive positions with the same international corporation or organizations where they were continuously employed for the previous year.

B. APPLYING FOR "PRE-CERTIFICATION" & "BLANKET" LABOUR CERTIFICATION APPROVAL IN SCHEDULE A OCCUPATIONS

The following is a brief summary of the procedure for assuring labour pre-certification (also called 'automatic' or 'blanket' labour certification) in Schedule A occupation situations:

●The alien must (usually) have first applied for a job with his (her) potential U.S. employer and secured a job offer, or a pre-arrangement or some proof thereof that the employer has a "Schedule A" type position available. (Note that the normal formalities involved in the recruiting of U.S. workers (see pp.147-9) do not apply with respect to Schedule A occupations).

●The U.S. employer completes only Part A of the application form, FORM ETA 750; and the alien completes Part B of the form.

(See pp.129-132 for an illustrative sample of this form. Note that when such Schedule A applications are filed, they are often accompanied by a petition for an immigrant Third or Sixth PREFERENCE classification (pp.43-5) and, in some cases, by an application for ADJUSTMENT of status (pp.161). When that is the case, then attach the applicable application forms and their supporting documents. See "Explanatory Note" on p. 119.)

●All required documentations (most are specified in the instructions on the application Form) are attached to the form, listing the job descriptions, working conditions, the alien's qualifications for the particular job sought, etc. To be attached, also, is proof that the employer has a position of "Schedule A " type available.

●The application forms, and all supporting documents, are forwarded to the Immigration and Naturalization Service (INS) office covering the area where the job is located in the U.S., or, in some very limited cases, to the U.S. consul in the alien's home country. NOTE that this application is not filed with the local Employment Service Office or the U.S. Department of Labour, as is the case in the regular labour certification cases (pp 147-8).

●The INS, upon determining that the alien is fully qualified and able to perform the duties for the Schedule A job, will approve the application, or delay it.

●If approved, then the next step for the alien would be for him to now commence the procedures for applying for an immigrant visa (pp.112; if denied, the alien may do one of three things: either seek another route or basis by which to gain eligibility for an immigrant visa other than a job-related basis (see pp. 34 for other such basis), or, alternatively, request an APPEAL with the Immigration Service (none could be filed when ever the U.S. consul abroad is the party to whom the application is submitted) for a review or reconsideration of the alien's case (see pp. -), or, thirdly, simply have the employer make, at once, a regular labour certification application for the job to the local Employment Service in the U.S. (see pp.147) without having to wait for the regular 6-months waiting period.

(The detailed procedures by which the overwhelming majority of Labour Certification applications are made by or for aliens are outlined in pp.147-9)

C. SCHEDULE "B" JOBS: THOSE JOB CATEGORIES FOR WHICH YOU MAY POSSIBLY NEED A LABOUR CERTIFICATION

To put it simply, **"SCHEDULE B"** occupations are exactly the opposite of the "Schedule A" occupations just discussed above. In other words, this schedule contains occupations about which the U.S. Department of Labour has determined that **there are generally sufficient U.S. workers** who are able, willing, qualified and available to do them. Schedule B normally covers skilled, semi-skilled and unskilled worker, as can be seen from the listing below. HERE'S WHAT IS IMPORTANT ABOUT IT, THOUGH: ordinarily, alien labour certification CANNOT be applied for or granted for Schedule B occupations.

That is the general rule—the "theory" of it all. But wait a minute. Is that the end of the story? Not at all! In practice, you (basically your employer) still may be able to apply and to get labour certification for a Schedule B job—if you have the "right" conditions. **HERE'S THE KEY RULE:** If your prospective U.S. employer can show that he or she has tried exhaustively to obtain a worker for the job involved but without success in finding one, then, in that event, he is permitted to apply for a "waiver" that, in effect, frees him to go ahead and apply for an "affirmative" labour certification for the job. To put it in a different way, *the central key is to be able to make a credible case (or, more accurately, a documented case) that a prospective employer has not been able to find, at the prevailing wages and working conditions, a United States worker for the occupation he seeks to fill!* A prospective U.S. employer able to present such a situation, may apply for a waiver of the general rule regarding Schedule B jobs and, with that, the door is wide open for him to apply for the "affirmative" labour certification for the Schedule B job in question.

What follows below are the jobs currently designated under SCHEDULE B, and their descriptions.

TABLE 8
SCHEDULE "B" JOB CLASSIFICATIONS
(LIST AND DESCRIPTION OF THE JOBS ON SCHEDULE "B")

(1) *"Assemblers"* perform one or more repetitive tasks to assemble components and subassemblies using hand or power tools to mass produce a variety of components, products or equipment. They perform such activities as riveting, drilling, filing, bolting, soldering, spot welding, cementing, gluing, cutting and fitting. They may use clamps or other work aids to hold parts during assembly, inspect or test components, or tend previously set-up or automatic machines.

(2) *"Attendants, Parking Lot"* park automobiles for customers in parking lots or garages and may collect fees based on time span of parking.

(3) *"Attendants (Service Workers such as Personal Service Attendants, Amusement and Recreation Service Attendants)"* perform a variety of routine tasks attending to the personal needs of customers at such places as amusement parks, bath houses, clothing check-rooms, and dressing rooms, including such tasks as taking and issuing tickets, checking and issuing clothing and supplies, cleaning premises and equipment, answering inquiries, checking lists, and maintaining simple records.

(4) *"Automobile Service Station Attendants"* service automotive vehicles with fuel, lubricants, and automotive accessories at drive-in service facilities; may also compute charges and collect fees from customers.

(5) *"Bartenders"* prepare, mix, and dispense alcoholic beverages for consumption by bar customers, and compute and collect charges for drinks.

(6) *"Bookkeepers II"* keep records of one facet of an establishment's financial transactions by maintaining one set of books; specialize in such areas as accounts-payable, accounts-receivable, or interest accrued rather than a complete set of records.

(7) *"Caretakers"* perform a combination of duties to keep a private home clean and in good condition such as cleaning and dusting furniture and furnishings, hallways and lavatories; beating, vacuuming, and scrubbing rugs; washing windows, waxing and polishing floors; removing and hanging draperies; cleaning and oiling furnaces and other equipment; repairing mechanical and electrical appliances; and painting.

(8) *"Cashiers"* receive payments made by customers for goods or services, make change, give receipts, operate cash registers, balance cash accounts, prepare bank deposits and perform other related duties.

(9) *"Charworkers and Cleaners"* keep the premises of commercial establishments, office buildings, or apartment houses in clean and orderly condition by performing, according to a set routine, such tasks as mopping and sweeping floors, dusting and polishing furniture and fixtures, and vacuuming rugs.

(10) *"Chauffeurs and Taxicab Drivers"* drive automobiles to convey passengers according to the passengers' instructions.

(11) *"Cleaners, Hotel and Motel"* clean hotel rooms and halls, sweep and mop floors, dust furniture, empty wastebaskets, and make beds.

(12) *"Clerks, General"* perform a variety of routine clerical tasks not requiring knowledge of systems or procedures such as copying and posting data, proofreading records or forms, counting, weighing, or measuring material, routing correspondence, answering telephones, conveying messages, and running errands.

(13) *"Clerks, Hotel"* perform a variety of routine tasks to serve hotel guests such as registering guests, dispensing keys, distributing mail, collecting payments, and adjusting complaints.

(14) *"Clerks and Checkers, Grocery Stores"* itemize, total, and receive payments for purchases in grocery stores, usually using cash registers; often assist customers in locating items, stock shelves, and keep stock-control and sales-transaction records.

(15) *"Clerk Typists"* perform general clerical work which, for the majority of duties, requires the use of typewriters: perform such activities as typing reports, bills, application forms, shipping tickets, and other matters from clerical records, filing records and reports, posting information to records, sorting and distributing mail, answering phones and similar duties.

(16) *"Cooks—Short Order"* prepare and cook to order all kinds of short-preparation-time foods; may perform such activities as carving meats, filling orders from a steam-table, preparing sandwiches, salads and beverages, and serving meals over a counter.

(17) *"Counter and Fountain Workers"* serve food to patrons at lunchroom counters, cafeterias, soda fountains, or similar public eating places; take orders from customers and frequently prepare simple items, such as dessert dishes; itemize and total checks; receive payment and make change; clean work areas and equipment.

(18) *"Dining Room Attendants"* facilitate food service in eating places by performing such tasks as removing dirty dishes, replenishing linen and silver supplies, serving water and butter to patrons, and cleaning and polishing equipment.

(19) *"Electric Truck Operators"* drive gasoline- or electric-powered industrial trucks or tractors equipped with forklift, elevating platform, or trailer hitch to move and stack equipment and materials in a warehouse, storage yard, or factory.

(20) *"Elevator Operators"* operate elevators to transport passengers and freight between building floors.

(21) *"Floorworkers"* perform a variety of routine tasks in support of other workers in and around such work sites as factory floors and service areas, frequently at the beck and call of others; perform such tasks as cleaning floors, materials and equipment, distributing materials and tools to workers, running errands, delivering messages, emptying containers, and removing materials from work areas to storage or shipping areas.

(22) *"Groundskeepers"* maintain grounds of industrial, commercial, or public property in good condition by performing such tasks as cutting lawns, trimming hedges, pruning trees, repairing fences, planting flowers, and shoveling snow.

(23) *"Guards"* guard and patrol premises of industrial or business establishments or similar types of property to prevent theft and other crimes and prevent possible injury to others.

(24) *"Helpers (any industry)"* perform a variety of duties to assist other workers who are usually of a higher level of competency or expertness by furnishing such workers with materials, tools, and supplies, cleaning work areas, machines and equipment, feeding or offbearing machines, and/or holding materials or tools.

(25) *"Hotel Cleaners"* perform routine tasks to keep hotel premises neat and clean such as cleaning rugs, washing walls, ceilings and windows, moving furniture, mopping and waxing floors and polishing metalware.

(26) *"Household Domestic Service Workers"* perform a variety of tasks in private households, such as cleaning, dusting, washing, ironing, making beds, maintaining clothes, marketing, cooking, serving food, and caring for children or disabled persons. This definition, however, applies only to workers who have had less than one year of documented full-time paid experience in the tasks to be performed, working on a live-in or live-out basis in private households or in public or private institutions or establishments where the worker has performed tasks equivalent to tasks normally associated with the maintenance of a private household. This definition does not include household workers who primarily provide health or instruc-

tional services.

(27) *"Housekeepers"* supervise workers engaged in maintaining interiors of commercial residential buildings in a clean and orderly fashion, assign duties to cleaners (hotel and motel), charworkers, and hotel cleaners, inspect finished work, and maintain supplies of equipment and materials.

(28) *"Janitors"* keep hotels, office buildings, apartment houses, or similar buildings in clean and orderly condition, and tend furnaces and boilers to provide heat and hot water; perform such tasks as sweeping and mopping floors, emptying trash containers, and doing minor painting and plumbing repairs; often maintain their residence at their places of work.

(29) *"Keypunch Operators"*, using machines similar in action to typewriters, punch holes in cards in such a position that each hole can be identified as representing a specific item of information. These punched cards may be used with electronic computers or tabulating machines.

(30) *"Kitchen Workers"* perform routine tasks in the kitchens of restaurants. Their primary responsibility is to maintain work areas and equipment in a clean and orderly fashion by performing such tasks as mopping floors, removing trash, washing pots and pans, transferring supplies and equipment, and washing and peeling vegetables.

(31) *"Laborers, Common"* perform routine tasks, upon instructions and according to set routine, in an industrial, construction or manufacturing environment such as loading and moving equipment and supplies, cleaning work areas, and distributing tools.

(32) *"Laborers, Farm"* plant, cultivate, and harvest farm products, following the instructions of supervisors, often working as members of a team. Their typical tasks are watering and feeding livestock, picking fruit and vegetables, and cleaning storage areas and equipment.

(33) *"Laborers, Mine"* perform routine tasks in underground or surface mines, pits, or quarries, or at tipples, mills, or preparation plants such as cleaning work areas, shoveling coal onto conveyors, pushing mine cars from working faces to haulage roads, and loading or sorting materials onto wheelbarrows.

(34) *"Loopers and Toppers"* (i) tend machines that shear nap, loose threads, and knots from cloth surfaces to give uniform finish and texture, (ii) operate looping machines to close openings in the toes of seamless hose or join knitted garment parts, (iii) loop stitches or ribbed garment parts on the points of transfer bars to facilitate the transfer of garment parts to the needles of knitting machines.

(35) *"Material Handlers"* load, unload, and convey materials within or near plants, yards, or worksites under specific instructions.

(36) *"Nurses' Aides and Orderlies"* assist in the care of hospital patients by performing such activities as bathing, dressing and undressing patients and giving alcohol rubs, serving and collecting food trays, cleaning and shaving hair from the skin areas of operative cases, lifting patients onto and from beds, transporting patients to treatment units, changing bed linens, running errands, and directing visitors.

(37) *"Packers, Markers, Bottlers, and Related"* pack products into containers, such as cartons or crates, mark identifying information on articles, insure that filled bottles are properly sealed and marked, often working in teams on or at end of assembly lines.

(38) *"Porters"* (i) carry baggage by hand or handtruck for airline, railroad or bus passengers, and perform related personal services in and around public transportation environments.

(ii) Keep building premises, working areas in production departments of industrial organizations, or similar sites in clean and orderly condition.

(39) *"Receptionists"* receive clients or customers coming into establishments, ascertain their wants, and direct them accordingly; perform such activities as arranging appointments, directing callers to their destinations, recording names, times, nature of business and persons seen and answering phones.

(40) *"Sailors and Deck Hands"* stand deck watches and perform a variety of tasks to preserve painted surfaces of ships and to maintain lines, running gear, and cargo handling gear in safe operating condition; perform such tasks as mopping decks, chipping rust, painting chipped areas, and splicing rope.

(41) *"Sales Clerks, General"* receive payment for merchandise in retail establishments, wrap or bag merchandise, and keep shelves stocked.

(42) *"Sewing Machine Operators and Hand-Stitchers"* (i) operate single- or multiple-needle sewing machines to join parts in the manufacture of such products as awnings, carpets, and gloves; specialize in one type of sewing machine limited to joining operations; (ii) join and reinforce parts of articles such as garments and curtains, sew button-holes and attach fasteners to such articles, or sew decorative trimmings on such articles, using needles and threads.

(43) *"Stock Room and Warehouse Workers"* receive, store, ship, and distribute materials, tools, equipment, and products within establishments as directed by others.

(44) *"Streetcar and Bus Conductors"* collect fares or tickets from passengers, issue transfers, open and close doors, announce stops, answer questions, and signal operators to start or stop.

(45) *"Telephone Operators"* operate telephone switchboards to relay incoming and internal calls to phones in an establishment, and make connections with external lines for outgoing calls; often take messages, supply information and keep records of calls and charges; often are involved primarily in establishing, or aiding telephone users in establishing, local or long distance telephone connections.

(46) *"Truck Drivers and Tractor Drivers"* (i) drive trucks to transport materials, merchandise, equipment or people to and from specified destinations, such as plants, railroad stations, and offices. (ii) Drive tractors to move materials, draw implements, pull out objects imbedded in the ground, or pull cables of winches to raise, lower, or load heavy materials or equipment.

(47) *"Typists, Lesser Skilled"* type straight-copy material, such as letters, reports, stencils, and addresses, from drafts or corrected copies. They are not required to prepare materials involving the understanding of complicated technical terminology, the arrangement and setting of complex tabular detail or similar items. Their typing speed in English does not exceed 52 words per minute on a manual typewriter and/or 60 words per minute on an electric typewriter and their error rate is 12 or more errors per 5 minute typing period on representative business correspondence.

(48) *"Ushers (Recreation and Amusement)"* assist patrons at entertainment events to find seats, search for lost articles, and locate facilities.

(49) *"Yard Workers"* maintain the grounds of private residences in good order by performing such tasks as mowing and watering lawns, planting flowers and shrubs, and repairing and painting fences. They work on the instructions of private employers.

D. CLASSES OF IMMIGRANTS WHO MAY NEED LABOUR CERTIFICATION

In the first instance, a central point to remember is this: that with perhaps one exception, namely, H-2 temporary worker, labour certification does not apply to any alien or visa category of <u>nonimmigrant</u> classification. It applies only to aliens seeking to become Permanent Residents of the United States —that is, to IMMIGRANT or "GREEN CARD" applicants.

The second point of relevance to remember in this regard is that, by and large, the alien who needs a labour certification should have lacked the other basis for immigrant visa eligibility other than the work-related basis —namely, he shall have lacked the family-oriented, or "special immigrant" or refugee grounds for eligibility (see pp. 34, 42 & 46).

Thirdly, the labour certification process essentially applies only to the THIRD and SIXTH preference categories within the immigrant preference classes (pp.43-5).

To summarize, the following are the classes of aliens needing a labour certification in qualifying for an immigrant visa:

i) Aliens falling under the "IMMIGRANT INVESTOR" classification (pp. 55 above);

ii) Aliens falling under the THIRD PREFERENCE category outlined on pp.43 (member of the professions or persons of exceptional ability in the sciences and the arts);

iii) Aliens falling under the SIXTH PREFERENCE category outlined on pp. 45 (skilled and unskilled workers for which there's shortage in the U.S.); and

iv) Aliens falling under the FOREIGN MEDICAL GRADUATE classes (see pp. 55 above).

E. STEP-BY-STEP PROCEDURES FOR APPLYING FOR AN AFFIRMATIVE LABOUR CERTIFICATION

The following is a summary of the applicable procedures for obtaining an "affirmative" labour certification:

FIRST: The employer-to-be in the U.S. fills out in duplicate the Department of Labour's (DOL'S) FORM ETA 750, Part A, while the alien job applicant fills out Part B of the form. (Pick up this Form free of charge at your state's local Employment Service Office, for which the main offices are listed on pp. 181-2 below, or at U.S. consular offices abroad. Illustrative sample of the form is reproduced on pp.129-132.)

SECOND: The U.S. employer (actual or prospective) submits ("files") the form at no charge, with all necessary supporting documentary evidence fully attached, to the local State Employment Service Office. Include also among the submissions (except if Schedule A or Household domestic jobs are involved) a copy of signed statement by the employer, the POSTED NOTICE (see sample copy on pp.152).

THIRD: The local State Employment Service Office reviews the application and the supporting documents, with particular attention paid to verifying the minimum requirements and wages. If the job appears to the reviewer to be a "Schedule B" type job (this is not applicable to "Schedule A" jobs), the Employment Service will notify the employer that he must advertise the job and try to find a U.S. worker for the position.

Assuming that the application is alright, the Employment Service will write up a job order for the position, assign a "JOB ORDER NUMBER" to it, and list the job with the Service's "Job bank" for 30 days, during which period the Service will try to find a qualified U.S. worker to fill the job. However, if the application is found unacceptable, the Employment Service may return the application to the employer for correction, or for additional documentation or information.

FOURTH: It is possible for an employer to get a "reduction" or a "waiver" permitting him to suspend further recruitment efforts early on in the process. If, for example, you (i.e. the employer) have made sufficient recuitment efforts before you filed the labour application, you can request (by including a letter of request to that effect with the application) that additional recruiting by the Employment Service be reduced. (You will have to supply extensive documentation and other proof (copies of the advertisements, letters of previous experience at recruiting posted notices, etc.) showing that you made sufficient test of the labour market and had no luck in filling the job opening and showing that further recruiting effort on your part is unlikely to locate a qualified U.S. worker. Note that no "reduction" can be made for any job on Schedule B, however).

NOTE: The employer often has an option to try to find a U.S. worker before he files the application with the Employment Service. Nevertheless, he runs the risk that the Employment Service may not accept the recruitment effort as satisfactory, or that he may later be required to advertise the job. This will prolong the processing time.

FIFTH: Should the Employment Service be unsatisfied with the adequacy of the recruitment effort already made by the employer at finding a U.S. worker, it may require further advertising of the job. The employer may be required to advertise in a local newspaper, professional journal, or whatever other medium that is most used for the particular occupation, all within 30 days of the labour application filling date. (To save yourself the expense of possibly having to re-run a job advertisement, it is often advisable to <u>first</u> check with the Employment Service for the requirements).

SIXTH: Upon satisfaction that sufficient U.S. recruitment effort have been made by the employer (recruitment effort does not apply in Schedule A jobs), the Employment Service forwards the labour application, including the employer's report of his recruiting efforts and the supporting documentations thereof, to the Regional Office of the U.S. Department of Labour (DOL) for the area where the job is to be performed.

SEVENTH: The DOL certifying officer reviews the labour application. It may issue a **NOTICE OF APPROVAL** (if the certifying officer is satisfied from the facts of the case that sufficient recruitment efforts had been made, and that no qualified U.S. applicants either did apply or met the minimum qualifications), thereby granting the labour certification. (See samples on pp. 92 & 153)

Alternatively, the DOL's certifying officer may issue a notice that the application is unsatisfactory and spell out the basis on which it is so determined, and allow the said employer a specified amount of time within which to correct the deficiencies named by the certifying officer. The employer may attempt to make such correction of the specified deficiencies by sending a letter and supplying additional documents (a "rebuttal" response) to show why he nevertheless deems it deserving that the labour certification be issued. Now, if the employer's rebutal response adequately corrects or addresses the deficiencies to the certifying officer's satisfaction, a Labour Certification will be issued. If not, the certifying officer will at this point issue a **FINAL DETERMINATION** denying the granting of labour certificate.

EIGHT: If certification is denied, the employer has the right, if he so chooses, (and if he had sent in a rebuttal response on time), to make an **APPEAL** of the "Final Determination" to an Administrative Law Judge of the Department of Labour in Washington D.C. To do this, it will be sufficient if the employer makes a request in writing for a review of the denial detailing his grounds, and sends it by certified mail to the address listed on the Final Determination notice within the time allowed for such an appeal. Be forewarned, however, that such appeals rarely succeed, if ever!

F. POINTERS FOR SUCCESSFULLY APPLYING FOR A LABOUR CERTIFICATION

Certain "practice pointers" (some call it 'trade secrets') that are often better known to lawyers and immigration consultants and other practitioners in the field, may be helpful in enabling the intending U.S. employer or the alien to file a more successful or smoother-running Labour Certificate application.

Among the major ones are the following:

● It cannot be emphasized enough: the crucial key for success in any filing is presentation of *adequate supporting documentations*. Most applications fail or succeed based on this factor. Documentation is required showing that the alien has the necessary training and previous experience to qualify for the job in question: letters and affidavits from former tutors or employers or recognized experts in the field all testifying to the alien's technical training or specialized experience; copies of licenses held; copies of school diplomas and other records received; published materials by or about the alien; copies of advertisements and proof of other recruiting efforts for the job, if any, etc. *In a word, the more massive the documentation you can supply, the better!*

● It's helpful to include in the labour certification application (except for Schedule A or Household Domestic jobs), the following additional documents: a copy of the POSTED NOTICE (see a sample on P. 52), and a copy of the alien's PROOF OF PRIOR EXPERIENCE signed by the employer (see a sample on pp. 86 & 134)

● *Give a lot of advance thought and advance planning to each and every step and requirement involved* in the labour application. For example, think through what the term "job description" should entail in your particular case. As no two jobs or aliens are ever exactly alike, you (and/or the alien) should endeavor to prepare a set of papers, personality profiles, educational, training and job experience, that will be unique for the job being offered. Think of any special attributes possessed or equipment operated by the alien— some skills or knowledge not usually found among U.S. workers, e.g. knowledge of a foreign language, a foreign dance or culture, or the ability to prepare foreign dishes.

●‑ Preferably, seek to fill occupations for which U.S. workers are traditionally not readily available at the "prevailing wages"— live-in domestic workers, welders, or auto mechanics, for example. (The local Employment Service could help with information about a job's "prevailing wages" for your area.)

● In working up the requirements, descriptions and duties of particular jobs or the description for the position you seek to fill, consider consulting the **DICTIONARY OF OCCUPATIONAL TITLES (DOT)** – a widely accepted guide published by the U.S. Department of Labour and generally available in public libraries and at local Employment Service Offices.

● If the job being offered involves a "combination of duties"–that is, if it either calls for two separate job titles in the DOT (e.g. chauffer/mechanic),or calls for duties from two jobs (say, an accountant's position whose duties includes answering the phone and serving as a receptionist)–then, papers must be attached to the application showing why such an arrangement is necessary, a so-called "BUSINESS NECESSITY" letter of justification. A "Business Necessity" letter of explanation should also be attached when the job being offered has a description or requirement significantly different from that found in the DOT. (See illustrative sample copy of a 'combination of duties' letter on p.152. and of a business necessity letter on pp. 91 & 102).

● When the position involved is a Household Domestic Worker title: Note that, as a rule, virtually all present-day labour certification applications for such workers now contain a "live-in" requirement in the employer's job description, for it has become common knowledge that U.S. workers would usually be available to fill such a position when no live-in condition is required.

● The employer's recruitment effort should include whatever normal and usual methods that are used to find workers for the position involved: advertisement in professional, trade or ethnic publication, depending on the nature of the job involved; listing among associates and employment agencies, newspaper advertising (required in almost all cases), and if such job is unionized and the union is a customary source of jobs for workers, then an arrangement may have to be made with the union for it to refer applicants.

● A very wise practice idea is to consult with and discuss the job description, wage offer, and your plans for recruiting with the local Employment Service – even before you ever start anything. This way, you will be able to get an official guidance on what would constitute an approvable recruiting effort or methods, the methods by which to advertise, and so on. It could possibly save you a lot of unnecessary expenses or wasted efforts down the road!

● Finally, if you should receive the DOL's NOTICE OF FINDING and it appears to you (from the seriousness or weight of the evidence outlined thereof) that your application simply has no chance of being approved, then seriously consider withdrawing the whole application immediately. Submit a letter of its withdrawal at once–that is, before you can get the Final Determination notice. The significance of this has to do with *a rule that every one should be aware of, namely, that once a Final Determination is issued denying an application, and the reason is for anything other than that the wage offered was below the prevailing wage, then the employer is prohibited from filing another labour certification application for the same job opening for 6 months as from the date of the denial.* Hence, by withdrawing the application in advance, you will be able to avoid the 6 months waiting period to refile. (A sample NOTICE OF FINDING is reproduced on p. 154)

G. THE SIGNIFICANCE OF HAVING A LABOUR CERTIFICATION IN HAND: IT ONLY PUTS YOU IN A POSITION TO BEGIN THE PETITION FOR A VISA.

The process involved in merely trying to obtain an alien labour certification could often be so tedious, complex and prolonged for the average applicant. Consequently, it is no wonder, then, that many aliens and U.S. employers who have gone through the grueling certification process, often have the tendency to instinctively view the labour certification application as the actual petition for the visa itself.

The true reality needs to be borne in mind, however. *All that issuance of a labour certification document means or represents is this: an official confirmation to the Immigration and Naturalization Service - the only agency having the responsibility to decide on your eligibility for issuance of a visa –that, in the assessment of the Department of Labour Officials, there is truly no American worker readily willing or available to fill a particular job opening for which you, an alien, indicated an interest or qualification for.*

That's all that the labour certification means, in essence! In fact, certification does not even touch upon or address the issue of whether or not you are, or will be ultimately found to be, eligible for issuance of a visa itself. For, the fact is that when you eventually get to "petition" for an immigrant visa, it will be to a different agency altogether that you will apply to, namely to the Immigration and Naturalization Service (INS), and not to the Department of Labour (DOL).

In deed, one other additional point of relevance ought to be borne in mind in this connection, and that is that, according to the courts' interpretations in many legal decisions,* while the DOL's certification may carry a great deal of influence with the INS, *such certification is nevertheless not binding on the INS, and the INS may (and does) if and when it pleases, re-evaluate the basis of such labour certification and may invalidate a certification for a number of grounds* — fraud or wilful misrepresentation of facts made in an underlying application, or a holding that the prospective employer will be unable to pay the prevailing wage, or simply that the alien is judged unqualified for the position in question.*

The central point of all these, then, is simple. It is simply to say that we should remind ourselves always that even at best, the fundamental task of hopefully securing a Third or Sixth preference immigrant visa to the U.S. is only just begun, even with the securing of an approved LABOUR CERTIFICATION. With the Labour Certificate obtained, the alien and/or the U.S. employer is only then in a position to begin to file his petition for the real thing - the visa itself. And, now it's time you get on with it!

NOTE: It's most important that you be reminded that the law was changed as recently as June 20, 1986. Thus, effective thereafter, the new rule is that anyone who files for and receives labour certification from the Department of Labour, must file the visa petition (Form 1 - 140) within 60 days of receiving certification even if a visa number is not available. And if this is not done, the person will lose his "priority date" for a visa number, which was established when the certification application was filed with the DOL.

---

* In Madany v. Smith, 696 F.2d 1008 (D.C. Cir. 1983), the court, addressing the issue of INS authority to review an alien's qualification following an approved labour certification, held that the INS is not statutorily bound by the conclusions of the Dept. of Labour, and reasons that the DOL looks solely to the position offered when issuing a labour certification, while the INS looks to the individual seeking to fill the position when granting a Third or Sixth preference petition.

CONTRACT OF EMPLOYMENT   (A SAMPLE)

THIS is a Contract of Employment between Mr/Ms _____,
who resides at_____(address?)_____, City of_____, State of
_____ (hereinafter called "**EMPLOYER**", and Mr/Ms_____,
who resides at_____, city/town of_____,
State of_____Zip_____(hereinafter called "EMPLOYEE").

The Employer hereby agrees to employ the Employee as a live-in domestic worker in the Employer's home at the above address, at a salary of $_____ per hour for the first forty (40) hours worked, and $_____ per hour, for the next four (4) hours worked, if any, up to the required forty-four (44) hours per week. The Employer also agrees to pay the Employee at the same "overtime" rate of $_____ per hour for all time worked over forty-four (44) hours per week. The regular weekly wage (i.e., without overtime) is $_____. The Employee will be given private room and board at no expense to the Employee.

The duties of the Employee will consist of the following: general household work, cleaning, laundry, shopping, cooking and serving meals, child care, answering the door and phone, and running general errands, lawn tending.

Household equipments which the Employee will operate are: dishwasher, vacuum cleaner, washing machine and dryer, lawn mower.

The hours of employment will be fortyfour (44) per week, from _____ A.M. to _____P.M., daily, 5 days per week, with a 2 hour rest period and 2 hours for meals each day. The Employee will work a guaranteed minimum of four (4) hours overtime per week at an hourly rate of $_____. The Employee agrees to live on the premises of the Employer. Employee is totally free to leave the premises at all times which are not working hours.

The Employer and the Employee, each agrees to give the other a two-week notice of intent to terminate the employment herein.

The Employer and the Employee, each acknowledges the receipt of a duplicate of this Contract, and each asserts that he/she entered into and signed this document freely, willingly, and voluntarily, after having first read, considered, and understood the contents thereof.

SIGNED: SIGNED:

_____   _____
(Employer)   (Employee)
Dated:_____199___.   Dated:_____199___.

"BUSINESS NECESSITY" LETTER   (A SAMPLE)
(On the Employer's Letterhead)

Date:_____

Local Employment Service
Address:_____
City._____ State _____
   Zip._____

                      Re: Business Necessity
                         Employee: Jozef Braun
                         Employer: Castle Export Corp.
                         Job: Supervisor, Export Department

Gentlemen:

We have required that the person who is in the position of Supervisor in the Export Department be able to speak French fluently.

This requirement is necessary for us since about 70% of our business is to buyers in France. The buyers do not speak English very well and always prefer to deal in French, their native language.

We have two other people in the Export Department who will be supervised by Mr. Braun. Both of these people speak some French but are not fluent. Our business has suffered in the past because of the language problem.

In addition to his supervisory duties, you will also note that his job includes receiving and processing orders, shipping documents, and other papers related to the export function. Many of these documents are in French. We have attached samples of documents we have received in the past. Sometimes we have had the documents translated by outside personnel at great cost of time and money.

Unless the Supervisor can speak and write French fluently, it will hurt our business very much and make it not possible for us to continue to compete.

                    Very truly yours,

                    Roger Perter
                    President

NOTE: This sample letter is cited, with permission for which we are most grateful to the Publisher, from the 'Green Card Book".

NOTICE OF JOB OFFERING

COOK, GREEK STYLE FOOD. A job is open for a cook of Greek style food. Prepare Greek dishes such as spanakopita, keftedakia, stuffed grape leaves, and others. Requires two years experience in a similar job. Uses commercial cooking equipment including ovens, mixers, food processors, and other restaurant kitchen equipment. 40 hours per week at $250.00 per week. Call Mr_____ at phone No:_____, if interested. Phone between the hours of _____ and _____

To the Labour Department: this notice was posted on the Bulletin Board of the Greek Spoon Restaurant from _____ to _____ There were no responses.

Signed: _____
Name Signed & Your Title:_____

CERTIFICATE OF APPROVED LABOUR CERTIFICATION
(OR, OF DENIED LABOUR CERTIFICATION)

U.S. DEPARTMENT OF LABOR
EMPLOYMENT AND TRAINING ADMINISTRATION
1515 Broadway
New York, N.Y. 10036

Date: _____

In reply refer to:DD/CB

TO: ABC Restaurant, Inc
Address: _____

_____

John Doe , SPECIALTY COOK FRENCH/THAI
Alien's name and occupation

DEC 15, 1980
Date of acceptance for processing

The Department of Labor has made a determination on your application for alien employment pursuant to Title 20, Code of Federal Regulations, Section 656.21 and as required by the Immigration and Nationality Act, as amended. Final action has been taken as follows:

☑ 1. Form ETA 7-50 has been certified and is enclosed with the supporting documents. All enclosures should be submitted to the Immigration and Naturalization Service District Office for consideration of alien's application for adjustment of status (I-485) or with your petition (Form I-140).

☐ 2. Form ETA 7-50 has been certified and forwarded to the .... Consulate at which the alien has indicated he will file a visa application. The Consular Officer will inform the alien of any additional documents to be submitted and steps to be taken in order to apply for an immigrant visa.

☐ 3. Form ETA 7-50 has not been certified and is being returned. A certification cannot be issued as required by Section 212(a)(14) of the Immigration and Nationality Act, as amended, on the basis of information available for the following reasons:

☐ a. There are U.S. workers available who are able, willing, and qualified for the job.

☐ b. The employment of aliens would have an adverse effect on wages and/or working conditions of U.S. workers similarly employed.

The wage offer of .... is below the prevailing rate of ....
for this occupation in the proposed area of employment.

Prevailing wage was determined by ....
....

Sincerely,

Bette F. Roy

BETTE F. ROY
Certifying Officer

cc: State ES Agency

CC: John Doe

Request for a review of a denial of certification may be made. A request for review of a denial may only be made in writing addressed to the Chief Administrative Law Judge, Department of Labor, and submitted by certified mail to the Certifying Officer who denied certification within 35 days of date of this denial for transmittal and shall: (1) Clearly identify the particular certification determination for which review is sought; (2) set forth the particular grounds on which the request is based; and (3) include all documents which accompanied the denial of certification.

ETA 7-145 (Dec. 1976)

FORM ETA 7145

NOTE: The above document, set forth herein for illustrative purposes, is reproduced here by courtesy of and from "The Greencard Book," by Richard Madison (Visa Publishing Co., New York N.Y.), p.73. A few minor modifications have been made herein by the present publisher.

NOTICE OF FINDINGS

U.S. DEPARTMENT OF LABOR
EMPLOYMENT AND TRAINING ADMINISTRATION
1515 Broadway
New York, N.Y. 10036

Date: _____   In reply refer to: **DD/CB**

John Doe _____ /Spec. Cook French/Thai

Alien's name and occupation   12/15/80

TO: ABC Restaurant, Inc.   Date of acceptance for processing

Address: _____

_____

The Department of Labor has considered your application for alien employment certification. In accordance with Title 20, Code of Federal Regulations, Section 656.25(c)(3), we hereby issue our Notice of Findings. You have until **September 20, 1981** .... to submit documentary evidence to rebut the findings outlined below by certified mail on or before date specified above. If the rebuttal evidence is not received by certified mail on or before this Notice of Findings automatically becomes the final decision to deny labor certification.

(1) Pursuant to 20 CFR 656.21(b)(7) the Revised Federal Requirements employer must document that if labor certification is granted, the wage rate paid will equal or exceed the prevailing wage applicable at that time. The statement will equal or exceed. The said prevailing wage at the time "is not satisfactory,

(2) Pursuant to 20 CFR 656.21(b)(15) employer has documented that he will be able to place the alien on the payroll on or before his date of proposed entry into U.S. It is noted that alien has been employed since March 1, 1978, therefore employer should document that alien is presently on the payroll.

(3) Pursuant to 20 CFR 656.21(b)(9) employer has documented "subsequent to filing with my local employment service office. I placed a further advertisement in a newspaper of general circulation directing applicants to report to the local office of the employment service." This documentation was signed on 10/4/80 the job order was not placed until 11/30,/80 and the additional ad on May 23, 1981, therefore this is not a bonafide statement.

(4) Pursuant to 20 CFR 656.21(b)(10) employer has stated he posted a notice. A copy of this notice and the results of its posting must be submitted.

(5) Item 31, Form MA 7-50B, pertaining to education and training requirements, have not been answered. If none required so state.

(6) Items 5 and 6 of Form MA 7-50A, pertaining to names of schools attended or special qualifications and skills has not been answered.

(7) Should employer choose to comply with the above and/or rebut these findings he may address his letter to this office.

Sincerely,

Sincerely,

[signature]

BETTE F. ROY
Certifying Officer
cc: State E. S. Agency

FORM ETA 7-145A   ETA 7-145A (Dec. 1976)

NOTE: The above document, set forth herein for illustrative purposes, is reproduced here by courtesy of and from "The Greencard Book," by Richard Madison (Visa Publishing Co.), p.72 . A few minor modifications have been made by the present Publisher herein.

CHAPTER  9

ENTERING THE UNITED STATES: THE PROCESS OF GETTING ACTUALLY ADMITTED INTO THE COUNTRY AFTER YOU'VE GOT YOUR VISA

Alright. So you've gone through all those lengthy formalities and hassles customarily involved in applying or petitioning for a visa to enter the United State. And, at long last, let's say you have been granted the visa; and shortly thereafter, you left your home country and are now at a U.S. border port of entry with your "almighty" U.S. entry permit in your hands seeking to physically enter the United States! Are you automatically guaranteed or entitled to admission just because you have a valid visa in hand?

The answer is a resounding: No! GET THIS POINT VERY CLEAR: think of the process of your admission into the U.S. as a TWO-step process; in this two-step process, the issuance of a visa to you is only the first of the two steps! All that your possessing the visa does for you, in practical terms, is enable you to – accord you the right to– come to a border port of entry to the United States. And then, while you are at such border or port of entry, you may then "apply" for actual admission into the country; and, what is more important, you will have to demonstrate your qualification and eligibility for admission into the U.S. all over again for a second time, to the satisfaction of the U.S. immigration officers there at the border. And only then may you finally gain entry into the United States!

A.   EVIDENCE OF YOUR VISA ISSUANCE

Upon the approval of your visa petition or application in a foreign country by a U.S. Consul there, if the visa granted you is a NONIMMIGRANT type, the consul shall have typically stamped your passport with a notation indicating for how long the visa is valid, the approved visa classification to which you belong, number of entries you are permitted into the United States. And if the Visa granted you is an IMMIGRANT type, the Consul shall have typically issued you an immigration form, FORM 1–551,the Alien Registration Receipt Card, more commonly known as the "GREEN CARD", complete with your photograph, date and country of birth, and your "A" (immigrant) classification number.

B.   GOING THROUGH INSPECTION AT THE PORT OF ENTRY

In all the time the alien visa seeker is in his home country, or is in any country whatsoever so long as it is outside the United States, the agency of the U.S. Government with the sole jurisdiction or authority over matters concerning the processing of the alien's visa application in the foreign country in question is the Consular office, an arm of the U.S. Department of State. However, once the alien sets his or her foot on a port of entry in the United States (at a land border, an airport or a seaport), from that moment on it is the Immigration and Naturalization Service (INS),an arm of a different agency of the U.S. Government, namely, the Department of Justice, that now takes over and automatically assumes the decision-making powers as to all matters concerning your admission or admissability, and decides whether you may be admitted or excluded from admission and the grounds thereof. *The key point to remember here, is that though you have your visa in hand at a port of entry quite properly issued you by a consulate official abroad, that, nevertheless, is not a guarantee that you will necessarily be found acceptable for admission by the immigration officials at the port of entry, or that you will necessarily be allowed entry into the United States.*

Here's The way the Admission Process Works, in brief:

●Upon your (the alien's) arrival at the U.S. port of entry, you will have to undergo a "secondary inspection", meaning that you will have to be examined one more time to determine your entitlement to enter the U.S., this time, though, by INS as opposed to consular inspectors or examiners. You report for "inspection and admission" procedure before the INS inspector; you surrender your passport and your visa (and any other relevant or applicable documents, e.g. information on school admission or report of medical examination) to the INS inspector, and, upon the inspector reviewing your documents, he'll probably ask you a number of questions regarding your eligibility to enter the United States.

●Your name is checked against a "lookout book" the INS maintains for aliens who may be excludable and for other persons for whom government agencies have requested a "lookout". You may possibly (though not commonly) be required to take a complete medical and physical examination by a Public Health Service Officer, and may be subject to background investigations.

●In some cases, the immigration inspector may possibly decide that the alien is not eligible for admission. He may determine, for example, that the alien's record, in some way, is in violation of some requirements for which an "exclusion" from entry into the United States is called for under the immigration laws or regulations, or that some material documentation required from the alien has either not been provided or is incomplete or unsatisfactory.

Essentially, to be admitted into the United States, here is what you are required to satisfy the immigration inspector of: that you are "clearly and beyond doubt entitled to land in the United States"— in other words, that you basically meet the necessary qualifications as provided for under the law for the type of visa you hold, and that there truly are no legal barriers that would prevent you from being admitted into the United States.

C. ADMISSION OR DENIAL OF ADMISSION

In the end, assuming that the immigration inspector approves your being admitted, in that event if you are being admitted in one of the nonimmigrant classifications, the immigration inspector will at that time grant you the specific length of time you will be allowed to stay in the U.S. in accordance with the particular type of visa you were issued. (This, and various other types of information designed to stand as evidence of the alien's lawful admission into the U.S., is either stamped in his passport or, more typically, it is entered on a FORM 1 - 90 Departure Card and stapled to the inside of his passport). If, on the other hand, you are admitted as an immigrant, you may either be issued an Alien Registration Receipt Card (the "GREEN CARD") on the spot,. or a rubber stamp will be placed in your passport to serve as your temporary Green Card; the actual card will then be manufactured and sent to you thereafter by mail at your designated address in the United States.

D. IF DENIED ADMISSION, YOU COULD SEEK A REVIEW: AN "EXCLUSION" HEARING.

What happens if the immigration inspector conducting the initial examination at your port of entry were to determine that you are not admissible, and therefore "excludes" you – that is, denies you entry into the United States? Usually, you would probably be advised to appear for a *"secondary"* (i.e., a more formal) *examination,* if the port of entry at which you arrived is a land border; or, if your place of arrival is at an INS office other than at an airport or seaport, you may be given a *"deferred inspection".* Thereafter, if you are still found inadmissible, you are ordered "excluded" (i.e., barred from entry), at which point you are given a choice: either voluntarily return to your home country at your own expense, or your case is referred to an immigration judge for a hearing, the so-called *EXCLUSION HEARING PROCEDINGS.*

An "exclusion" hearing is the hearing of relevance to an alien who is refused entry at a port of entry, as opposed to *"deportation"* hearing (pp.158). In a word, an EXCLUSION hearing is one held to determine an alien's right merely to enter the United States; it takes place BEFORE the right to enter is offically granted. It technically differs from a DEPORTATION hearing (pp.158-9), in that deportation has to do with determining the alien's right to remain in the U.S. AFTER he shall have already been admitted into the U.S. by an immigration officer and has probably lived in the country for a while.

E. RIGHTS OF DETAINED ALIENS & THE PROCEDURES IN EXCLUSION HEARINGS

To be sure, exclusion proceedings (and, in deed, the related subject of deportation proceedings) are clearly beyond the very limited scope of the present book, and an alien faced with such a circumstance may well be better advised, anyway, to seek the help of a competent immigration lawyer and immigration social services organizations. Here, therefore, we can only present *a brief outline of the alien's rights and the procedures involved:*

1. In exclusion hearings, it is the alien himself, and NOT the Immigration Service (INS), that has t h e big burden of proving that he or she is otherwise eligible for admission to the U.S. and that he has actually not violated any immigration laws. And he or she must make this proof by a "clear and convincing evidence".

2. Basically, under the premise that the alien in an exclusion hearing is a person merely "at the door" but who is not yet in, aliens in exclusion hearings are viewed as a group not entitled to the usual constitutional guarantees; hence, the normal constitutional protections do not apply in exclusion hearings, inasmuch as admitting foreigners to the U.S. is said to be a "privilege" granted only at the pleasure of, and on the terms and conditions set by, the U.S. government.

3. *The INS District Director has a right to, if he so chooses, and may in his discretion, either hold you in an immigration detention facility pending the conclusion of the hearing, or release you on a bond or on your own personal recognizance.*

4. *The hearing takes place before a U.S. immigration judge; and you may (you have a right to, if you wish) represent yourself in the case, or be represented by a friend or a lawyer of your choice, providing you can pay such a lawyer out of your own resources.*

5. You are entitled to be told the charges made against you, and to be given the opportunity to present evidence in defense of yourself, and to confront and question any evidence presented or any witnesses who appear or testify against you.

6. Aside from other remedies you may consider, one thing you may do at this hearing is to make an *application for political asylum (political asylum procedures are outlined on pp. 46-54.)*

7. *In the end, whatever the decision arrived at by the hearing judge, it must be based solely on the* evidence presented at the hearing and must be adequately supported by such evidence, and be supported in such a way that it can be rationally inferred that you (the alien) are not entitled to admission.

8. If the decision of the judge is that you be excluded from admission, he will issue an *ORDER FOR EXCLUSION* (ORDER OF DEPORTATION, if a deportation case) against you to that effect.

9. You have a right (except if you are a crewman, stowaway or a person excluded on security or *medical disqualification grounds) to appeal the decision of the immigration judge to the next level,* namely, *to* the *Board of Immigration Appeals in Washington D.C. (To appeal, you must do so* immediately, at the conclusion of the hearing, if the decision is oral, or within 10 days of the decision, if the decision is a written one. Initiate the process by serving a written *NOTICE OF APPEAL* upon the INS promptly.)

10. If you fail to appeal the immigration judge's ORDER FOR EXCLUSION (or DEPORTATION) or fail to do so on time, you will immediately be deported — returned, in this instance, to the country from which you came to the U.S.

11. The judge may, at his "discretion", either decide to allow you to post a bail bond, or to release you on parole with or without a bond.

12. *On appeal, the following are a few grounds on which you can base your claim that the decision of the immigration judge deserves to be reversed or set aside: (i) that there were "improper procedures" at the hearing (i.e., that you had an unfair hearing or that it did not follow the legal and agency requirements set for such hearings); (ii) that the judge's ORDER OF EXCLUSION (or Deportation) was based on "mistake of fact" or "errors of law" (i.e., that the judge applied an incorrect meaning or interpretation of the relevant laws and regulations); (iii) that the decision did not have "adequate support in the evidence" or was rendered with "unwarranted disregard of the evidence" or was not based on "proper standard of evidence" (i.e., not having a substantial and reasonable basis in the evidence); and iv) that there was on the part of the judge on "arbitrary excercise of discretion" or "failure to excercise discretion" (i.e., that either no reason is given for the decision rendered, or the reason given is irrational or out of keeping with established policy, or discriminatory or based on improper grounds).*

13. In exclusion hearings, if you appeal an immigration judge's decision to the Board of Immigration Appeals and the Board's decison still remains unfavorable to you, you have only one final right of appeal: the right to petition a court of law for a judicial review. This petition, called a *WRIT OF HABEAS CORPUS,* is filed with the U.S. District Court in the hearing area, the object being for the court to review the administative action taken in the exclusion hearings and to establish that the order of Exclusion is valid.

F. IF DENIED THE RIGHT TO REMAIN IN THE U.S., YOU COULD SEEK A REVIEW: DEPORTATION PROCEEDINGS

A "deportation" proceeding, as previously explained in pp. 156 of this chapter, is primarily concerned with determining the alien's right (or lack of it) to remain in the United States AFTER he shall have already been duly admitted into the U.S. by the immigration officials. In short, whereas you'll seek an exclusion hearing if you have a valid visa but are denied entry into the U.S., a deportation hearing is what you seek to have when you are denied or threatened with denial of the right to remain in the U.S. at any time after you have gained formal admission into the country. Usually, a deportation proceeding comes about because the immigration service, probably contending that an alien who had been duly admitted to the country has committed some acts which violate certain immigration laws or the terms upon which the alien had ben granted his visa, has initiated a move to send the alien back to his home country.

G. RIGHTS OF ALIENS & PROCEDURES IN DEPORTATION HEARINGS

The following is a brief outline summarizing the alien's rights and the procedures involved in *deportation hearings:*

1. *An important preface is appropriate here: aside from a few important areas of differences, by* and large the rights of aliens involved in deportation hearings and the procedures thereof, are essentially the same as those of aliens involved in exclusion hearings, and the procedures thereof. In the interest of brevity and to avoid unnecessary repetition, here's what you do: simply read all the rights and hearing procedures outlined on pp. 157-9 above for the alien facing an "exclusion" hearing, and treat the said facts (pp. 157-8) as equally applicable with respect to the alien facing deportation hearings, except for just a few differences as specified below.

(2) The significant points of departure regarding the alien involved in deportation proceedings are as follows:

i) Contrary to the situation prevailing in exclusion proceedings (see paragraph 2 on P.157), the alien involved in deportation hearings is entitled to, and is accorded, all constitutional rights, protections and privileges that a U.S. citizen has, such as the right not to self-incriminate oneself. In deed, this is probably the overriding distinguishing factor between the two types of hearings.

ii) One manifest way by which the deportation-bound alien enjoys superior constitutional privileges not extended to the exclusion-bound alien, is this: in deportation hearing, it is the immigration service, and NOT the alien, as in the case of aliens facing exclusion, that has the burden of proving, by a "clear and convincing evidence", that the alien is deportable and/or has actually violated specific immigration laws.

iii) Among the remedies open for consideration to the alien in a deportation proceding, are the following "discretionary relief": aside from being able to apply for political asylum in the U.S., you may apply for a "stay (suspension) of deportation" (File immigration FORM 1 -256); and you may apply to have your status adjusted from nonimmigrant to immigrant status, if qualified. (See Chapter 10 on adjustment of status, at pp. 161-170)

iv) Just as in exclusion hearings, you can appeal a decision by a U.S. immigration judge in a deportation hearing to the *Board of Immigration Appeals* in Washington, D.C. under basically the same grounds and ground rules (paragraphs 9 thru 12 on P.157 above). However, the final appeal in deportation proceedings is not from the Board's decision to the area's U.S. District Court, but to the area's *U.S. Court of Appeals.* You file for such review of the Board's decision by filing within 6 months after the Board's ruling a *"PETITION TO REVIEW DEPORTATION ORDER"*

NOTE: The Court of Appeals in this instance, will look only at the previously assembled record of the appealed proceedings, with no new evidence submitted or considered. To apply for suspension of deportation, you need to be able to show: that you were continuously present in the U.S. for the previous 7 years or that you performed honorable service in the U.S. armed forces for at least 24 months; that you are of good moral character; how and why your deportion would result in "exceptional and extremely unusual hardship" to yourself or to a U.S. citizen or permanent resident to whom you are closely related by blood or marriage. As usual, massive documentations of sorts would have to be assembled and be presented to the judge at the hearing to prove such contentions: police records, affidavits of good character from respectable U.S. citizens, and of employment from an employer, records of permanent entry into the U.S., birth and/or marriage certificate, bank books, rent receipts, lease, licenses, church and school records, tax receipts, etc, showing continuous residence in the U.S.

v) If you should fail to appeal the INS Board's FINAL ORDER OF DEPORTATION (or, before that, the INS judge's Order), or fail to appeal on time, you have a right in deportation hearing to, upon application during the proceedings, be deported to any country of your choice (this contrasts with an alien's right in an exclusion case), or you may be granted a right to depart voluntarily (an *ORDER OF VOLUNTARY DEPARTURE) at your own expense, and thus avoid being deported. This is a very important right, the difference being that an alien who is deported requires a special permission by the INS to return to the U.S. in the future, but an alien who leaves voluntarily does not.*

vi) *If all else fails, there's still one ultimate relief that a person facing deportation may seek: you may contact your area's Congressman or Senator and request him or her to introduce a "private immigration bill"* in Congress to relieve you from deportation or otherwise permit you to "stay" the deportation or otherwise permit you to stay in the U.S. Upon the introduction of such a bill in Congress for an alien, as a rule, the INS will usually stay the deportation of the alien, and, if the bill is neither voted down nor tabled nor withdrawn, and is acted upon favorably at the close of Congress and signed by the president, the alien beneficiary of the bill is rendered eligible to remain in the United States.

H. A WORD OF ADVICE FOR PERSONS SEEKING ENTRY OR FACING EXCLUSION OR DEPORTATION

To conclude this chapter, certain words of caution seem fitting as a guide for aliens in dealing with the immigration officials at the port of entry for purposes of admission, or in going through an exclusion or deportation proceeding, if need be. Much is often made about the supposed "imperial" powers said to be possessed by immigration officers (and even more so, by the consular officers) over decisions as to whether a visa application is to be granted, or about whether a visa-holding alien gets admitted into the country. True, the fact that the powers granted the immigration officers to exclusively decide on such matters are officially sweeping, cannot at all be disputed. Nevertheless, that aside, it is still most important that an alien facing an official encounter with the immigration officer in any of the above treated contexts should have the proper attitude and the right psyhological mind-set for productively dealing with the immigration personnel.

To begin with, it is most important that the alien bears in mind that most immigration officials they encounter at the port of entry (or at exclusion or deportation proceedings or elsewhere) are generally fair-minded; that they are simply workers with no special axe to grind who are employed to do a job, and are honestly attempting to do just that the best way they can.

Sure, the decision as to whether to admit or to exclude a particular alien may often be "discretionary", even "subjective", and is for the most part based on the immigration official's past experiences which are necessarily limited. Nevertheless, in practice, the factual reality has been that by and large in those instances where aliens appear to have been granted special discretionary relief or favourable rulings by immigration officials, certain common denominators appear to have been present. Typically, to approve an admission, the INS officials would look for a showing of certain objective attributes[*]—such as a good moral character, close bona fide family ties in the United States, the existence of certain humanitarian reasons for which admission could be allowed, such as probability of hardship resulting to the alien or close relatives in the event of the alien being excluded or deported, and the like. On the other hand, most denials of entry into the U.S. have by and large been based on objective reasons, among the most common of them being the following: violation of immigration requirements (such as engaging in unauthorized work in the U.S.), being previously excluded or deported from the U.S., entering the U.S. as a visitor but with the seeming intention to remain permanently, making false or contradictory statements and misrepresentations to consular and immigration officers or in connection with present or previous applications for visa, failure to make full disclosure of information regarding political or other associations with those having an ideology deemed unacceptable by the U.S. (e.g., past membership in, say, the Communist or Nazi

---

[*] In deed, the long-standing policy of the INS has been to grant an alien's application for the relief requested, except where there are specific reasons for it to be rejected. And such policy has been reinforced by a widely influencial decision by the Board of Immigration Appeals. (See In Matter of Aral, 13 I & N Dec. 49)

party), likelihood of an alien becoming a "public charge" and not being able to financially support himself, physical or mental disease, alcoholism, drug convictions, a record or history of immorality or of unacceptable criminal convictions (or conduct), especially if involving "moral turpitude" (defined as "a crime of baseness, vileness or deprevity in the private or social duties" of a person), and so on.

The point of all this, simply, is that aliens facing the port-of-entry admission process should approach the process with the proper attitude calculated to enhance, not hurt, their cause: they should have the psychological mind-set, and project the attitude that in the final analysis, the decision of the border immigration officer regarding one's admission to (or exclusion from) the United State, will by and large be based on the objective qualities possessed by the alien himself and on the image and background the alien projects to the officer. It is most important that you be absolutely open and truthful with the immigration inspectors (or interviewers); that you be patient, polite, positive and cooperative with them, and be forthcoming in answering their questions. And, though it cannot be said that such attitude will necessarily guarantee that admission will materialize, it will nevertheless guarantee that you will enhance your case and minimize your potential losses and frustrations with the immigration officials.

CHAPTER  10

"ADJUSTMENT OF STATUS": HOW A NON-IMMIGRANT ALIEN CAN CHANGE TO IMMIGRANT OR PERMANENT RESIDENCY STATUS WHILE IN THE U.S.

Ordinarily, the authorized legal process by which an alien gets admitted to the United States as a PERMANENT RESIDENT (i.e., as an "immigrant" or "Green Card" holder), is for the alien to apply for and obtain an immigrant visa in a foreign country outside the United State, usually at a U.S. Consulate in a foreign country, and to then be admitted into the United States as an "immigrant" by virtue of the immigrant visa. However, suppose the alien is already physically present in the United States in a non-immigrant status of one kind or another. Can he or she then change to an immigrant status at some point along the line? The answer is, YES. He may apply to do so— under certain conditions.

The process by which a nonimmigrant changes his or her status to an immigrant status (i.e., to the status of a lawfull permanent resident of the U.S.), is called *ADJUSTMENT OF STATUS*.

A. ALIENS WHO ARE NOT ELIGIBLE TO APPLY FOR ADJUSTMENT OF STATUS

As conceived under the relevant immigration laws and policies of the United States, adjustment of status is viewed as a form of relief from deportation and as a "privilege" which is granted only in the discretion of the Attorney-General of the United States. It is held that adjustment of status is a "privilege" in that it relieves the alien of the potential burden of having to return to his home country to make an application there for an immigrant visa. A trip to the alien's home country to make such a visa appointment, for example, may well have interfered with the alien's present business activities and could be prohibitively expensive, according to this line of reasoning. In light of such fundamental premise that permitting adjustment of status is a "privilege" and not a right, certain legal requirements and restrictions are therefore imposed upon the nonimmigrant alien with respect to being permitted to adjust his or her status.

Aliens (or other persons) falling under any of the following categories are NOT eligible to apply for (or to be granted) adjustment of status:

1. Aliens who at the time of entering the United Status had gained entry surreptitiously as stowaways or without inspection at the U.S. port of entry. (You must, in other words, have been "inspected" by an immigration officer at the entry time, and been either admitted in some nonimmigrant classification or been "paroled" into the U.S. (i.e. allowed in, pending decision in a deportation or exclusion hearings)

2. Aliens who last entered the U.S. officially as CREWMEN in any capacity on board a ship or aircraft.

3. Nonimmigrant aliens, other than those qualifying as "immediate relative" or "special immigrants", who have worked in the U.S without permission at any time falling after January 1977. (Unless, in other words, you had worked with specific permission to do so by the INS, e.g., as an F - 1 student or J-1 or J-2 exchange visitor; or you hold a nonimmigrant visa whose category has a standing permission to work in the U.S., e.g., those holding E-1 or E-2, or H-1 or H-2 or H-3 or L visas, and the like.)

4. Aliens (except for "immediate relatives" of U.S. citizens only) who are NOT in legal immigration status at the time that they apply for change of status, or who have failed (other than by no fault of their own) to maintain continuons legal status since entry into the U.S.

5. Aliens who entered the U.S. "IN TRANSIT", that is, who entered while enroute to another country and merely stopped off to transfer in the U.S. while going to another destination.

6. Aliens who entered the U.S. as, or had their status changed to, J-1 or J-2 EXCHANGE VISITORS (p. 21), and were subject to the requirement of having to return to their own countries to live for a 2-years period before applying for a change of status, unless they had been granted a waiver of that requirement.

7. Aliens who would not have been admissible to the U.S. anyway, based on any part of Section 212 (a) of the Immigration and Nationality Act—that is, the laws listing the grounds for, and the classes of aliens subject to "exclusion" from admission, as in pp. 179-180 below.

8. Aliens who are granted "conditional resident" status (pp   of this manual), or are admitted as fiances or fiancees pending the conferral of full permanent residency status. (Adjustment of status is prohibited to those aliens who seek permanent residence based on a marriage entered into while administrative or judicial proceedings are pending regarding the alien's right to enter or remain in the U.S.)

B. WHY SEEKING THE IMMIGRANT STATUS BY "ADJUSTMENT" METHOD FROM WITHIN THE U.S. MAY BE BETTER THAN APPLYING FOR IT FROM THE OUTSIDE

Many experts contend that seeking to gain immigrant status by the "adjustment" process from within the United States, held certain advantages over seeking the same objective through the normal process— that is, by applying for the immigrant visa from outside the United States. Consequently, seeking such a visa by adjustment of status in the U.S., has been said to be "preferable" by legal practitioners and immigration experts.

The following are among the major advantages of securing an immigrant status visa via the "adjustment of status" route from within the U.S.:

1. By adjusting status from within the U.S., the alien needs not have to travel to a U.S. consulate in his home country or other foreign country to apply for the immigrant visa, thereby saving on travel expenses, and relieving him from having his business activities or family life disrupted.

2. As a rule, the adjustment of status process frequently leads to a speedier and faster grant of the permanent residency (i.e. immigrant) status than does regular visa processing, depending on the type of petition filed and the consular post abroad in which the visa application would otherwise have been made.

3. For those classes of aliens whose claim for eligibility for admission as immigrants are based on occupational qualifications, the alien filing for adjustment of status (i.e. from within the U.S.) can usually be granted employment authorization as early as the date of filing of the adustment of status application; whereas, with regard to visa petitions filed from foreign countries, as a general rule no explicit employment authorization is granted the alien during the processing of the application.

4. *Perhaps the most important advantage lies in the far greater legal constitutional protections that the alien filing from within the U.S. could enjoy over one doing so from a foreign country.* To put it simply, as an alien seeking adjustment of status from within the U.S., you are automatically allowed all the privileges and immunities of the United States constitution, the same as a person would enjoy who is fully a U.S, citizen.

To begin with, once you have been inspected at a port of entry and been properly admitted into the U.S., if the immigration officials should at any time thereafter deny you a visa to remain in the country, it is on the shoulders of the immigration officials themselves, and NOT on yours, that the burden now squarely falls to show that you are indeed a person deserving to be deported. In deed, under the applicable law, in a "deportation" hearing to determine your immigration status you need not even have to show (as you will have to in an "exclusion" hearing situation) that you are a person absolutely entitled, beyond a reasonable doubt, to enter the United States.

The second point is that if you filed a visa petition in the United States and it is denied, access to the Federal Courts, as well as to formal administrative appeals bodies, are readily available to you in full. Just like any regular U.S. citizen, you yourself are entitled to hire an experienced immigration lawyer, or to seek the aid of any of the many domestic U.S. immigration organizations involved in protecting the rights of aliens in the U,S.   You may have such experts or organizations represent you and fight on your behalf to secure your rights through the courts and administrative bodies. Thus, if, for example, the first INS officer to rule on your adjustment application case (he's usually the area's District Director) turns you down, then you are at least in a position to appeal your case to higher authorities—first, to a U.S. immigration Judge, and if still unsatisfied, then next to the Board of Immigration Appeals in Washington D.C., and if need still be, then finally to the U.S. Court of Appeals.

In contrast to the above situation, for an alien who applies for the immigrant visa through a U.S. consulate in a foreign country, the decision of one official and one official alone—the U.S. consul- is, for all practical purposes, final and virtually unappealable to any higher authority!*

---

*Sure, in theory at least, a Consul's decision can be reviewed by the U.S. Department of State in Washington D.C. But the Department's role is only advisory and the Department may not order the Consul to approve a petition. Secondly, most aliens residing in a foreign country will hardly ever dare, much less afford, the expense or trouble to challenge a Consul's negative decision before a U.S. government agency located for away in alien Washington D.C.

C. CATEGORIES OF ALIENS WHO MAY APPLY FOR ADJUSTMENT OF STATUS

The following broad classes of nonimmigrant aliens may seek, and frequently do seek, to adjust their status to immigrant status while residing in the U.S.

Temporary visitors (pp.18-19)
Aliens who are married to U.S. citizens or permanent residents after coming to the United States on a temporary visit.
Aliens who came to the U.S. as nonimmigrants but have changed their intention AFTER (but not before) they were admitted to the U.S.
Brothers and sisters of U.S. citizens who are 21 years of age or older.
Business people who entered the U.S. for business purposes on B-1 visas (pp.18-19)
Executives and managers who entered the U.S. as Treaty Traders or Investors (pp. 26-8) or as
L-1 Intra-company Transferees of foreign international corporation having subsidiaries in the U.S. (pp.25-6)
Aliens on J-1 or J-2 Exchange visitor visas, who have been granted a waiver of the 2-year foreign residency requirement (see pp.21-2)

D. STEP-BY-STEP PROCEDURES FOR APPLYING FOR ADJUSTMENT OF STATUS

So you want to adjust your status to an IMMIGRANT status while you are already living in the United States? Follow the following general procedures in the exact order in which they are listed below:

step 1: DETERMINE THAT YOU MEET THE GENERAL ELIGIBILITY REQUIPMENTS TO APPLY FOR ADJUSTMENT OF STATUS

See Sections A, B, and C of this chapter, at pp. 161-3. Do you, hopefully, fall under one or more of the categories of aliens who may apply (p.163)?

step 2: OBTAIN THE NECESSARY APPLICATION FORMS FOR THE TYPE OF VISA YOU SEEK.

For the added convenience of the readership, Do-it-yourself Legal Publishers makes available to its readers the standard, fully pre-sorted, all-in-one package of forms—containing the proper forms necessary for the particular type of visa you designate.

To order the Publisher's standard "all-in-one" immigration forms package, just complete the Order Form on p.191-2 and send it to the Publisher's legal Forms Division.

step 3: PROPERLY FILL OUT THE APPLICATION FORMS & BEGIN TO ASSEMBLE THE NECESSARY SUPPORTING DOCUMENTATIONS.

Here are the initial forms needed:

(i) FORM I-130 , "Petition to classify status of Alien Relative For Issuance of Immigrant Visa" to be filled out by the sponsoring petitioner. (Applicable only in situations when a Preference Petition based on a family relationship to a U.S. citizen or permanent resident,is being used. See p.120 for illustrative sample of form).

(ii) FORM I-140, "Petition to Classify Preference status of Alien on Basis of Profession or Occupation", to be filled out and signed by the prospective U.S. employer (Applicable only in situations when the basis for the alien's application is job skills or employment, i.e. to establish a Third or Sixth Preference (pp, 43-5). See pp.123-5, 126-7 for illustrative sample of form.

(iii) FORM I-485 , "Application for Status as Permanent Resident", to be filled out by the alien "beneficiary" (See pp.135-6 for illustrative sample of the form).

(iv) FORM G-325A, "Biographic Data", to be filled out by the alien. (Sample of form is on p.110)

NOTE: Note a few general rules in regard to completing the immigration forms. A truly important aid to anyone in preparing all such forms are the "blocks" provided on the forms; such blocks are generally self-explanatory and quite explicitly indicate the exact information required to be entered, and the order in which such information is to be put in in order for the information to contain in the space. Secondly, almost every immigration form has a set of "INSTRUCTIONS" on the body of the form, clearly telling the reader the purpose(s) for which the form is appropriate and giving some pointers on how to complete or file them, and guidelines on the information and supporting documents required to be furnished.

Hence, the first rule in completing the forms in this: in all instances, always be absolutely sure to read the forms and thoroughly understand the information required of you before filling them out. Be deliberately careful. Remember this: that the initial batch of forms you complete and submit are what is known as the "primary" documents, meaning that this is the documentary source which the consular and immigration authorities will probably go back to and refer to again and again, and against which they will cross-check any future documents and information from you for consistency. (In submitting supporting documents to the consular or INS officers, make it a point always, especially with regard to irreplaceable documents, to file only photostatic copies of the originals by first presenting the originals to them for their personal inspection and certification that the copies are the true copies. This precaution is necessary because the immigration services have a history of chronically losing important, often irreplaceable documents submitted by aliens. Furthermore, for any documents written in a foreign language, always submit a certified English translation as well).

DETERMINE THAT THIS IS A PROPER TIME WHEN YOU MAY FILE AN ADJUSTMENT APPLICATION.

Next, before you rush to go file the completed initial application forms, there is one thing you had better done first: determine that you have either an approved (or approvable) immediate relative or preference petition, or, if your case is one for which no preference petition is required (e.g. as in the case of NONPREFERENCE classification or SPECIAL IMMIGRANTS), then you need only be able to present appropriate evidence of eligibility for such nonpreference or special immigrant status. In simple terms, here's what you do: First, check the latest U.S. Department of State's Visa Bulletin. Is an immigrant visa number available to you under the category for which you qualify at the time of this application? (See p. 11 for how to do this). If it is, then this is the proper time for you to file your adjustment application. And if it is not, then it is not the proper time for you to file. Secondly, are you going to file, as most people have to do, under one of the eight immigrant PREFERENCE categories (p.**7**)? (And you probably will — unless you happen to be among the relative few who qualify as "immediate relative"and"special immigrant" who are exempt from the numerical limitation requirement outlined on p. 6 & 8). If you are, then here's what you have to do: either you shall have previously filed the visa petition under your chosen preference classification and secured an approval for it, or, if that is not the case, then simply prepare the visa petition and be prepared to submit it concurrently with your application for adjustment.

Recall a basic rule of relevance here: namely, that an adjustment application may be accepted only if the alien applicant has shown that he is qualified for the immigrant visa at the time of the application (or will be when the papers already on file in a pending application are approved). If the applicant does not have a nonpreference priority date (from having an approved Labor Certification, for example), and does not have a nonpreference petition on file with the INS, then the applicant cannot qualify for an immigrant visa, meaning that the adjustment application cannot be accepted. If there is an immigrant visa "available" to the alien, the alien who believes he meets the qualifications for adjustment can file his adjustment application at the same time that he files the petition that will make him eligible for the preference classification. He does not have to wait for the preference petition to be approved so long as he will be eligible for an immigrant visa if and when the petition is approved.

Example: let's say you are going to file a "Schedule A" labour certification application and a Third Preference petition. Now, if according to figures from the latest Visa Bulletin the Third Preference is "current" (meaning available) for your home country, this means that approval of your Third Preference petition will make you eligible for an immigrant visa immediately; hence, under this situation you CAN file an adjustment application *at the same time* that you file your Schedule A application and the Preference Petition.

Let us say that, on the other hand, everything else remains the same as in the above example but except for one thing:

that the latest Visa Bulletin shows that Visas are NOT "current" for the Third Preference category for your country. Then, in that case, approval of your Third Preference petition will not make you eligible for an immigrant visa immediately, and hence you CANNOT file an adjustment application at this time, and you must wait and file when a visa is available for you. Now, suppose a visa number becomes available while your Schedule A application and Preference petition are awaiting approval? You can then do one of two things: either file the adjustment application and ask the INS to put it together with your previously filed Schedule A application and preference petition papers; or, in the alternative, you can wait and file the adjustment application after the Schedule A application and preference petition have been approved — so long as a visa is immediately available to you and you continue to meet all the adjustment requirements.

 FILE THE ADJUSTMENT APPLICATION, WITH THE SUPPORTING DOCUMENTS ATTACHED

You are now in the position to submit ("file")·your application for Adjustment of Status to the INS. What do you do? You submit the papers outlined in STEP 3 above (could be done in person or by mail , depending on the procedures of the particular local INS office) to the office of the Immigration and Naturalization Service (INS) covering the alien's place of residence in the U.S. (see listing on pp.183-4)

If the Form 1 — 140 preference petition is applicable, and is being filed at the same time as the application for adjustment, both papers should be filed at the same INS office; if it is being filed without the application for adjustment, the filing would be with the INS office covering the place of the alien's intended employment. A nominal fee is charged by the INS for the filing of the adjustment application. A separate application need to be submitted for each member of the alien's family (the spouse and unmarried children under 21 years of age) being applied for.

Documents you may attach:

A number of supporting documents and forms often have to accompany the primary adjustment application forms. Thus, along with the applicable forms listed in STEP 3 above, you may also attach the following to your submission, as and if applicable:

- The alien's (each alien's) BIRTH CERTIFICATE or an equivalent
- 3 passport - size color PHOTOGRAPHS of each alien
- INS Form G - 325A, BIOGRAPHIC INFORMATION, to be filled out by the alien beneficiary. (sample is at p.110·)
- INS Form 1 - 94, "ARRIVAL — DEPARTMENT RECORD", which must have been obtained by the alien at the time of his original entry into the United States.

● The Alien's PASSPORT (used for proof of the alien's identity and nationality)

Documentary evidence that you (the alien) will not become a "public charge" in the United States - typically, it's either an AFFIDAVIT OF SUPPORT sworn to and given on the alien's behalf by a close relative in the U.S. and his/her spouse, if married, (same as FORM 1 —134 sampled on pp79-80), or an OFFER OR EMPLOYMENT LETTER from a U.S. employer, as in sample on pp. 134 & 151-2, for example, or both.

● FINGERPRINT **CARD**(same as FORM FD - 258 sampled on p. 72). The fingerprinting may be made either at a local INS office or at a local police department, and the fingerprint card duly filled out and signed by the official who did the fingerprinting. (Fingerprinting not applicable for aliens 14 years of age or younger.)

● Report of MEDICAL EXAMINATION. (The exam. must be done by a doctor or medical facility specifically designated by the INS to perform such service, and the report is usually made by the examining doctor on FORM FS 398, Forms 1-486A, OF 157, 1-693, or an equivalent .)

ADDITIONAL Documents Particular to Petitions Based on Family Relationships:

● BIRTH CERTIFICATE (or other equivalents, such as baptismal certificates, military service records, and the like) for both the petitioner and the alien "beneficiary" of the petition, to establish the relationship between the U.S. petitioner and the alien, if any.

● PROOF OF U.S. CITIZENSHIP OF PETITIONER, or of his/her U.S. Permanent Residency status (Form 1-551, the "Green Card")

● MARRIAGE CERTIFICATE of the petitioner to the alien, if applicable.

● PROOF OF AGE of each alien (e.g. birth certificate or Declaration of age).

● ADOPTION DECREE (or other proof of legal adoption), if the alien is said to be an adopted child.

● DIVORCE DECREE (or death certificate thereof) from prior marriages by the petitioner and/or the alien, if any.

● MARRIAGE CERTIFICATE OF THE COMMON PARENTS of the petitioner and the alien(s), in cases, for example, involving a brother or sister sponsoring a brother or sister.

● "SECONDARY EVIDENCE" type of data — such as affidavits (sworn statements) from people attesting to the necessary facts as to the close family relationship claimed, or letters, correspondence and other proof of communications which had existed between the petitioner and the alien.

● For an alien family member (a child or a spouse) accompanying or following to join an alien already qualified for visa issuance in the U.S., you must further furnish such documents as are necessary to establish the family relationship claimed: birth certificates, marriage licences, sworn statements (affidavits), letters and proof of other forms of communications which had existed between the petitioner and the alien.

ADDITIONAL Documents Particular For Petitions Based on Job-related 3rd or 6th Preference Visa Categories:

● Alien LABOUR CERTIFICATION (if applicable); with the underlying documentary evidence upon which the certification had been obtained attached. (See Chapter 8 at pp. for the labour certification procedures) See illustrative sample of Approved LABOR CERTIFICATION on pp.133 & 153)

● STATEMENT OF QUALIFICATION OF ALIEN, Form ETA750B. (See illustrative sample on pp.134)

● JOB OFFER FOR ALIEN, Form ETA-750A. (See illustrative sample on pp.129-130))

● Certified copies of CERTIFICATES, DIPLOMAS, SCHOOL TRANSCRIPTS, and other documents and proofs of educational qualification, job skills or professional status. (See, for example, "Explanatory Note" on p. 119, paragraph 3 thereof)

●**AFFIDAVIT FROM CREDIBLE AUTHORITIES OR EXPERTS** testifying to alien's technical training or specialized experience.

●**PUBLISHED MATERIALS BY OR ABOUT THE ALIEN** in newspapers, magazines, professional journals, and the like.

● Proof of **PROFESSIONAL LICENSES**, membership in professional societies, achievement awards, and the like.

● Affidavits from present or former employers, professors or professional colleagues. (See examples on pp. 134 & 152)

● EMPLOYER'S SUPPORTING LETTER OR OFFER OF EMPLOYMENT) from the alien's U.S. petitioner-employer. (For samples, see pp. 134 & 151-2)

● CERTIFICATE AWARDS from trade union or technical schools, apprenticeship schools, etc.

●LICENSES or trade union certificates.

step : **THE IMMIGRATION OFFICER EXAMINES YOUR APPLICATION & THE DOCUMENTATIONS FILED**

What happens next, after you've filed your adjustment-of-status application papers with the INS office? The INS examiners will take a quick look at your submission and make a preliminary assessment, and, assuming that the examiners are able to determine (from the figures from the Department of State's Visa Bulletin) that a visa number is immediately available to the alien at the particular time of the filing of the said application, the application will be considered properly filed and hence will be retained for processing.

Following that, the INS visa processing examiners will more closely examine the application papers to evaluate the alien's eligibility for admission. *Among the key questions they would seek answers to are such questions as the following:* is it clear in the given case that there are no grounds on which the alien can be excluded from the U.S. under Section 212 of the Immigration Act? Does the alien seemingly meet the qualifications under all immigration laws and regulations? Did he (she) come into the U.S. properly, after having undergone an inspection at a U.S. port or through being paroled into the U.S., pending an exclusion hearing? Are there any indications, or reasons to believe, that the alien has entered the U.S. with a <u>preconceived</u> intent to beome an immigrant and permanently reside in the U.S.? Has he in the past ever overstayed the time authorized him under the nonimmigrant visa he currently or previously had? Has the alien engaged in unauthorized employment after January 1, 1977? Has he maintained a valid status since entry into the U.S. and as of the time of the adjustment application? In other words, to put it in one sentence: does the alien lack any of the important qualifications for adjustment of status, or violate any of the conditions and prohibitions for gaining eligibility, enumerated in this chapter, at pp. 179-180 above?

step 7: ATTEND THE IMMIGRATION   VISA INTERVIEW

You (the alien and each one applying with him or her) will need to be interviewed by the INS following the preliminary screening of the application. The Immigration and Naturalization Service (INS) district office, upon scheduling the interview, will usually send or give you an interview appointment notice telling you the date and place set for the adjustment interview to be held. Indeed, the INS would usually send the alien the MEDICAl EXAMINATION AND IMMIGRATION INTERVIEW form (Form 1-486 or 1-693 or equivalent), with the date and place for the alien to appear for the immigration interview marked on the said Form. (The approved doctor, upon completion of the medical exam., completes Form 1 - 486A and returns it to the alien in a sealed envelope to deliver to the INS at the interview).

Now, depending on the procedures followed by your particular INS office, the interview may be held on the same day as the date of the filling of the application, or, more often than not, it may be scheduled weeks or even months later. If applicable in your situation, the interview may also cover the 1 - 140 Preference Petition filed by you, in which case the U.S. employer may also have to be invited for the INS interview.

The primary objective of the interview should be well understood. It is essentially this: to enable the interviewing officers to better determine whether the facts set forth by the alien in his underlying visa petition papers are accurate, or whether fraud is involved, and whether the alien meets the qualifications for adjustment as set forth under the law, or is deserving of being granted an adjustment anyway as a matter of discretion. Hence, the interviewer basically uses the face-to-face meeting and exchanges to counter-check any questions or apparent contradictions for consistency the aim being to fill in any material gaps or omissions on any questions occuring from the documentations submitted.

Again, depending on the precise processing procedure employed in the given INS district office of your filing, the required security clearances, which take 60 days to complete, may be made either prior to the interview or thereafter. In any case, whether made prior to or after the interview, the process by which such security checks are made are essentially the same: the INS forwards copies of the alien's Biographic Information form, FORM G - 325A, to the FBI, the CIA, and the consular office located in the alien's country of nationality or last residence, and waits for at least 60 days. (Such checks are limited only to applicants over 14 years of age.) If no response is received within the 60 days period, then it is assumed that no adverse information exists against the alien(s) in question.

Finally, the INS examiner will contact the State Department's Visa Section (usually by telephone and on the day of the interview) to assure that a visa number is available for the applicant. Now, assuming that a visa number is available, upon the conclusion of the interview the INS official may inform you (the alien) there and then that your adjustment application is approved. Or, the INS official may inform you that the decision will be sent you in the mail. If the adjustment application is granted, the INS officer will usually stamp your passport (or your Form 1 - 94) with employment authorization notation, and you will be assigned an "A" (file) card number which will become your permanent resident identification number on your GREEN CARD upon the finalization of your visa processing.

WHAT ARE THE CHANCES THAT THE INS MAY NOT RULE ON YOUR ADJUSTMENT APPLICATION FAIRLY OR OBJECTIVELY?

True, the granting of an alien's application to allow him to change from nonimmigrant to immigrant status is considered a "privilege" extended by the immigration service, rather than a right, and the INS officer is deemed to have sweeping "discretionary" powers either to grant such application or to deny it. Admittedly, it is to be clearly borne in mind that even when the alien can show that he or she meets all the statutory requirements called for to warrant the granting of adjusment, it is still possible, in deed totally within the realm of the INS's "discretaion", that the INS may still refuse to grant the adjustment, should it's officers simply feel, for example, that the alien does not deserve such a privilege. Nevertheless, with all that said, it should be stated, in all fairness to the INS, that as a practical matter by and large the rules under which the INS decides the fate of adjustment applicants hardly ever allow the INS to deny such applications on arbitrary basis – that is, without some good reason.* (Such reasons as, say, violation of the prohibition against unauthorized employment, or of having entered the U.S. with a pre-conceived intent to remain permanently resident there, or of making material false statements to a U.S. Consul in the alien's home country or in the adjustment application, or of failing to have maintained valid nonimmigrant status since entry in the U.S., and the like, for example.)

Probably the most common basis for denying an adjustment application is ENGAGING IN UNAUTHORIZED EMPLOYMENT on the part of an alien. Nevertheless, even in such cases the general rule followed by the INS in addressing them is that in the absence of some "adverse factor", approval of adjustment application is usually granted, and even in those circumstances where such adverse factors are present, the principle is that those adverse factors are weighted against any "unusual or even outstanding equities" (i.e., factors that are favorably countervailing) in the alien's favour in determining whether to grant adjustment.

The second most prominent basis for denying adjustment applications by the immigration service, is ENGAGING IN SHAM MARRIAGES. As a rule, immigration officials scrutinize adjustment applications that are based on marriage of the alien to a U.S. citizen or permanent resident alien, more carefully. The belief, common among immigration officials, is that this category of immigrant visas (that is, those based on marriage relationships) is the most abused among all immigrant visa categories, and that many such aliens enter into sham marriages simply for the purpose of securing immigrant visa eligibility through the marital relationship. Consequently, if you are an alien in a marriage relationship situation you should generally expect to be questioned closely regarding what your preconceived intention might have been at the time of your last entry into the U.S. as a nonimmigrant, the objective being to ascertain that the marriage was not entered into fraudulently, solely for the purpose of gaining eligibility for an immigrant visa, and that you and your supposed spouse truly intend to establish a life together in a bona fide marital relationship at the time when you entered into the marriage.

For a helpful insight, you'll find reproduced on pp. 172-3 a QUESTIONNAIRE used by consular and immigration officials in interviews and investigations where the bona fides (the honesty or legitimacy) of a marriage is a concern.

---

*See In the Matter of Arai, 131 & N. 494, 496 (B.I.A. 1970)

Format of suspected "Marriage Fraud" Interviews & INS Investigations.

Typically, in an immediate relative situation where both the alien and his/her U.S. citizen or permanent resident spouse live in the United States, the format is to interview the spouses separately. At the interview, the couple will be separated*and exactly the same questions will be asked each one on various specific personal issues about their relationship. The questions are normally diverse enough as to preclude the possibility that the spouse could anticipate or prepare the answer in advance of the interview, and, except for questions of sexual nature concerning the sexual habits of the couple, virtually every area of the couple's marital relationship could be probed. The questions asked will basically relate to matters which spouses who actually live together should normally know about each other and that perhaps no one else would know.

Typical questions will relate to matters such as: the divison of household chores, the food preferences of the spouses, what type of food was eaten by the couple on a particular day or occasion, the nature and setting of the couple's living room, questions about where things are kept, the number of rooms in the couple's marital residence, on which side of the sitting room or on which chair the respective spouses sit, the color preferences of the parties, on which side of the bed the respective spouses sleep, what time of the day each spouse typically wakes up to prepare for work or goes to sleep or returns from work, the kinds of sports programs or T.V. programs or movies preferred by each, and matters of this nature.

Then, following the separate questioning, the interviewer compares the answers of both spouses to the questions to determine that there are no serious inconsistencies between the two sets of answers. And if the immigration (or consular) examiner should be left with some serious doubts as to the legitimacy of the marriage, he can do one of two things: either deny the visa application outright, or refer the case to the Investigation Section of the INS which then assigns the matter to inspector for a "field investigation" of the marriage relationship. Such investigations would often involve things like making unannounced visits to the couple's designated home address at unusual hours (e.g. in early mornings or late at night) to determine if the parties really lived together, visiting the spouses' place of employment to check the information listed in the employment records regarding marital status, contacting the landlord of the couple's residence or the neighbors to ask questions about the couple, etc.

Indeed, the immigration and consular authorities hav designed a list of factors — "WARNING SIGNS"— as a guide for them in determining whether a given marriage may have been fraudulently entered into for purposes of getting an immigration benefit. They are: (1) that the couple has not knowneach other for very long; (2) they have only seen each other for a brief period or a few times prior to the marriage; (3) they do not presently live together or have never lived together; (4) they married only after the alien spouse becames the subject of a deportation proceeding; (5) they come from very different racial, cultural or religions backgrounds; (6) they do not speak a common language; (7) there is a big age difference between the couple; and (8) the alien spouse paid a large sum of money to the U.S. citizen or Permanent Resident.

The Principal "Discretionary" Factors Considered by the INS in Deciding on Adjustment Applications.

As summarized from the relevant major court and administrative decisions on the matter, the following are the principal factors which influence the decision of the immigration officials as they excercise administrative "discretion" on an adjustment application:

1. The existence of true family ties in the United States
2. Likelihood of hardship resulting to the alien and the petitioner and difficulty in traveling abroad
3. Length of residence in the U.S.
4. Evidence of preconceived intent to remain permanently in the U.S. at the alien's time of last entry into the U.S. as a nonimmigrant (e.g. entering the U.S. as a nonimmigratnt just weeks before making application for adjustment of status.)
5. Repeated violations of the immigration laws or entry into the U.S. as an undesirable nonimmigrant
6. Whether the applicant is a person of good moral character

---

*In situation where the alien spouse (or finance(s) lives in her native country, the alien spouse is interviewed alone there, and the U.S. relative who resides in the U.S. is not usually required to attend the interview.

7.   The candor of the applicant at the adjustment interview and in his application papers

8.   Circumstances clearly demonstrating, through the timing of the filing of the adjustment application, for example, that the only reason the alien entered the U.S. was to make his application for permanent resident. (For example, entering the U.S. as a nonimmigrant, and within a relatively short time marrying a U.S. citizen (or permanent resident) who had borne the alien a child and whom he had known for considerable length of time before the marriage, would raise a question of preconceived intent to marry a citizen and remain in the U.S. permanently)

On the other hand, immigration experts knowledgable in the matter suggest certain conditions as being helpful in getting a more favorable disposition by immigration officers in visa cases based on marriage relationship: existence of photographs that show the spouses together, such as wedding album or marriage reception pictures, guest list of persons who attended the wedding and letters, gifts and greeting cards which have been exchanged between the couple; keeping a joint bank account or joint credit cards by the couple, having mutual wills, use of the husband's last name by the wife, and evidence that the parents and families of the parties have met and approved of the marriage.

step 8: WHAT ARE YOUR REMEDIES IN THE EVENT YOUR APPLICATION IS DENIED?

A few courses of action are open to you should your application for adjustment be turned down for whatever the reason. First, you may simply forget about the application that had been filed on your behalf in the United States altogether, and just make out another application for immigrant visa and file it anew at the U.S. consulate in your home country. (Follow same procedure as in pp. 111-7). Or, alternatively, you may seek a re-consideration of your Application for Adjustment: you simply appeal your case firstly to the Board of Immigraton Appeals in Washington D.C., and following that, you may make a second but final appeal to the U.S. Court of Appeals, if need be. (See pp. 155-160 for detailed discussion of immigration appeals and hearing procedures.

EXPLANATORY NOTE (to the forms and procedures used in Chapter 10)

"**Adjustment of Status**" procedures (the subject matter of Chap. 10, at p.161-170), are very closely similar to the same procedures described with respect to the filing of Mr. Arun (Doe's) petition for 3rd Preference immigrant visa, as set forth in "Explanatory Note" on p.119 , starting especially from paragraph 3 thereof.

In that specific case discussed in "Explanatory Note" on p.119 , an actual case previously and successfully processed, Mr. Arun (Doe), an Indian national who had first come into the U.S. on an F-1 student visa, had, upon obtaining advanced degrees in Engineering, subsequently applied for and obtained a change of status to the non-immigrant **H-1 (temporary worker)** status. Thereupon, the alien's employers subsequently sought to get him a permanent residence - a 3rd preference visa - that would ensure his services to them on a permanent basis.

First, the employers applied for and obtained a labor certification approval from the U.S. Department of Labor for the position in question, following essentially the same procedures as those outlined in Chap. 8 of this manual, pp. 141-154. Then, **secondly,** at the same time, immediately after receiving the labor certification (i.e., no later than 60 days of that), the employers filed the **immigrant visa petition, Form I-140,** with the Immigration Service in Denver, Colorado, requesting to classify Mr. Arun (Doe) under the 3rd (it could also have been the 6th) preference visa category. (See sample Form I-140 for Arun reproduced on pp. 126-7, but note that the newer edition form currently in use, is reproduced on pp. 123-5 ; sample labor certification application Forms ETA 750A & B used for Arun are reproduced on pp.129-132, and the sample letter from the Dept. of Labor approving certification is reproduced on p.133).

And **thirdly,** at the same time the I-140 petition was filed, the alien "beneficiary" of the petition also filed an application to adjust his status to that of a Permanent Resident, Form I-485 (see pp. 135-6)) from within the U.S., and to this petition the alien attached the relevant supporting documents - the employer's letter of offer of employment (see copy on pp. 134), the alien's Biographic Information Form G-325A (a blank copy of this form is on p. 110), the alien's letter of approved Labor Certification (see pp. 133), and the underlying documents on which it was granted, fingerprints, photographs, birth certificate, passport, medical examination report, certified copy of alien's college degrees and diplomas and his Arrival-Departure Record, Form I-94, etc.

In this particular instance, the alien was able to **simultaneously** file for adjustment of status (Form I-485) with the visa petition (Form I-140), because he was in a position to do so in that the petition was for the 3rd preference for which there is relatively little or no backlog of visa numbers. In contrast, however, the 6th preference category job positions are generally noted for having chronic backlogs of visa numbers, and had the petition been filed in the 6th preference category, Mr. Arun (Doe) would not have been eligible to adjust his status from within the United States; rather, he would have had to designate in his petition (paragraph 18 of the current Form I-140 at p. 124) an American Consulate abroad closest to his residence to which the visa case should be sent for processing upon approval of the petition.

CONCERNING FAMILY-BASED IMMIGRANT VISA PETITIONS

What if this adjustment of status petition was based, not on employment or occupation, but on a marriage or blood relationship to a U.S. citizen or a Green Card holder - essentially those falling under the **1st, 2nd, 4th** and **5th preferences, and the "immediate relatives" and "special relatives" categories**? In such a situation, the procedures would remain basically the same as those outlined above, **EXCEPT** that: i) Rather than provide evidence of professional or job qualifications, such as a Labor Certification or school diplomas and the like, you merely have to provide evidence relevant to establishing the claimed family relationship, such as marriage and birth certificates, adoption papers, and the like; and ii) you'd have to file visa petition Form I-130, "Petition For Alien Relative," (see sample on pp. 120-2), rather than the petition Form I-140. The rest of the usual procedures will remain essentially the same as are outlined in Chap. 7 (pp. 111-7) and/or Chap. 10 (pp.161-170) of this manual for either category as the basis of qualification.

QUESTIONNAIRE USED TO ESTABLISH INTENTIONS
OF MARRIED COUPLE

Name_____   Date_____

File No._____

1. State your true and full name and any other names by which you are known.
2. State your spouse's full name and any other names by which he or she is known.
3. What is his/her date and place of birth?
4. Where do you presently reside? With whom and for how long?
5. When, where and how did you meet your spouse for the first time?
6. Who introduced you to him/her?
7. For how long did the courtship last? And how was it done?
8. How long did the two of you go steady before marriage?
9. Did you have any dates prior to marriage? Where and what did you do on those dates?
10. Who made the necessary arrangements for your wedding?
11. Where and when did you get married (specify place, time and date)?
12. What is the name of the officer, judge, priest or minister who solemnized your marriage? And who contracted him?
13. Approximately how many people were present during the wedding? If there are eight or less people who attended, list their names and your relationship to them.
14. What are the names of the witnesses at your wedding? And who chose them?
15. If a reception was help after the wedding, list the place, time and number of people who attended.
16. Were there pictures of the wedding, and/or the reception? If there were, pictures should be shown to the interrogation officer.
17. Where and for how long did you spend your honeymoon? Was the marriage consummated?
18. List all the places where you lived with your spouse and the inclusive dates when you lived at such places.
19. Aside from the two of you, who else lived in the above listed places?
20. Where are you presently working? What is the nature of your job? What hours do you work? And how much do you receive a month?
21. Where does your spouse work? What is the nature of his/her job? What hours does he/she work? And how much does he/she earn?
22. What are your parents names and present whereabouts?
23. What are your sibling's names and their addresses?
24. Was your spouse ever introduced to your parents and siblings? (If so, when and where?)
25. What are your spouse's parents' names and present addresses?
26. What are your spouses siblings' names and present addresses?
27. Have you ever been introduced to your spouse's parents and siblings? (If so, when and where?)
28. Did you give or receive a wedding ring or an engagement ring?
29. Was the ring engraved? Where was it purchased?
30. How many children do you have? List all their names, ages and present addresses.
31. By what means and how often did you hear from your spouse before and after your marriage?
32. If your spouse has already left for the U.S., how often has he/she visited you?
33. Where did you stay during those visits and what did you do?
34. Have you given or sent any gifts to your spouse? (What and when?)
35. Have you received any gifts or presents from your spouse? (What and when?)

36. Who is arranging for your travel documents? Any travel agent or atorney?
37. Who filled out the petition for you? Where was it filled out?
38. How often did you and your spouse go to your travel agent/attorney?
39. Who paid for your travel agent or attorney?
40. Who will pay for your traveling expenses and how?
41. Monetary support. How much and how often?
42. The following documents and/or papers were shown to the interviewer/witness:

	Date	Quantity
Letters	_____	_____
Photos (Wedding)	_____	_____
(Reception)	_____	_____
Money Order Receipts	_____	_____

I have read the foregoing statement and it is a true and correct record of my declaration.

_____
Signature (of alien spouse)

Subscribed and sworn before me on_____ at_____

_____
Signature (of INS officer)

Witnessed by:_____

_____
Signature
CLERK

_____   _____
                                                  Title

FORM I-485

U.S. Department of Justice
Immigration and Naturalization Service (INS)

–174–

Application for Permanent Residence

P.I.
OMB # 1115-0053

DO NOT WRITE IN THIS BLOCK

Case ID#	Action Stamp	Fee Stamp
A#		
G-28 or Volag#		

NOTE: This is the last revised version of this Form. The preceding Form (before 2/27/87) is reproduced on pp. 135-6. Before completing Form, first read the INSTRUCTIONS accompanying Form

Section of Law
- ☐ Sec. 209(b), INA
- ☐ Sec. 214(d), INA
- ☐ Sec. 13, Act of 9/11/57
- ☐ Sec. 245, INA
- ☐ Sec. 249, INA

Country Chargeable _____

Eligibility Under Sec. 245
- ☐ Approved Visa Petition
- ☐ Dependent of Principal Alien
- ☐ Special Immigrant
- ☐ Other _____

Preference _____

A. Reason for this application

I am applying for lawful permanent residence for the following reason: (check the box that applies)

1. ☐ An immigrant visa number is immediately available to me because
   - ☐ A visa petition has already been approved for me (approval notice is attached)
   - ☐ A visa petition is being filed with this application
2. ☐ I entered as the fiance(e) of a U.S. citizen and married within 90 days (approval notice and marriage certificate are attached)
3. ☐ I am an asylee eligible for adjustment
4. ☐ Other: _____

B. Information about you

1. **Name** (Family name in CAPS)   (First)   (Middle)

2. **Address** (Number and Street)   (Apartment Number)

   (Town or City)   (State/Country)   (ZIP/Postal Code)

3. **Place of Birth** (Town or City)   (State/Country)

4. **Date of Birth** (Mo/Day/Yr)

5. **Sex**
   - ☐ Male
   - ☐ Female

6. **Marital Status**
   - ☐ Married
   - ☐ Widowed
   - ☐ Single
   - ☐ Divorced

7. **Social Security Number**

8. **Alien Registration Number** (if any)

9. **Country of Citizenship**

10. **Have you ever applied for permanent resident status in the U.S.?**
    - ☐ Yes   ☐ No
    (If Yes, give the date and place of filing and final disposition)

11. **On what date did you last enter the U.S.?**

12. **Where did you last enter the U.S.?** (City and State)

13. **What means of travel did you use?** (Plane, car, etc.)

14. **Were you inspected by a U.S. immigration officer?**
    - ☐ Yes   ☐ No

15. **In what status did you last enter the U.S.?**
    (Visitor, student, exchange alien, crewman, temporary worker, without inspection, etc.)

16. **Give your name EXACTLY as it appears on your Arrival/Departure Record (Form I-94).**

17. **Arrival/Departure Record (I-94) Number**

18. **Visa Number**

19. **At what Consulate was your nonimmigrant visa issued?**   Date (Mo/Day/Yr)

20. **Have you ever been married before?**   ☐ Yes   ☐ No

If Yes.   (Names of prior husbands/wives)   (Country of citizenship)   (Date marriage ended)

21. **Has your husband/wife ever been married before?**   ☐ Yes   ☐ No

If Yes.   (Names of prior husbands/wives)   (Country of citizenship)   (Date marriage ended)

INITIAL RECEIPT	RESUBMITTED	RELOCATED		COMPLETED		
		Rec'd	Sent	Approved	Denied	Returned

FORM I-485 (REV. 2-27-87)N

–OVER– →

22. List your present husband/wife, all of your sons and daughters, all of your brothers and sisters (If you have none, write "N/A")

Name	Relationship	Place of Birth	Date of Birth	Country of Residence	Applying With You?
					☐ Yes ☐ No
					☐ Yes ☐ No
					☐ Yes ☐ No
					☐ Yes ☐ No
					☐ Yes ☐ No
					☐ Yes ☐ No
					☐ Yes ☐ No
					☐ Yes ☐ No
					☐ Yes ☐ No
					☐ Yes ☐ No

23. List your present and past membership in or affiliation with every organization, association, fund, foundation, party, club, society or similar group in the United States or in any other country or place, and your foreign military service (If this does not apply, write "N/A")

A _____ 19 _____ to 19 _____
B _____ 19 _____ to 19 _____
C _____ 19 _____ to 19 _____
D _____ 19 _____ to 19 _____
E _____ 19 _____ to 19 _____
F _____ 19 _____ to 19 _____
G _____ 19 _____ to 19 _____

24. Have you ever, in or outside the United States:

a) knowingly committed any crime for which you have not been arrested? ☐ Yes ☐ No

b) been arrested, cited, charged, indicted, convicted, fined, or imprisoned for breaking or violating any law or ordinance, including traffic regulations? ☐ Yes ☐ No

c) been the beneficiary of a pardon, amnesty, rehabilitation decree, other act of clemency or similar action? ☐ Yes ☐ No

If you answered Yes to (a), (b), or (c) give the following information about each incident

	Date	Place (City)	(State/Country)	Nature of offense	Outcome of case, if any
1)					
2)					
3)					
4)					
5)					

25. Have you ever received public assistance from any source, including the U.S. Government or any state, county, city or municipality?

☐ Yes ☐ No   (If Yes, explain, including the name(s) and Social Security number(s) you used.)

26. Do any of the following relate to you? (Answer Yes or No to each)

A Have you been treated for a mental disorder, drug addiction, or alcoholism? ☐ Yes ☐ No

B Have you engaged in, or do you intend to engage in, any commercialized sexual activity? ☐ Yes ☐ No

C Are you or have you at any time been an anarchist, or a member of or affiliated with any Communist or other totalitarian party, including any subdivision or affiliate? ☐ Yes ☐ No

D. Have you advocated or taught, by personal utterance, by written or printed matter, or through affiliation with an organization:

1) opposition to organized government ☐ Yes ☐ No

2) the overthrow of government by force or violence ☐ Yes ☐ No

3) the assaulting or killing of government officials because of their official character ☐ Yes ☐ No

4) the unlawful destruction of property ☐ Yes ☐ No

5) sabotage ☐ Yes ☐ No

6) the doctrines of world communism, or the establishment of a totalitarian dictatorship in the United States? ☐ Yes ☐ No

E. Have you engaged or do you intend to engage in prejudicial activities or unlawful activities of a subversive nature? ☐ Yes ☐ No

F. During the period beginning March 23, 1933, and ending May 8, 1945, did you order, incite, assist, or otherwise participate in persecuting any person because of race, religion, national origin, or political opinion, under the direction of, or in association with any of the following:

1) the Nazi government in Germany ☐ Yes ☐ No

2) any government in any area occupied by the military forces of the Nazi government in Germany ☐ Yes ☐ No

3) any government established with the assistance or cooperation of the Nazi government of Germany ☐ Yes ☐ No

4) any government that was an ally of the Nazi government of Germany ☐ Yes ☐ No

G. Have you been convicted of a violation of any law or regulation relating to narcotic drugs or marijuana, or have you been an illicit trafficker in narcotic drugs or marijuana? ☐ Yes ☐ No

(Continues) ➔

H. Have you been involved in assisting any other aliens to enter the United States in violation of the law? ☐ Yes ☐ No

I. Have you applied for exemption or discharge from training or service in the Armed Forces of the United States on the ground of alienage and have you been relieved or discharged from that training or service? ☐ Yes ☐ No

J. Are you mentally retarded, insane, or have you suffered one or more attacks of insanity? ☐ Yes ☐ No

K. Are you afflicted with psychopathic personality, sexual deviation, mental defect, narcotic drug addiction, chronic alcoholism, or any dangerous contagious disease? ☐ Yes ☐ No

L. Do you have a physical defect, disease, or disability affecting your ability to earn a living? ☐ Yes ☐ No

M. Are you a pauper, professional beggar, or vagrant? ☐ Yes ☐ No

N. Are you likely to become a public charge? ☐ Yes ☐ No

O. Are you a polygamist or do you advocate polygamy? ☐ Yes ☐ No

P. Have you been excluded from the United States within the past year, or have you at any time been deported from the United States, or have you at any time been removed from the United States at government expense? ☐ Yes ☐ No

Q. Have you procured or have you attempted to procure a visa by fraud or misrepresentation? ☐ Yes ☐ No

R. Are you a former exchange visitor who is subject to, but has not complied with, the two-year foreign residence requirement? ☐ Yes ☐ No

S. Are you a medical graduate coming principally to work as a member of the medical profession, without passing Parts I and II of the National Board of Medical Examiners Examination (or an equivalent examination)? ☐ Yes ☐ No

T. Have you left the United States to avoid military service in time of war or national emergency? ☐ Yes ☐ No

U. Have you committed or have you been convicted of a crime involving moral turpitude? ☐ Yes ☐ No

If you answered Yes to any question above, explain fully (Attach a continuation sheet if necessary)

_____

_____

_____

_____

27. ☐ **Completed Form G-325A (Biographic Information) is signed, dated and attached as part of this application.** Print or type so that all copies are legible.   ☐ **Completed form G-325A (Biographic Information) is not attached because applicant is under 14 or over 79 years of age.**

Penalties: You may, by law, be fined up to $10,000, imprisoned up to five years, or both, for knowingly and willfully falsifying or concealing a material fact or using any false document in submitting this application.

Your Certification

I certify, under penalty of perjury under the laws of the United States of America, that the above information is true and correct. Furthermore, I authorize the release of any information from my records which the Immigration and Naturalization Service needs to determine eligibility for the benefit that I am seeking.

Signature _____ Date _____ Phone Number _____

Signature of Person Preparing Form if Other than Above

I declare that I prepared this document at the request of the person above and that it is based on all information of which I have any knowledge.

_____   _____   _____   _____
(Print Name)   (Address)   (Signature)   (Date)

G-28 ID Number _____

Volag Number _____

Stop Here

(Applicant is **not** to sign the application below until he or she appears before an officer of the Immigration and Naturalization Service for examination)

I, _____ swear (affirm) that I know the contents of this application that I am signing including the attached documents, that they are true to the best of my knowledge, and that corrections numbered (   ) to (   ) were made by me or at my request, and that I signed this application with my full, true name:

_____
(Complete and true signature of applicant)

Signed and sworn to before me by the above-named applicant at _____ on _____
                                                                                        (Month)   (Day)   (Year)

_____
(Signature and title of officer)

(End of Form)

FORM I-693

U.S. Department of Justice
Immigration and Naturalization Service

(Front page)

OMB #1115-0134

Medical Examination of Aliens Seeking Adjustment of Status

(Please type or print clearly)
I certify that on the date shown I examined:

1. Name (Last in CAPS)

(First)   (Middle Initial)

2. Address (Street number and name)   (Apt. number)

(City)   (State)   (ZIP Code)

3. File number (A number)

4. Sex
☐ Male   ☐ Female

5. Date of birth (Month/Day/Year)

6. Country of birth

7. Date of examination (Month/Day/Year)

General Physical Examination: I examined specifically for evidence of the conditions listed below. My examination revealed;

☐ No apparent defect, disease, or disability.   ☐ The conditions listed below were found (check all boxes that apply).

Class A Conditions

☐ Chancroid
☐ Chronic alcoholism
☐ Gonorrhea
☐ Granuloma inguinale

☐ Hansen's disease, infectious
☐ HIV infection
☐ Insanity
☐ Lymphogranuloma venereum

☐ Mental defect
☐ Mental retardation
☐ Narcotic drug addiction
☐ Previous occurrence of one or more attacks of insanity

☐ Psychopathic personality
☐ Sexual deviation
☐ Syphilis, infectious
☐ Tuberculosis, active

Class B Conditions

☐ Hansen's disease, not infectious   ☐ Tuberculosis, not active

☐ Other physical defect, disease or disability (specify below).

Examination for Tuberculosis - Tuberculin Skin Test

☐ Reaction _____ mm   ☐ No reaction   ☐ Not done

Doctor's name (please print)   Date read

Examination for Tuberculosis - Chest X-Ray Report

☐ Abnormal   ☐ Normal   ☐ Not done

Doctor's name (please print)   Date read

Serologic Test for Syphilis

☐ Reactive Titer (confirmatory test performed)   ☐ Nonreactive

Test Type

Doctor's name (please print)   Date read

Serologic Test for HIV Antibody

☐ Positive (confirmed by Western blot)   ☐ Negative

Test Type

Doctor's name (please print)   Date read

Immunization Determination (DTP, OPV, MMR, Td-Refer to *PHS Guidelines* for recommendations.)

☐ Applicant is current for recommended age-specific immunizations.

☐ Applicant is not current for recommended age-specific immunizations and I have encouraged that appropriate immunizations be obtained.

REMARKS:

Civil Surgeon Referral for Follow-up of Medical Condition

☐ The alien named above has applied for adjustment of status. A medical examination conducted by me identified the conditions above which require resolution before medical clearance is granted or for which the alien may seek medical advice. Please provide follow-up services or refer the alien to an appropriate health care provider. The actions necessary for medical clearance are detailed on the reverse of this form.

Follow-up Information:
The alien named above has complied with the recommended health follow-up.

Doctor's name and address (please type or print clearly)   Doctor's signature   Date

---

Applicant Certification:
I certify that I understand the purpose of the medical examination, I authorize the required tests to be completed, and the information on this form refers to me.

Signature   Date

Civil Surgeon Certification:
My examination showed the applicant to have met the medical examination and health follow-up requirements for adjustment of status.

Doctor's name and address (please type or print clearly)   Doctor's signature   Date

---

The Immigration and Naturalization Service is authorized to collect this information under the provisions of the Immigration and Nationality Act and the Immigration Reform and Control Act of 1986. Public Law 99-603.

OVER→

(Back Page)
Medical Clearance Requirements
for Aliens Seeking Adjustment of Status

Medical Condition	Estimated Time For Clearance	Action Required
*Suspected Mental Conditions	5 - 30 Days	The applicant must provide to a civil surgeon a psychological or psychiatric evaluation from a specialist or medical facility for final classification and clearance.
Tuberculin Skin Test Reaction and Normal Chest X-Ray	Immediate	The applicant should be encouraged to seek further medical evaluation for possible preventive treatment.
Tuberculin Skin Test Reaction and Abnormal Chest X-Ray or Abnormal Chest X-Ray (Inactive/Class B)	10 - 30 Days	The applicant should be referred to a physician or local health department for further evaluation. Medical clearance may not be granted until the applicant returns to the civil surgeon with documentation of medical evaluation for tuberculosis.
Tuberculin Skin Test Reaction and Abnormal Chest X-Ray or Abnormal Chect X-Ray (Active or Suspected Active/Class A)	10 - 300 Days	The applicant should obtain an appointment with physician or local health department. If treatment for active disease is started, it must be completed (usually 9 months) before a medical clearance may be granted. At the completion of treatment, the applicant must present to the civil surgeon documentation of completion. If treatment is not started, the applicant must present to the civil surgeon documentation of medical evaluation for tuberculosis.
Hansen's Disease	30 - 210 Days	Obtain an evaluation from a specialist or Hansen's disease clinic. If the disease is indeterminate or Tuberculoid, the applicant must present to the civil surgeon documentation of medical evaluation. If disease is Lepromotous or Borderline (dimorphous) and treatment is started, the applicant must complete at least 6 months and present documentation to the civil surgeon showing adequate supervision, treatment, and clinical response before a medical clearance is granted.
**Venereal Diseases	1 - 30 Days	Obtain an appointment with a physician or local public health department. An applicant with a reactive serologic test for syphilis must provide to the civil surgeon documentation of evaluation for treatment. If any of the venereal diseases are infectious, the applicant must present to the civil surgeon documentation of completion of treatment.
Immunizations Incomplete	Immediate	Immunizations are not required, but the applicant should be encouraged to go to physician or local health department for appropriate immunizations.
HIV Infection	Immediate	Post-test counseling is not required, but the applicant should be encouraged to seek appropriate post-test counseling.

*Mental retardation; insanity; previous attack of insanity; psychopathic personality, sexual deviation or mental defect; narcotic drug addition; and chronic alcoholism.

**Chancroid; gonorrhea; granuloma inguinale; lymphogranuloma venereum; and syphilis.

Form I-693 (Rev. 09/01/87) N

APPENDIX A

1. GROUNDS FOR EXCLUSION FROM THE UNITED STATE

The exclusion provisions of the Immigration and Nationality Act do not apply to citizens of the United States.

Any alien found to be inadmissible shall be referred to an Immigration Inspector for further examination. Bear in mind that presentation of appropriate documents or examption from the necessity for presenting such documents does not entitle any alien to enter the United Sates if he falls within any of the classes which are excludable by law.

Of the thirty-one classes of excludable aliens listed in Section 212(a), twenty-one deal with classes of aliens who are considered *personally undesirable.* The first six of these are in Section 212 (a)(1) through 212 (a) (6) and relate to aliens who are physically or mentally deficient.

(1) Aliens who are mentally retarded
(2) Aliens who are insane
(3) Aliens who have had one or more attacks of insanity
(4) Aliens who are afflicte with psychopathic personality, sexual deviation, or mental defect.
(5) Aliens who are drug addicts or chronic alcoholics
(6) Aliens who are afflicted with any dangerous contagious disease

The exclusion of aliens under the above paragraphs (1) through (6) **can be only on the basis of a Class "A" certificate issued by the Public Health Service.**

The next four undesirable **classes based on economic factors are listed in Section 212 (a) (7), (8), (14), and (15) as follows:**

(7) Aliens who have a physical defect that may affect ability to earn a living
(8) Aliens who are paupers, professional beggars or vagrants
(14) Aliens whose employment in the United States may adversely affect similarly employed United States citizens or lawful permanent resident aliens
(15) Aliens who are likely to become public charges

The exclusion of an alien under (7) is based on a Class "B" certificate issued by the Public Health Service. Only certain specified classes of immigrants are excludable under (14), generally, aliens in those specified classes who are seeking employment in the United States must get a certification from the Secretary of Labour that his employment will not adversely affect United States Labour.

The next six undersirble **classes based on criminal or immoral grounds** are listed in Section 212(a)(9) through (13) and in Section 212(a)(23).

(9) Aliens who have committed a crime involving moral turpitude
(10) Aliens who have been convicted of two or more offenses for which the aggregate sentences to confinement actually imposed were five years of more
(11) Aliens who are polygamists or who practice or advocate the practice of polygamy.
(12) Aliens who are prostitutes or connected with prostitution or unlawful commercialized vice
(13) Aliens who have been convicted of a narcotics law or are engaged in illicit traffic of narcotics

Many decisions have been published establishing standards and guidelines in determining "crimes," "moral turpitude", "admission of crimes", "prosptitution", "immoral sex act," "narcotics", etc. These decisions are available in Immigration offices and may be discussed in more detail with an officer of the Immigration Service.

Polygamists who enter the United States as nonimmigrants are exempted from Section 212(a)(11). The next undersirable class is found in Section 212(a)(25) and is **based on illiteracy.**

(25) Aliens over sixteen years of age, physically capable of reading, who cannot read and understand some language or dialect

Lawful permanent residents returning from a temporary visit abroad are exempted from Section 212(a)(25). There are several other exemptions, such a nonimmigrants and aliens with close familial ties in the United States.

The next three underirable classes are found in Section 212(a)(27) through (29) and relate to subversives or aliens whose entry would be contrary to the best interests of the **United States.**

(27) Aliens who seek to enter the United States to engage in activities prejudicial to the public interest

(28) Aliens who are Communists or subversives

(29) Aliens who might engage in espionage, sabotage, public disorder, or in other subversive activity

The last of the twenty-one personally undesirable classes of aliens is found in Section 212(a)(31) and relates to smugglers.

(31) Aliens who smuggle or assist other aliens to enter the United States in violation of law

The above section of law has particular application along our land borders because of the activity of known smugglers in nearly countries.

The next five classes of aliens are **excludable because of improper manner of arrival** and are found in Section 212(a)(16), (17), (18), (24), and (30).

(16) Aliens who have been excluded and deported within the past year

(17) Aliens who have been arrested and deported

(18) Aliens who are stowaways

(24) Aliens who arrival in adjacent islands or contiguous territories on nonsignatory carriers

(30) Aliens accompanying other aliens who have been ordered excluded and deported

Aliens who fall within (16) and (17) may overcome their inadmissibility by obtaining permission from the Attoney General to reapply for admission. Alien nonimmigrant stowaways found on board are not entitled to an excluson hearing before a special Inquiry Officer. Section 212(a)(24) is not applicable to aliens seeking entry as nonimmigrants.

Aliens who are **excludable for documentary reasons** fall within the next four classes listed in Section 212(a)(19), (20), (21) and (26)

(19) Aliens who have obtained visas or other documents by fraud

(20) Alien immigrants who at time of application for admission do not have proper documents

(21) Alien immigrants who have visas that are not issued in compliance with Section 203 of the Immigration and Nationality Act

(26) Alien nonimmigrants who are not in possession of proper documents

Paragraphs (20) and (26) are brought into use more than any other section. However, there are provisions for waiver of documents that may be applied to correct the majority of cases. Section 212(a)(21) is rarely found applicable as a ground of exclusion. Section 212(a)(19) has also resulted in a number of published decisions establishing standards and guidelines.

The last of the listed classes in Section 212(a) is in Section 212(a)(22) and is based on ineligibility for citizenship.

(22) Aliens who are ineligible for citizenship or who have evaded service or training in the armed forces of the United States.

The above section of law embraces those aliens who apply for exemption or discharge from training or service in the Armed Forces on the ground of alienage and who are relieved or discharged as a result of the application.

It is important to reflect that diplomats and international organization nonimmigrants properly documented under classifications A-1, A-2, G-1, G-2, G-3, or G-4 are exempt from practically all of the above exclusionary provisions.

NOTE: All thirty-one paragraphs of Section 212(a) have been discussed in brief. It must be stressed there are many exception, exemptions, and waivers that may be applicable in a given case. This is one reason that aliens who are thought to be excludable should be referred to an inspector of this Service.

APPENDIX B
MAIN OFFICES OF EACH STATE'S EMPLOYMENT SERVICES IN THE UNITED STATES

ALABAMA
Dept. of Industrial Relations
649 Monroe Street
Montgomery, Alabama 36130

ALASKA
Employment Security Div.,
Department of Labor
4th & Harris Sts.
P.O. Box 3-7000
Juneau, Alaska 99811

ARIZONA
Dept. of Economics Security
P.O. Box 6123
Phoenix, Arizona 85005

ARKANSAS
Employment Security Commission
P.O. Box 2981
Capitol Mall
Little Rock, Arkansas 72203

CALIFORNIA
Employment Development Dept.
800 Capitol Mall
Sacramento, California 95814

COLORADO
Division of Employment & Training
251 E. 12th Avenue
Denver, Colorado 80203

CONNECTICUT
Employment Security Division
Hartford, Connecticut 06115

DELAWARE
Department of Labor
801 West Street
Wilmington, Delaware 19899

DISTRICT OF COLUMBIA
D.C. Department of Manpower
500 C Street, NW
Washington, DC 20001

FLORIDA
Department of Commerce
Collins Building, Suite 510
Tallahassee, Florida 32304

GEORGIA
Employment Security Agency
290 State Labor Building
Atlanta, Georgia 30334

GUAM
Department of Labor
Government of Guam
P.O. Box 2950
Agana, Guam 96910

HAWAII
Dept. of Labor and Industrial Security
825 Mililani Street
Honolulu, Hawaii 96813

IDAHO
Department of Employment
317 Main Street
P.O. Box 35
Boise, Idaho 83707

ILLINOIS
Bureau of Employment Security
910 South Michigan Avenue
Chicago, Illinois 60605

INDIANA
Employment Security Division
10 North Senate Avenue
Indianapolis, Indiana 46204

IOWA
Iowa Dept. of Job Service
1000 East Grand Avenue
Des Moines, Iowa 50319

KANSAS
Division of Employment
Dept. of Human Resources
401 Topeka Avenue
Topeka, Kansas 66603

KENTUCKY
Dept. of Human Resources
Bureau for Manpower Services
275 E. Main Street
Frankfort, Kentucky 40621

LOUISIANA
Dept. of Employment Security
1001 N. 23rd Street
Baton Rouge, Louisiana 70804

MAINE
Employment Security Commission
20 Union Street
Augusta, Maine 04332

MARYLAND
Employment Security Administration
1100 North Eutaw Street
Baltimore, Maryland 21201

MASSACHUSETTS
Division of Employment Security
Charles F. Hurley ES Building
Boston, Massachusetts 02114

MICHIGAN
Michigan Employment Security Comm
7310 Woodward Avenue
Detroit, Michigan 48202

MINNESOTA
Dept. of Employment Services
390 N. Robert Street
St. Paul, Minnesota 55101

MISSISSIPPI
Employment Security Commission
1520 W. Capital Street
P.O. Box 1699
Jackson, Mississippi 39205

MISSOURI
Div. of Employment Security
421 E. Dunklin Street
P.O. Box 59
Jefferson City, Missouri 65101

MONTANA
Employment Security Division
Corner of Lockey & Roberts
P.O. Box 1728
Helena, Montana 59601

NEBRASKA
Division of Employment
550 S. 16th Street
P.O. Box 94600
Lincoln, Nebraska 68509

NEVADA
Employment Security Dept.
500 East 3rd Street
Carson City, Nevada 89713

NEW HAMPSHIRE
Dept. of Employment Security
32 S. Main Street—Room 204
Concord, New Hampshire 03301

NEW JERSEY
Dept. of Labor & Industry
John Fitch Plaza
P.O. Box V
Trenton, New Jersey 08625

NEW MEXICO
Employment Security Commission
401 Broadway NE
P.O. Box 1928
Albuquerque, New Mexico 87103

NEW YORK
Department of Labor
State Campus, Building 12
Albany, New York 12240

NORTH CAROLINA
Employment Security Commission
P.O. Box 25903
200 W. Jones Street
Raleigh, North Carolina

NORTH DAKOTA
Employment Security Bureau
1000 E. Divide Avenue
P.O. Box 1537
Bismarck, North Dakota 58505

OHIO
Bureau of Employment Services
145 S. Front Street
P.O. Box 1618
Columbus, Ohio 43216

OKLAHOMA
Employment Security Commission
Will Rogers Memorial Office Bldg.
Oklahoma City, Oklahoma 73105

OREGON
Employment Division
875 Union Street NE
Salem, Oregon 97311

PENNSYLVANIA
Bureau of Employment Security,
Labor & Industry Bldg.
7th and Forster Streets
Harrisburg, Pennsylvania 17121

PUERTO RICO
Bureau of Employment Security
414 Barbosa Avenue
Hato Rey, Puerto Rico 00917

RHODE ISLAND
Dept. of Employment Security
24 Mason Street
Providence, Rhode Island 02903

SOUTH CAROLINA
Employment Security Commission
1550 Gadsden Street
P.O. Box 995
Columbus, South Carolina 29202

SOUTH DAKOTA
Employment Security Department
607 North Fourth Street
Aberdeen, South Dakota 57401

TENNESSEE
Dept. of Employment Security
536 Cordell Hull Building
Nashville, Tennessee 37219

TEXAS
Employment Commission
638 TEC Building
15th & Congress Avenues
Austin, Texas 78778

UTAH
Dept. of Employment Security
174 Social Hall Avenue
P.O. Box 11249
Salt Lake City, Utah 84147

VERMONT
Dept. of Employment Security
5 Green Mountain Drive
P.O. Box 488
Montpelier, Vermont 05602

VIRGINIA
Employment Commission
703 East Main Street
P.O. Box 1358
Richmond, Virginia 23211

VIRGIN ISLANDS
Employment Security Agency
35 Norre Gade Street
P.O. Box 1092
Charlotte Amalie
St. Thomas, Virgin Islands 00801

WASHINGTON
Employment Security Department
ES Building—212 Maple Park
Olympia, Washington 98504

WEST VIRGINIA
Dept. of Employment Security
112 California Avenue
Charleston, W. Virginia 25305

WISCONSIN
Job Service Department
201 E. Washington Avenue
P.O. Box 7398
Madison, Wisconsin 53701

WYOMING
Employment Security Commission
ESC Bldg.—Center & Midwest St.
P.O. Box 2760
Casper, Wyoming

APPENDIX C
IMMIGRATION AND NATURALIZATION SERVICE
OFFICES IN EACH STATE

The District Offices are open usually Monday through Friday, 9:00 a.m. or earlier until about 4 or 5:00 p.m. Some offices are so crowded that to keep order, a number is given to those waiting.

Numbers are not given out after a certain time of the day in the busiest offices. People should arrive early and be prepared to stay most of the day.

DISTRICT OFFICES:

Begin address with: "Immigration and Naturalization Service"

New Federal Building
701 C Street, Rm. D229
Anchorage, **Alaska** 99513

Federal Building
230 North First Avenue
Phoenix, **Arizona** 85025

300 North Los Angeles Street
Los Angeles, **California** 90012

880 Front Street
San Diego, **California** 92188

Appraisers Building
630 Sansone Street
San Francisco, **California** 9411

17027 Federal Office Building
Denver, **Colorado** 80202

900 Asylum Avenue
Hartford, **Connecticut** 06105

25 E Street, N.W.
Washington, D.C. 20538

155 South Miami Avenue
Miami, **Florida** 33130

Richard B. Russel
Federal Office Building
75 Spring Street, Rm. 1408
Atlanta, **Georgia** 30303

P.O. Box 461
695 Ala Moana Boulevard
Honolulu, **Hawaii** 96809

Dirksen Federal Office Bldg.
219 South Dearborn Street
Chicago, **Illinois** 60604

Postal Service Building
701 Loyola Avenue
New Orleans, **Louisiana** 70113

76 Pearl Street
Portland, **Maine** 04112

E.A. Garmatz Federal Building
100 South Hanover Street
Baltimore, **Maryland** 21201

E.A. Garmatz Federal Building
100 South Hanover Street
Baltimore, **Maryland** 21201

John Fitzgerald Kennedy
Government Center
Boston, **Massachusetts** 02203

Federal Building
333M. Elliott Street
Detroit, **Michigan** 48207

932 New Post Office Building
180 East Kellogg Boulevard
St. Paul, **Minnesota** 55101

Suite 1100
324 E. Eleventh Street
Kansas City, **Missouri** 64106

Federal Building, Rm. 512
Drawer 10036
301 South Park
Helena, **Montana** 59626

106 South 15th Street
Room 1008
Omaha, **Nebraska** 68102

Federal Building
970 Broad Street
Newark, **New Jersey 07102**

68 Court Street
Buffalo, **New York 14202**

26 Federal Plaza
New York, **New York** 10007

Rm. 1917, Anthony J. Celebreeze
Federal Office Building
1240 East 9th Street
Cleveland, **Ohio 44199**

Federal Office Building
511 N.W. Broadway
Portland, **Oregon** 97209

Room 1321, U.S. Courthouse
Independence Mall West
601 Market Street
Philadelphia, **Pennsylvania** 19106
GPO Box 5068

San Juan, **Puerto Rico** 00936

Room BA12, Federal Building
1100 Commerce Street
Dallas, **Texas** 75242

P.O. Box 9398
343 U.S. Courthouse
El Paso, Texas 79984

719 Grimes Avenue
Harlington, Texas 78550

Federal Building
U.S. Courthouse
P.O. Box 61630
515 Rusk Avenue
Houston, **Texas** 77208

U.S. Federal Building
Suite A301
727 East Durango
San Antonio, **Texas** 78206

Federal Building
P.O. Box 591
St. Albans, **Vermont** 05478

815 Airport Way, South
Steattle, **Washington** 98134

LOCAL OFFICES:

104 Federal Building
507 State Street
Hammond, **Indiana** 46320

Room 423
U.S. Courthouse and Customhouse
1114 Market Street
St. Louis, **Missouri** 63101

Federal Building
U.S. Courthouse
300 Las Vegas Boulevard South
Las Vegas, **Nevada** 89101

Suite 150
350 South Center Street
Reno, **Nevada** 89502

Room 220, U.S. Post Office & Courthouse
445 Broadway
Albany, **New York** 12207

Charles R. Jones Federal Bldg.
P.O. Box 31247
401 West Trade Street
Charlotte, **North Carolina** 28231

P.O. Box 537, 5th & Walnut Streets
U.S. Post Office and Courthouse
Cincinnati, **Ohio** 45201

2130 Federal Building
1000 Liberty Avenue
Pittsburgh, **Pennsylvania** 15222

Federal Building, U.S. Post Office
Exchange Terrace
Providence, Rhode Island 02903

814 Federal Office Building
167 North Main Street
Memphis, Tennessee 38103

Room 4103 Federal Building
125 South State Street
Salt Lake City, Utah 84138

Norfolk Federal Building
200 Granby Mall
Norfolk, Virginia 23510

691 U.S. Courthouse Building
Spokane, Washington 99201

Room 186, Federal Building
517 East Wisconsin Avenue
Milwaukee, Wisconsin 53202

APPENDIX D

WHO'S WHO FOR ALIENS

The cast of persons dealing with the problems of aliens is as extensive as the interests of the alien. The agencies that deal with the right of aliens to come to the United States include the State Department, which is responsible for the issuance of visas; the Department of Justice, which determines eligibility to obtain various types of visas and whether an alien may be admitted into the United States; the Department of Labor, which decides, in certain situations, whether aliens may enter the United States to be employed; the Department of Health, Education, and Welfare, which conducts medical examinations of aliens, administers Social Security laws, and determines standards for various health and welfare benefits. In addition, the attorney general for each state enforces laws that may affect the rights of aliens in that state.

Listed below are specific *officials* who are responsible for various matters involving the needs of aliens.

OUTSIDE THE UNITED STATES:

Consul: Ranking officer in each consulate of the United States, who supervises issuance of immigrant and non-immigrant visas. Consulates are located in each country with which the United States has diplomatic or consular relations.

Vice consul for immigrant visas: Officer responsible for issuing immigrant visas for aliens seeking admission to the United States as permanent residents.

Vice consul for nonimmigrant visas: Officer responsible for issuing nonimmigrant visas for aliens seeking to enter the United States temporarily.

District director or officer in charge, INS: Located in Athens, Greece; Frankfurt, Germany; Guadalajara, Mexico; Hamilton, Bermuda; Hong Kong, B.C.C.; Manila, Philippine Islands; Mexico City, Mexico; Monterrey, Mexico; Montreal, Canada; Naples, Italy; Nassau, Bahamas; Ottawa, Canada; Palermo, Italy; Rome, Italy; Tijuana, Mexico; Tokyo, Japan; Toronto, Canada; Vancouver, Canada; Victoria, Canada; Vienna, Austria; Winnipeg, Canada. The district director or officer in charge is responsible for decisions on petitions for immediate relatives, requests for waivers of visas and passports, waivers of certain grounds of excludability, and applications to extend reentry permits. In addition, the INS officers in Athens, Frankfurt, Rome, Vienna, and Hong Kong are authorized to grant permission to refugees to enter the United States.

Public Health Service officer or contract surgeon: Physician who conducts medical examination of aliens seeking to enter the United States. In most cities, the physician is in private practice but has been designated by the Public Health Service to conduct the examination for a prescribed fee paid by the alien.

IN THE UNITED STATES:

Attorney General of the United States: Designated by the Immigration and Nationality Act as the officer responsible for the administration and enforcement of the law. He has delegated authority to the commissioner of the INS to administer and enforce the statute and to determine appeals of decisions, with certain exceptions, to the Board of Immigration Appeals.

Attorney general of each state: Chief legal officer in each state of the United States. Responsible for legal determinations of the rights of aliens under any state law. In the District of Columbia, the corporation counsel serves this function.

Board of Immigration Appeals: Established by the Attorney General to review on appeal decisions rendered by immigration judges in exclusion and deportation proceedings, including release from custody on bond, decisions involving visa petitions for immediate relatives, and certain other decisions rendered by district directors.

Border Patrol agent: Patrols U.S. borders with Mexico and Canada to detect illegal entries of aliens to the United States. Authorized to arrest aliens entering the United States illegally or believed to be unlawfully in the United States. Empowered to enter, without warrant, private lands within 25 miles of border to prevent illegal entry of aliens.

Bureau of Security and Consular Affairs: Designated by the Immigration and Nationality Act as the State Department bureau responsible for regulations and policies governing the issuance of visas. Advisory Opinions Section within the Visa Office of the Bureau may review refusal by consul to issue visa.

Commissioner of Immigration and Naturalization: Chief executive officer of the INS.

Customs officer: Inspects personal effects and luggage and customs declarations of persons arriving in the United States to determine whether import duties are to be collected.

District director, officer in charge of INS district office: The district director is responsible within his area for enforcement and administration of immigration laws and for determinations made by the examining officers, investigators, and the detention-deportation officers regarding aliens. District offices are located in 36 cities in the United States and in selected foreign countries: St. Albans, Vermont; Boston, Massachusetts; New York, New York; Philadelphia, Pennsylvania; Baltimore, Maryland; Miami, Florida; Buffalo, New York; Detroit, Michigan; Chicago, Illinois; St. Paul, Minnesota; Kansas City, Missouri; Seattle, Washington; San Francisco, California; San Antonio, Texas; El Paso, Texas; Los Angeles, California; Honolulu, Hawaii; Phoenix, Arizona; Denver, Colorado; Newark, New Jersey; Portland, Maine; Hartford, Connecticut; Cleveland, Ohio; Washington, D.C.; Atlanta, Georgia; San Juan, Puerto Rico; New Orleans, Louisiana; Omaha, Nebraska; Helena, Montana; Anchorage, Alaska; Houston, Texas; Portland, Oregon; Hong Kong, B.C.C.; Frankfurt, Germany; Mexico City, Mexico; Rome, Italy.

Detention and deportation officer: Officer in INS district office responsible for arranging for deportation of aliens from United States. Authorizes permission for aliens to remain in the United States after entry of order of deportation or order that alien depart voluntarily.

Examining officer: Officer in INS district office who renders decisions on extensions of stay in the United States for nonimmigrants; on petitions by immediate relatives on behalf of aliens; petitions based upon occupation of aliens; and applications for changes of status to other nonimmigrant status or to permanent residence.

Exchange Visitor Waiver Review Board: Determines whether to recommend waiver of two-year foreign residence requirement for government-sponsored and other exchange visitors to become eligible for permanent residence in the United States. The board, which passes upon most requests, is within the Department of Health, Education, and Welfare and makes its recommendations for that department. Other departments have established similar boards.

Facilitative Services staff: Administers international programs for exchange visitors, and makes determination on behalf of State Department whether to recommend foreign residence waivers for exchange visitors.

Foreign consul: Consular officer in the United States of foreign governments. Usually notified when citizen of consul's country is arrested and detained by immigration officers. Available for assistance to alien. Serves function of issuing and revalidating passports and travel documents for nationals of his country to travel, and where required, to remain in the United States.

Foreign student advisor: Administrative officer or faculty member at educational institution usually available to assist foreign students with advice regarding immigration status.

Investigator: Immigration officer responsible for detecting aliens illegally in the United States. Authorized to arrest aliens, with or without warrants of arrest, whom he believes to be present in the United States illegally. Conducts investigations in connection with eligibility for benefits under the immigration laws, including naturalization.

Local State Employment office: Office of State Employment Service in area where an alien seeking immigration status based upon occupation wishes to work. Local office determines availability of labor in area to fulfill job requirements and employment conditions, including wages, for position; and transmits application for alien employment certification, with relevant information, to Regional Employment and Training Administrator of United States, ETA Administration.

Naturalization examiner: INS officer who conducts interviews to determine alien's eligibility to become United States citizen or entitlement to derivative citizenship through parents. Prepares recommendations to courts.

Public Health Service officer—contract surgeon: Conducts medical examinations, when required, of aliens in the United States. Aliens are referred by INS offices to designated medical laboratories for serology, chest X rays, and reports. Medical examinations are usually performed by private contract physicians designated by the Public Health Service.

Regional commissioner: Supervises operations of district offices within his region and determines appeals of certain decisions by district directors. The United States is divided into four regions: Eastern, Northern, Southern, and Western.

Regional Employment and Training administrator: Acts upon applications for alien employment certifications that are required for intending immigrants whose permanent residence is to be based upon their occupation. The United States is divided into ten regions.

Secretary of State: Designated by the Immigration and Nationality Act as responsible for the regulations governing operations of Bureau of Security and Consular Affairs and the conduct of diplomatic and consular officers, including the determination of nationality of persons outside the United States.

Selective Service Local Board: Registration office for male aliens between the ages of 18 and 26.

Social Security Administration office: Issues Social Security cards to aliens authorized to accept employment, those who require Social Security numbers for bank accounts and investment income, and to permanent resident aliens.

Your Representative in the House of Representatives: Every member of the House of Representatives provides assistance to aliens who live in his congressional district. Members of Congress from areas that have large foreign-born populations usually employ case workers who are trained to assist aliens in their problems with government agencies, including the Immigration and Naturalization Service. When helpful, a member of the House of Representatives can introduce legislation in Congress to relieve an alien from deportation or provide other assistance. An alien who needs assistance may write, telephone, or visit the Representative from his congressional district either at the congressional office in the district or at the House of Representatives in Washington.

Your Senators in the United States Senate: Senators perform similar services. However, a Senator's office may sometimes refer an alien to the member of the House of Representatives who represents his congressional district. Most Senators, however, have staff persons who can provide assistance to aliens in their dealings with government agencies.

APPENDIX ^E

GLOSSARY OF TERMS & SOME RELEVANT DEFINITIONS

ACCOMPANYING OR FOLLOWING TO JOIN: Immediate family members who travel to the U.S. with the principal alien, or who arive in the U.S. after the principal alien. Does not include those who come to the U.S. before the principal alien.

ADMITTED: An alien who has been inspected and allowed to enter the U.S. in an Immigrant or non-Immigrant status.

ADJUSTMENT OF STATUS: The procedure for changing an alien's non-Immigrant status to an Immigrant status while in the U.S. (see p. 161 of text)

ADVISORY OPINION: A procedure which allows the Visa Office in Washington, D.C. (part of the U.S. State Department) to review the decision of a U.S. Consul. A Consul is generally not obliged to change the decision even after an Advisory Opinion is issued. (see p. 147 of text)

ALIEN: A person who is not a Citizen or National of the U.S. (see p. 1 of text)

APPEAL: A procedure allowed in certain cases for a superior person or board to review the decision and papers in a case. After review, the person or board can return the papers for further action, allow the original decision to stand, change the decision in whole or in part. (see pp. 143 & 157 of text)

ATTORNEY: A lawyer admitted to practice law in any jurisdiction in the United States.

BOARD OF IMMIGRATION APPEALS: The part of the U.S. Justice Department responsible for review of decisions on Preference Petitions and for certain other appeals from the Immigration and Naturalization Service.

BRIEF: The paper or letter accompanying an appeal or motion which contains the facts or rebuttal.

BUSINESS NECESSITY: A justification for requiring a Combination of Duties, foreign language requirement, or other special requirement not found in the Dictionary of Occupational Titles. Business Necessity arises when the absence of the requirement would tend to undermine the business. Business Necessity can also refer to a situation in a private household when a Live-in requirement for a domestic worker is essential to the household. (See p. 149 of text)

CERTIFYING OFFICER: The employee of the U.S. Labor Department responsible for issuing the Labor Certificate and for affixing the Certifying Stamp to the Application Form. (see p. 147 of text)

DICTIONARY OF OCCUPATIONAL TITLES: A publication of the U.S. Government listing job titles and descriptions. It is used as a guide by the local Employment Service offices and the U.S. Department of Labor. It is available for examination in many Public Libraries, government agencies. The Dictionary is for sale by the Superintendent of Documents in Washington, D.C., and in U.S. Government Book Stores in larger U.S. cities. (see p. 149 of text)

EXCEPTIONAL ABILITY: (See discussion in text , at pp. 44-5)

EXCLUDABLE: An excludable alien is barred from entering the U.S. Some excludable aliens are barred permanently; others may enter after receiving a waiver. (See discussion in Chap. 9 and Appendix A of text)

GREENCARD: A card identifying the holder as being registered as a Permanent Resident of the U.S. The color of the card is no longer green, but the name has remained. The GreenCard is officially a Form I-551 "Alien Registration Receipt."

IMMEDIATE FAMILY: An alien's spouse and children. The spouse must be the legal spouse. The children must be under 21 years of age, unmarried, and be considered legitimate by the Immigration Service or U.S. Consul.

IMMIGRANT: An alien who intends to remain in the U.S. for an indefinite time.

IMMIGRANT VISA: The type of Visa issued to persons who are qualified for U.S. Permanent Residence.

IMMIGRATION AND NATURALIZATION SERVICE: A part of the U.S. Department of Justice responsible for implementing and enforcing most of the Immigration laws. (INS)

IMMIGRATION SERVICE: See Immigration and Naturalization Service.

INS: See Immigration and Naturalization Service.

INSPECTION: The procedure which occurs when an alien is questioned (or allowed to pass without questioning) by an Officer of the U.S. Immigration Service at a Port of Entry. No "Inspection" occurs if the alien falsely claims to be a U.S. Citizen or evades a proper examination.

INTERNATIONAL ORGANIZATION: See discussion in the text, at p. 29)

LABOR CERTIFICATE: Issued by the U.S. Department of Labor after it finds that U.S. workers will not be adversely affected if an alien fills a particular job. The finding is shown by the placement of a special Stamp upon the application form. The Stamp contains the words of the Certificate and the Signature of the Certifying Officer. (See Chap. ;8 of text)

LIVE-IN JOB: A job which requires the employee to live on the employer's premises as a condition of employment. (see p. 149)

LOCAL EMPLOYMENT SERVICE OFFICE: The unit responsible for the initial receipt and processing of applications for Labor Certificates except for Schedule A Occupations. These offices are part of a State or other non-Federal employment service (except in Washington, D.C.). It is distinct (separate) from the U.S. Department of Labor but acts as a pre-processor of Labor Certificate applications on behalf of the U.S. Department of Labor. (See Appendix B of text)

MOTION: A written request made to a government agency as part of an application procedure.

NON-IMMIGRANT: An alien who intends to depart from the U.S. after completing the purpose of his trip of limited duration.

NOTICE OF FINDING: (See discussion in text, at p. 149.)

NUMERICAL LIMITATION: See p. 6 of text)

PAROLE: A status granted by the Immigration Service to an alien who has been inspected and who is allowed to enter the U.S. for a particular purpose even though the alien lacks required documents or visa. As examples, parole status may be granted by the Immigration Service at the Port of Entry to allow an alien to apply for political asylum, testify at a judicial proceeding, or receive necessary medical treatment. It is also granted to allow an alien to complete a pending Adjustment of Status application upon his return to the U.S. if the alien had been given Advance Parole before departing.

PETITION: A form used to apply for a preference under the Immigration law. Refers to the Form I-140 Petition for Third or Sixth Preference, or Form 1-130 for family-based petitions.

PREFERENCE: One of the categories in which an alien may qualify for an Immigrant Visa (for Permanent Residence).

PREFERENCE DATE: The date which determines an alien's place on the list for a Preference. (See discussion in the text at pp. 11-12

PRINCIPAL ALIEN: An alien who has qualified for U.S. Permanent Residence directly and not derivatively. As an example, the alien who has an approved Labor Certificate and an approved Preference Petition is the Principal Alien, while his or her spouse and minor unmarried children are not principal aliens but obtain their right to an Immigrant (Resident) Visa derivatively. The derivative aliens are usually those who will accompany, or follow to join, the Principal Alien.

PRIORITY DATE: See Preference Date.

REBUTTAL: The written response to a Notice of Finding by the U.S. Labor Department. (See discussion in text at p. 148)

RECONSIDERATION: The procedure for having the papers in a case re-examined by the Government agency so that a more favorable decision will be made.

REOPENING: The procedure which allows additional facts or papers to be added to the record of a case.

REGIONAL OFFICE: An office of the Employment and Training Administration of the U.S. Department of Labor responsible for final processing and issuing regular Labor Certificates. The Certifying Officer is an employee in the Regional Office. There are several Regional Offices in the U.S.

REGULAR LABOR CERTIFICATE: A Labor Certificate for a job *not* on Schedule A. (see Chap. 8 of text)

SCHEDULE A: A list of occupations for which an alien employee can receive a Labor Certificate without recruiting U.S. workers.(see Chap. 8 of text)

SCHEDULE B: A list of occupations for which an alien employee cannot receive a Labor Certificate without a waiver.

SIXTH PREFERENCE: The Immigrant category for skilled and non-skilled workers. (Also includes everyone who is qualified for the Third Preference. (See discussion in the text e.g. pp. 43-5)

THIRD PREFERENCE: The Immigrant category for professional employees. (See discussion in the text at pp. 43-5)

TRWOV or TWOV: *TR*ansit *W*ith*O*ut *V*isa. Refers to an alien who is allowed to enter the U.S. without a visa while in transit between airplane flights or between ships.

U.S.: United States.

U.S. CONSUL: An employee of the U.S. State Department posted at a Consulate or Embassy of the U.S. abroad, responsible for approving and issuing Immigrant or non-Immigrant Visas.

U.S. DEPARTMENT OF LABOR: Refers to the section of the U.S. labor department responsible for processing and issuing Labor Certificates. It is part of the Labor Department's Employment and Training Administration.

U.S. EMPLOYER: Any person with a U.S. location authorized to offer a job to an alien for Labor Certificate purposes. Can be an individual, corporation, or other legal person. Does *not* include an alien temporarily in the U.S. even though authorized to work.

U.S. WORKER: A person who is authorized to work in the U.S. including U.S. Citizens and U.S. Permanent Residents. Does not include an alien temporarily in the U.S. even though authorized to work.

VISA APPOINTMENT: The procedure which occurs when an applicant for U.S. immigrant (residence) status appears before a U.S. Consul abroad to allow the Consul to determine if the alien is qualified for an Immigrant Visa.

VISA BULLETIN: A publication issued each month by the U.S. State Department which gives the status of Immigrant Visa priority dates. (see pp. 11-15 of text)

WAIVER: Special permission issued by a U.S. government agency to allow an alien to receive a privilege or benefit that the alien could not get without the waiver. For example, a Labor Certificate cannot be issued for a job on Schedule B without special permission (a waiver) from the Labor Department. Some excludable aliens can be admitted to the U.S. if they receive a waiver.

APPENDIX **F**

ORDERING YOUR IMMIGRATION FORMS

The following is a list of IMMIGRATION VISA and related forms or documents obtainable from the Do-It-Yourself Legal Publishers.

(Customers: For your convenience, just make a xerox copy of this page and send it along with your order. **All prices quoted here are subject to change without notice.**)

TO: Do-It-Yourself Legal Publishers (Legal Forms Division)
298 Fifth Avenue, N.Y. N.Y. 10001

Please send me the Publisher's Complete Package of Standard Forms to File for the Visa or Visas indicated, as Checked Off ☑ below:
[PRICES]: $15.95 (in US dollars or convertible equivalence) per Set, for each set checked off. Persons ordering from outside the U.S.,please add $1.90 per set for shipping & handling]

Forms For "K" Visa.(Fiance(es) Engaged to Marry U.S. Citizens):

Check off which one S. please ☑ ☑

Form: I-129F, Petition to Classify Status of Alien Fiance(es) for Issuance of Non-Immigrant Visa.
G-325A, Biographic Information
FD-258, Fingerprint Card
I-134, Affidavit of Support
OF 157, Medical Examination of Applicants for U.S. Visas; OR, I-486A, Medical Examination & Immigration Interview

Forms For B-1 & B-2 Temporary Visitor Visa:
Form:: 156, Nonimmigrant Visa Application
FD-258, Fingerprint Card
G-325A, Biographic Information
I-134, Affidavit of Support
OF 157, Medical Examination of Applicants for U.S. Visas; OR, I-486A, Medical Examination & Immigration Interview
I-539, Application to Extend Time of Temporary Stay

Forms for F, M, & J Student & Exchange Visitor Visas:
Form: I-20AB, Certificate of Eligibility for Nonimmigrant (F-1) Student Status for Academic & Language Students
I-20MN, Certificate of Eligibility for Nonimmigrant (M-1) Student Status for Vocational Students
IAP-66, Certificate of Eligibility for Exchange Visitor (J-1) Status
FD-258, Fingerprint Card
G-325A, Biographic Information
I-134, Affidavit of Support
OF 157, Medical Examination of Applicants for U.S. Visas; OR, I-486A, Medical Examination & Immigration Interview
I-538, Application by Non-immigrant Student (F-1) for Extension of Stay, School Transfer or Permission to Accept or Continue Employment
I-612, Application for Waiver of the Foreign Residence Requirement

Forms For H-1, H-2, & H-3 Temporary Worker and L-1 Intra-Company Transferee Visas:
I-129B, Petition To Classify Non-immigrant as Temporary Worker or Trainee
ETA-750A & B, Application For Alien Labor Certification
FD-258, Fingerprint Card
G-325A, Biographic Information
I-134, Affidavit of Support (Optional)*
OF 157, Medical Examination of Applicants for U.S. Visas; OR, I-486A, Medical Examination & Immigration Interview
I-539, Application to Extend Time of Temporary Stay

Forms for Treaty Trader (E-1) or Investor (E-2) Visas:
I-506, Application for Change of Non-Immigrant Status
I-126, A Report of Status by Treaty Trader or Investor
FD-258, Fingerprint Card
G-325A, Biographic Information
I-134, Affidavit of Support (Optional)*
OF 157, Medical Examination of Applicants for U.S. Visas; OR, I-486A, Medical Examination & Immigration Interview
I-539, Application to Extend Time of Temporary Stay

Forms for 1st,2nd,4th & 5th Preference (Family Relationships) IMMIGRANT Visas:
I-130, Petition for Alien Relative
FD-258, Fingerprint Card (or, Form ID-258)
G-325A, Biographic Information
I-134, Affidavit of Support
OF 157, Medical Examination of Applicants for U.S. Visas; Or, Form I-486A, Medical Examination & Immigration Interview
230, Application for Immigrant Visa & Alien Registration
I-600, Petition to Classify Orphan as an Immediate Relative(if applicable)
I-600A, Application for Advance Processing of Orphan Petition (if applicable)

NOTE: some of the *forms and* documents listed here may not apply or be required for your own particular visa classification or in your own particular case or consulate, and are only listed here as a general all-inclusive guide. Ultimately, the best source of what would specifically be required in a given case, is your consular official, and he will usually advice you of such details at the appropriate time.

*Not necessary, if you've other proofs of income, resources,or U.S. employment.

Forms for 3rd & 6th Preference (Job or Skill-Related) IMMIGRANT Visas:
    ETA-750A & B, Application for Alien Labor Certification
    I-140, Petition for Prospective Immigrant Employee
    FD-258, Fingerprint Card (or, Form ID-258)
    G-325A, Biographic Information
    I-134, Affidavit of Support (Optional)*
    OF 157, Medical Examination of Applicants for U.S. Visas; OR, I-486A,
            Medical Examination & Immigration Interview
    230, Application for Immigrant Visa & Alien Registration (Often optional)

Forms for U.S. Alien Labor Certification:
    ETA- 750A & 750B, Application for Alien Labor Certification

Forms for "SPECIAL IMMIGRANTS*" Immigrant Visa (see pp.6, 42-3 of manual)
    I-485, Application for (Adjustment of) Status as a Permanent Resident
    FD-258, Fingerprint Card (or, Form ID-258)
    G-325A, Biographic Information
    I-134, Affidavit of Support (Optional)*
    OF 157, Medical Examination of Applicants for U.S. Visas; or, Form I-486A,
            Medical Examination & Immigration Interview

Forms for IMMIGRANT INVESTOR Immigrant Visa:
    I-526, Request for Determination that Prospective Immigrant is an Investor
    OF 222, Preliminary Questionnaire To Determine Immigrant Status
    FD-258, Fingerprint Card (or, Form ID-258)
    G-325A, Biographic Information
    OF 157, Medical Examination of Applicants for U.S. Visas; Or, Form I-486A,
            Medical Examination & Immigration Interview
    ETA 750A & B, Application for Alien Labor Certification

Forms for "Adjustment of Status" from Non-immigrant to IMMIGRANT Visa:
    I-130, Petition for Alien Relative (only if alien is being sponsored as a
           Family "relative" of a U.S citizen or Green Card holder.)
    I-140, Petition for Prospective Immigrant Employee (applicable only if alien
           is being sponsored as employee of a US employer under 3rd or 6th Pref.)
    I-485, Application for Status as a Permanent Resident
    FD-258, Fingerprint Card (or, Form ID-258)
    G-325A, Biographic Information
    I-134, Affidavit of Support (Optional)*
    OF 157, Medical Examination of Applicants for U.S. Visas; Or, Form I-486A,
            Medical Examination & Immigration Interview

Forms for Refugee or Asylum Status Visa under the 7th Preference:
    I-589, Request for Asylum in the U.S., & the Addendum to Form I-589
    FD-258, Fingerprint Card (or, Form ID-258)
    G-325A, Biographic Information
    OF 157, Medical Examination of Applicants for U.S. Visas; Or, Form I-486A,
            Medical Examination & Immigration Interview
    I-570, Application for Issuance or Extension of Refugee Travel Document
    I-590, Registration for Classification as Refugee
    I-591, Assurance by a U.S. Sponsor in Behalf of an Applicant for Refugee
           Status
    I-602, Application by Refugee for Waiver of Grounds of Excludability

Forms for Deportation or Exclusion Proceedings, Appeals, and the Like:
    I-212, Application for Permission to Reapply for Admission Into the U.S.
           after Deportation or Removal
    I-246, Application for Stay of Deportation
    I-256A, Application for Suspension of Deportation
    I-290A, Notice of Appeal to the Board of Immigration Appeals
    I-290B, Notice of Appeal to Commissioner

*Not necessary, if there're other proofs of income, wealth, or U.S. employment.

Note a few general rules in regard to competing the immigation forms. A truly important aid to anyone in preparing all such forms are the "blocks" provided on the forms; such blocks are generally self-explanatory and quite explicitly indicate the exact information required to be entered, and the order in which such information is to be put in inorder for the information to contain in the space. Secondly, almost every immigration form has a set of "INSTRUCTIONS" on the body of the form, clearly telling the reader the purpose(s) for which the form is appropriate and giving some pointers on how to complete or file them, and guidelines on the information and supporting documents required to be furnished

FORMS Order Form

APPENDIX G

OTHER PUBLICATIONS FROM
DO-IT-YOURSELF LEGAL PUBLISHERS:

1. HOW TO DRAW UP YOUR OWN LEGAL SEPARATION, PROPERTY SETTLEMENT, OR COHABITATION AGREEMENT WITHOUT A LAWYER
2. HOW TO WIN YOUR LEGAL RIGHTS AS A TENANT WITHOUT A LAWYER
3. HOW TO PROBATE AND SETTLE AN ESTATE WITHOUT A LAWYER ($29)
4. HOW TO ADOPT A CHILD WITHOUT A LAWYER
5. HOW TO FORM YOUR OWN PROFIT/NON-PROFIT CORPORATION WITHOUT A LAWYER
6. HOW TO DRAW UP YOUR OWN WILL WITHOUT A LAWYER
7. HOW TO DECLARE YOUR PERSONAL BANKRUPTCY WITHOUT A LAWYER
8. HOW TO BUY OR SELL YOUR OWN HOME WITHOUT A LAWYER OR BROKER ($29)
9. HOW TO FILE FOR CHAPTER 11 BUSINESS BANKRUPTCY, WITH OR WITHOUT A LAWYER ($29)
10. HOW TO LEGALLY BEAT THE TRAFFIC TICKET WITHOUT A LAWYER (forthcoming)
11. HOW TO SETTLE YOUR OWN AUTO ACCIDENT CLAIMS WITHOUT A LAWYER (forthcoming)
12. HOW TO OBTAIN YOUR U.S. IMMIGRATION VISA WITHOUT A LAWYER ($29)
13. HOW TO DO YOUR OWN DIVORCE WITHOUT A LAWYER

PRICES: ● *Each* book, except for those specifically priced otherwise, costs $25, plus $1.95 per book for postage and handling. [All prices quoted here are subject to change without notice]. New York residents please add 8¼% sales tax for the "Big Apple" ($2.06 per $25 book, and $2.39 per $29 book.)

All publications sold with a 10-day money-back guarantee

(Customers: Please make and send xerox copy of this page with your orders)

Order Form

TO: **Do-It-Yourself Legal Publishers**
298 Fifth Avenue
New York, N.Y. 10001

Please send me the following:

1. _____ copies of _____
2. _____ copies of _____
3. _____ copies of _____
4. _____ copies of _____

Enclosed is the sum of $_____ to cover the order.
Mail my order to:

Mr/Mrs/Ms/Dr. _____

Address (include zip code please): _____

_____

Phone #( ) _____
Incl. area code:

Only orders placed by mail will be honored, please.

Index